I0759683

CRYPTIC

CRYPTIC

From Voynich to the Angel Diaries, the Story of the World's Mysterious Manuscripts

GARRY J. SHAW

YALE UNIVERSITY PRESS
NEW HAVEN AND LONDON

For information about this and other Yale University Press publications, please contact:
U.S. Office: sales.press@yale.edu yalebooks.com
Europe Office: sales@yaleup.co.uk yalebooks.co.uk

Set in Adobe Caslon Pro by IDSUK (DataConnection) Ltd
Printed and bound in the UK using 100% renewable electricity at CPI Group (UK) Ltd

Library of Congress Control Number: 2025931216
A catalogue record for this book is available from the British Library.
Authorized Representative in the EU: Easy Access System Europe, Mustamäe tee 50, 10621 Tallinn, Estonia, gpsr.requests@easproject.com

ISBN 978-0-300-26651-1

10 9 8 7 6 5 4 3 2 1

This book is dedicated to the memory of my father,
Rodney Shaw

CONTENTS

ACKNOWLEDGEMENTS

I would like to thank Heather McCallum, the managing director and publisher at Yale University Press, London, for giving me the opportunity to write about this wonderful selection of mysterious manuscripts, and her team for making this book a reality. The Vatican Apostolic Library provided me with helpful advice, and Montpellier University's Bibliothèque universitaire historique de médecine made manuscript H.505 available online, enabling me to make progress with my research into the writings of Johannes Heckius. I am also grateful to the anonymous referees who read and commented on the initial proposal and, later, the finished book, and who provided suggestions for improvement; and to the book's copyeditor, Hester Higton. My thanks also go to Verena Priem for asking me to include her in these acknowledgements – here you go (!) – and to my wife, Julie Patenaude, for reading and commenting on the drafts of this book, and for our conversations about the topics covered within.

Lille, France
November 2024

INTRODUCTION

Hidden Knowledge

Skeletons dance beneath enciphered words. Secret messages hide in the letters of demonic magic. An elegant but unreadable script flows beside unusual plants, their roots resembling animals or sprouting human heads. Beautiful. Intriguing. But what does it all mean? What knowledge lies hidden behind such strange symbols, words, and illustrations. And, perhaps most importantly, who created the mysterious manuscripts that protect these secrets – and why?

Over the centuries, authors have devised many ways to keep their knowledge hidden. Their attempts have created some of medieval and early modern Europe's most enigmatic writings – unique manuscripts and documents that were meant to be read only by certain eyes. But these texts are much more than just historical novelties. They reflect a real or imagined need for secrecy, providing an insight into their authors' lives and the times in which they were produced. Secret writings do not exist in a vacuum; they shine a light on society. To fully understand their content, we need to examine the lives of those who produced them.

Consequently, *Cryptic* focuses less on the methods used by people in the past to hide information, and more on the individuals themselves and what they chose to keep secret. As we shall see, their hidden knowledge covers a wide variety of themes, from the occult, alchemy, and religion, to science, engineering, and medicine. In their writings, we find attempts to summon demons, contact angels, and keep alchemical secrets, and descriptions of innovative inventions, medical recipes,

1. A small green dragon and a plant, from the Voynich Manuscript's herbal section.

religious revelations, scientific explorations, and linguistic experimentations. The authors' secrets lie behind ciphers, codes, unusual alphabets, illustrations, and invented languages. And sometimes their manuscripts are hoaxes – attempts to exploit this fascination with mysterious languages and secret scripts to deceive or manipulate people.

THE CREATORS OF MYSTERIES

Across *Cryptic*'s chapters, passing through time, we will explore the unknown alphabet and language of the German nun Hildegard of Bingen, who experienced religious visions from a young age; the extensive enciphered writings of the prank-loving Italian physician Giovanni Fontana; and the life of the German monk Johannes Trithemius, who invented ways to hide information in plain sight, but was lambasted as a summoner of demons. From there, we meet the English polymath John Dee and his attempts to receive the language and alphabet of angels; the fraudsters behind a historical forgery, designed to improve the lives of Spanish Muslim converts to Christianity; the English mathematician Thomas Harriot's attempt to create a universal alphabet, inspired by his interactions with the Algonquin; the wanderings and enciphered travel notebooks of the unstable Dutch doctor Johannes Heckius, a founding member of one of Europe's earliest scientific societies; and the multiple levels of alchemical symbolism encoded into the creative books of the unlucky German alchemist Michael Maier. Each life story reveals why they wrote their 'mysterious manuscripts' – the circumstances behind their creation.

And then there is the Voynich Manuscript, subject of Chapter 2. Written in a unique script and filled with unusual illustrations, it has been dubbed the world's most mysterious manuscript. From page after page of unusual plants, to complex astrological scenes, and what appear to be recipes for unexplained concoctions, it has hypnotized everyone who has seen it for centuries. All, however, have the same question in the end: what does it all mean?

Myriad other cases of hidden knowledge, based around the same themes as each chapter's featured manuscript, provide a wider background to the stories told in *Cryptic*. Among them, we will find the enciphered writings of a group of early fifteenth-century alchemists, recorded in a notebook under the title *Alchymey teuczsch*; the Rohonc Codex, a work once believed to be a gibberish-filled hoax, but now revealed to be an encoded manuscript; and the entirely faked life of George Psalmanazar, who invented a language and script to add authenticity to his claim that he came from the island of Formosa (Taiwan). We will also explore the seventeenth-century fascination with devising a universal language and alphabet, a craze that even swept up the young Isaac Newton, and the methods of secrecy used by natural philosophers such as Galileo Galilei, who hid news of his discoveries in anagrams. Secret societies used ciphers too, among them the Highly Illuminated Order of the Oculists from Wolfenbüttel, Germany, who obscured the details of their initiation ritual in a manuscript dated to the eighteenth century.

Throughout these stories, kings and queens, emperors and popes lurk behind the scenes, impacting the lives of people across Europe. There are tensions between Catholics and Protestants, between the advocates of natural and ceremonial magic, between science and religion. We will travel across the continent, from Prague Castle in Czechia, a magnet for the occult and everything mysterious, to fifteenth-century Venice in Italy, to the house of John Dee at Mortlake in England, and even across the Atlantic Ocean, as far as the east coast of what is now the USA. Each manuscript also has a journey through time to the present day. We will see how they survived the centuries to reach the libraries that now protect them, learning whose hands they have passed through and the marks that these individuals left on their pages. In many cases, the manuscripts' journeys are just as turbulent as the lives of their creators. Each highlighted text has also been the subject of recent or ongoing research that has either solved a long-standing mystery or revealed deeper ones.

INTRODUCTION

WORLDWIDE ENCHANTMENT

Cryptic writings continue to fascinate people across the globe. The digital edition of the Voynich Manuscript is among the most-viewed pages on the Beinecke Rare Book and Manuscript Library's website. This most mysterious of manuscripts has inspired novels, the plots of TV shows, and even music, and any intriguing attempt at unlocking its secrets is swiftly reported by journalists.[1] Of the subjects covered in this book, perhaps only Hildegard of Bingen and John Dee can match it for fame – the latter even had an opera devoted to him, featuring music composed by Damon Albarn. Secret writing is also a staple of books and documentaries on the Second World War, which often detail the work of codebreakers – in particular, those of Bletchley Park, in the UK, and their attempts to crack the Nazi Enigma machine. Mysterious ciphers, anagrams, and codes are popular plot devices in fiction too, from the works of Edgar Allen Poe to Arthur Conan Doyle, but perhaps most famously in the puzzles faced by the symbologist Robert Langdon in the novels of Dan Brown.[2]

Enigmatic manuscripts have also inspired art. Perhaps the best-known modern 'mysterious' book is *Codex Seraphinianus*, written by the architect and artist Luigi Serafini and published in 1981. Its unusual illustrations fuse the recognizable with the fantastical: a rhino with a horn connected to its tail; humans with wheels for feet; a couple who transform into a crocodile while making love. These images are accompanied by headers, labels, lists, and seemingly explanatory text, all written in a curious invented script of curling cursive characters that appears to explain what is going on, but has not yet been decrypted – if it even can be. The *Codex*'s encyclopaedia-like arrangement, spread across eleven chapters and three hundred pages, entices the reader to look closer; after all, books of this genre are supposed to provide information. But cut off from reading the text, our usual window into a book's content, we instinctively search for meaning in the illustrations and find our own interpretations.[3] Decades may have passed since *Codex Seraphinianus*'s publication, but it is still discussed today – often in conjunction with the Voynich Manuscript.

BEING CRYPTIC

My aim with this book is twofold. Firstly, I want to explore the fascinating world of medieval and early modern Europe's mysterious writings and secret scripts – primarily those produced from the twelfth to seventeenth centuries – and to reconstruct the lives of the people who wrote them. These individuals did not produce these

2. Concentric circles bearing Voynich characters, with four figures at the centre, from the Voynich Manuscript.

works of hidden knowledge without a clear motivation – they are responses to a need. But what factors triggered this need? On a wider scale, I also want this book to be a voyage of discovery through the eclectic range of topics connected with the manuscripts I discuss. Consequently, each individual and the manuscript they created serve as a launching point for exploring a theme or genre of hidden knowledge. For example: Hildegard of Bingen's *lingua ignota* and *litterae ignotae* provide an opportunity to examine the topic of medieval artificial languages and scripts; the alchemical works of Michael Maier let us explore the myriad ways by which alchemists hid their knowledge from the unworthy; and the enciphered notebooks of Johannes Heckius open a window onto the secret communication methods of natural philosophers and doctors.

Secondly, studies of the Voynich Manuscript tend to conclude that it is either an enciphered or encoded text, an artificial language and script, or a hoax. One way to narrow down these possibilities – to say what the Voynich Manuscript might be and what it is not – is to look at other texts that fall into these categories, produced in roughly the same centuries. The manuscripts examined over the course of *Cryptic*'s chapters provide this opportunity. Some of them have appeared repeatedly in discussions of the Voynich Manuscript, others not at all.[4] I am not trying to solve the Voynich mystery – that is not an aim of this book; I simply want to know if an understanding of why these authors wrote their texts, and how they used them, suggests a likely option. My thoughts on this problem serve as the book's conclusion.

So let us begin our journey. In our first chapter, we will visit a small town in medieval Germany, where a young girl's miraculous visions will eventually propel her to fame – and to create her own mysterious language and script.

1

THE *LINGUA IGNOTA* AND *LITTERAE IGNOTAE* (1150–8)

Medieval Secret Scripts and Artificial Languages

In the year 1101, when Hildegard was only three years old, she saw a bright light shimmering before her. It shone with such intensity that she felt her soul shake. It was a life-changing event but, because of her youth, she could not find the words to describe what had happened. As she grew up, she experienced further visions, found that she could predict the future, and said things that confused people around her. When she asked her nurse if she could see one particular vision, at that moment, clearly present in Hildegard's eyes, the nurse replied with a puzzled 'no'. Nothing unusual was happening. Perhaps sensing how people might treat her if she continued to talk about the marvels she witnessed, Hildegard decided to keep her visions to herself. They would be for her alone. She kept this vow for decades, while living away from the world in a convent, only divulging her secret to the head nun, or magistra, Jutta, who in turn told a monk named Volmar.[1] This continued until Hildegard was forty-two years and seven months old, when a divine voice told her to reveal her visions to the world. She followed the divine instruction with trepidation. Would everyone think she was mad?

She need not have worried. Over the years that followed, Hildegard transformed from a recluse into one of the medieval world's greatest religious thinkers, a woman who corresponded with archbishops and popes, whose advice was sought for exorcisms and healing, who composed beautiful music and extensive works on natural science, and who founded and managed her own convent. But among her works was something more obscure, which remains little known, even today: Hildegard invented her own language and alphabet, known as her *lingua ignota* and *litterae ignotae* – her Unknown Language and Unknown Letters. Why she did this and how she used them remains a mystery. Were they ways of hiding knowledge? A method of secret communication? The language of God? Whatever the case may be, it is clear that she saw both, like her visions, as divinely inspired. Only three manuscripts are known to have preserved these enigmatic creations. One of them vanished two hundred years ago and, as we will see, it is a miracle that the grandest among them – the *Riesencodex*, or 'Giant Codex' – survives at all.

FROM CONFINEMENT TO FAME

Hildegard of Bingen was born in 1098, perhaps in the small wine-growing village of Bermersheim, near Mainz, in western Germany. She was the tenth child of a wealthy family, and her parents showed their thanks to God by sending Hildegard to become an anchoress – a religious recluse – at the newly built Benedictine monastery of Disibodenberg, named in honour of the Irish monk Saint Disibod, who was buried at the site. Although the monastery was primarily inhabited by monks, it had a small cell for nuns, where they lived separate from the men. On 1 November 1112, Hildegard crossed the threshold of this holy space and left the world behind – forever, she probably imagined – to live, study, and pray under the nuns' magistra, Jutta of Sponheim. The entry rituals were performed as if she were attending her own funeral; she may even have heard a choir singing funerary songs and have received rites for the dying, as was traditional. When the cell door shut and the key turned in the lock, sealing her inside like the lid of a coffin, she was reborn into a new existence. For the next twenty-four years, Hildegard communicated with the outside world through a single tiny window, lived her life entirely within the grey stone walls of the cell illuminated by candlelight, and followed a strict religious regime devised by Jutta.[2] When Jutta died in 1136, Hildegard, now thirty-eight, replaced her as the nuns' magistra in what had grown into a small convent.[3] Her first act was to soften Jutta's austere rules. Under Hildegard's management, the convent would enter a new, more open, phase.

It was a divine vision that spurred on these changes. At the age of forty-two, Hildegard saw a great light descend from the sky. She describes it as entering her heart and mind, and although the flame was searing hot, it did not burn her, though it did change the way that she engaged with the world. Suddenly, despite her lack of training and education, she found that she could better understand the Bible and the writings of saints and philosophers; and she began to compose music. At the same time, a voice told her to write down everything that she had seen and heard in her visions, and to tell the world all that she had experienced.[4] Hildegard was afraid. After spending decades hiding her visions, she did not want to follow the divine command. She delayed and worried, and then fell ill. The sickness had to be a punishment from God, she decided, brought down upon her for not doing as instructed. Hildegard only recovered when she started work on a manuscript detailing her visions and experiences – experiences that she emphasized occurred in her soul when fully awake, rather than in a trance or dream. She toiled away on this manuscript for the next ten years.[5] It would be called *Scivias*, and would launch her new career as a prophet.

While penning *Scivias*, Hildegard managed her convent, which continued to grow in size and fame. Between 1147 and 1148, Pope Eugene III, fresh from launching his (catastrophic) Second Crusade, learned of Hildegard's visions and despatched a group of high-level clergy to the monastery at Disibodenberg to investigate. They returned with a section of *Scivias*, which the pope read to his assembled archbishops and cardinals in Trier, Germany. Eugene was satisfied that this was truly divine work, and he gave his papal seal of approval for Hildegard to continue writing.[6] To be accepted in this way, it probably helped that Hildegard wrote in Latin, the language of the elite, rather than in German. Although the average person did not understand her words, the religious authorities certainly did. Her choice of language ensured that she would be taken seriously (and perhaps reveals her intended audience). That she wrote on theology was also radical: not just because she was a woman, writing in a time when this was highly unusual, but because she regarded herself as uneducated. To medieval thinkers, theology was one of the most advanced areas of study, a subject only reached after completing years of education and mastering other topics. Hildegard circumvented the problems that she would have faced because of her sex and education by proclaiming that her visions were the work of God, and that it was God himself who wanted her to write down what she saw.[7]

Around 1147, as *Scivias* progressed, the now forty-nine-year-old Hildegard decided – as usual, through divine command – that she and her nuns needed a new convent. Disibodenberg's cell was not big enough for them, so she would rebuild a destroyed monastery at Rupertsberg, 25 kilometres to the north-east, overlooking the green and picturesque spot where the River Nahe meets the Rhine. This location would give her independence from the Disibodenberg monks, who, even after her rise to fame, still controlled her finances. She had the backing of the Archbishop of Mainz, but her announcement caused fury among the monks, who knew that they would lose income and status if the increasingly famous Hildegard abandoned them. Her presence alone attracted rich patrons to the monastery.[8] Upon hearing their protests and anger, Hildegard fell sick and blind, and only recovered when the monastery's abbot personally witnessed her condition and, against his monks' appeals, approved her plan for relocation.[9]

Based in Rupertsberg from 1150 or 1151, Hildegard and her nuns built a new home for themselves among the rubble and ruins. The convent's furnishings were awful, we are told, as were the general conditions. Some of the nuns quit the convent in disgust – this was not what they had signed up for – and donors expressed concerns that their money, meant for Disibodenberg, was being diverted to

Rupertsberg. Hildegard weathered these storms. Over the years, heralded by the sounds of wood-sawing and stone-carving, the buildings were reborn, creating space for fifty nuns and servants, and rich families buried their dead in its cemetery, giving the revitalized convent much-needed legitimacy. There was even running water. Eventually, the Archbishop of Mainz accepted that Hildegard's Rupertsberg should be fully financially independent from the monks of Disibodenberg, freeing her from the final links that chained her to her old life.[10] With her freedom assured for the first time, it was at Rupertsberg that Hildegard would produce two of her most mysterious creations: her Unknown Language and Unknown Letters.

THE *LINGUA IGNOTA* AND *LITTERAE IGNOTAE*

Hildegard developed her Unknown Language, or *lingua ignota*, between 1150 and 1158.[11] It consists of 1,011 nouns, which are categorized from the most divine – beginning with God and angels – down to the lowliest creatures. Notes in German and Latin explain the meaning of her mysterious words. Hildegard's word for angel, for instance, is 'Aiganz' in one manuscript, and 'Aleganz' in another. God is 'Aigonz'. The devil is 'Díuueliz'.[12] Other words are more down to earth: there are 48 trees, 60 birds, and 130 herbs and plants.[13] Some words are repeated with different meanings, so that 'Scolmiz' can be both 'vestment' and 'plough handle'. The plant lovage and the word for duck are the same: 'Luschia'.[14] To inspire her new words, Hildegard appears to have drawn from German and Latin, but it is not clear what rules she followed when forming them. As for her word selection, her choice appears to have been influenced by similar dictionary-like works, known as summaria, but perhaps above all, the seventh-century *Etymologies* of Bishop Isidore of Seville, and a later adapted version of it called the *Summarium Heinrici*, which was popular in Germany during the twelfth century. Hildegard followed the structure of these summaria, which cover subjects as diverse as the divine, family members, parts of the body, and weapons.[15]

3. Entries from Hildegard of Bingen's *lingua ignota*, from the *Riesencodex*.

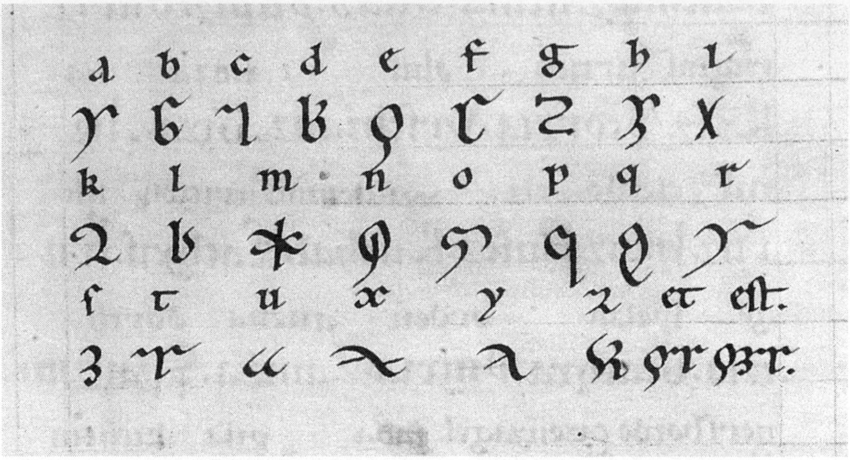

4. Characters from Hildegard of Bingen's *litterae ignotae*, from the *Riesencodex*.

For now, the sole known use of Hildegard's Unknown Language is in her song 'O Orzchis Ecclesia', which was perhaps performed during the consecration of a church, beyond the inner circle of her nuns at Rupertsberg, implying that it was not for her community alone. In the song, interspersed among the expected Latin, are her invented words, many absent from the *lingua ignota* list; this suggests that this list was just one source of her language, or is incomplete, rather than its main source.[16]

Hildegard's *litterae ignotae*, meaning 'unknown letters', consist of twenty-three symbols, each standing for a letter of the alphabet, with the letters j, v, and w omitted.[17] A later version includes two extra symbols, representing 'et' and 'est', based on a Latin shorthand system called Tironian Notes (see below).[18] The inspiration for the design of Hildegard's characters is hard to pinpoint. She seems to have been influenced by Greek letters, and perhaps Aramaic and Hebrew, while certain letters resemble what would later be called 'Theban Writing'.[19] The earliest known use of the Unknown Letters is in a letter from Hildegard to the monks of Zwiefalten in south-west Germany, written sometime between 1153 and 1154, in which they name the recipients:

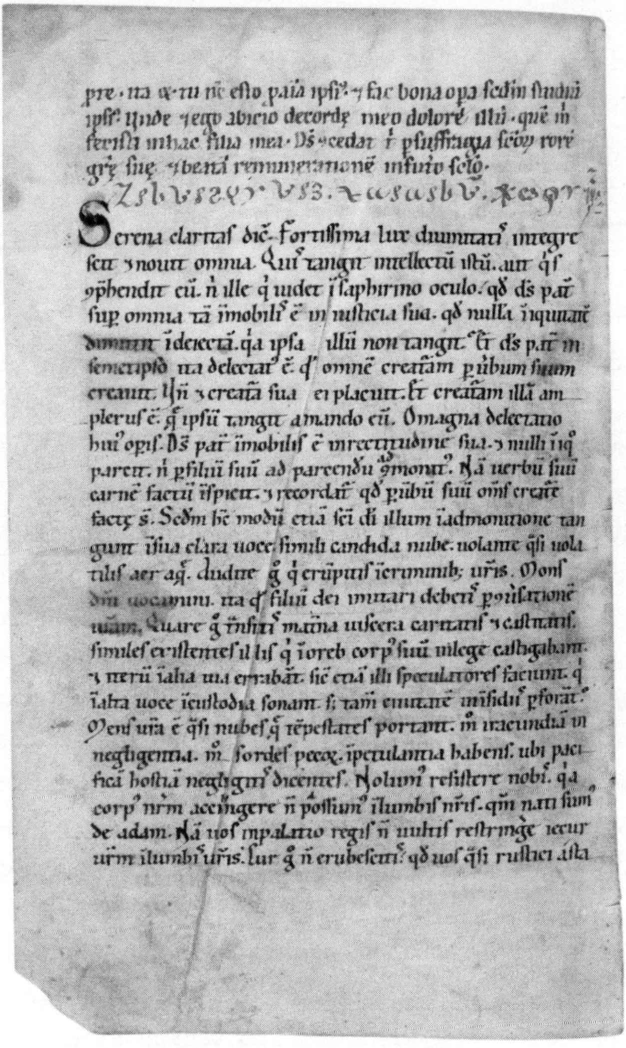

5. Hildegard of Bingen's *litterae ignotae* (fifth line), used in a letter.

the monks. In the letter, Hildegard scolds the monks for abandoning their chastity and committing sins.[20] As she spells out words in Latin, rather than in her Unknown Language, it is a mystery why she chose to use her invented alphabet here. The symbols may have already been associated with her, adding an extra special level of authority or power to the letter, or it is possible that the abbot simply knew how to read them.[21] Because the letter's content was critical of the monks, perhaps Hildegard wanted to hide the identity of the recipients from anyone who might happen to see it.[22] In another letter, her symbols are written in the margin, and again they 'decrypt' into Latin, seemingly to address a bishop.[23] It is probable, then, that the Unknown Letters were aimed at a monastic audience: monks and nuns.[24] The only other examples are found among the later collected editions of her works,[25] and (more oddly) spread across the pages of a codex.[26]

The existence of the Unknown Letters and Unknown Language was not a secret. In 1153, Hildegard mentioned both in a letter to the elderly pope, Anastasius (Eugene III's successor).[27] This is the first known reference to either. The next time they are mentioned is a decade later, in 1163, when, in a preface to her *Liber vitae meritorum*, Hildegard wrote that the language and letters came to her in a vision.[28] Scholars have interpreted Hildegard's invention in different ways. Perhaps she believed her language to be the one spoken by virgins in heaven, or maybe it was a form of speaking in tongues (unlikely, as this would surely have been recorded by one of her biographers).[29] Maybe it was cryptography: secret words used by Hildegard's nuns for communicating among themselves. Or perhaps it was her attempt to recreate the language of Adam – the perfect language that existed at the beginning of time. Against this argument is the fact that Hildegard, or at least one of the later compilers of her thoughts, believed that Adam and Eve spoke German. Elsewhere, she wrote that Adam knew all world languages. Another explanation is that she perhaps wanted to replace Greek in her macaronic poetry – that is, poetry that mixes together multiple languages – with her own, divinely inspired language.

Although Hildegard understood German and Latin, she did not known Greek, a language that was often included as an ornament in Latin poetry and reflected high learning. The use of her own language would bypass this problem, while highlighting her own special connection with the divine.[30] What is at least certain is that, to Hildegard, her Unknown Language and Unknown Letters were divine revelations, direct from God. They were later accepted as miracles and therefore became one of the reasons for her canonization.[31]

MEDIEVAL INVENTED ALPHABETS, CODES, AND SHORTHAND

Where might Hildegard have found her inspiration? And what other alphabets and languages were invented in the years before and after her death? For her influences, in addition to the summaria mentioned above, she appears to have read the writings of the Benedictine monk Raban Maur. Born in the eighth century, Maur wrote *De inventione linguarum*, in which he discusses various alphabets and secret writing systems, and includes word lists for parts of the human body and the months of the year, just as Hildegard does. Maur also describes a mysterious alphabet that consists of twenty-two signs, each associated with an equally mysterious-sounding word. This alphabet is first found in *Cosmographia*, a work on the universe and geography that presents the world as flat, ascribed to the fictional eighth-century philosopher Aethicus Ister. Ister's alphabet has similarities to Glagolitic script, an early Slavic alphabet.[32] Glagolitic script is said to have been devised in the ninth century by a Greek missionary named Constantine (later Saint Cyril), who was sent to a part of what is now Czechia from Constantinople. He appears to have drawn from various scripts, including Greek, Armenian, and Coptic, to create this alphabet to write down Slavonic, which had no previous written form, and through it he translated various religious works from Greek. His motivation for creating this script was spreading the word of Christianity.[33]

Medieval scribes often borrowed letters from other alphabets – particularly Greek – to write their names in the manuscripts they copied. This made it obvious to any reader that their personal additions were separate from the main content. They used runes and imaginary scripts for the same purpose, or to obscure the meaning of certain words; an extra benefit was that these characters added to the

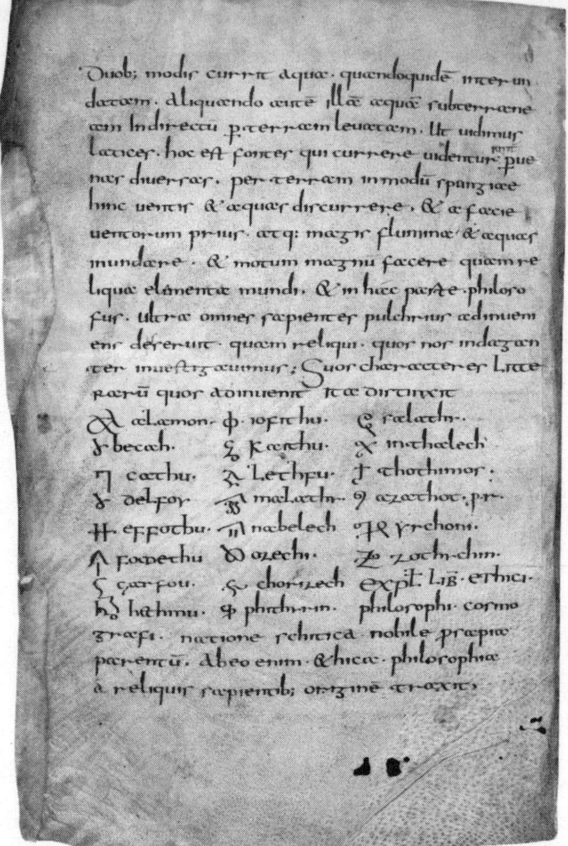

6. The script of Aethicus Ister.

page's beauty. Hugeburc, a nun based in Heidenheim, Germany, who lived around the year 800, took this all a step further. She developed her own script, replacing vowels with shortened versions of Latin ordinal numbers, and added a line of text to her manuscript of the *Vitae Willibaldi et Wynnebaldi* – a work describing the lives of her monastery's founder and his brother – explaining that she was its author. Clearly, Hildegard was not the only nun with an interest in scripts and a creative streak. Other popular secret writing systems include *Notae Bonifatii*, in which different numbers of dots represent vowels, and the Caesar Cipher. In this latter system, in its simplest form, the scribe swapped each letter in a sentence with the letter that immediately followed it, so that 'a' became 'b', 'b' became 'c', 'c' became 'd', and so on. Other substitution methods involved scribes replacing vowels with consonants ('e' becoming 'f', for example), or switching them with 'G's, in which 'a' as the first vowel in the alphabet became 'G', while 'e', as the second, became 'GG', and so on.[34]

As Greek and Hebrew characters can also represent numbers, scribes wrote strings of numbers to hide their messages too.[35] At the same time, numbers themselves could be presented in unusual ways. From the thirteenth century to the fifteenth, monks used a set of symbols formed of a line (or stem), with lines and squares branching off it, to represent numbers. The number, whether 1 or 4,632, was represented by a single symbol, or single 'block' of individual symbols combined together. So, for the number 4,632, you would find in one symbol the combined symbols for 4,000, 600, 30, and 2. This system has various names, but it is sometimes referred to as St Alban's Numerals or Basingstoke.[36]

At first glance, medieval shorthand can also appear like secret scripts and ciphers. This is the case with one ninth-century psalter (a book that contains the Old Testament Book of Psalms), but the symbols are actually Tironian Notes, a shorthand system used by medieval scribes to replace Latin words, parts of words, or letters.[37] Scribes often used Tironian Notes to record comments in the margins or between the lines of their manuscripts, or in school texts to identify useful information. As a shorthand system, it made best use of the space available.[38] In later centuries, however, prayer books could be truly enciphered, hiding writing in Latin and English.[39]

In the century after Hildegard's death, the English Franciscan friar and philosopher Roger Bacon wrote his *Epistle on the Secret Works of Art and of Nature and on the Nullity of Magic*. Within it, he describes the wonders that technology can bring to the world, from submarines to aeroplanes. But, he warns, these mechanical marvels might be presented as magic in the wrong hands. Bacon was strongly against the uneducated or untrustworthy gaining access to scientific and technological knowledge because he was sure that they would abuse it; so he suggested that writers on these subjects should use a variety of cryptographic methods to hide their learning – this would keep it (and everyone) safe. To help his readers, Bacon provides some handy examples for how a person can hide the true content of their writing. He suggests writing in verse (perhaps more accurately meaning complex jargon), or omitting the vowels, making the words harder to read. You can mix different languages together – perhaps with Latin, Hebrew, and Greek characters – invent entirely new letters, or draw geometric shapes instead. Shorthand can be used, Bacon writes, as can fake magic spells, or figurative language, presenting metaphors that only a select few can understand.[40] Bacon's work on cryptography only became widely read when it was translated from Latin to English and published as a book in 1659. Apparently, it had been copied by a person called T.M. from a manuscript owned by the Elizabethan polymath John Dee (the subject of Chapter 5).

During the first millennium AD, and for a few centuries afterwards, the greatest advances in secret writing and scripts came from the Arab world, not Europe. The eighth-century linguist and philologist Al-Khalil wrote a manuscript on cryptography, though no copies are known to exist, while, in the following century, the philosopher Al-Kindi discussed techniques for breaking ciphers, types of ciphers, and the use of statistical analysis in cryptography, such as letter frequencies. Some Arab cryptoanalytical techniques even treated dead languages as ciphers to be broken and read. In the tenth century, Ahmad ibn Wahshiyyah wrote a book on languages that included ninety-three alphabets.[41] Among them was 'dâwoûdî', also called 'rihani', a script that is often found in magical texts and was formed by changing the appearance of Hebrew letters.[42] In the thirteenth century, both Ibn Adlan and Ibn Dunainir wrote guides to breaking ciphers, and in the fourteenth century, Ibn Ad-Duraihim discussed different systems of encipherment, including the use of invented symbols in place of letters.[43] Clearly, then, by the time that Hildegard invented her Unknown Language and Unknown Letters, many others had already experimented with languages and alphabets, both in Europe and in the Arab world.

HILDEGARD'S LATER WRITINGS

Hildegard continued to write in her later years, despite the worsening of the illnesses that had plagued her all her life. She completed *Scivias* in 1151 and immediately moved on to other, shorter works. Among them was the *Subtilitatum diversarum naturarum creaturarum*, written between 1151 and 1158, which today only survives divided in two as the nine-book *Physica* and the six-book *Causae et curae*. In *Physica*, Hildegard writes on different aspects of nature, listing everything from plants, reptiles (including dragons), and animals to various metals and minerals, such as gemstones that scare away the devil. In her entries, she comments on whether whatever she describes is hot or cold, wet or dry, and sometimes on how they can be used as medical cures. If you have worms in an ulcer, she writes, emerald (*smaragdus*) can help. If a person is bewitched, you should utter prayers, pass a type of zircon called hyacinth over a cross cut into the top of a loaf of bread, and feed them the bread. Unicorns can be trapped by a virgin, and their hooves can detect poison. In *Causae et curae*, meanwhile, Hildegard describes the structure of the cosmos, problems from daily life (such as hair loss and toothache), and the causes of diseases, how to diagnose them, and cures, before finishing with a section on how astrology can predict a person's personality. (Along the way, she notes that dragons hate people.)

Hildegard also wrote commentaries on the gospels and on the Rule of Saint Benedict, and composed works of music.[44] She developed her Unknown Language and Unknown Letters during her busy years writing these diverse works, providing an insight into her interests at the time.

After *Scivias*, Hildegard's second major visionary work was her *Liber vitae meritorum*, which she spent five years writing, from 1158 to 1163. This 'Book of Life's Merits' was centred on six visions and discussions on virtues and vices, and includes detailed descriptions of punishments for sins, such as thieves being whipped with flames while being consigned to deep pits.[45] Her third, and final, visionary work was the *Liber divinorum operum*, 'The Book of Divine Works', which she started in 1163. This presents ten visions covering a variety of topics, all connected by the importance of the Gospel of John's statement that in the beginning was the Word – perhaps another sign of Hildegard's interest in word and alphabet creation.[46] Here, she discusses humanity, the natural order of the cosmos, the passage of time, and salvation, and she brings together much of her thinking from the decades of her life spent pondering the universe, the mind, the body, and theology.[47]

In between her time spent with parchment and quill in hand, Hildegard is said to have performed miracles, healing the sick of their fevers and bleeding through religious gestures and written commands, or even by offering a braid of her own hair. Her powers expanded into exorcism too. On one occasion, the Abbot Geldof of Brauweiler brought a woman named Sigewize to Hildegard, so that she could exorcize a demon that had possessed Sigewize for eight years. An earlier effort, in which Hildegard sent instructions on how to help Sigewize, ultimately failed, leading to the possessed woman having to travel to Rupertsberg, where Hildegard and seven priests successfully expelled the demon. Hildegard also found time to travel. Accompanied by two nuns, she visited communities across Germany and preached to crowds about the state of both the world and the Church.[48] After so much time locked inside, she made the most of her later years.

Hildegard died at the age of eighty-one on 17 September 1179 – a day that she is said to have predicted – and was buried at Rupertsberg beside other saints. As the years passed, people came to visit her grave and experienced miracles, including the exorcism of a demon from a woman called Mechthild, who had travelled from nearby Laubenheim.[49]

THE JOURNEY OF THE *RIESENCODEX*

Towards the end of Hildegard's life, her followers tried to bring together all of her writings to prove her prophetic skills. Three of the resulting codices contain Hildegard's Unknown Language and Letters. One of these was kept in the Austrian National Library in Vienna, but vanished between 1800 and 1830.[50] Another was created by two scribes in around 1220, forty years after Hildegard's death. It spent some time in a monastery near Trier before entering the possession of the Jesuits of Agen in south-west France. By the middle of the nineteenth century, it belonged to Thomas Phillipps, a British baronet, in Cheltenham, UK, who was famous for his bibliomania; later, it passed to the German kaiser, Wilhelm II. The manuscript reached its final destination in 1912, when it became part of the Berlin State Library collection.[51] This was quite a journey, but the third codex, known as the *Riesencodex*, meaning 'Giant Codex', had a far more adventurous life.

The most impressive surviving collection of Hildegard's works, the *Riesencodex* is a monumental manuscript, 481 parchment folios long, and weighing a massive 15 kilograms. Six scribes at Rupertsberg's scriptorium copied out the texts, mainly from older sources, though the musical section already existed and was reused (for this, all they needed to do was to write over it in darker ink, and then insert the pages into the codex).[52] They probably had not originally planned to include the *lingua ignota* and *litterae ignotae*, for both were only introduced at a late stage in the codex's development.[53] There are also some quite untidy additions. On one folio page, a scribe decided to write some extra content. At first, he followed the limits of the text column, but, after realizing that his sentences would not fit, he wrote to the edge of the page, ruining the design.[54] Once complete, the *Riesencodex* appears to have been kept at Rupertsberg Monastery, where, in the fifteenth or sixteenth century, it was bound between two wooden covers, each wrapped in pigskin. A chain, attached to the bottom of its back cover, kept the codex joined to a desk in the library or scriptorium, suggesting that it was accessible to interested readers as a *liber catenatus*, or chained book. People certainly consulted the *Riesencodex*, because some of them made copies of its sections; others even wrote their names on its pages.[55]

One of the most famous people to study the *Riesencodex* was the Benedictine monk Johannes Trithemius (the subject of Chapter 4), who commissioned his own copy of most of its content in 1487. Oddly, despite his interest in secret writing and languages, this did not include the *litterae ignotae* and the *lingua ignota*. It is possible that the scribes copying the codex for him did not understand the purpose of these pages and dismissed them as unnecessary.[56] Other writers wrote their own extra content into the *Riesencodex* itself. On the recto of the first folio, a scribe added an account of the opening of Hildegard's grave on 17 November 1489. The Abbess of Rupertsberg, Adelheid von Reiffenberg, oversaw the exhumation, along with the Archbishop of Mainz, Berthold of Henneberg. Both hoped that they would find a canonization document buried alongside Hildegard.[57] Nine years later, in 1498, the archbishop opened Hildegard's grave again, this time to perform an 'elevatio' – the lifting of her bones – which was an informal way of canonizing her. He was accompanied by the above-mentioned Trithemius, who, as thanks for his prayers, was awarded one of Hildegard's arms.[58]

A second addition to the *Riesencodex* was made during the Thirty Years' War, after Easter 1632, when Rupertsberg monastery was destroyed by the Swedish army. Caspar Lerch von Dirmstein, a brother of the monastery's abbess, wrote the forty-two-line account of these events.[59] Following the monastery's destruction, the nuns of Rupertsberg hauled the *Riesencodex* to Eibingen monastery on the other side of the Rhine, but this monastery fell out of use in the nineteenth century.[60] So, in 1814, the codex entered the collection of the Öffentliche Landesbibliothek in Wiesbaden, which later became the Hochschul- und Landesbibliothek RheinMain – Wiesbaden's state library.[61]

But the *Riesencodex*'s story does not end there. Amid the chaos of the Second World War, Gustav Struck, the director of Wiesbaden's state library, feared for his city's safety. Even if only the occasional bomb fell on Wiesbaden, it could be disastrous for the many precious manuscripts in his care, so he organized for the *Riesencodex* to be sent to Dresden, where he believed it would be safe. By 1942, the precious 900-year-old manuscript found itself sealed in a specially crafted metal box and stored in a vault within the Girozentrale Sachsen bank, along with various other manuscripts. Nobody expected Dresden to be bombed, though the director of the city's Sächsische Landesbibliothek expressed his shock and concern that the *Riesencodex* had been taken to that particular bank, given that it was a tall building near the town hall. Of course, in February 1945, Dresden was devastated by one of the most intense bombing raids of the whole war. The bank was flattened but, amazingly, as the flames roared all around, the vault survived intact among the rubble. Even more astonishing, when looters stole the manuscripts from the vault, they left the *Riesencodex* untouched.[62]

After the war, the Americans installed Franz Götting as the new director of the Wiesbaden state library, who tried to recover the *Riesencodex* from Dresden. The Soviet authorities, now in control of the city, refused. In their eyes, the manuscript was their property, and they transferred it to the Sächsische Landesbank, the Saxon State Bank. Attempts to convince the Soviets to return the *Riesencodex*, including by the nuns of the Abbey of Saint Hildegard at Eibingen, built between 1900 and 1904 as a successor to the earlier dissolved Eibingen monastery, were unsuccessful.[63]

Things were looking bleak until the arrival in the story of Margarete Kühn, a medievalist and follower of Hildegard, who worked in Berlin's Soviet sector on a project called Monumenta Germaniae Historica. The project had written to the nuns at Eibingen, asking for photographs of the *Riesencodex*, who, in turn, contacted Franz Götting in Wiesbaden. Despite no longer having the manuscript in his collection, Götting sent a letter of authority to Kühn, in the hope that it might help her gain access to the *Riesencodex* in Dresden. To everyone's surprise, the Soviet authorities not only let Kühn see the manuscript, but they also gave her permission to take it to Berlin's Soviet sector too. This was the opportunity that everyone had been waiting for. Without delay, Kühn passed the manuscript to the wife of an American general, who removed it from the Soviet Zone and delivered it – perhaps accompanied by Kühn – to the nuns at Eibingen. The *Riesencodex* was in the Abbey of Saint Hildegard as of 11 March 1948 and, after some extra travels for it to be microfilmed, it returned to Wiesbaden a year later, in March 1949.[64]

But the story was still not over. By April 1949, the Soviet authorities in Dresden had repeatedly asked for the *Riesencodex* to be returned from Berlin. Worse, news of the manuscript's presence in Wiesbaden had been published in a journal. The cat was out of the bag, leaving Kühn in a difficult situation. She could not return a manuscript that she did not have. There was only one solution: to send a substitute codex in its place. In Wiesbaden, Götting searched through his library collection and identified a manuscript that looked similar enough to the *Riesencodex* that it might do the job; he just needed to add a chain. Once the lookalike codex was ready, they delivered it to Berlin, and from there it was taken to Dresden. The ruse was not revealed until January 1950, when the Soviet authorities wrote to Kühn demanding an explanation. It was just a mix-up, everyone was assured. Surprisingly, this led to a negotiation, which concluded with the *Riesencodex* remaining in Wiesbaden, where it has been ever since. Meanwhile, Kühn continued to work on the Monumenta project until the end of her life, at the age of ninety-two.[65]

Today, the *Riesencodex* is in the Hochschul-und Landesbibliothek RheinMain in Wiesbaden, Germany, under call number HS 2.[66]

In our next chapter, we will visit fifteenth-century Italy, where five scribes are busy producing the most mysterious manuscript of all: the Voynich Manuscript.

2

THE VOYNICH MANUSCRIPT (*c.* 1404–38)

The World's Most Mysterious Manuscript

Sometime between 1404 and 1438, somewhere in northern Italy, five scribes gathered together to create a unique manuscript. For its material they chose calfskin parchment, which had been soaked in water and lime, and smoothed with a knife. It was an expensive undertaking, for they had purchased enough for eighteen quires – long folded pages which, when ready, would be sewn together at the spine. There was enough material to include foldout sections, which would add to the manuscript's beauty.[1] The scribes – one of whom might also have been its artist – or whoever commissioned the manuscript wanted its pages to boast a great many illustrations on various subjects, from plants and astrology to bathing.[2] The drawings, executed using iron gall ink, were the first task to be completed on each page, leaving enough space around them for the text, which, itself, would be unlike anything else ever written. Six hundred years later, the meaning of these enigmatic illustrations and words is still debated, and the work as a whole has been dubbed the world's most mysterious manuscript.[3] Today, it is known as the Voynich Manuscript.

The manuscript's creators dedicated its first and longest section (folios 1r–66v) to plants, drawing attention to their roots and highlighting the shape and appearance of their leaves and flowers. Snakes or worms with spotted bodies and pronounced lips wrap themselves around one plant's roots (folio 49r); balloon-shaped human heads grow from another (folio 33r); and certain roots vaguely resemble animals (folios 34v, 46v, 90v).[4] A tiny dragon exhales the leaves of one plant, as if breathing them out as fire (folio 25); elsewhere, a person lies ill, reclining in pain as they hold their stomach with their right hand (folio 66r).[5]

The next section (folios 67r–73v) is dedicated to astronomy, cosmology, and astrology. Here, the artist drew page after page of concentric circles and elaborate spirals. Some pages unfold to reveal yet more circles, each filled with stars, tubes, wavy lines, and round faces representing suns and moons – usually with blank expressions, or perhaps looking slightly worried. One set of seven stars might be the Pleiades star cluster (right side of folio 68r),[6] while ten rings feature signs of the zodiac, embellished with circles of nude women, who stand or sit in barrels, holding stars on stalks that look like daffodils. The artist drew Aries as a ram, Taurus as a bull, Libra as scales, all according to tradition, but, more unusually, presented Sagittarius as a man wearing a Florentine archer's hat, typical of the fifteenth century (folio 73v).[7]

The next section, sometimes referred to as the balneological or biological section (folios 75r–84v), centres on bathing and is filled with nude women, often up to their thighs in green or blue pools of water. On one page (folio 79v), a woman holds a cross, while, below her, water flows through tubes and falls on to the face of a woman lying beneath, who grasps a ring. Blue water descends through strange tubes and pours into a green pond inhabited by four-legged creatures with long snouts, where a final bathing woman is eaten by a giant fish. A canopy rests above the scene, doubling as a rain cloud – the origin of the water.[8]

The cosmological illustrations (folios 85r–86v) in the next section, inked out by the artist on large foldout sheets, present nine connected circles, sometimes referred to as rosettes. Each circle is unique and joined to the others by ramparts or bridges, perhaps flanked by water, and viewed from above. Although most of the circles enclose complex patterns of ovals, rings, crescents, and stars, others present buildings. Towers emerge from castles and ramparts, and there are turrets and tubes. The central, and largest, circle includes structures with

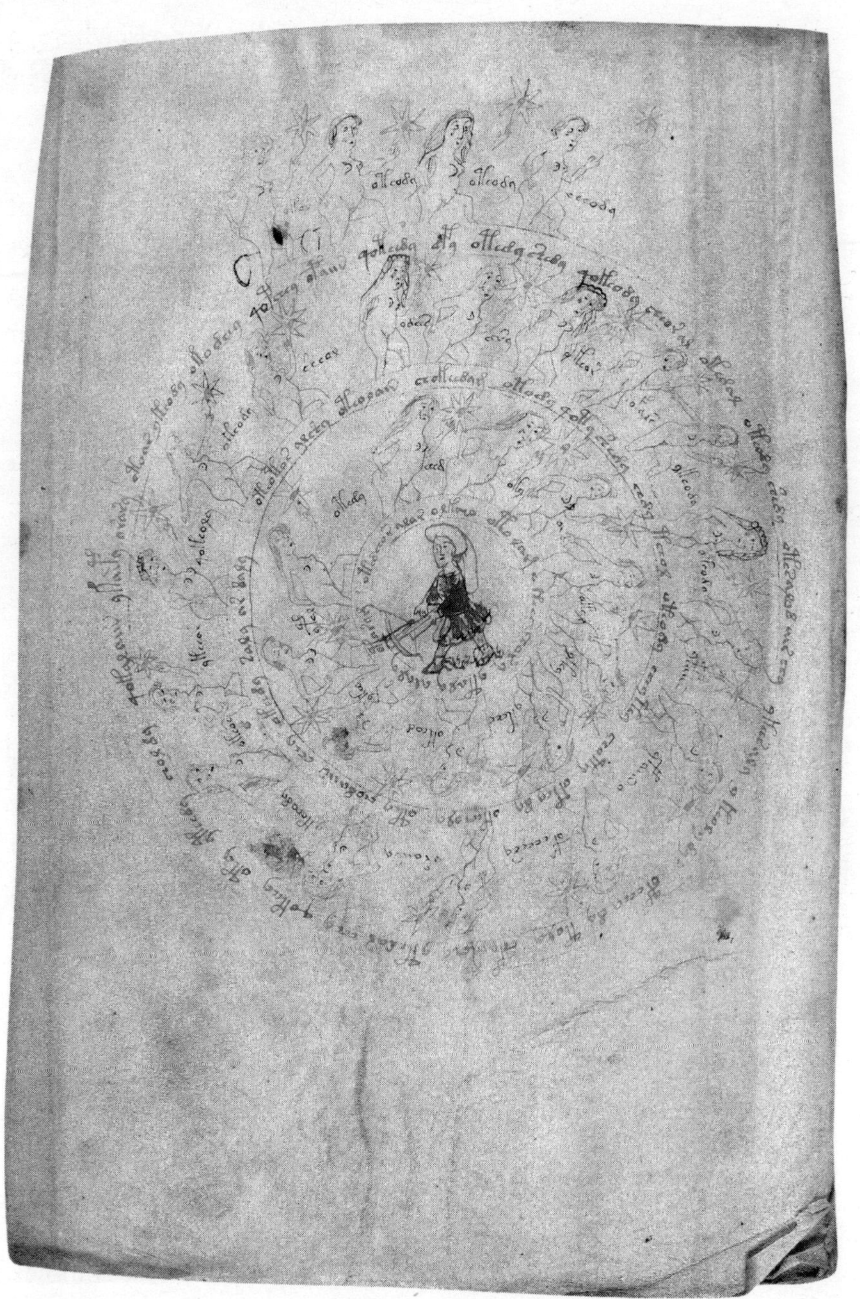

7. Sagittarius, from the Voynich Manuscript.

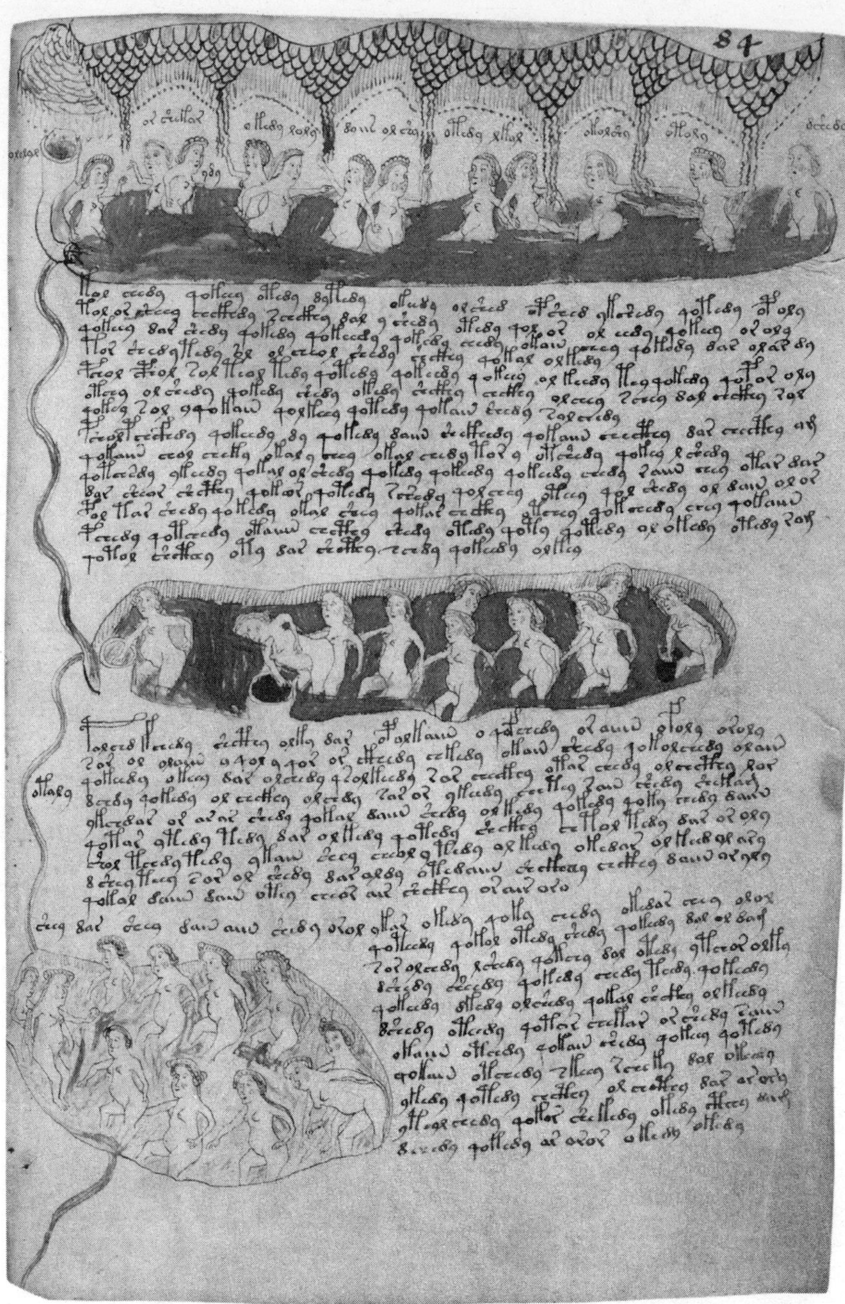

8. Bathing women, from the Voynich Manuscript.

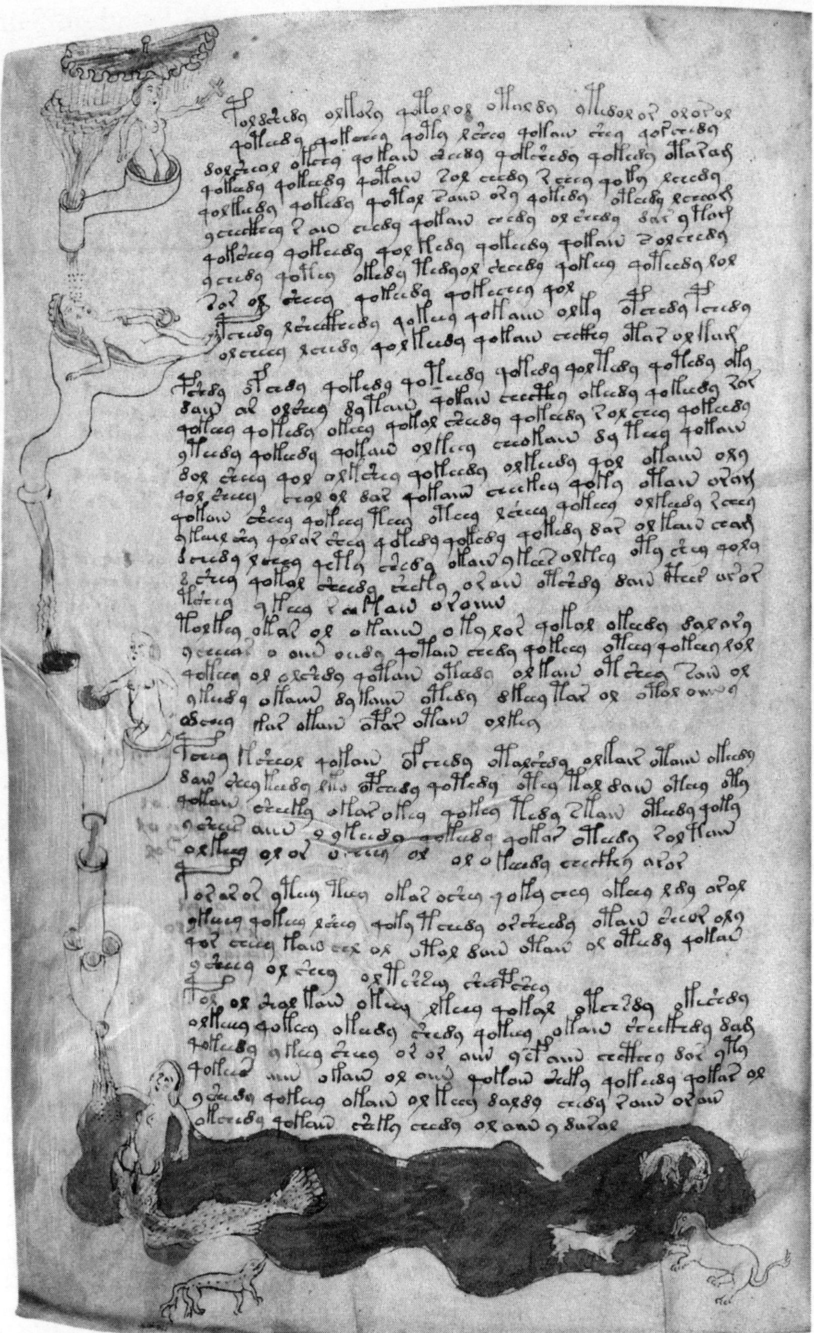

9. Water flows while women bathe, from the Voynich Manuscript.

'onion'-domed towers topped by crosses (like those found on Saint Basil's Cathedral in Moscow). Each feature is accompanied by a label, as if the diagram as a whole is a plan or a map.

In the pharmaceutical section that follows (folios 87r–102v), the artist drew ornate pots, which are fused together like interlocked drums or tubes, often painted in red and blue. In rows beside them are various plants, presumably meant to be ingredients for concoctions (folios 99r–102v).[9] There is a frog or toad on one page (folio 102r), and we again find human heads connected to the roots of plants (folios 89r1 and 101v1). The manuscript's final section (folios 103r–116r) appears to be a long list of recipes, each introduced by a star.

If these illustrations were not bizarre enough, the scribes also took the decision to write the entire manuscript in an unusual, invented script. Some of the characters resemble Arabic numerals, like '4', '8', and '9', while others take their inspiration from the Latin alphabet, such as 'o', 'a', and 'c'. There is a small upside-down 'v', and a character that looks like two 'P's, one backwards, one forwards, linked by a horizontal line at their looped peaks. Certain characters resemble Latin abbreviations, such as 'cc', sometimes connected by a line.[10] Others are quite elaborate, sporting flowing curving lines, or can be as simple as an 'x' with a looped top. The scribes made virtually no corrections when writing these characters; each of them must have been proficient in its peculiarities by the time their quills touched the parchment. Depending on how you separate one symbol from another, the Voynich alphabet, which could possibly include capitalized forms and numerals, consists of roughly thirty-four to seventy characters.[11] Its words appear familiar, as if you should be able to read them with ease, yet are different enough to be exotic and enticing.

The five scribes wrote the text in brown-black iron gall ink and, because the manuscript covered a wide variety of topics, they divided the job of writing its content among them, with one acting as manager. The herbal section, dedicated to plants, was the longest part, so they shared the duty of writing it. The astronomical, cosmological, and astrological section fell to a second scribe, and a third wrote out the bathing section. Another wrote the recipes introduced by stars, though the work here was helped by the managing scribe. Intriguingly, one scribe appears to have written his or her sections in a different dialect from the others.[12] Once they had completed the illustrations and text, the team bound the quires together to create the final manuscript. They sewed the folio pages with bast-fibre threads onto flax-fibre cords; at the top and bottom of the spine, the bookbinder added endbands to secure the pages, held in place with pink threads. Wooden boards decorated with leather served as the manuscript's covers.[13]

The manuscript was ready – but for what purpose? Did the unique script have meaning, and, if so, why was its content restricted to a small group of people? Why did the knowledge within, apparently covering a wide variety of topics, need to be kept secret? Such questions would plague anyone who saw the manuscript for centuries to come.

THE FIRST KNOWN OWNER?

Around 150 years after its creation, the Voynich Manuscript surfaced in the Czech city of Prague. Nothing firm is known about its whereabouts over the intervening years but, based on the most convincing current evidence, its earliest-known owner was Carl Widemann, who lived in the prosperous Bavarian city of Augsburg in the late sixteenth century. A physician and alchemist, Widemann owned around a thousand books – enciphered manuscripts among them – and made extra income on the side as a manuscript dealer to important people, including King James I of England and King Philip IV of Spain. In 1599, Widemann sold a collection of manuscripts – referred to in the records as rare books – to the Holy Roman Emperor Rudolf II for 600 gold florins, doubling his personal wealth in the process.[14] A later record refers to the sale as raising 600 ducats, another type of gold coin in circulation at the time.[15]

Widemann already knew Rudolf, for he had served at the emperor's court in the 1580s and collaborated on alchemical work in Prague with Edward Kelly – best known as the scryer for the polymath John Dee (whom we will meet in Chapter 5). The sale's middleman was Zacharias Geizkofler, manager of Rudolf's state finances, who had already sourced a book from Augsburg for the emperor in 1597. Once they had agreed this latest transaction, the collection of rare manuscripts was piled into a barrel for transport and sent from Widemann in Augsburg to Rudolf in Prague.[16]

If this reconstruction is correct, it might be possible to push back the Voynich Manuscript's earliest ownership even further. One option is that Widemann received the manuscript from his father, a barber surgeon, who might have bought it hoping to gain some medical knowledge from its herbal section. Another is that the manuscript came to Widemann from the botanist and traveller Leonhard Rauwolf, who served as an Augsburg physician before him, and into whose house Widemann had moved. Rauwolf had died in 1596, followed by his wife in 1597 – the year that Rudolf bought his first book from Augsburg. Rauwolf's family may have decided to sell the book collection they had inherited and approached Widemann, who was well known for his manuscript dealings, leading to the sale to Rudolf.[17]

Whatever the case may be, during the period between the manuscript's production and its appearance in Prague, its original binding was removed, and its page order was mixed up, never to be corrected. Someone added quire numbers to this newly arranged version of the manuscript and, later, page numbers too. Afterwards, a paint wash of green, red, yellow, and blue was applied to the illustrations, making them stand out more. Faint instructions in German, telling the painter which colours to use, were left on the pages; if correctly read, among them appear to be 'Rot' for 'red', and the letter 'G' for 'Grün' ('green'). Some sections were lost before the manuscript was rebound, or perhaps its owner simply discarded them.[18] These have never been found.

THE VOYNICH MANUSCRIPT (*c.* 1404–38)

THE PRAGUE YEARS

Crowned Holy Roman Emperor in 1576, the melancholy Rudolf II was bewitched by the arts, sciences, and the occult. He wanted to solve the mysteries of the world, so, after moving his court to Prague in 1583, he transformed the city into a centre of learning dedicated to this goal. Artists, alchemists, and natural philosophers flocked to Prague from across Europe, usually in the hope of securing work at his court; whether Protestant or Catholic, all were welcomed equally, as long as they had something to contribute. Astrologers and astronomers, such as Tycho Brahe and Johannes Kepler, observed the skies. Doctors searched for new cures to illnesses. Artists filled the walls of Rudolf's castle with paintings; among them was Giuseppe Arcimboldo, who painted Rudolf's face and torso assembled from vegetables, fruits, and flowers, presenting him as the Roman god of the seasons, Vertumnus, much to Rudolf's delight.[19] On Prague's Golden Lane, just outside the castle, alchemists practised their divine art, searching for the philosopher's stone, while the sounds of exotic animals drifted across the air from the nearby royal menagerie.[20]

Rudolf was also an obsessive collector, and famous across Europe for his 'Kunstkammer', or Art Chamber.[21] He had filled this royal art collection with objects of every kind, from paintings and bronzes to skeletons and armour, all spread across four rooms in his palace at the castle. Among his treasures were an agate bowl that he had identified as the Holy Grail, and an object he believed to be a unicorn horn.[22] In this world of magic, alchemy, and mystery, the Voynich Manuscript would have fitted in perfectly, though it is unclear whether the emperor kept it in his Kunstkammer or elsewhere.[23]

One of the key men at Rudolf's court was Jacobus Horčický, a plump man with a round face, features emphasized by his arched eyebrows and moustache. Said to be kind and polite, he started his career as a child servant working in a kitchen. There, the Jesuits spotted his intelligence and helped him to gain an education at their college in Krumau. He eventually became a chemist at the college, before moving to Prague to study philosophy. When outside class, he worked in the seminary kitchen in the old town and conducted his own studies into chemistry and herbs. Over time, he gained a reputation as a skilled healer and people started to call him Sinapius, from *sinapi* – Latin for mustard, which was the meaning of his surname, Horčický. After leaving Prague to build his name as a chemist, he returned to serve in Rudolf's court and cured the emperor of a serious illness. In 1608, he received the honour of a title: de Tepenec. It was sometime between this event and Rudolf's death in 1612 that the Voynich Manuscript passed into Horčický's hands. He signed his name on one of its pages, along with his new official title, and added a number, representing its position in his library.[24] In 1622, Horčický departed for his estates in Melnik, but a fall from his horse left him close to death. He returned to Prague and died there. He left his fortune to the Jesuits and was buried in the Old Town's church of St Salvator.[25]

There is no information on how the Voynich Manuscript passed from Jacobus Horčický to its next known owner, the alchemist and legal scribe Georgius Barschius. Barschius had the manuscript in his possession by 1637 and dedicated a great deal of his time to breaking its code. In late 1637, he asked his friend the Jesuit mathematician Theodor Moretus to write to the Jesuit polymath Athanasius Kircher in Rome, to see if he could help him understand its bizarre content. Kircher had a strong scholarly reputation and a history of mastering mysterious writings, such as Egyptian hieroglyphs. Rather than send him the whole manuscript, Barschius copied out a section and sent it with Moretus's letter.[26] In March 1639, Kircher replied, saying that he had perused the pages but had not managed to translate them. A month later, Barschius sent another letter to Kircher, but no response is known.[27]

Barschius died around 1662, still no wiser about the contents of his enigmatic manuscript. He left it and all of his other books to his old friend Johannes Marcus Marci, a physician and natural philosopher in Prague, who served as the Dean of the Faculty of Medicine at Charles University from 1638 and who had developed a friendship with Kircher during a visit to Rome. Following in Barschius' footsteps, the seventy-year-old Marci wrote to Kircher on 19 August 1665, again asking for the great scholar's thoughts. He explained how the manuscript had been sold to Emperor Rudolf for 600 ducats and that its author was believed to be the Franciscan friar and philosopher Roger Bacon. He also included something extremely important with his letter – the entire manuscript, which was carried to Rome by a priest who managed the Jesuits' work in Bohemia. Kircher, who had written a book on cryptography a couple of years earlier, appears not to have responded but, ever the careful archivist, he kept the letter with the manuscript. In 1666 and 1667, when Marci was suffering from failing eyesight and ill health, his friend Godefrid Alois Kinner sent two extra letters as reminders on his behalf. Again, no response is known. Marci died in 1667; like his friend Barschius, he had come no closer to unlocking the manuscript's secrets.[28]

ONWARDS TO ROME

And so, from 1665, the Voynich Manuscript ended up in the possession of the illustrious Athanasius Kircher in Italy. Born in Germany in 1601, Kircher had lived in Rome since 1634, initially taking up a position at the Collegio Romano teaching mathematics, before becoming a full-time researcher. Over the years, he published on a huge range of subjects, from Noah's Ark and magnetism to cryptography and Chinese culture. But he had a particular interest in world languages, ancient and modern, through which he hoped to access the knowledge given to Adam by God. His attempt to understand ancient Egyptian hieroglyphs – to Kircher, an important step towards Adam's original language – was published as *Oedipus Aegyptiacus* in 1652, making him famous across Europe. From 1651, he also ran his own museum, the *Museo Kircheriano*, housed at the Collegio Romano, which exhibited objects from Greece, Egypt, and Italy, but also from the Far East.

There were obelisks, statues, masks, the skeleton and tail of a siren, and an endlessly burning lamp. Such wonders gripped visitors. Although there is no indication that Kircher ever displayed the Voynich Manuscript, inventories and catalogues for the museum's earliest incarnation are lacking, leaving many questions about how he organized his exhibitions and what people could see. Nonetheless, it did have a small library, where visitors could read Kircher's own writings – his books and correspondence – and view select rare manuscripts.[29]

By this point in the manuscript's journey, the many hands that it had passed through had added their own scribbles on its pages.[30] Sometimes, these are the 'artefacts' of attempts to decipher its text. Marci appears to have written letters of the alphabet and Voynichese characters in columns in the margin of the manuscript's first page (folio 1r).[31] Elsewhere, there is what might be Greek writing, now very faint, along with a doodle of a shield (folio 17r).[32] In the astrological section, a reader, perhaps of northern French origin, added month names to the zodiacs.[33] A faint circle, divided into three parts, was drawn at the centre of one astrological page; this is a medieval symbol for the inhabited world, but also the alchemical symbol for soapstone. It is found again, very lightly visible, on other pages, along with what might be Arabic writing.[34] In addition to the German instructions for colours, mentioned above, other apparently German writing appears at the end of the manuscript (folio 116v), and the writing next to one illustration has been interpreted to read 'mus del' (folio 66r), but why it says this or what it truly means is unknown.

When Kircher died in 1680, the Voynich Manuscript entered one of the Jesuit libraries, most probably at the Collegio Romano, uncommented upon by anyone who happened to see it. It remained there until 1873, when the Italian government confiscated the Jesuits' documents and manuscripts to form part of their envisioned national library. But the Voynich Manuscript was not among them, for it had been moved to the personal collection of Petrus Beckx SJ, a priest of Belgian origin who had led the Jesuits since 1853. This collection appears to have been kept for safety in Villa Torlonia, in the town of Castel Gandolfo, south-east of Rome. In 1903, after Beckx's death, the Jesuits wanted to sell 380 of their manuscripts to the Vatican Library, and the Voynich Manuscript is listed in the sale catalogue. But the transaction was delayed by nine years, during which time they sold some of the manuscripts in secret to the book dealer Wilfrid Voynich, triggering the next major phase in the manuscript's eventful life.[35]

WILFRID VOYNICH AND HIS 'ROGER BACON CIPHER MANUSCRIPT'

Wilfrid Voynich was born in 1864 in Telšiai, Lithuania, to a Polish family. He joined the movement for Polish independence from Russia, but was arrested for revolutionary activity in 1885. After spending eighteen months imprisoned in Warsaw, he was sent to the icy outer reaches of Siberia to serve a five-year sentence. However, within a

10. Wilfrid Voynich in his London office.

couple of years, he escaped. Voynich travelled west and ultimately made his way to England, joining other exiles dedicated to revolution in Russia. Through his newfound connections, he rose in society and, following the advice of a friend, he decided to get involved in the antique book trade, with the intention of selling books and manuscripts in London. His shop opened in London's Soho Square in 1898 and became his life's focus. A few years later, in 1902, he married the famous novelist Ethel Boole. As his business grew and flourished, he moved to new premises on London's Shaftesbury Avenue, where there was more space for his stock. Voynich's willingness to travel in search of books and his knowledge of multiple languages were keys to his success, as were his deep knowledge of the books themselves and his good relations with his customers.[36] With each success, he sought rarer books – ones that went beyond the norm.

In 1912, Voynich arrived at the gates of Villa Torlonia in Castel Gandolfo, Italy. Nestled among the green hills south-east of Rome, overlooking Lake Albano, this picturesque town is best known as the location of the pope's summer residence. The Jesuits, strapped for cash, had decided to sell off some of their centuries-old rare manuscripts and books, which by this time had been kept hidden at Villa Torlonia for nearly forty years. Voynich had been invited to inspect a selection of these manuscripts by one of the Jesuit monks, Father Joseph Strickland, but, not wanting to bring attention to themselves – there was still the danger that the government might confiscate the collection – the Jesuits asked Voynich to keep the transaction a secret.[37]

To maintain this secrecy and add some deflection, Voynich's published account of his discovery simply describes him finding the manuscript 'in an ancient castle in Southern Europe'.[38] He says that, in one of the castle chambers, he rooted through dusty old chests, removing the manuscripts from within to peer at their contents. They had belonged to important families, he noticed; some pages still bore their coats of arms. Then, much to his pleasure, he came across a selection of beautifully illustrated manuscripts. One stood out from the rest – an 'ugly duckling' in Voynich's words. He inspected it, and discovered that the whole manuscript appeared to be written in cipher. He flicked through its 240 folio pages, observing the unusual calligraphy, the colours, and the drawings. His eyes fell on plants, a tiny dragon, castles. It could be a work of natural philosophy, he figured, perhaps from the thirteenth century based on its vellum, calligraphy, illustrations, and pigments. Voynich's next thoughts turned to authorship. Who had lived during the thirteenth century who could have written this mysterious manuscript? Perhaps it was the great philosopher and theologian Albertus Magnus, he wondered, or maybe Roger Bacon, a famous Franciscan friar believed to have practised black magic.[39] These thoughts marked the modern beginning of the quest to discover the manuscript's secrets.

After buying the manuscript, along with a number of others, Voynich researched its history. During one inspection, he took a closer look at a letter attached to the front cover, which he had previously largely ignored. It was the letter sent from Marci to Kircher with the manuscript, centuries earlier. Its content confirmed Voynich's suspicion that the manuscript was the work of Roger Bacon. He also began to suspect that the Elizabethan polymath John Dee, who had lived in Prague during Rudolf's reign, had sold the manuscript to the emperor, and that Dee himself had received it from the family of the Duke of Northumberland. He theorized that it probably entered this family's possession following the Dissolution of the Monasteries, so it must have been kept in a monastery beforehand.[40]

With the eruption of the First World War in 1914, Voynich started operating from New York. From there, he criss-crossed the United States, endeavouring to sell his 'Roger Bacon Cipher Manuscript', but could not find a buyer, perhaps due to his asking price, an astonishing $100,000. When lung cancer claimed his life in 1930, Voynich was laid to rest in New York and his manuscript remained unsold. In his will, he stipulated that his cipher manuscript should go to a public institution. His wife, Ethel, and the manager of his New York office,

Anne Nill, inherited the manuscript, and the decision on its fate would be decided by the two of them, with the aid of three friends as advisors. This ultimately led to nothing. Ethel died in 1960; a year later, Nill sold the manuscript to the book dealer H.P. Kraus for $24,500, who, like Voynich before him, could not find any buyers, perhaps again because of his hefty asking price: up to $160,000. It was Kraus who gave the Voynich Manuscript to Yale University's Beinecke Rare Book and Manuscript Library in 1969, where it remains today. Intriguingly, before Ethel passed away, she wrote a letter, to be opened only after her death, in which she explains some of the details surrounding the sale of the manuscript to her husband. She writes that Wilfrid had found it in Italy around 1911, possibly in a castle, and that it had belonged to the Vatican. Father Strickland had been the intermediary in the sale, she adds, but her husband had been sworn to secrecy.[41]

DECIPHERING THE VOYNICH MANUSCRIPT

Voynich had regarded the bizarre content of his manuscript as a cipher, in which the readable letters of its language had been switched for other characters; as a result, it became of interest to cryptographers. The first real attempt to decrypt its content was in the early 1920s by the University of Pennsylvania's William Newbold, whose solution was to see a form of microscopic shorthand. According to Newbold, each Voynich character was formed from around ten tiny signs that were abbreviations based on Greek. The reader needed a microscope to discern these signs, and had to decide at what position in the larger characters to begin identifying the tiny characters. Once the decipherer had noted these abbreviations and placed them in the correct order, they could construct a translation in Latin. This all seems a bit far-fetched; but what makes it even more unbelievable is that, because Newbold believed Roger Bacon to be the manuscript's author, this thirteenth-century friar would have first needed to invent the microscope. Newbold's solution was unusual, to say the least, but it was accepted until after his death. Only later in the 1920s did another scholar dismantle Newbold's arguments, and (politely) claim that his colleague's conclusions had been mistaken.[42]

John Manly, the scholar who dismantled Newbold's arguments, was also the one who set in motion the next attempt at decryption, when he sent photos of the manuscript to the codebreakers William and Elizebeth Friedman. Captured by its tantalizing script, they would spend the next decades of their lives examining the manuscript; William even founded a Voynich Manuscript Study Group in 1944, and the two of them later used computers to help with their decipherment work. During this time, the general consensus became that the manuscript was produced sometime in the sixteenth century, probably in northern Italy or southern Germany. In 1959, the Friedmans wrote an article together, which ended with an anagram. This was said to give their final thoughts on the Voynich Manuscript, but the solution was sealed in an envelope, held by the journal's editor, and would only be opened after William's death. That solution was published in 1970. Their conclusion? That the authors of the Voynich Manuscript had attempted to create an artificial or universal language, unconnected to any that existed.[43]

The next major investigation was by Mary D'Imperio, a cryptologist working for the US National Security Agency, who published a book about the manuscript in 1978. In great depth, she examines its illustrations, makes comparisons to other manuscripts, and describes attempts to decrypt its content.[44] D'Imperio also presents the conclusions of Prescott Currier, who showed that multiple hands worked on the manuscript and, based on differing patterns in the arrangement of the letters, spotted the presence of two 'languages'.[45] Scholars also analysed the manuscript's illustrations over the decades. According to one newspaper article, a Danish botanist named Holm recognized sixteen European plants in its illustrations and argued that the rest were composites of various plants or were imaginary.[46] Ethel Voynich tried to match the illustrations to known plants.[47] Meanwhile, the botanist Hugh O'Neil argued that the illustrations included a sunflower and a pepper plant, with the ramification that its creators were aware of New World plants, placing its production after 1492.[48]

In the 1970s and '80s, Robert Brumbaugh, a professor of medieval philosophy, was the next scholar to investigate the Voynich Manuscript and offer a method of decryption.[49] He saw each Voynich character as representing a number from 0 to 9, and each number representing three letters. The character he identified as '7', for example, stood for 'G', 'P', and 'Y', while '2' was 'B', 'K', and 'R'. To read a word, you first had to translate each character into its number and then write out the three possible letters beneath each one; this led to a grid of options. You then looked along the rows and chose the letters that revealed the word – one letter might come from the top row, the next from the bottom, the next from the middle, and so on. To make things even more complex, the words themselves were written in an artificial pseudo-Latin and often had spelling mistakes.

Using this method, Brumbaugh decrypted the text beside the illustration of a plant controversially identified as a capsicum pepper, a genus unknown in Europe before 1493. This revealed the word 'pepper'. When he applied the same approach to other words on the page, he found misspellings of plants like Papavayjs for Papaversus, meaning poppy.[50] Brumbaugh also used his decryption method to translate the words beside the nude women holding stars in the zodiac rings. He found that each was associated with the name of a famous person from the past, such as Alexander the Great or Julius Caesar, and suggested that these could be souls connected to the stars. Because Arab philosophers are among the names, he added that this section may have been copied from a twelfth- or thirteenth-century document of Spanish origin.[51] Brumbaugh also suggested that whoever created the Voynich Manuscript played on Roger Bacon's association with finding the elixir of life and produced a manuscript that appears to hold its secret.[52]

Despite his promising findings, in the 1980s Brumbaugh changed his conclusions; unfortunately, having tried his decryption method on the main text, he overall found nonsense. He noted that many words ended in '-us', that there were the names of some countries, and that there were words that tantalizingly appeared to spell 'elixir' – but nothing else. Ultimately, Brumbaugh concluded that the manuscript was a hoax with little meaning to be found. He suggested that it was created by John Dee and Edward Kelly in the sixteenth century to make money out of Emperor Rudolf II, and he linked the timing of the sale with a sudden rise in the two men's fortunes.[53]

THE ROHONC CODEX: THE WORLD'S SECOND-MOST MYSTERIOUS MANUSCRIPT

Before we continue the Voynich Manuscript's journey into the twenty-first century, for any readers worrying that its mystery might never be solved, we will briefly take a look at the world's second-most mysterious manuscript: the Rohonc Codex. With obscure origins, this manuscript was first investigated by scholars after being inherited by the Hungarian Academy of Sciences, along with 30,000

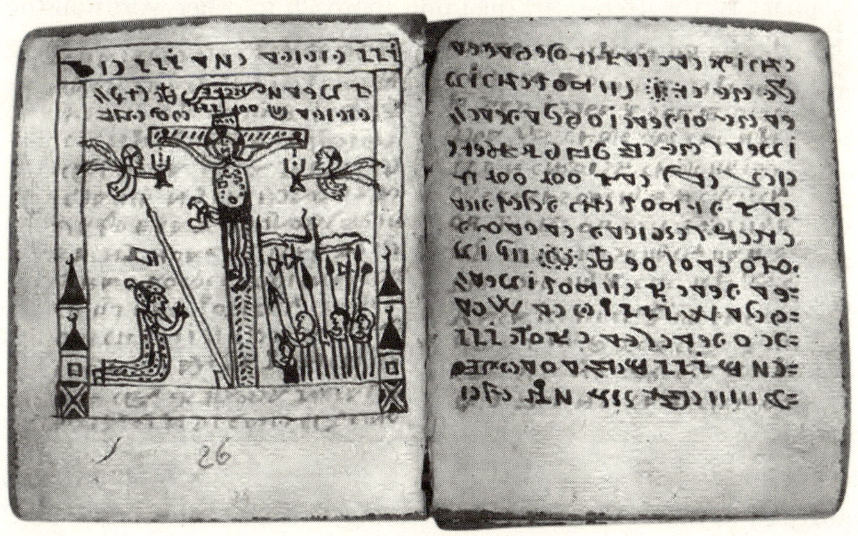

11. Two pages from the Rohonc Codex, one bearing an illustration of the crucifixion.

other volumes, following the death of Count Gusztáv Batthyány, a nobleman from what in those days was Rohonc in Hungary.[54] The 450-page manuscript, featuring around ninety illustrations, is entirely written in mysterious symbols, seemingly in more than one hand, or by one person who varied the speed of their writing. Based on watermarks on its pages, it was perhaps produced during the sixteenth century, while the paper itself appears to have been made in northern Italy or in Salzburg in Austria.[55] Religious scenes are among the illustrations, including the crucifixion, Jesus with the crown of thorns upon his head, the resurrection, and the star of Bethlehem, although the manuscript's overall theme is less clear in other places. The weapons and architecture reflect those of central Europe during the sixteenth and seventeenth centuries. The Rohonc script itself, meanwhile, consists of around eight hundred symbols, written from right to left, starting at the top of the page, and without any breaks or punctuation to separate the words and sentences.[56]

When discovered in the library of the Hungarian Academy of Sciences, the Rohonc Codex generated a great deal of interest among scholars. In the 1840s, the historian János Jerney suggested that the text might be a cipher or that it was perhaps written by Tartars using an Asian script. The artist Mihály Munkácsy studied the manuscript in Paris between 1890 and 1892; later, Kálman Némäti argued that the text was ancient Hungarian. At the end of the nineteenth century, a team of palaeographers concluded that the Rohonc Codex was a forgery and that its symbols were meaningless. During the twentieth century, Ottó Gyürk realized that certain symbols could be read as numerals, showing that there might be meaning behind them after all. One researcher later argued that the manuscript was written in a form of vulgar Latin, while in the 2000s another said it was Sanskrit. As the twenty-first century continued, researchers used computer analyses to better understand the Rohonc Codex's mysterious text; notably, Miklós Locsmándi identified its numbers in 2004. The historian Benedek Láng then undertook extensive research into the codex, tracing its history, discussing its possible contents, and reviewing the attempts to break its code.[57]

In recent years, breakthroughs have been made towards understanding the Rohonc Codex, spearheaded by the researchers Levente Zoltán Király and Gábor Tokai. Initially working separately and then together, they revealed that its mysterious characters were in fact a code, in which each group of symbols signified a word, be it a noun like 'bread', a verb like 'give', or prepositions. There were symbols that stood for names, such as Pilate or Longinus; others for places; and some for numerals. Sometimes, different symbols had the same meaning – for example, there are three symbols for 'Jesus'. This accounted for why there were around eight hundred different symbols across the manuscript. The researchers also noticed that the folios were in the wrong order and that at least twenty-two are missing, so they reconstructed its original structure. Overall, as expected from the illustrations, the manuscript appears to present biblical stories, mainly from the New Testament, but with some Old Testament content too. They include the life of Jesus, the crucifixion, Jesus's teachings and miracles, prayers to Mary, and the period from the resurrection to Pentecost, among other subjects. Intriguingly, certain details within these stories are unique, indicating a local influence. The decoded dates suggest that the manuscript was produced in 1593, confirming the earlier argument for a sixteenth-century origin, but it is not yet possible to identify which language was used or where the manuscript was created. It was most probably written by a person from central Europe who visited Italy, given that the themes in its illustrations suggest a knowledge of Italian thirteenth- and fourteenth-century paintings.[58]

'VOYNICHESE' IN THE TWENTY-FIRST CENTURY

Unlike the Rohonc Codex, recent analyses of the Voynich Manuscript's unusual script have reached conflicting conclusions about whether a true language lies behind its characters, or if it is nothing but gibberish. Over the years, researchers have studied the occurrence of words in paragraphs, the characters or their similarity to the scripts of various world languages, and the structure of the text itself. Sometimes, these studies conclude that 'Voynichese' has the characteristics of a real enciphered text, but they do not always present a conclusion about which language (or languages) it hides, or offer a decryption and translation.[59] One paper, written by Luke Lindemann, compares the Voynich Manuscript's word distribution to that of 160 modern languages and those found in certain historical manuscripts, and concludes that it is closest to medieval Germanic languages.[60] Another, by Ivan Zelinka and colleagues, used computer analysis to see how similar Voynich characters are to the scripts of various world alphabets, but as this was just a test – a proof of concept – they only included ancient Indian dialects (in which case, its closest match was the Khojki Jiva dialect).[61]

A 2011 study by Sravana Reddy and Kevin Knight argues that there appear to be two 'languages' in the Voynich Manuscript, just as Prescott Currier had earlier proposed; this could be because its content is different languages or dialects, or simply because it covers a variety of subjects with their own vocabularies. The researchers see the Voynich script as an abjad: a script in which the vowels are typically omitted, as is the case for those used by Semitic languages like Arabic.[62] Claire L. Bowern and Luke Lindemann, the authors of a 2021 paper, also see two 'languages' in the Voynich Manuscript, and suggest that this is the result of its creator(s) using different encryption methods for one or more natural languages.[63] Another study, written by Andrew Caruana and colleagues, looks at the occurrence of pairs of words across multiple texts, and highlights that certain words tend to occur together in a particular order. When they applied their results to the Voynich Manuscript, the researchers concluded that a linguistic structure was present, and therefore a true language.[64] Finally, in a paper from

2020, Lisa Fagin Davis identified the handwriting of five scribes in the manuscript, showing that they shared the task of producing its content.[65]

Some researchers have offered decipherments. Rainer Hannig has suggested that the language underlying the Voynich script is Hebrew.[66] Gerard Cheshire has argued that it is a form of Proto-Romance, and has since developed his theory to identify it as Galician-Portuguese, with additions from Latin, Greek, and Arabic.[67] Nicholas Gibbs has proposed that the Voynich script is a collection of Latin abbreviations and ligatures;[68] while Jules Janick and Arthur O. Tucker have argued that it is a synthetic language created from different languages found in New Spain, or that it is a form of Nahuatl (Aztec) lingua franca, with the addition of words from Spanish and maybe Arabic.[69] Tucker and Janick have also concluded that all but one of the Voynich botanical illustrations show New World plants or are circumboreal.[70]

Perhaps the most intriguing recent decipherment proposal was made by Stephen Bax, who argued that he had managed to read fourteen of the Voynich characters and ten of its words. He began by looking at the herbal section, where he found an illustration that resembles juniper leaves and certain symbols that he thought might spell out the Arabic/Hebrew word *arar* – 'juniper'. He then turned to the astrological section and identified the word Taurus. Next, taking the characters he had assigned a sound value, he applied his method to other pages in the herbal section. In the end, Bax concluded that Voynichese was probably developed to write a language that had no script, perhaps by a small group of people who died out before passing their knowledge on. He could not be certain which language lies behind the script, but he argued that it was probably not European, suggesting Near Eastern, Caucasian, or Asian languages as options.[71] Although a fascinating proposal, like all the above proposed decipherments, Bax's arguments have not been widely accepted.[72]

Other researchers have argued that the Voynich Manuscript contains nothing but gibberish and have provided counterarguments to the above theories.[73] Statistical analyses of the text have concluded that there is no hidden meaning,[74] while one study, by Andreas Schinner, argues that it was made using a 'stochastic process' – roughly meaning that the scribes developed a method to produce random text.[75] Another study, by Torsten Timm, showed that the distribution of words throughout the manuscript does not follow the expected pattern for natural languages.[76] But if there is no meaning behind the words, how did the scribe or scribes create so much content? One suggestion, proposed by Timm and Schinner, is through 'self-citation'. In this method, the scribes created new words based on the model of those on the lines above, simply switching a character or two to make them appear new and different, yet still similar to the ones that came before. Using this technique, the scribes could quickly generate new words, page after page. They did not need to actively or purposefully follow this method; it could just have been an instinctive way to continuously invent words with ease.[77] Another method, proposed by Gordon Rugg and Gavin Taylor, is that the scribes could have used a table bearing Voynich symbols and a series of grilles, each with three holes in different formations. These grilles, when placed on the table, would only reveal three symbols at a time, which could then be combined to form a Voynich word. A statistical analysis of text produced by this method replicated features found in the Voynich Manuscript.[78]

An experiment involving volunteers writing a few pages of gibberish revealed surprising similarities to the Voynich Manuscript's text. By analysing these pages, Daniel E. Gaskell and Claire L. Bowern showed that the volunteers' meaningless sentences could quite closely replicate the appearance of a true language and Voynichese. At the same time, unlike true languages, which usually mix long and short words in a sentence, the Voynich Manuscript often has a sequence of long words followed by short words; it is as if the writer(s) noticed that they were overusing long words and corrected themselves. This phenomenon was also found in the gibberish texts produced by the study's volunteers. The Voynich Manuscript has only short words beside illustrations, as if they were designed to fit the available space; volunteers who included drawings on their pages did likewise. Also, if a volunteer wrote a gibberish word in a heading, they repeated it, or a very similar word, in the text they produced on that same page; again, this is found in the Voynich Manuscript. Intriguingly, too, volunteers intuitively generated new words by looking at ones they had written earlier, effectively following the 'self-citation' method.[79]

STUDYING THE VOYNICH ILLUSTRATIONS AND MATERIALS

The Voynich Manuscript's illustrations have also received attention from researchers. In 2016, the medical historian Alain Touwaide noted that its herbal illustrations share a lot in common with those found in botanical works of the fourteenth and fifteenth centuries, adding that the astrological section might have been included because a physician could use the stars to make predictions about patients' health. As for the bathing section, Touwaide suggests that it relates to thermal baths, and that the women represent elderly people relaxing. The pharmaceutical section's plants might refer back to those in the first part of the manuscript, while the final section, usually identified as recipes, might be an index and synopsis of the whole manuscript. Touwaide notes that the manuscript is similar to medical manuals and proposes that its illustrations might have been painted a second time at some point in its history.[80]

Certain illustrations have provided researchers with clues to the manuscript's origins, inspirations, and function. A small drawing of a castle bears distinctive swallowtail (also called Ghibelline) merlons that form its crenellations (folio 86r6). As highlighted by René Zandbergen, this architectural feature is typically seen in northern

Italy, particularly around Verona, as well as in central Europe, but its presence in drawings is usually found in manuscripts produced in northern Italy.[81] Koen Gheuens and Cary Rapaport recently analysed the canopies drawn on various pages of the manuscript, suggesting that they were inspired by medieval parasol-roofed tents, and that this may be part of a metaphor in which the sky is seen as a tent.[82] Keagan Brewer has noted that many of the images of nude women break medieval taboos. One woman points a phallic object towards her genitals, for example (folio 80r). Such imagery could associate the Voynich Manuscript with sexological texts, or books of women's secrets, translated into vernacular languages and commissioned by the nobility of the fifteenth century. Writings of this type regularly obscured taboo topics, such as sex and genitalia, from words to whole recipes, using ciphers.[83] Brewer and Michelle L. Lewis have also argued that the Voynich rosettes might represent coitus and conception.[84]

Scientific analyses of the manuscript itself have revealed that its current cover is not original and that certain folios are missing. In fact, the original cover was probably made from wood lined with leather. Fibre threads bind the manuscript's pages to flax cords, rather than the more usual leather strips used in the era it was produced; and certain threads that held the book together were pink. To help shape the manuscript's spine, its binders put pieces of paper between its supports. This too is surprising, because parchment or leather usually served this purpose. The calfskin parchment chosen by the scribes was expensive, but not the finest quality that could be bought; and, although the presence of foldout sections was not unusual, particularly in manuscripts that included calendars to predict the future or in handbooks consulted by doctors, the parchment used to make these sections would have been costly. Finally, expert analysis of the ink and paint shows their ingredients to be consistent with fifteenth-century examples, while carbon-14 dating of the parchment gives a date range of 1404 to 1438.[85]

NEXT STEPS?

Each of these modern studies has brought something new to the unfolding Voynich mystery, chipping away at its wall of silence. But with such contradictory results, ranging from the almost certain presence of languages to it being total gibberish, there is still a great deal of confusion. This is surprising, given the length of the time that the text has been scrutinized by professional codebreakers, and the hefty computing power now available to researchers. At the same time, despite the large number of studies, none have yet managed to fully explain the Voynich Manuscript's function. Why would someone have gone to the effort of producing this manuscript in the first place? Although researchers have made great progress, none have yet managed to fully unravel the mystery of the manuscript. The work of Newbold, the Friedmans, D'Imperio, and Brumbaugh has, however, laid out the main categories into which it could fall: it could be an enciphered or encoded natural language, like Latin or Spanish; it could be an artificial or universal language and script; or it could be a hoax. We will return to this problem in Chapter 10.

The Voynich Manuscript is today housed in Yale University's Beinecke Rare Book and Manuscript Library, with the call number Beinecke MS 408.[86]

In our next chapter, we will travel to early fifteenth-century Venice to meet Giovanni Fontana, an Italian doctor with a mind for invention and mischief, whose enciphered manuscripts cover diverse topics, from the art of memory to weapons of war.

3

BELLICORUM INSTRUMENTORUM LIBER (1420–30)

Ciphers and the Secrets of Engineering and Technology

It was the day of Saint Lawrence, 10 August 1410, when the waters of Venice, normally so serene, turned turbulent. A ferocious wind roared across the city, taking everyone by surprise. It was so sudden that many Venetians were still on their boats. Those sailing from Mestre – the mainland to the west of Venice's islands – sank to the bottom of the lagoon. Around three hundred men, women, and children died. People would later find bodies floating in the San Segondo Canal. Sister Bartolomea Riccoboni watched the storm from the convent of Corpus Domini, on the north-west edge of Venice's main island, facing the Grand Canal. At around sunset, during vespers, a huge gust of wind slammed into the convent. The belfry broke away and crashed down onto the new dormitory. A chimney smashed through the roof of the old dormitory. Trees toppled and a wall collapsed, leaving the convent open to thieves.

Another witness to the storm was a teenager called Giovanni Fontana. As he travelled over land and water that August day, he watched the wind terrorize the city. He saw sailors washed away by the rising flood waters, huge trees uprooted, and terracotta tiles flying from the roofs of buildings. The air was filled with the fragments of bricks and stones. All around him, houses collapsed and the spires of towers fell to the ground. Amid the chaos, he watched people pray. This was the wrath of God, they had decided. Venice would be destroyed. Witnesses claimed to have seen devils flying among the clouds, and heard screaming in the sky. The young Fontana disagreed.

Through all the madness, he saw a purely natural phenomena. The disturbance had been caused by winds, blowing from different directions, meeting and swirling rapidly into the sky, he argued. There was no need to blame God, Satan, or any other heavenly or hellish force. Even so, Fontana believed that he only survived that day thanks to divine mercy.[1]

This mixture of the scientific and the devout, of practical knowledge gained from experiments and observations of nature combined with a belief in the supernatural, was characteristic of Fontana. He was a true pre-Renaissance man. He was entranced by the natural magic of mechanical creations and hydraulics, the weather, clocks and fountains, and the possibility of flight or of being able to dive to the bottom of the sea. But he was a world-class prankster too, happy to poke fun at the elite, a showman, and a Christian, who claimed that a spirit taught him how to thicken mercury.[2] He was also fascinated by ciphers. He had two of his Latin manuscripts copied in a cipher of his own devising, a pioneering idea in a time when ciphers were mainly used to hide the content of diplomatic correspondence, intelligence, and merchants' business secrets. He dedicated one of these enciphered works to the art of memory, the other to his imagined machines, filling its pages with sketches of complex mechanisms – from mechanical witches to siege engines and rocket-powered chairs. Today, it is known as the *Bellicorum instrumentorum liber*, the 'Book of the Instruments of War'.

FONTANA'S EARLY YEARS AND STUDIES

Giovanni Fontana was born around 1395, probably in Venice, adding to its 120,000-strong population.[3] His father was Michele da Venezia, but nothing else can be said about him. His mother's identity is unknown.[4] At the time of Fontana's birth, Venice was experiencing a boom. The Venetian Republic's phase of expansion was in full swing, with key locations like Crete and Corfu already under its sway. A maritime empire had formed.[5] Sailors travelled the known world from Venice's ports, returning with exotic goods to be sold at stalls in the bustling Rialto market. Travellers and merchants from East and West spread the latest news and gossip – important in the world of commerce, where information was power.[6] Along the Grand Canal, the city's main conduit, wealthy merchants had raised grand palazzos of red brick and white limestone with roofs of terracotta tiles; the fanciest had street and canal access. Some of these buildings fused Eastern style and Gothic design, creating a uniquely Venetian architecture. The Doge's Palace (Palazzo Ducale), Venice's centre of government, had already overlooked St Mark's Square for centuries, which then, as today, was dominated by the Byzantine architecture of St Mark's Basilica. Across the city, gondolas and flat-bottomed boats bobbed on the water, passed over by small wooden bridges that spanned the canals, intersecting the floating city, to provide access to its labyrinthine streets.[7]

During his teenage years, Fontana moved to Padua, 35 kilometres west of Venice. This city had fallen under Venetian control in 1405, when Francesco Novello, the Seigneur of Padua, was imprisoned in Venice and strangled, probably just a few years before Fontana's arrival. Fontana studied art and medicine at the University of Padua under the famous philosopher, astrologer, and mathematician Biagio Pelacani and the philosopher and theologian Paul of Venice; like other students of his time, he would have paid his professors' wages directly to them. The university was still relatively young in the early fifteenth century, having been founded in 1222 by academics and students from Bologna University who wanted more freedom in their teaching and study.[8] Unlike Bologna, the university was open to people of all religions, though female students were forbidden.[9]

If you visited Padua in the 1410s, it would have been easy to spot Fontana. When not studying, he could be found standing beside the River Bacchiglione, dropping lead-weighted fish into its depths to measure the speed of descent. You might have had to dodge a rocket-propelled rabbit sent hurtling towards you while Fontana measured the length of time it took to travel the distance from him to you. He also had rocket-propelled birds among his oeuvre so, even from above, you would not have been safe. On one occasion, he terrified an inquisitive monk with a particularly devilish creation. In preparation for the monk's visit, Fontana took a pair of bat wings, bird legs, and some horns, and attached them to a body made from furry leather. He added eyes of glass and red crystal and, as the *pièce de résistance*, stuffed the body with gunpowder. When the monk stepped into the room, Fontana lit his monstrous invention and threw it into a water-filled barrel. The monk leapt back in terror. A shrieking creature writhed in the water before him – a true demon, the monk exclaimed! It twisted and shook. Flames burst from its lips. The smell of sulphur filled the room. Fontana laughed. Through his inventions, he could convince even Padua's wisest men that he had the power to summon the supernatural.[10] It is no surprise that, in his writings, he had to dedicate space to emphasizing his lack of heresy. He did not deal in black magic, demons, or raising the dead, he explained. Apparently, he just thought it was funny.

The places that Fontana experienced and the people whom he met during his years in Padua crept into his writing. He mentions the spiral staircases inside the Basilica of Sant'Antonio,[11] and his friend the painter Jacopo Bellini, for whom he wrote a treatise on perspective.[12] He describes how he watched rainwater pooling on the stone slabs lining the ground at Piazza delle Erbe and pondered its movements in puddles. As he left that piazza, he would have joined the throngs of people passing in and out of the market that separates it from the nearby Piazza della Frutta, and perhaps he might have taken the time to admire the grand Palazzo della Ragione above the market, where Padua's courts met in a hall decorated with astrological themes. Nearby, on Via Marsilio da Padova, he perhaps even watched the annual competition to be the first to climb a greasy pole; the winner won a pair of gloves and some gold coins.

Fontana's deep interest in experiments and discovery was perhaps inspired by the intellectual changes happening in society all around him. Not only had he grown up in Venice, a crossroads between East and West, but the early fifteenth century in northern Italy was a time of rediscovery, when ancient Greek knowledge resurfaced and translations of medieval Arabic works enhanced the study of the natural world. In 1405, Giovanni Aurispa had brought copies of Theophrastus's botanical writings from Constantinople; in 1417, Poggio Bracciolini discovered a copy of Lucretius's *On the Nature of Things* at a monastery near Lake Constance; and in 1426, Guarino of Verona brought from Constantinople a work on surgery by Celsus. These discoveries, and many more like them, began an era of lost manuscript mania. From Rome to Florence, Padua, and Venice, people actively sought out old manuscripts, rediscovered lost knowledge, and wrote new works with the potential to upturn everything scholars accepted as fact. Everywhere, people questioned, tested, experimented, and disproved or built upon the work of classical writers.[13] For a young person with a scientific mind like Fontana, it must have been a vibrant time to be alive. Anything seemed possible.

As the years went by, Fontana remained in Padua to study for a doctorate in liberal arts. He passed his examination at the city's episcopal palace in June 1418 and officially received his qualification the day after, during a public ceremony at the cathedral next door.[14] He was then elected by the university's students to be the Rector of the Arts in Padua from July 1418 to July 1419, a position that changed holder annually.[15] Rectors were sworn in at Padua's cathedral in the presence of the city's dignitaries, after which they had to throw an expensive feast and provide gifts to the electors and other guests.[16] For his year in office, Fontana, like all rectors of the arts, would have had to wear expensive scarlet robes (with thicker ones during the winter). He would certainly have stood out in the city's streets.[17] Afterwards, he remained in Padua to complete a doctorate in medicine, passing his examination in May 1421.[18]

FONTANA'S EARLIEST MANUSCRIPTS

Fontana's years in Padua were a productive time in his side career as an author. Writing for friends, he dedicated one of his earliest works to mechanisms run by gear wheels, such as mechanical clocks, and included seventy drawings. Within the text, he describes the various ways in which these devices can be powered, from simple muscle power to steam, water, wind, magnets, and even hot air produced by candles.[19] As early as 1416 or 1417, he wrote a treatise on water clocks with alarms, and then dedicated another manuscript, completed in 1418, to the subject of sand clocks. Here, he mentions his plan to write a manuscript on war machines and his belief that it is possible to build a perpetual motion machine. Given Fontana's early interest in mechanisms and clocks, we can imagine that, after his return to Venice in the 1420s, he spent time around the Rialto market watching the two mechanical clocks that helped Venice's citizens to keep an eye on the timing of the tides and to schedule trading negotiations. The one at San Giovanni Elemosinario was built in 1394; the second, on San Giacomo di Rialto was erected during Fontana's lifetime, in 1422.[20]

Shortly after 1418, while still living in Padua, Fontana wrote a manuscript on science and engineering called the *Tractus de pisce, cane, et volucre*. He dedicated this primarily to measurements of height, depth, and distance using devices made to appear like animals; to measure depth, for instance, he sank a weighted fish. He writes on hot air balloons (which he felt would be too difficult to control), the possibility of breathing underwater using machines, and his creation of rocket devils, made from wood and paper, that launched into the sky with fire blasting from their rear ends, creating a foul smell.[21] Here, again, Fontana mentions his plan to pen a manuscript on war machines and equipment.[22]

Based on his writings and the sources he drew from, Fontana's interests and reading were wide. Mechanisms, hydraulics, meteorology, the measurement of time, fountains, mirrors, flight, diving – there was nothing beyond his curiosity. He made his own instruments to refine his experiments and observations, and never solely relied on the writings or words of others. The technical subjects he investigated were not covered in university curricula of the early fifteenth century; even so, scholars did take an interest in mechanical devices, continuing the research of Greek and Roman authors. Giovanni Dondi wrote on wheel clocks in 1365; in the same century, Pierre de Maricourt explored how magnets can create motion. In the first half of the fourteenth century, Guido of Vigevano designed a wind chariot. Often, these musings were not just out of academic curiosity. Any innovation in these fields could give a warring state an edge over its rivals. For example, before the fall of Padua to Venice, the soon-to-be-strangled Seigneur of Padua asked Konrad Gruter, a German expert in mechanical devices who would later write a book on the subject, to take a look at his state's war equipment.[23] It was a smart idea, even if it did not change Padua's fate.

WRITING THE *BELLICORUM INSTRUMENTORUM LIBER*

After completing his studies in Padua, Fontana appears to have returned home to Venice, perhaps to work as a doctor while continuing his scientific experiments. It was there, probably during the 1420s and still in his mid-twenties, that he started writing his *Bellicorum instrumentorum liber*.[24] Although that was not its original title, and not every design is dedicated to warfare, weapons of war were a major concern; given the violent years in which Fontana lived, this was a clever tactical move. There was money to be made from war. Over the decades from 1389, the Venetian Republic had aggressively expanded westward, transforming from a primarily maritime republic, with its eyes to the East, into one of the five powerful states of Italy. While Fontana wrote his manuscript, the republic absorbed the Friuli region, north-east of Venice, and spread west into Brescia and Bergamo.[25] There was also Venetian expansion along the Adriatic coast.[26]

But to make money from war, you first had to grab the attention of a powerful patron. These competed to hire the greatest skilled artists, engineers, and architects of their day, commissioning them to realize important projects, from designing churches, palaces, and fortifications to preparing creations meant as entertainment for the elite. But it was weapons of war they most desired; and it was probably the hope of securing such a wealthy patron that inspired Fontana to write his *Bellicorum instrumentorum liber* – such manuscripts were good advertisements for a person's talents. Fontana's intended reader is not named in the manuscript, but they appear to have been on friendly terms – the two had enjoyed discussions together, we are told, and the reader had already received other manuscripts from him. If securing patronage was indeed Fontana's aim, he would have joined many others elbowing through the crowd to make their names known in a century that gave birth to a plethora of famous innovators: from Mariano Taccola, a contemporary of Fontana's from Siena who, like him, wrote illustrated treatises on machines and devices, to – of course – Leonardo Da Vinci, who was born midway through the century and designed a wide range of fantastic machines (among his many other achievements). In all cases, the key to success was an interest in experimentation: trying a new approach, rather than simply relying on the writings of classical authors. Curiosity and questioning were rewarded.[27]

And Fontana's *Bellicorum instrumentorum liber* is filled with invention. The wealthy Italian prince looking to enhance his weapons of war could find a gigantic tower-shaped battering ram on wheels (folios 1v–2r); a giant flame-throwing machine (again on wheels) (folios 2v–3r); a building armed with weapons that automatically fired and reloaded, powered by ropes, with cannons on the first floor, spears on the second, and arrows on the third (folios 6v–7r); a massive cannon, attached to a castle, that fired flaming balls into a nearby river to disrupt the water and unbalance the boats (folios 12v–13r); and weapons disguised as tools (folio 50r).[28]

12. An amphibious ship, from Giovanni Fontana's *Bellicorum instrumentorum liber*.

Beyond war machines, we can find Fontana's glowing bishop's mitre (folio 19v), his surgical equipment (folio 45v), his fountains (e.g. folios 22v–23r), and his designs for labyrinths (folios 9v and 10r), for which he offers both round and square versions and mentions having written a short treatise on the subject already (now unfortunately lost).[29] There is a design for lock picks (folio 36r), and a complex set of accoutrements for helping a person balance on a tightrope (a setup that he had not yet attempted himself) (folios 33v–34r).[30] Other designs represent means of transport, from his amphibious ship, which looks like a large galleon warship on wheels (folios 37v–38r), to his chair on wheels, fitted with gears to make them spin – in effect, an early car (folios 17v–18r).[31] Fontana comments that his chair moves faster than a galloping horse and can be difficult to stop when it hurtles down a slope – or even when the terrain is level. Perhaps he should have invented brakes first. He also includes a rocket-propelled dove and rabbit, with flames coming out of the rabbit's rear end and its legs fixed to a form of fifteenth-century skateboard (folio 37r).[32]

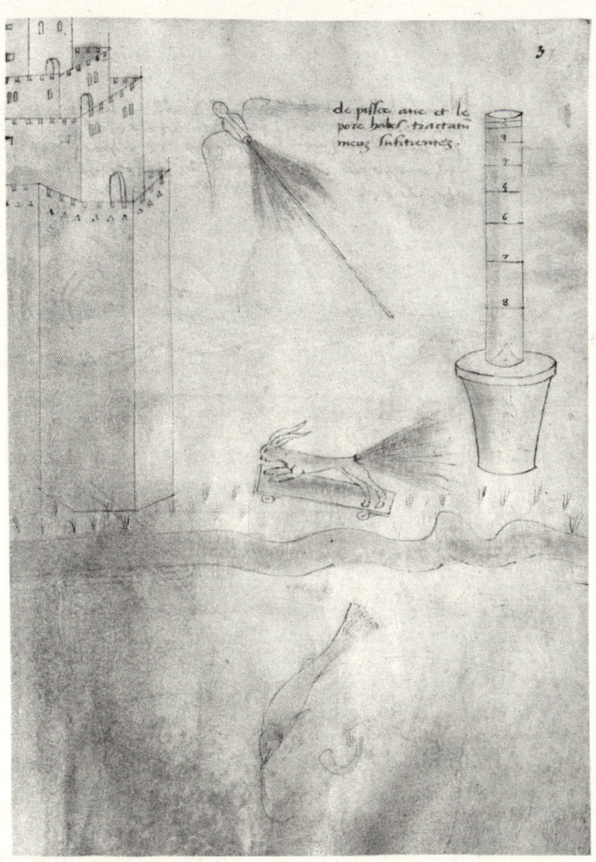

13. Rocket-propelled animals, from Giovanni Fontana's *Bellicorum instrumentorum liber*.

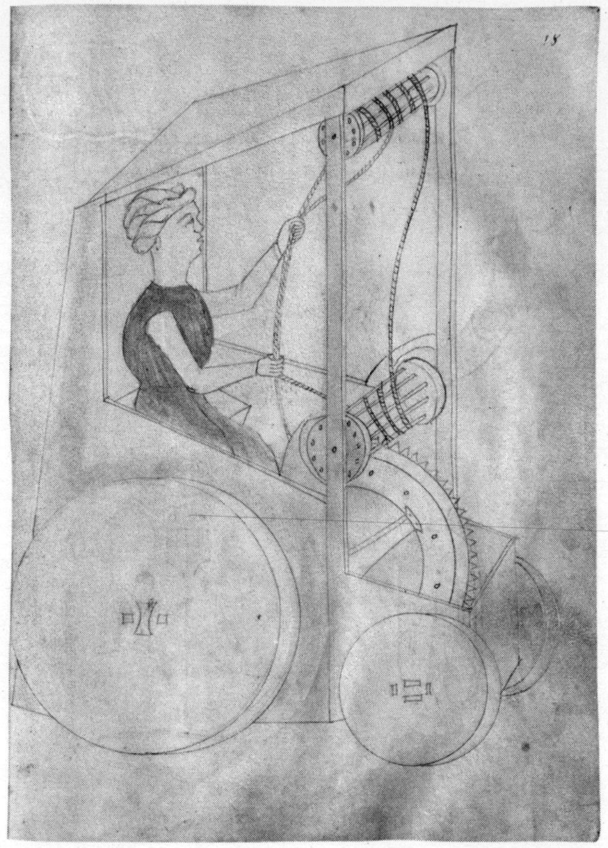

14. A chair on wheels, fitted with gears to make them spin, from Giovanni Fontana's *Bellicorum instrumentorum liber*.

But perhaps Fontana's most intriguing designs are those meant to excite or frighten an audience. One presents an artificial way of raising the dead. Two painted wooden skeletons rest in a box; beneath them is a clock-like mechanism with wheels, which, when turned, makes the skeletons move (folio 51r).[33] Then there is Fontana's mechanical devil, which, he writes, was specifically made to scare people. This seated, winged monster, with three faces on its head, has moveable joints, tongue, horns, and wings, all pulled by ropes (folios 59v–60v).[34] The design for his fire-breathing witch (folios 63v–64r) demonstrates that

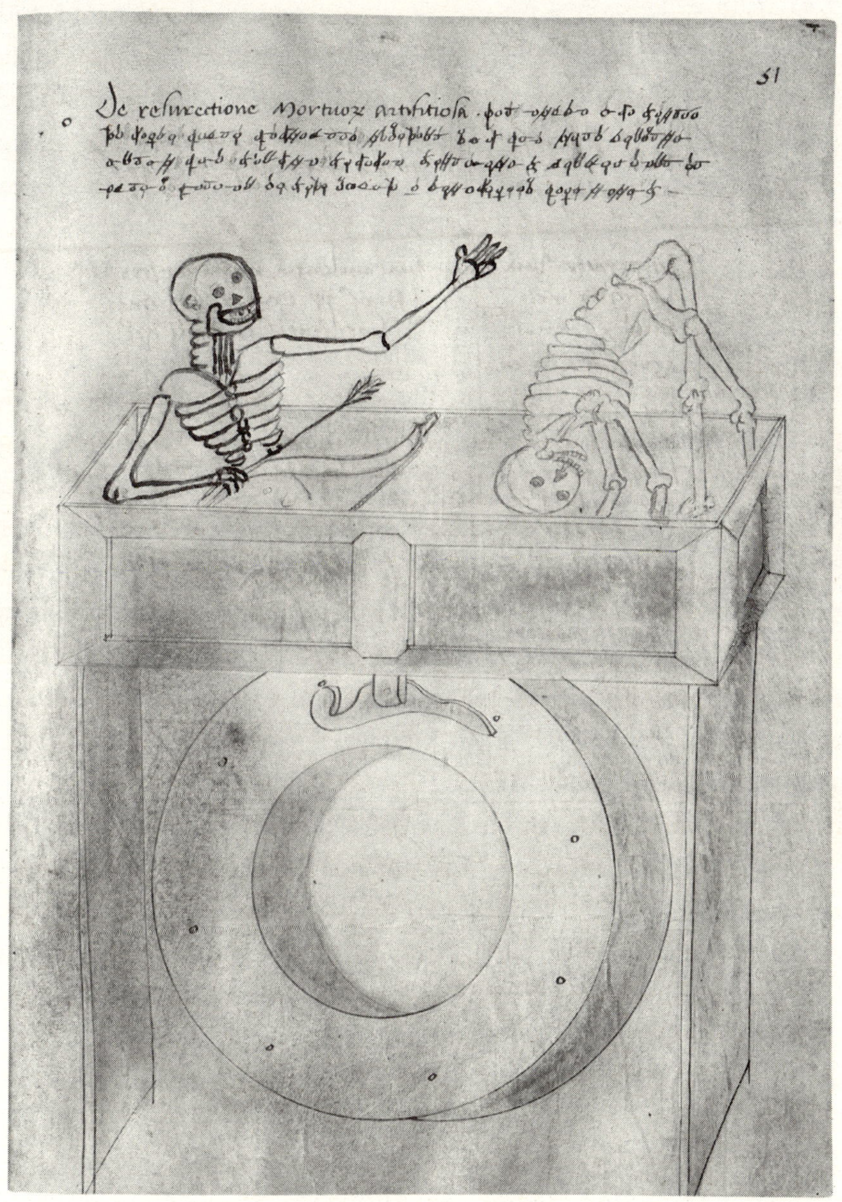

15. Two painted wooden skeletons in a box, from Giovanni Fontana's *Bellicorum instrumentorum liber*.

Fontana planned for it to travel along a track while its head, wings, and tail all moved. Rockets blew fire from its mouth and ears; a candle inside the witch's body made it glow; and the audience could marvel as springs made it throw small explosives.[35] He also designed a magic lantern that cast a devil intended to terrify viewers at night (folios 69v–70r).[36] Fontana relished designing such monstrous creatures; his aim was to recreate the types of supernatural events that scared people, but using mechanical – non-magical – means.[37] If he lived today, he would probably be making special effects for horror movies.

Alongside each invention in his *Bellicorum instrumentorum liber*, Fontana wrote an introduction in Latin, readable to anyone flicking through, but gave extra detail in a cipher of his own devising, masking further Latin text. Using this cipher, he swapped each Latin letter for one of his own symbols, which could be written in a number of variations to add to the text's complexity. This made it harder to decipher. He also added unnecessary vowels to make the job even more difficult. All of Fontana's characters are based around circles with straight or squiggly lines reaching off them, which distinguish one symbol from another. His 'a', for example, is a circle with a straight line branching off its left side, while his 't' is a circle with a flat line resting on top of it.[38]

Fontana's illustrations are also unusual for the time. They represent his inventions in two different ways: the item in action, and its mechanism. So, his mechanical witch is shown advancing, clawed feet gripping its track, fire exploding from its mouth and ears, and flapping its wings, but it is also presented from 'behind the scenes', with ropes tied to parts of its body, a hidden candle, and pipes for blasting the flames.[39] Fontana poured his heart into this manuscript, and even splashed out on expensive parchment, but it was not written in his own hand.[40] Instead, he gave the work of copying out the text to scribes, who cannot have been fluent in his unique cipher system, because their errors crept into the text.[41]

Why Fontana chose to encrypt a large portion of his manuscript is hard to explain, for it was not normal for early fifteenth-century natural philosophers and engineers to hide their work in this way. It is probable that he wanted to protect his ideas from being stolen by others, while simultaneously bringing attention to his own inventiveness. His cipher system was not complex, but it was unique and eye-catching – a tease. It showed potential patrons that there was more to say. Anyone educated could read the Latin and understand the basic purpose of Fontana's inventions, but it was the hidden text that often gave the key information on how it all worked; on the other hand, sometimes it added little of importance, as if the author could not think of anything significant to write but wanted to include his cipher anyway. Whatever the case, if a patron was interested, to gain access to these secrets he would have to hire Fontana. The colourful illustrations, probably drawn by a hired painter, similarly served to intrigue.[42]

Fontana's unusual symbols might have appealed to the aristocrats of Venice and academics of Padua who, during his lifetime, had developed a great interest in 'exotic' languages. People sought out manuscripts that bore ancient or unusual writings in the belief that early alphabets had power, and could perhaps even provide an insight into God's creation.[43] Fontana's cipher, then, was probably just another way to make his inventions more noticeable: just as he enjoyed dressing a rocket as a witch or demon, he masked his writings in mysterious symbols.[44] It could even be interpreted as a game – some fun for the manuscript's unnamed recipient, who appears to have known Fontana.[45]

Ciphers have a long history in Italy. As far back as 1226, Venetians replaced vowels with crosses in their correspondence. In the fourteenth century, code words or syllables were introduced in place of frequently written words in messages, such as 'Pope' or specific locations. There were also simple substitution ciphers, in which a single letter of the alphabet was switched for another letter or symbol. At the end of the thirteenth century, Venetians also sometimes used Greek or Hebrew letters to hide certain words or sentences from potential readers.[46] During Fontana's lifetime, the use of codes and ciphers tended to be restricted to intelligence gathering and diplomacy. In particular, the cryptologists of the Duchy of Mantua, just west of Venice, were innovative in their creation of homophonic substitution alphabets, a system in which, at its simplest, consonants are switched for other letters or symbols, and multiple characters represent each vowel. This all made it harder for anyone who intercepted the message to decipher its meaning. The earliest-known European use of this system was in 1401, when Simeone de Crema enciphered a message sent to the Duchy of Mantua's captain general, Francesco Gonzaga. Over the early fifteenth century, this encipherment system spread across Italy and became increasingly complex. Eventually, each consonant could be replaced by multiple characters, with even more symbols for the vowels; symbols could represent doubled letters or syllables; there were signs for frequently written names, places, and titles; and there were nulls – symbols that had no meaning.[47]

Intriguingly, given that he developed a cipher with a similar method of encryption, Fontana did have a connection with the diplomatic service. The Doge of Venice sent him on a diplomatic mission to meet the captain general of the Milanese army, the Count of Carmagnola, Francesco Bussone, in Brescia.[48] As Bussone switched his allegiance to the Venetians in 1425, this mission must have occurred before that time, placing the meeting exactly when Fontana was writing his *Bellicorum instrumentorum liber*. Perhaps this is when Fontana was first exposed to homophonic substitution ciphers? Then again, Venetian merchants had long used ciphers to hide their business secrets, and even invented their own systems. Since Fontana had grown up in Venice, this is another possibility.[49] He may also have read the cryptographic works of Arab writers. He certainly owned translated works of Arabic, including some by the ninth-century Iraqi polymath Al-Kindi, who wrote on cryptography.[50] For now, all that can be said with certainty is that Fontana's creation of book-length works in cipher is unique in early fifteenth-century Europe. Only the Voynich Manuscript is similar in time, location, and its extensive use of encipherment – and only then if we accept that it is written in cipher.

FONTANA'S TRAVELS AND LATER WORKS

In 1430, after completing his *Bellicorum instrumentorum liber*, Fontana wrote a second work in enciphered Latin, using a system that was similar to, but not exactly the same as, the one he had invented for his earlier manuscript.[51] This new volume was dedicated to the art of memory and was called the *Secretum de thesauro experimentorum ymaginationis hominum*. The sole surviving manuscript copy is 140 parchment pages long. After a summary of the contents, it begins with a passage in praise of God – perhaps Fontana again wanted to prove his piety against accusations of heresy. He then moves on to his main subject: artificial memory. He gives reasons for why this area of study is important, from its relevance to ancient writers, to how we are each already surrounded by manifestations of artificial memory, such as paintings and statues. He goes on to stress the value of strengthening a person's memory, and how this can help when speculating on things, especially as memory can fail or become obscured, forgotten, or unclear. He then discusses various instruments or machines that can help to artificially aid memory and encrypt information; and he not only describes these devices but illustrates them.[52] Although much of the text is written in cipher, certain parts, including the table of contents, the titles, and the colophon, as well as some of the names of the authors that he mentions, are in plain Latin text, making it clear to any reader what the book is about.[53] For his inspiration, Fontana drew on medieval and classical sources, and was perhaps introduced to the subject by Peter of Civitavecchia, who taught on the subject of memory in Bologna and wrote a work entitled *Ars memorie artificialis* (of which Fontana might have owned a copy). Other contemporaries in northern Italian cities had also written on this subject, so Fontana was not unique in his interest.[54]

Fontana travelled widely over the course of his life, but it is difficult to pinpoint the exact timings of his movements. In Italy, he visited Rome and the Vatican, and there saw the Meta Romuli, an ancient Roman tomb better known as the Vatican Pyramid, which was later demolished to make way for Via della Conciliazione.[55] He also made journeys to Brescia and Ravenna in northern Italy, and reports seeing an unusual alchemical furnace in Bologna. Perhaps, like other artists and engineers of his generation, Fontana was travelling his home country in search of inspiration from ancient Roman ruins.[56] He travelled abroad too, in particular to Crete and the Middle East, and perhaps as far as Egypt.[57]

Along the way, Fontana enjoyed hearing stories about other cultures. He was told that in Asia there were rivers inhabited by fish that looked like humans, while during his trip to Carmagnola, near Turin, he heard of men who devoured their enemies' young. Elsewhere, he tells the story of a man who asked to be interred in the wall of a building in Venice because he did not want his body to get wet, touch the air, be eaten by worms, or come into contact with another corpse. Fontana wrote that he visited the spot where the man's body was eventually walled up, which was near San Salvador church, close to the door that leads to the cloisters.[58]

During the 1430s, Fontana moved to Udine, north-east of Venice, to work as a doctor; by the time of his arrival, this city had been part of Venice's expanding republic for around twenty years. Despite the lack of grand libraries, he continued to write and make his observations of nature. He reached out to contacts to source books for his research, and penned a work on conic sections and parabolic mirrors called *Speculi almukefi compositio*.[59] A later manuscript, *Tractatus de trigono balistario*, is dated to 28 February 1440, and covers methods of measuring height, depth, and distance using techniques devised by Fontana himself. He wrote this manuscript for the mathematician Domenico Bragadin. Despite being 222 pages long, it is an abbreviated version of a lost, much longer work on the same subject, and contains many crossed-out sentences and words, as well as additional thoughts in its margins. Fontana crossed out one entire page with a large X – he must have been unhappy with what he had written.[60]

Ten years later, in about 1450, Fontana completed his next major work, an encyclopaedia called *De omnibus rebus naturalibus*.[61] Within it, he drew from existing information to try to compile everything that was known about the world – an ambitious and monumental task. He begins with a discussion of the creation of the Earth in six days, following the Bible, and places it at the centre of the cosmos. He writes about demons, angels, and goblins, but also about geography, arguing that the Indian Ocean must be entirely surrounded by land. He describes the world as being like a mechanical clock operated by angels; he associates angels with the zodiac; and he discusses the influences they have on humans, adding that certain spirits have the power to move people great distances and that a spirit taught him how to make mercury thicker.[62] He goes on to write about the nature of wind, thunder, and lightning; on making sea water drinkable; and on optics, refraction, and water, and how refraction can change the appearance of things. To prove his point, he explains that prostitutes appear more attractive at night because of the evening humidity, and this is also why butchers try to shift their bad meat at night. Fontana encourages his readers to leave their homes and travel, so that they can experience for themselves differences in customs, languages, birds, animals, herbs, and fruits – and so that they can see what is possible in the world.[63]

THE FORGOTTEN AUTHOR

It is not clear when or where Giovanni Fontana died, but the final definite date when he was alive is 1454.[64] Afterwards, he simply vanishes from history. What is clear though is that the manuscripts he wrote and owned became widely dispersed. The only known copy of the *Bellicorum instrumentorum liber*, for instance, entered Germany or Austria during the fifteenth century. It passed into the hands of an unknown alchemist, who cracked Fontana's cipher and wrote fifteen lines of magical recipes, partly using his cipher system, partly in German and Latin, on what would become the manuscript's title page; below, he also jotted down a line of Fontana's symbols. Another unknown fifteenth-century reader added a comment to the bottom of a different page, paraphrasing a line of the cipher text (folio 10v).[65] The manuscript later entered the collection of Albert V, Duke of Bavaria, who founded his court library in Munich in 1558. In 1582, the manuscript was embellished with velvet bindings, and the librarian Wolfgang Prommer assigned it the grandiose title *Bellicorum instrumentorum liber cum figuris et (partim) fictitiis literis conscriptus* ('A Book of Instruments of War with Figures and (Partially) Fictitious Letters').

Fontana's manuscript only came to the interest of scholars in the late nineteenth century, when it was studied by the librarian and philologist Wilhelm Meyer, who broke the cipher, and also Henri Omont, a librarian with the Bibliothèque nationale de France. In 1910, a Viennese colonel, Heinrich Schulte, transcribed the text and compared Fontana's cipher to other examples.[66] Through all of these centuries, because Fontana's name was written in the *Bellicorum instrumentorum liber*, his authorship was never in doubt. The same cannot be said for his other works, most of which have only been identified as his over the past 120 years.

Take his *Secretum de thesauro experimentorum ymaginationis hominum*, for example. This is only known from a single, anonymous manuscript, produced by a group of scribes who made various errors, including misspelled words. It is not clear whether they copied out an already encrypted text, making their mistakes as they progressed, or if they were given a plain-text Latin version and made the errors while enciphering it in Fontana's unfamiliar symbols. Whatever the case may be, the scribes left spaces for the illustrations, which were drawn during the final stage of the manuscript's production.[67] In the centuries after its creation, parts of the text were erased and, in the seventeenth century, a certain 'Simon Castello Jerolimus' scribbled his name on one of the pages (folio 5r). Later, in 1721, Count Giovanni Carlo Lisca wrote his own name and the year in the manuscript, as well as page numbers, and added new ink wherever Fontana's words had grown faint with time, making them more legible. Lisca broke the cipher too, and used it to write a comment, saying that he did not approve of Fontana's art of artificial memory (folio 128r). An unfavourable review, but one that Lisca soon regretted for, in an enciphered comment on a later page, he wrote that he had changed his mind (folio 140r).

During the eighteenth century, a reader believed that the manuscript contained alchemical secrets and was much older than it really is, for they wrote 'Alchimia' on its spine and the year 'MCCC'. Then, in 1897, a bookseller in Venice sold the manuscript to the Bibliothèque nationale de France. It was bought for the library by the above-mentioned Henri Omont, a curator in the manuscript department, who soon after published an article about the text. At some point in the manuscript's long history, Fontana's name had been removed from its pages, leaving it anonymous. It was only in 1898, when Omont suggested him as its author, that Fontana regained his lost position. The fact that the text was written in Fontana's unique cipher confirmed Omont's argument.[68]

Then there is the case of Fontana's encyclopaedia, the *Liber de omnibus rebus naturalibus*. Because it was printed as a book, this became Fontana's most read creation. Unfortunately for him, his name was again absent from its pages. What happened is unclear, but in 1544 Fontana's manuscript was published in Venice, attributed to an otherwise unknown author, Pompilius Azalus of Piacenza. For anyone who scrutinized the text, however, it quickly became obvious that its author had not lived in the sixteenth century, but one hundred years earlier, and that he did not come from Piacenza but Venice. Even so, Pompilius was credited as its author until the twentieth century. It was only in 1931 that the historian Lynn Thorndike assembled the author's biographical clues from the text and realized that they mirrored Fontana's life story.[69] The book's publisher must somehow have come into possession of Fontana's manuscript, removed his name, and decided to make some money out of it, expecting that no one would ever find out.[70]

Even today, works by Fontana continue to be identified. Most recently, he was shown to be the author of *Speculi almukefi compositio*, a manuscript discussing the construction of parabolic mirrors. Although scholars had earlier suggested Fontana as its author, this was only confirmed in 2016 thanks to a study of additional documents by the researcher Horst Kranz. Previously, the main contender for its authorship had been an unknown monk.[71] As a man dedicated to discovery, Fontana would no doubt appreciate the detective work that has gone in to re-establishing his place in history.

Today, Giovanni Fontana's *Bellicorum instrumentorum liber* remains in the Bayerische Staatsbibliothek, Munich, under call number BSB Cod.icon. 242.[72]

In the next chapter, we will travel to Germany, to meet the Benedictine monk Johannes Trithemius, who is busy developing an innovative form of secret writing – one in which hidden messages remain visible in plain sight.

4

STEGANOGRAPHIA (1499)

The Magic of Hiding Words in Plain Sight

In February 1482, Johann Heidenberg, better known as Johannes Trithemius, left the university city of Heidelberg, its centuries-old streets sandwiched between the south bank of the River Neckar and its grand hilltop castle, to return to his home town of Trittenheim. He was only twenty-one, and had spent the last few years studying across Europe, beginning in Trier, before heading to the Netherlands, and then on to Heidelberg. Along the way, he had become intrigued by humanism, and had made strong connections with like-minded scholars. He was on a path towards a good career. The future was bright but, for now, it was time to return home. Joined by a travelling companion, he trekked across the forests and green hills of south-west Germany towards their destination. One evening, tired from the road, they decided to spend the night in Sponheim, a tiny village with a largely ignored Benedictine monastery called St Martin's. The monastery, founded in 1124, was not of major importance, but the monks were kind and offered Trithemius and his companion a place to sleep for the night.[1]

Well rested, the next morning the two men thanked the monks for their generosity and continued on their way. When they reached Bockenau, about an hour's walk across the hills from the monastery, a snowstorm struck. Neither man could see the way ahead. Trithemius convinced his companion to continue onwards – to try to push through. It would be humiliating to return to the monks for help, he said. But the snow continued to fall, accumulating into a freezing,

16. St Martin's Monastery at Sponheim, engraving by Matthäus Merian, seventeenth century.

unpassable barrier. Trithemius admitted defeat. The two men trudged their way back across the icy hills to Sponheim, where, once again, the monks offered them refuge. In that moment, Trithemius experienced a profound realization: his return to the monastery was a sign from God. This was where he was meant to be. He immediately changed his plans. Instead of going home, he would live out his days in Sponheim as a Benedictine monk.[2] A year later, Trithemius was appointed abbot. He would hold this position for twenty-three years.[3]

To Trithemius, standing in the snowy grounds of St Martin's Monastery, his arrival at Sponheim and promotion to abbot was the second miracle he had experienced in his short lifetime. He was born to a poor family in Trittenheim in 1462, his father dying before his first birthday. Fearing how a stepfather might treat her young son, his mother, Elizabeth, refused to remarry until she could no longer support the family herself. It was not until Trithemius was around the age of seven that she married again, to a man with the surname Zell or Zeller. He was against his stepson learning to read and write, and whipped Trithemius whenever he saw him doing so. But Trithemius could not be dissuaded. Any time he had the chance, he sneaked out of his home and was taught by a friend. It was then, at age fifteen, that the first miracle happened. One night, while Trithemius slept, a young man appeared to him, holding two tablets in his arms. In his true inquisitive fashion, Trithemius inspected them. One was covered in letters, he noticed, while the other bore images. 'You must select one of these tablets', the young man told Trithemius. This was an easy choice: he picked the one inscribed with writing. 'God has listened to you', the young man said. And not only that but he would give Trithemius everything he wanted, and more. With that, the young man vanished.[4] These two miraculous events had led Trithemius to becoming Abbot of Sponheim – and he had big plans for his new home.

As the years passed, Trithemius transformed St Martin's into the greatest place of learning in Germany. He criss-crossed Europe, travelling from monastery to monastery in search of manuscripts to bring home: not solely religious works, but those covering the liberal arts and medicine too. If he came across a particularly intriguing book, he bought or swapped it for another in his possession; if that was not possible, he had a copy made. Meanwhile, back in Sponheim, his monks wrote incessantly, working their fingers to the bone producing manuscripts of all kinds for his ever-growing library. Their work was relentless – Trithemius was a man who believed that lazy monks should not eat. Indeed, he was so dedicated to manuscript copying and collecting that, in 1492, he wrote a pamphlet arguing against that newfangled technology the printing press (despite later printing many of his works and finding wider fame as a result).[5]

Over time, Trithemius built up a collection of around two thousand manuscripts and printed volumes in a variety of languages – Hebrew, Greek, and Latin, and others too. One visitor to Sponheim reported seeing books in five languages, while a letter written by Trithemius mentions works in Arabic, Indian, and Tartaric. The fame of his collection attracted travellers from far and wide, and transformed his monastery from a dilapidated backwater into a beacon of learning.[6] The monastery became so famous that the chaplain of the Archbishop of Trier, Jason Alpheus, wrote a fifty-line poem about Trithemius's dog and its knowledge of Greek: apparently, Trithemius had taught his pet to respond to Greek to impress his friends.[7]

But it was not Trithemius's library collection that brought him the most attention. Nor was it his extensive writings on history, religion, and the Church. Despite his protests and attempts at damage control, he was infamous for another work produced by his own hand, a manuscript so dangerous and mysterious that even he did not dare to publish it: his three-volume *Steganographia*, 'Concealed Writing'.

WRITING A CONTROVERSIAL MANUSCRIPT

What if you could communicate to others without speaking? Send messages by fire across the Earth, even to a person locked away in a dungeon? What if you could teach Latin or Greek to someone who lacked even the most basic training or education in a mere two hours? Or learn the mysteries of many kinds of secret writing?[8] These methods would be extremely useful to kings and emperors, but dangerous in the hands of enemies and adulterers. In the late 1490s, nearing the end of his thirties, Trithemius pondered these problems as he began writing his masterwork, *Steganographia*. Building on his much shorter experiments on the same subject – the *Clavis steganographiae*, dedicated to methods of encipherment, and the *Clavis generalis triplex*, which mixes codes and magic – he planned his opus to be four volumes, each providing the reader with seemingly supernatural abilities.[9] To an initiate in Trithemius's thinking, his manuscript would be filled with wonders. To the ignorant, it would be useless, confusing, and perhaps even mistaken for black magic.

In his preface, Trithemius explains that the point of his manuscript is to show readers how to hide and send their secrets to people who know his system, in such a way that their messages can travel long distances without being detected. To stop the ignorant from understanding, he has concealed his methods behind a veneer of demon magic. He expects his discovery of these techniques to be useful to the Holy Roman Empire, but he is afraid that if everyone adopts them, including those of bad character, it could lead to a collapse in trust. No one would believe what others write, Trithemius warns. Every word would be under suspicion. Fearing that his readers might misinterpret his writings as true necromancy – that is, associated with demons and superstitions – he adds a lengthy, almost contract-like, section to his preface, explaining how his work is perfectly in line with good Catholic belief. He asks his readers not to criticize the content before they have properly read and understood it – if you do not understand it, do not criticize it, but your own talents.[10] No demons were *actually* summoned during the writing of this manuscript.

Nonetheless . . .

In the first chapter of his first volume, Trithemius explains his method, alongside a disclaimer that evil demons might trouble the sender and read out their secret messages. (You can already see why people might have suspected him of black magic.) The first stage is to say a prayer to the Holy Trinity and write out a letter that anybody who happens to glance at the page can read, Trithemius says. This letter should not contain any information that you would worry about being discovered. Next, check which spirits oversee the direction that you are sending your letter towards, turn to face their direction, and say an incantation to them, reciting Trithemius's magical words. The spirits should appear; if they do not, keep trying: they will eventually turn up. After a while though, if they still do not manifest, stop, because they might be angry and hurt you. Assuming that the spirits do appear, tell them your secret message and send the letter, on which you should have written the symbols for the direction the spirits represent. Remember: if the symbols are incorrect, the recipient might summon the wrong spirits and be harmed by them. When the recipient receives your letter, they read the symbols, turn

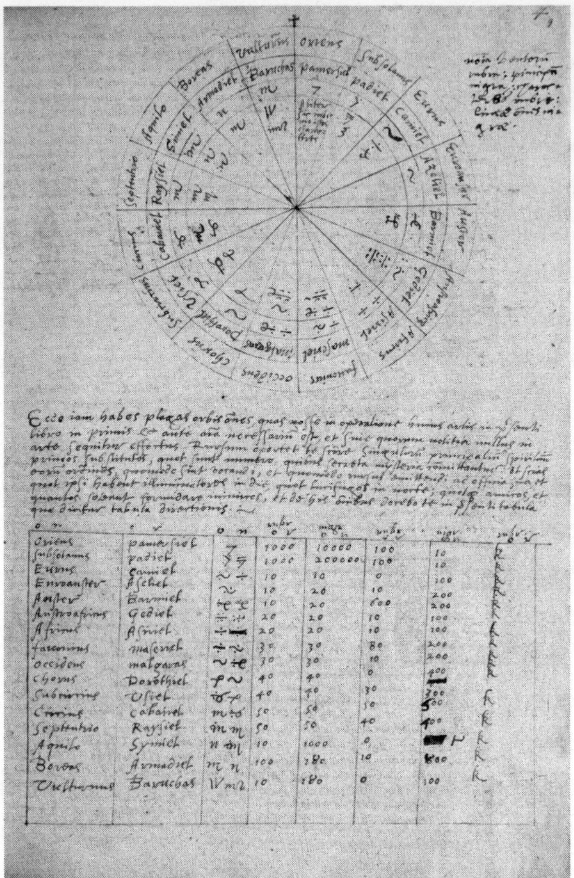

17. A page from John Dee's second copy of the first volume of Trithemius's *Steganographia.*

to face the appropriate direction, and recite another magic spell. The correct spirits should then appear and relay your secret message to them.[11]

This is all very fantastical. But the secrets hidden in Trithemius's manuscript are far more mundane, yet simultaneously ground-breaking. Certain passages, and especially his carefully worded magic spells with their addresses to spirits, actually contain hidden messages. These are revealed only when the correct letters in each word are read, ignoring the rest. Decoded, one concealed message in his first chapter tells people to read only the first letter of each word. To give an invented example of how this works, the gibberish Latinesque spell 'Halabus iropellocticon diplanus esparus' conceals the English word 'hide'. Trithemius's next spell, when deciphered, repeats his instructions, saying that the reader should convey the secret message using the first letter of each word. Intriguingly, in this case, it is actually every other letter of every second word that reveals his message, providing another combination for concealing secrets. Importantly, each spell – and so each method of encryption – was associated with a different directional spirit. By reading the name of the directional spirit summoned to 'send the message', the recipient learned which of Trithemius's enciphering systems the sender had used, and so which combination of letters to read and which to ignore – the spirit's name was the key to decryption. In his second chapter, Trithemius provides examples of what is possible using his method. Spread across one spell, he hides a message telling the recipient of a letter that he should imprison the messenger who brought it;[12] in another, he gives the time and place for a secret meeting.[13]

Trithemius's second volume continues in a similar vein, but his third takes a different approach. Here, he tells his readers that they need to be aware of astronomical movements to send their messages over great distances, adding that his work in this volume is based on an ancient text, written by a philosopher called Menastor. To successfully send your messages, Trithemius writes, you first have to study large tables filled with numbers related to the spirits of the seven planets and their subordinates. In reality, certain numbers in these tables represent letters and sounds, which Trithemius uses to write his secret messages. In one example, he spells out his first name; in another, he presents a psalm that expels demons from the possessed.[14] Unfortunately, Trithemius never completed his third volume, only getting as far as writing his chapter on the spirits of Saturn and their associates. By this time, word of his arcane writings had spread, and trouble was brewing for him beyond the walls of Sponheim's monastery.

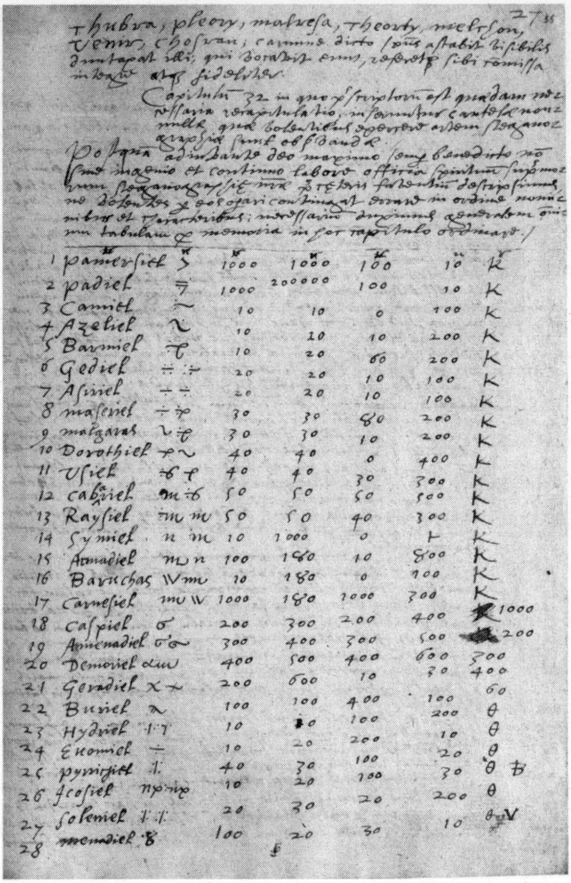

18. Directional spirits and their symbols: a page from John Dee's second copy of the third volume of Trithemius's *Steganographia*.

A MASTER OF CEREMONIAL MAGIC?

In 1499, Trithemius, excited about his developing manuscript, wrote a letter to Arnold Bostius, a Carmelite monk in Ghent, Belgium, who had expressed an interest in learning what his friend had been writing about recently. In his reply, Trithemius explained his plan for the four volumes of *Steganographia*, how each would have one hundred chapters, and the amazing impact that his book would have on its readers. He claimed that his ideas had come to him by revelation, passed on through the words of a mysterious entity that manifested while he slept. In short, the art of steganography came to him from God.[15] The letter never reached Bostius, who died on 4 April 1499. Others did read it, however. When the letter reached Bostius's convent, it was opened by the prior, who was appalled by what Trithemius had written. His claims were so extreme, the prying prior gasped, that the Abbott of Sponheim must be in league with demons! He shared the letter around, spreading news across Europe of Trithemius's occult leanings and obvious seduction by dark magic. Trithemius would never shake these accusations – not in his lifetime, nor to the present day.[16]

This invasion of privacy changed Trithemius. He became more selective of those he shared his knowledge with, and insisted that anyone who wanted to learn about magic and hidden writing from him had to visit Sponheim in person. He needed to trust a potential student before initiating them into his world; only then would he introduce them to his secret arts. One visitor to Sponheim appears to have been the influential doctor and alchemist Paracelsus, whose writings on medicine changed the discipline. Other students made copies of Trithemius's *Steganographia*, including Johannes Capellarius, Johannes Evriponus, and Heinrich Cornelius Agrippa, who let others copy his edition.[17]

Agrippa went on to write his own influential work on magic: his three-volume *De occulta philosophia*. Trithemius warmly received this manuscript, which was dedicated to him, in 1510. Within, among a vast array of topics, Agrippa presents various mystical alphabets, including the Theban alphabet, celestial characters, *transitus fluvii* writing, and Malachim writing.[18] With the importance of secrecy constantly on his mind, Trithemius urged Agrippa to keep his writings on magic hidden, and that he should not only explore natural magic – that is, magic that does not involve summoning demons and spirits – but magic as a whole, implying that he should experiment with its more dangerous forms. Like Trithemius's *Steganographia*, such knowledge was for 'initiates' only, spread through the copying of manuscripts, but never to be printed. (On an unrelated note, Agrippa was apparently the owner of a devil dog called Monsieur.)[19]

In either 1503 or 1504, the French philosopher and mathematician Charles de Bouelles (Carolus Bovillus in the Latin version) paid a visit to Trithemius in Sponheim. The two men must have got along swimmingly for, during the philosopher's two-week stay, Trithemius offered Bouelles his unfinished *Steganographia* to read. He wanted to know Bouelles's thoughts on the developing manuscript. Did he have any advice? To Trithemius's surprise, Bouelles freaked out. As he turned the pages, he saw demon magic in every word and feared the names of the unknown spirits penetrating his eyes. There were even instructions on how two lovers, kept apart and under surveillance, could meet in secret. The horror! To make his disgust abundantly clear, Bouelles threw the manuscript aside. It was not the most polite way to behave in front of his host. Worse, he later described his Sponheim experience in a letter to the French bishop Germain de Ganay, which the bishop shared around, leading to it being published in 1509. It was more bad press for Trithemius. This miserable situation gnawed at him so much that he wrote a response in his defence, and it bothered him until his dying days.[20]

NECROMANCY, WITCHES, AND DEMONS

Why did Bouelles panic? In Trithemius's time, although people regarded the miraculous and supernatural as a part of everyday life, the question was of how far good Christians could involve themselves with such forces. What was the difference between ceremonial magic, in which people summoned demons and spirits for their help, and natural magic, which did not rely on invoking demonic forces? Was the latter magic truly possible without supernatural aid? And what was a true miracle and what was deception? Trithemius took an interest in these problems from an early age. In his youth, he visited

Trier in south-western Germany, where he came across a crowd admiring a statue of the Virgin Mary that had been seen weeping. It drew the devout (and their donations) for months, and Trithemius himself even witnessed it crying. Naturally, the whole thing turned out to be a hoax. Someone had built a mechanism into the statue that made the Virgin cry her tears. But such fakery did not stop people believing other cases – Trithemius included. He fully accepted that a statue of Mary, kept in a monastery near Heilbronn, was capable of miracles, because credible witnesses had reported these events to him. He equally believed the miraculous stories surrounding a statue of Mary at a church in Dettelbach.[21]

In 1486, the influential philosophers Giovanni Pico della Mirandola and Marsilio Ficino had argued that practising natural magic was perfectly feasible; there was no need to call on demons or spirits to achieve your goals. Not all magic needed to be forbidden. It is perhaps no coincidence that Pico's and Ficino's support for natural magic happened at around the same time that Pope Innocent VIII had issued a papal Bull for the investigation and punishment of witches. With magic under close scrutiny, they wanted to reframe it, to rebrand it in a way that made it acceptable to everyone.[22] But to Trithemius, at least in private, magic always involved summoning supernatural beings. There was simply no other way. By writing *Steganographia* as a guide to using demons – even if this was just misdirection – he had knowingly entered a minefield. He had even included a hierarchy of demons in his manuscript, a devilish version of the hierarchy of heaven, more commonly found in necromancy manuals. With accusations everywhere, and a fine and unclear line between ceremonial and natural magic, not only his reputation but also his life was in danger. To fix this situation, one solution was for him to better define where natural magic met ceremonial magic, so that people everywhere could see that he was on the right and pious side, befitting an abbot. Another solution was to point his finger at everybody else. Trithemius tried both tactics.

Anybody invoking demons for magical purposes ran the risk of being accused of witchcraft or sorcery. This had been the case since before Trithemius's birth, but the persecutions had accelerated during the late fifteenth century. Trithemius was certainly aware of this, but continued to secretly promote ceremonial magic anyway. He unashamedly kept a large collection of magical works in his library, and lists and describes their content in his *Antipalus maleficiorum*, written in 1508.[23] Hypocritically, Trithemius simultaneously warned against owning books of magic, calling them dangerous and a temptation to those who did not know how to use them properly. Such restrictions did not apply to him, of course. His own magic – which involved astrological readings and the like – was natural, as he emphasized in public; he strongly condemned the use of ceremonial magic and its wicked recourse to demons. Angel magic – because, just as there were devilish demons around us, there were helpful angels – was perfectly fine, however. This was the work of God.[24]

The attitude that people like Bouelles had towards Trithemius's *Steganographia* was rooted in a deep fear of the power that manuscripts of demon magic possessed, a fear that existed throughout society, all the way up to kings. Demons lived within their pages, it was clear, and sometimes these books spoke to their readers. If the owner of such an evil manuscript was proven to have directed its power against others, they could be imprisoned or even executed; and the manuscripts themselves were scrutinized with equally intense suspicion. If manuscripts under investigation were found 'guilty' of being works of necromancy, they were burned, just like witches or heretics (even though many necromantic works were actually owned and used by lower-level clerics).[25] One necromancer's manual that escaped the flames is a fifteenth-century compilation of demonic magic from different sources. A glance through its contents reveals the types of things that worried concerned clerics and would-be book burners. If you wanted to become invisible, there was a spell for that. If you wanted to own a horse, a boat, or even a castle, there were spells for those too. Four

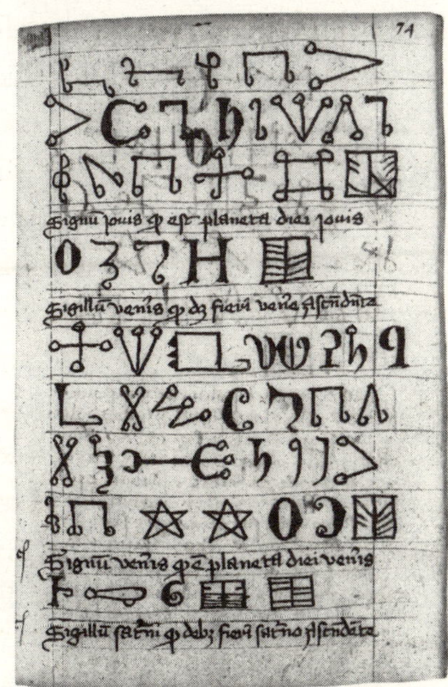

19. Pages from a fifteenth-century necromancer's manual.

spells caused a woman to fall in love with you. You could make friends fall out, or bring a dead person back to life. It was also possible to conjure Satan.[26] This was the sort of manuscript that petrified Bouelles.

People believed that demons were a real danger. In his *Hirsau Annals*, Trithemius writes that a demon caused havoc in the city of Mainz in 860: it hurled stones at people, made walls quake, and snuck into women's beds. In 1132, a demon called Hudeskin hassled the people of Hildesheim. But he explained that, to cause such havoc, demons needed to be invited by willing supporters: witches and sorcerers, often weighed down by sins such as lust, sorrow, and sloth. These practitioners were rewarded with supernatural powers, from invisibility to super speed. Children could also be bewitched, but this only happened when the child's parents had been sorcerers, or if the midwife had been a witch. Over the years, Trithemius wrote a number of books on demonology, and planned works on the subject that he never finished, such as his twelve-book *De demonibus*. Part of his reason for this deep dive into the occult was again, no doubt, to prove that his own brand of magic was safe and Christian, while accusing everyone else – particularly female witches.[27]

While researching and conducting his own ceremonial magic in secret, Trithemius published books that condemned witches, and carefully classified the types of demons with whom they interacted; he accused witches of spreading across the Holy Roman Empire in league with such demons to harm men. But, unlike others in his day, Trithemius stopped short of saying that all witches should be burned: exorcism was good enough in some cases.[28] A witch could be saved by pouring holy water around her home; this should be mixed with a powder derived from wax candles, burned during mass, and incense, among various other materials. A bath of clean river water, while the witch held holy items, helped too. For an exorcist faced with such a situation, the most important requirement was to be a truly pious man. The abbot Adam, who must have been as holy as they come, exorcized two convents full of demons in 1499, according to Trithemius.[29] But, if nothing could be done, Trithemius was not against executing witches, and his books on the subject contributed to the persecution of women for centuries.[30]

A NEW LIFE IN WÜRZBURG

Perhaps it was the increasing association between the dark arts and Trithemius, or perhaps they had simply grown tired of the heavy workload of endless study and manuscript copying commanded by him, but as the first years of the sixteenth century passed, the monks of Sponheim turned against their infamous abbot. Naturally, Trithemius himself took no responsibility for this situation and blamed an evil demon for their disloyalty. This began a period of illness and depression for him, only made worse when he slipped from his horse and seriously injured one of his legs.[31] But there were some positive developments too. In the middle of 1505, the Holy Roman Emperor, Maximilian I, sent for Trithemius, for he had questions about the biblical scriptures that he wanted answered. The abbot duly travelled to Cologne and spent a week with him in discussion. The emperor's questions covered a series of topics, from issues of salvation and black magic to witches and evil, which led Trithemius to write a major work on demonology, the *Liber octo quaestionum*. He dedicated the book to the emperor and presented it to him at his castle in Boppard in 1508. Trithemius's meetings with Maximilian later became the stuff of legend; one story relates that, during his visit, the magical abbot made the dead appear, including the emperor's wife, Mary of Burgundy, who had departed this world in 1482.[32]

Trithemius left his position at Sponheim in 1505, much to his monks' delight, and the following year he took up a new job as the abbot of a small monastery called St Jacob in the city of Würzburg, along the River Main in northern Bavaria. This move, 160 kilometres east of Sponheim, meant abandoning his beloved library; he left all but a few books behind, including many that he had laboriously copied by hand.[33] By this time, Trithemius had given up writing his *Steganographia*. In a letter sent to Rutger Sicamber in 1507, he says that he had planned on making his opus eight books long (doubling his earlier proclamations), but that, although he had written the first two, the third would remain incomplete. Finishing the project would be hard work, and he declared that there was little to be gained from the effort. So, unless a good reason came along, the manuscripts would be left untouched, and it would all remain unpublished.[34] It was during his Würzburg years that Trithemius completed the above-mentioned *Liber octo quaestionum*, as well as his *Antipalus maleficiorum*, and drafted the plan for his unfinished *De demonibus*. He also wrote an autobiography called *Nepiachus*, a work on demons and epilepsy called *De morbo caduco et maleficiis*, and a manuscript on astrology and kabbala called *De septem secundeis*, which features the angels from his *Steganographia*.[35]

But Trithemius's troubled experience penning *Steganographia* did not stop him from returning to the subject. In 1507, he started writing, and this time completed, another set of manuscripts dedicated to hidden writing. He called it *Polygraphia*. This work was stripped of the spirits and demon magic of its unfinished predecessor, saving him from further reputational harm (and perhaps even rehabilitating him). He did, however, reuse his idea of hiding messages in astral calculations based on planets, which originally appeared in *Steganographia*'s third volume.[36]

POLYGRAPHIA

Trithemius divided *Polygraphia* into six books, each presenting variations on methods for hiding information in plain sight.[37] The first book mainly consists of a long list of tables, each containing the letters of the alphabet and, beside them, different Latin words. To hide a message, you simply looked down the first table of letters and selected the word corresponding to the first letter in the message to be enciphered. For the next letter to be enciphered, you moved to the second table and, again, chose the word associated with the letter, and so on. Because Trithemius included 384 tables, you could get through 384 letters before starting again with table number one. So, to encipher the word 'apple', you look at the first table, and see that the word beside 'a' is 'Deus'. You then look for 'p' in the second table, and see that the associated word is 'fortissimus'. In the third table, 'p' is beside 'intuens'. In the fourth table, 'l' is 'terrena'; and in the fifth table, 'e' is 'concedat'. The enciphered word 'apple' thus becomes 'Deus fortissimus intuens terrena concedat', a phrase that would pass as a normal line of Latin in a religious text or prayer.[38] This was all part of Trithemius's ingenious plan. He designed the conjugation of the words in each of the tables to fit together and make sense to the reader. No one would suspect a thing.[39]

Trithemius presents similar tables in Books 2 to 4, but fills them with invented words rather than Latin, while in Book 5 he includes

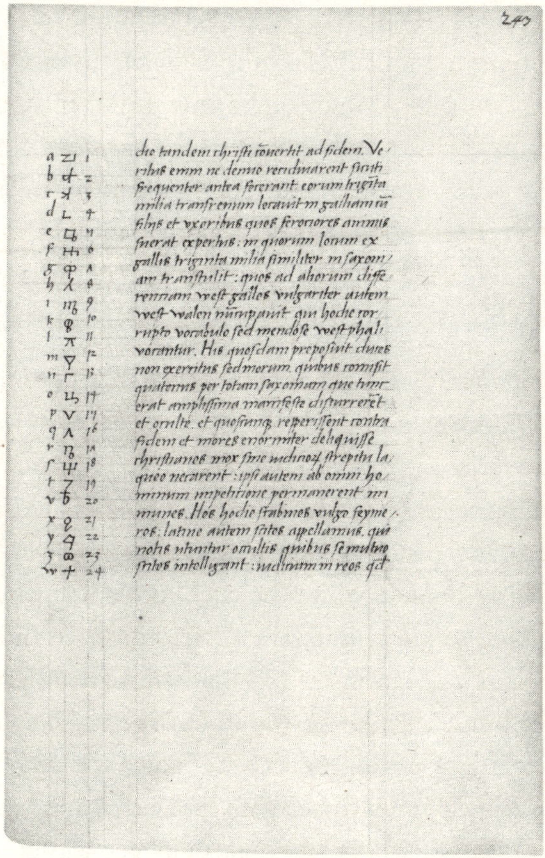

20. The alphabet of Otfrid, from Trithemius's *Polygraphia*, written in Trithemius's own hand.

transposition tables that enable the reader to generate polyalphabetic ciphers – the most basic consisting of tables in which, in each row, the alphabet progressively moves one step to the right. In Book 6, he introduces a variety of alphabets and number systems, which, he suggests, can be used to hide information. Among them, he includes Greek numbers; ancient Germanic alphabets, such as an alphabet said to have been devised by Charlemagne, found in a work by a Weissenburg monk called Otfrid; an alphabet of Trithemius's own creation; an alphabet consisting of symbols devised by Aethicus Ister;

and Norse runes.[40] When he completed work on this project, Trithemius presented an edition of *Polygraphia*, written in his own hand, to Emperor Maximilian on 8 June 1508, in either Linz am Rhein or Boppard. It then entered the imperial collection in Innsbruck, Austria.[41] Another edition, although made by a scribe, is filled with corrections penned by Trithemius himself.[42]

THE LAST YEARS OF TRITHEMIUS'S LIFE

Trithemius remained in Emperor Maximilian's favour during his years in Würzburg, and was eventually tasked with researching the history of the emperor's family line. Maximilian wanted proof that he was descended from the Trojans, which, naturally, did not exist. This forced Trithemius to fake historical documents and to invent a Frankish historian called Hunibald, whom he cited as his major source. When Maximilian asked to see Hunibald's work for himself, Trithemius was also forced to invent excuses; he said that the manuscript had been in his Sponheim library, which had now, sadly, been dispersed – sorry, emperor, blame those mean monks for ousting me.[43] He also appears to have faked correspondence between himself and learned and interesting people, many of whom suspiciously praise his skills and intelligence. He perhaps only shared these with select individuals, reducing his chance of being caught out, and never imagined that they would end up in print – which of course they did, but only after his death.[44] Certain people, however, were aware of his inclination towards inventing history, such as the astronomer and cartographer Johannes Stabius. This cannot have helped the abbot's damaged reputation.[45]

Over the years, people continued to ask Trithemius for copies of his now legendary *Steganographia*. They were usually disappointed. In 1515, when Germain de Ganay, the Bishop of Orleans and spreader of Bouelles's letter about Trithemius's occult leanings, requested a copy, he received *Polygraphia* instead.[46] Thanks to his many demonological publications, others approached Trithemius for advice on dealing with supernatural beings. In 1515, he received a letter from his friend the aristocrat Willibald Pirckheimer, who complained that heretics had summoned demons to Nuremberg. Pirckheimer begged Trithemius to send him one of the books that the infamous monk had penned on the subject, so that he could teach himself how to deal with the problem.[47] Incidentally, Pirckheimer had been caught up in an earlier supernatural event too. In 1503, the Bishop of Mainz had consulted Trithemius regarding a bizarre spate of crucifixes falling on people, particularly on children, one of which had dropped on a maid in Pirckheimer's house.[48]

With such issues on his mind, and after a lifetime of writing on and pondering the nature of demons, magic, and secret writing, Trithemius died in Würzburg on 13 December 1516. He was only fifty-four years old. He was interred at St Jacob's in Würzburg, but in 1720 was moved to a chapel in the city's Neumünster Church. His second library, collected during his Würzburg years, was dispersed after his death.[49]

FROM SOUGHT-AFTER MANUSCRIPT TO BANNED BOOK

Polygraphia was published in 1518, shortly after Trithemius's death, and again in 1550, with further editions following, including one in French from 1561.[50] These publications, but especially that of 1550, ensured the continuation of Trithemius's fame. The text also mentioned his unpublished *Steganographia*, generating intrigue among Europe's scholars, who scoured the continent for copies to study. In this manner, *Steganographia*'s reputation continued to precede it. In 1568, Ricardus Argentinus of Ipswich referred to it as a book of superstition; in 1580, Jean Bodin called it one of the most detestable books in the world; and in 1621, Sigismundus Scherertzius suggested that it should be burned.[51] Others looked at it with a cryptological eye, among them the French diplomat and cryptographer

Blaise de Vigenère, who, in 1586, wrote that he had seen copies in Germany and Italy, but could not understand it.[52]

One manuscript of *Steganographia*, perhaps even *the* original manuscript written in Trithemius's own hand, was once kept in a library in Heidelberg. This edition was apparently burned sometime between 1573 and 1576 by a librarian called Franciscus Junius, perhaps at the request of Count Frederic II.[53] Trithemius left another volume to his student Cornelius Agrippa in his will, along with the *Clavis steganographiae*.[54] In the 1530s, Johannes Wier, one of Agrippa's students, made an abridged copy of these manuscripts, which were copied by others, spreading their content further.[55] The Elizabethan polymath John Dee was so excited to find an edition in Antwerp in 1563 that he borrowed it from its owner, a Hungarian nobleman, and spent ten days copying it. Unfortunately, this was lost when Dee's library at Mortlake, near London, was looted,[56] so he made a second copy in 1591, apparently from a manuscript owned by Giacomo Castelvetro, an Italian author and teacher living in England.[57] Flicking through Dee's second *Steganographia*, the reader is met with his typically difficult handwriting, crossed-out and corrected words, and blotchy letters where his quill lingered.

In the late sixteenth century, *Steganographia* was read by southern Italian sorcerers, for its use is recorded in Inquisition documents;[58] and the Italian philosopher Giordano Bruno certainly had access to an edition sometime between 1586 and 1591, because he included material from it in his *De magia cabalistica*.[59] In 1600, Bruno was burned for his heretical beliefs in Campo de' Fiori in Rome. In 1591, in Vienna, Henry Wotton spent 7 florins having a copy made for Baron Edward la Zouche, while sometime before 1601, Friedrich IX, Count of Oettingen-Wallerstein, had a volume produced for himself.[60] A manuscript edition was translated into German sometime between 1577 and 1590.[61]

Steganographia was first printed as a book in 1606, with further print editions following over later years. These included copies of

Trithemius's shorter works, such as the *Clavis steganographiae*, which better explain his methods for hiding messages and provide solutions to the coded content. Unfortunately, the printed edition also included mistakes. The first chart, meant to present the names and locations of spirits, is mostly empty; and a note from the publisher points out spelling errors in the spirits' names – this was apparently the result of a careless engraver (*sculptoris incuria*).[62] There are also problems with a table of spirits on a later page, where the numbers and symbols do not always match those found in earlier manuscript editions, such as the one copied by John Dee.[63] Given that Trithemius warns readers to be careful about pronouncing the names and directions of spirits correctly, these are pretty serious mistakes and omissions for any would-be wizards. Even though this printed edition makes it clear to all readers that Trithemius's appeals to spirits are simply a cover for hidden messages, in 1609 the book still ended up on the *Index librorum prohibitorum* – the list of books that Catholics were banned from reading.

After the publication of *Steganographia* in 1606, Augustus II, Duke of Brunswick, better known as Gustavus Selenus, decided to write his own book on steganography, and set out to find earlier manuscript editions of Trithemius's work. He had noticed the flaws in the printed books, including the missing text and the problems with the published hidden messages. One manuscript copy he had bought included twelve extra chapters, totally absent from the printed version, and he wanted to compare this with other manuscript editions to identify which was the most accurate. To help, he asked an agent, Philipp Hainhofer, to scour Europe for copies. The search did not go well. Hainhofer heard that a copy was kept in Straubing, Germany, but, after investigating, found that it had been burned – people believed it had contained evil magic for contacting the dead. When he tracked down a copy in Tübingen, the librarian would not lend it to him because someone had once cut out four pages.

In the end, there was little that the duke could do but proceed with his research using the one manuscript he had managed to buy. With this, and the various printed editions, he completed his volume on steganography, which draws heavily from Trithemius's writings. Unfortunately for the duke, the twelve extra chapters in the *Steganographia* he had bought turned out to be the work of a forger. The enterprising hoaxer had copied a printed edition of *Steganographia* by hand and added the extra content himself. This was probably done specifically to interest the duke, making the unique manuscript all the more mysterious and worth his money. To add to its allure and authenticity, the forger even made reference to a person known to have corresponded with Trithemius, a certain Johannes de Woesbruck who worked in Bruges.[64]

Since solutions to the secret writing in *Steganographia*'s first two volumes were published with the main text, there was no mystery surrounding how Trithemius had hidden his messages. But for the third, unfinished volume there was no key, leading to centuries of speculation about its content. Were there actually secret messages there, or was it purely a work of magic? Speculation by various writers did not help the matter. In 1533, for instance, Agrippa wrote that both he and Trithemius had sent messages to recipients within twenty-four hours, no matter the distance.[65] In 1676, Wolfgang Ernst Heidel, a doctor of law from Worms, Germany, wrote a book called *Steganographia vindicata*, all about Trithemius and his *Steganographia*. In it he claims to have solved the mystery of *Steganographia*'s third volume, but hides his solution behind a polyalphabetic cipher. He did not want others to claim that they had revealed Trithemius's secrets before him.[66]

In the end, it took until the 1990s for the mystery of *Steganographia*'s third volume to be solved, when Thomas Ernst and Jim Reeds, working separately and independently, revealed that Trithemius had hidden his messages in the astrological tables.[67] At the same time, Ernst broke Heidel's cipher and compared the seventeenth-century solution to his own. It turned out that Heidel had been right all along.[68]

Various manuscript editions of *Steganographia* survive. They include the one copied out by the English polymath John Dee, now reference number Peniarth MS 423D in the National Library of Wales, Cardiff, UK.[69]

In the next chapter, we will visit Dee, who believes that he is being taught the celestial language and script of angels, and records their conversations in his diaries. Can these mystical discussions help him reveal the secrets of creation?

5

THE ANGEL DIARIES OF JOHN DEE (1583–7, 1607)

Inventing and Using a Celestial Language and Script

The angels introduced John Dee and Edward Kelly to their celestial alphabet on the morning of 26 March 1583, a Tuesday. As usual, the two men had taken their places around the holy table in Dee's house at Mortlake, situated on the bank of the River Thames just outside London, and Kelly had stared into the show stone, a round crystal, in which he saw the angels manifest. Dee himself saw nothing in the stone, and relied entirely on Kelly's descriptions when jotting down the day's angel encounters – or 'actions', as he called them – in his diary. On this March day, the angel Raphael appeared in a cloud and offered to help Dee. The best way to reduce ignorance is to learn celestial speech, Raphael told him; all languages spoken since the beginning of time are nothing but shadows of this original speech, used by Adam to name all things. The angels would teach this language to Dee, so that he could better understand the secrets of the cosmos. Raphael then revealed a golden book to Kelly, its pages filled with tables of forty-nine by forty-nine squares. When the angel passed a finger across one of the tables, celestial characters appeared. He pointed to the first, and glanced at Kelly; then to the next, and glanced at Kelly. The characters were red, like fresh blood. Raphael told Dee to record these mysterious symbols; so, one by one, as Kelly recited and described, Dee wrote out the twenty-two characters of the celestial alphabet. The angel then took a rod, pointed to each character in turn, and explained their pronunciation. Raphael told Dee to learn the names of these characters, so that he would not need to keep checking them in his notes.[1]

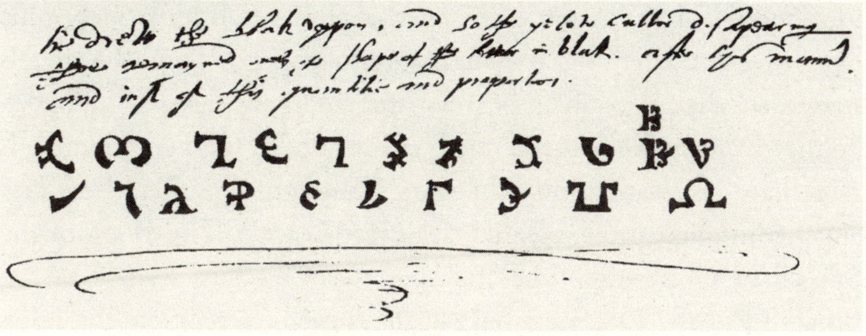

21. The celestial alphabet, written by Edward Kelly in one of John Dee's angel diaries.

Later that afternoon, when the angel encounter resumed, conversation quickly returned to the celestial alphabet. Raphael reminded Dee and Kelly that he had instructed them to learn the characters and their meaning by heart. Dee responded by saying that he had been too busy; earlier that afternoon he had attended a meeting about a planned search for America's north-west passage, and he simply had not had the time.[2] On 29 March, Good Friday, Raphael reappeared and began to dictate a text in the angelic language, naming each letter of the unfamiliar words. Dee realized that filling the forty-nine by forty-nine square was going to take forever, so he politely asked the angel if there was a faster way to receive his wisdom. Angered, Raphael severed contact; but when the communications eventually resumed, the angels used faster methods of dictation, including pronouncing whole words directly.[3] Afterwards, Kelly tried to neatly transfer the celestial words into the required table, but could not make them all fit, so instead he wrote them out as lines of text. This took ten whole pages.

Another ninety-five tables followed. The majority were formed of forty-nine by forty-nine squares, but some were much larger. Unlike the first table, which was meant to be filled with words, each square now contained nothing but a Latin letter or number, and was introduced by text written in the celestial alphabet. It took thirty-nine days to get everything transferred onto paper. When the angels suggested that the tables be rewritten in their celestial alphabet, neither Dee nor Kelly made much effort to fulfil their command – it must have all seemed too exhausting.[4] Brought together, these first angel communications created the *Liber Logaeth*, 'The Book of the Speech of God', sometimes referred to by modern writers as the Book of Enoch.[5] Dee must have been relieved to complete this book but, because the language was celestial, and there was no translation, he could not read it.

Over the next decade, the angels dictated further manuscripts to Dee, which, like the *Liber Logaeth*, he recorded in his angel diaries and extracted into separate books. Along the way, he quizzed the angels on a variety of topics, and carefully jotted down their every response, leading to the most unusual diaries ever written. This was all part of Dee's goal of glorifying God and understanding his divine creation – just in time for the coming apocalypse.

A REPUTATION FOR MAGIC

John Dee was born in London on 13 July 1527. He studied at Cambridge University, where he became infamous for sorcery after putting on a performance of Aristophanes' *Peace* in which he sent an actor flying into the air on the back of a giant mechanical dung beetle. The stunt was so astonishing that witnesses suspected Dee of using dark magic, despite his reassurance that it was purely engineering and mathematics. (Giovanni Fontana would have been proud.) From 1548, Dee travelled in Europe, spending time studying at the University of Louvain in Belgium, and giving lectures in Paris that attracted great crowds. He returned to England in around 1551, and impressed the young King Edward VI. In quick succession, he then worked for the Earl of Pembroke and the Duke of Northumberland, both Protestant.[6]

When Edward VI died in 1553 and the Catholic Queen Mary came to the throne, Dee's fortunes nosedived. Northumberland was executed for his role in trying to keep Mary from the throne and the authorities investigated anyone associated with him. Dee's father, Roland, was among those arrested; despite eventually being released from the Tower of London, he was ruined. The family lost everything and there was nothing left for John to inherit. John was also arrested, and held at Hampton Court Palace in May 1555, accused of using magic to harm the queen and casting horoscopes for Mary, her husband, Philip II of Spain, and Princess Elizabeth. Casting horoscopes of the queen's future was forbidden, for it was treated as a form of spying. He was later moved to the Palace of Westminster for interrogation, which led to nothing. He was then investigated as a heretic at St Paul's Cathedral. Again, nothing stuck. What probably saved Dee was his lack of enthusiasm for either side: he was Christian, but neither aggressively Catholic nor Protestant. To him, God could only be understood by looking deep into nature, at the world and cosmos around us. Luckily for Dee, Mary only reigned for five years. When Elizabeth ascended the throne in 1558, he regained his favour at court. The new queen even asked Dee to choose the most auspicious date for her coronation, based on his astrological calculations.[7]

In 1565, lacking a wealthy patron and without reliable income of his own, Dee and his first wife, Katherine Constable, moved back in with his mother, Jane. Her home was at Mortlake, near London, and it would remain Dee's residence for most of his life. There, he would conduct noisy and smelly alchemical experiments in the garden, converse with angels in a spare bedroom, write books, and assemble one of the greatest libraries in Elizabethan England, a dream of his since Queen Mary had turned down his request to form England's first national library. Buying books for his increasingly disorganized library was expensive, so Dee took on various freelance roles to make extra money, from interpreting clients' dreams to teaching. People came to visit him for all manner of reasons: some wanted their horoscopes cast, others arrived at Mortlake to discuss matters of mathematics and navigation. In 1558, Dee published a book called *Propaedeumata aphoristica*, in which he explains how rays are emitted by all things, like radiation. There are visible rays and supernatural rays, he writes; the heavenly bodies emit them, and this is how and why they affect people in their daily lives. Not only that, but angels travel on light. By using mirrors and lenses, people can affect supernatural rays, just like visible rays, a claim which led Dee into a study of optics.[8]

MONAS HIEROGLYPHICA

Written over the course of twelve days, Dee's *Monas hieroglyphica* was his next major work, published in 1564. He begins by looking at astronomical symbols, and asks if there is a greater power held within them: what if these symbols were all once part of a universal language? Through analysing their forms, and by studying subjects from mathematics to astrology and numerology, Dee argues that all astronomical symbols can be combined to make one ultimate symbol of power: the Monas. This new symbol takes existing symbols and restores them to their ancient, original forms. It combines them in such a way that it gives them a unity and power, understandable by all, irrespective of a person's origin. It is a symbol that reaches back to the very beginnings of language. Inspired by Kabbalistic techniques – methods of revealing hidden meanings in words, taken from Jewish mystical traditions and usually applied to Hebrew – as the book progresses, Dee investigates all aspects of his constructed symbol, taking it apart, reassembling it, and finding layer upon layer of concealed significance.[9]

Scholars in Dee's time were fascinated by the origin of the alphabet and language. They believed that tracing their roots would lead to a better understanding of nature and of God. After all, God spoke creation into existence, so which language did he use? And how was

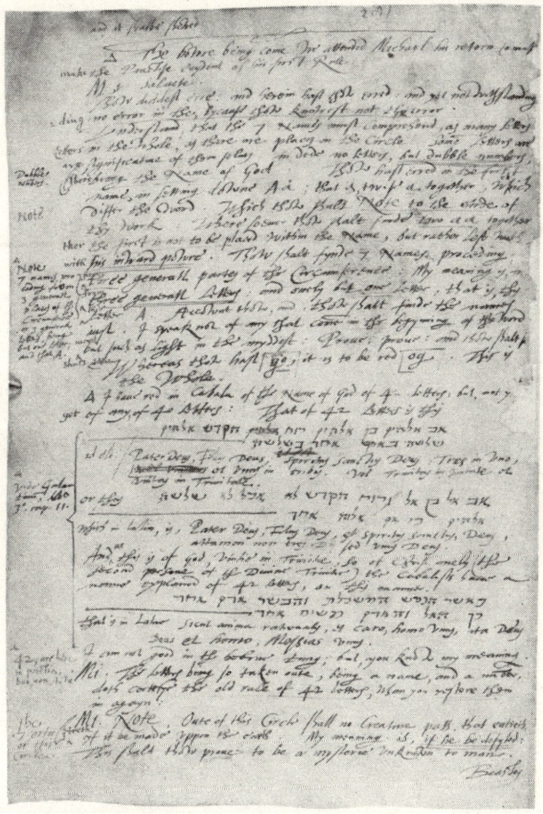

22. The angels and John Dee discuss the power of letters, including text in Hebrew, Latin, and English.

this language written? Initially, Hebrew was most often regarded as the earliest language, and this meant that mathematics was also built into creation, because Hebrew is alphanumeric – meaning that each letter can also be a number. But as time passed, and scholars collected alphabets and studied the evolution of languages, some argued that there were options with greater antiquity than Hebrew. Languages changed over time, they observed, so even known forms of Hebrew, contemporary or ancient, must be different from the original language of God. Perhaps by exploring the planet it might be possible to find people who still spoke the original language. Or perhaps, by studying

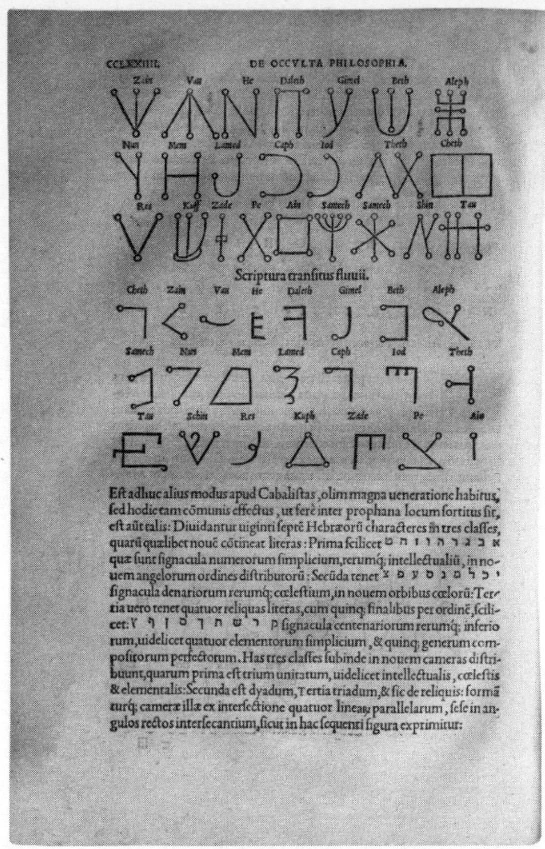

CCLXXIIII. DE OCCVLTA PHILOSOPHIA.

Zain Vau He Daleth Gimel Beth Aleph

Nun Mem Lamed Caph Iod Theth Cheth

Res Kuff Zade Pe Ain Samech Samech Shin Tau

Scriptura tranſitus fluuii.

Cheth Zain Vau He Daleth Gimel Beth Aleph

Samech Nun Mem Lamed Caph Iod Theth

Tau Schin Res Kuph Zade Pe Ain

Eſt adhuc alius modus apud Cabaliſtas, olim magna ueneratione habitus, ſed hodie tam cõmunis effectus, ut ferè inter prophana locum ſortitus ſit, eſt aũt talis: Diuidantur uiginti ſeptẽ Hebræorũ characteres in tres claſſes, quarũ quælibet nouẽ cõtineat literas: Prima ſcilicet א ב ג ד ה ו ז ח ט quæ ſunt ſignacula numerorum ſimplicium, rerumq́; intellectualiũ, in nouem angelorum ordines diſtributorũ: Secũda tenet י כ ל מ נ ס ע פ צ ſignacula denariorum rerumq́; cœleſtium, in nouem orbibus cœlorũ: Tertia uero tenet quatuor reliquas literas, cum quinq; finalibus per ordinẽ, ſcilicet: ק ר ש ת ך ם ן ף ץ ſignacula centenariorum rerumq́; inferiorum, uidelicet quatuor elementorum ſimplicium, & quinq; generum compoſitorum perfectorum. Has tres claſſes ſubinde in nouem cameras diſtribuunt, quarum prima eſt trium unitatum, uidelicet intellectualis, cœleſtis & elementalis: Secunda eſt dyadum, Tertia triadum, & ſic de reliquis: formãturq́; cameræ illæ ex interſectione quatuor linearũ parallelarum, ſeſe in angulos rectos interſecantium, ſicut in hac ſequenti ſigura exprimitur:

23. The third volume of Agrippa's *De occulta philosophia*, showing *scriptura malachim* and *transitus fluvii* writing.

ancient languages, they might be able to reconstruct their earliest forms. The more ancient the alphabet, the more powerful its use in magic might be too. Influential in this debate was Agrippa's third volume of his *De occulta philosophia* (*Of Occult Philosophy*), completed in 1533. Here, Trithemius's most famous student discusses ancient alphabets; among them is the *scriptura malachim* written by angels, and the *transitus fluvii* alphabet, believed to be a form of Hebrew from the time of Moses, or even further back, into the time of Abraham.[10]

On 14 June 1564, Dee visited Greenwich Palace to discuss his *Monas hieroglyphica* with Queen Elizabeth, who showed a great interest in his work. Unfortunately for Dee, England's scholars were not as impressed as their queen, so he accused them of not understanding what he had written.[11] Their lack of acceptance did not stop him from writing further influential works, however. In 1570, he contributed the preface to the first English translation of Euclid's *Elements of Geometry*, in which he describes the importance of numbers as intermediaries in creation for understanding nature.[12] And he wrote a book on navigation in 1577, illustrating the wideness of his learning. It was during these years, in 1575, that Dee's wife Katherine died. That same day, as a sign of her respect, Queen Elizabeth visited Dee's home to personally offer her condolences.[13] Three years later, on 5 February 1578, Dee remarried, this time to the twenty-three-year-old Jane Fromond, who worked at Elizabeth's court.[14] He was over twice her age.

SAUL, KELLY, AND THE ANGELIC SCRIPT

Over the course of the late 1550s and through the 1560s and 1570s, Dee had investigated the cosmos using all the means at his disposal, but had grown disillusioned. He now sought new ways to study the secrets of nature, and concluded that only contact with the divine could help him find the answers to his questions. This meant working with a scryer, a person who could see and interact with the supernatural. Though Dee might have employed scryers for a couple of years by this time, the earliest entry in his diary for an angel action is 22 December 1581, when he was fifty-four years old. His scryer was a man named Barnabas Saul, but their association only lasted a short time for, on 12 February 1582, Saul was charged with criminal behaviour, and mysteriously stopped being able to communicate with the supernatural.[15] Dee replaced Saul with Edward Kelly, who initially went by the name Edward Talbot – not at all suspicious.

They held their first session together on 10 March 1582, when Kelly impressed Dee by swiftly establishing a connection with the angel Uriel. Dee asked Uriel about 'The Book of Soyga', a mysterious manuscript in his library, filled with strange tables, that he had been trying to interpret and decipher. Uriel suggested that the archangel Michael could help him, and that he would appear to them as long as they both showed the proper piety and prayer. Michael manifested the next day, which Dee again took as a great sign of Kelly's abilities.[16]

All of this culminated on 26 March 1583, when Dee received the celestial alphabet, beginning a new phase in his investigations. Following Kelly's instructions, Dee jotted down the unfamiliar characters in a line. There were twenty-one distinct symbols, plus one duplicate differentiated by a dot, making a total of twenty-two characters. This was the same as Hebrew – which no doubt helped Kelly's claims to appear more authentic to Dee – and, like Hebrew, the script was read from right to left. Each character also had a name, but these had no connection to their pronunciation. To help him make sense of the angel's instructions, Dee sketched three columns in his diary: the first column presented the angelic symbols; the middle one, their names; and the last one, their English equivalents. The symbol called 'mals', which appears a bit like a Greek omega, stood for 'p'; the symbol 'veh', resembling a Latin 'k', represented 'c'; and 'drux', which looks like a backwards euro symbol, has the sound value 'n'. A day or two later, Dee wrote out the script again, this time placing the celestial characters in a row with their English equivalents beneath. As time passed, to help him remember the pronunciation of this angelic language, Dee wrote notes in the margins of his diary, using English words and sounds as his guide.[17]

The angels followed their gift of the celestial alphabet with lengthy dictations of angelic speech, which Dee and Kelly had to fit into ninety-five grids. Extracted from Dee's angel diary, this became 'The Book of the Speech of God', or *Liber Logaeth*.[18] Afterwards, Dee and Kelly diligently wrote out further books dictated by the angels. In the

De heptarchia mystica, for example, Dee collected together information on summoning specific spirits, gathered from his conversations. This included forty-nine seals of elemental angels (divided into kings and princes) and prayers, including the times and days to say them. Dee carefully drew some of these seals in his diary.[19] Intriguingly, despite the importance placed on the celestial alphabet, these books, and those that came later, made only a small use of it.

COMMUNICATING WITH ANGELS

For his angel actions to succeed, Dee had a number of requirements, revealed to him by Uriel through Kelly. He needed a quiet space, where he would not be interrupted, which at Mortlake he established in a spare bedroom (after first asking the angels if it would be suitable as long as he removed the bed).[20] The most important item was his show stone. This entered Dee's possession on 21 November 1582, when the angel Carmara told him that he needed a special stone for his actions, and asked Kelly to point to a spot beneath the room's west window. Dee could not see anything, but he got up anyway and crossed the room to investigate. As he got closer, he spotted a round shadow on the floor. He reached down and, to his surprise, discovered the stone.[21] From that moment on, Dee's scryers peered into this angel-gifted stone during their communications with the divine; to Dee, drawing from his study of optics, its surface collected supernatural rays, which were used by angels and emanated from and through all things.[22] Dee put the show stone on a wooden frame, which stood on a wax seal called the *sigillum dei*, its design described by the angels and noted in his diary.[23] In turn, this rested on a holy table, built and decorated according to angelic instruction (twice – because the angels decided that their first set of instructions were wrong).[24] Painted in blue, red, and gold, the table top was decorated with a pentagram, symbols called the seven Ensigns of Creation, and celestial writing, in which letters stood for angelic names.[25] Dee had to dress correctly

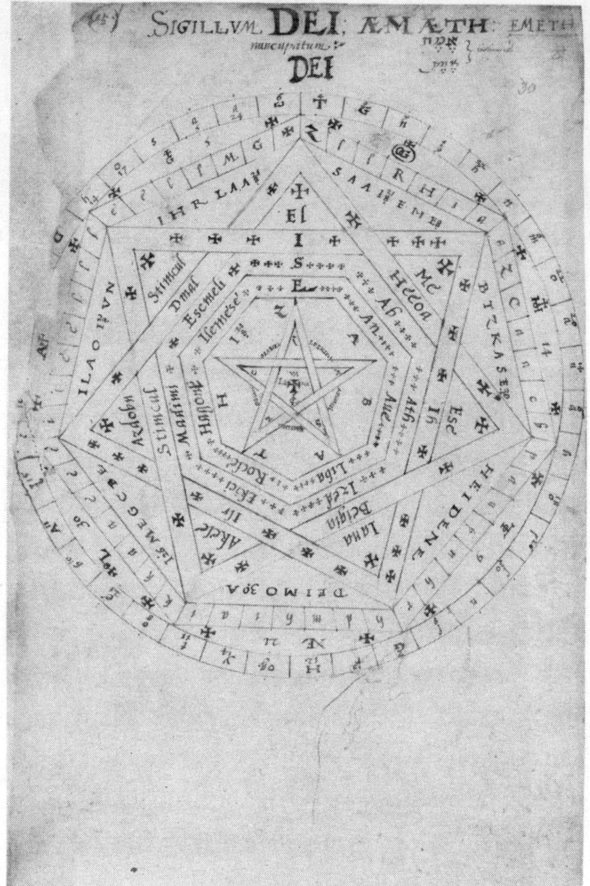

24. The *sigillum dei* from one of John Dee's angel diaries.

too. To keep himself safe from dangerous forces, he wore a gold ring with the word 'PELE' written on it and a triangular gold breastplate decorated with sigils, and he carried a rod.[26] With his long greying beard, he must have appeared quite the wizard.

During these celestial conversations, Dee sat beside Kelly and jotted down everything that was asked and said in one of his angel diaries. He added extra comments in the margins, sometimes after returning to the page later to clarify certain details. Dee wrote fast, his handwriting a blur of Latin, English, and angelic words. To keep up his speed, he

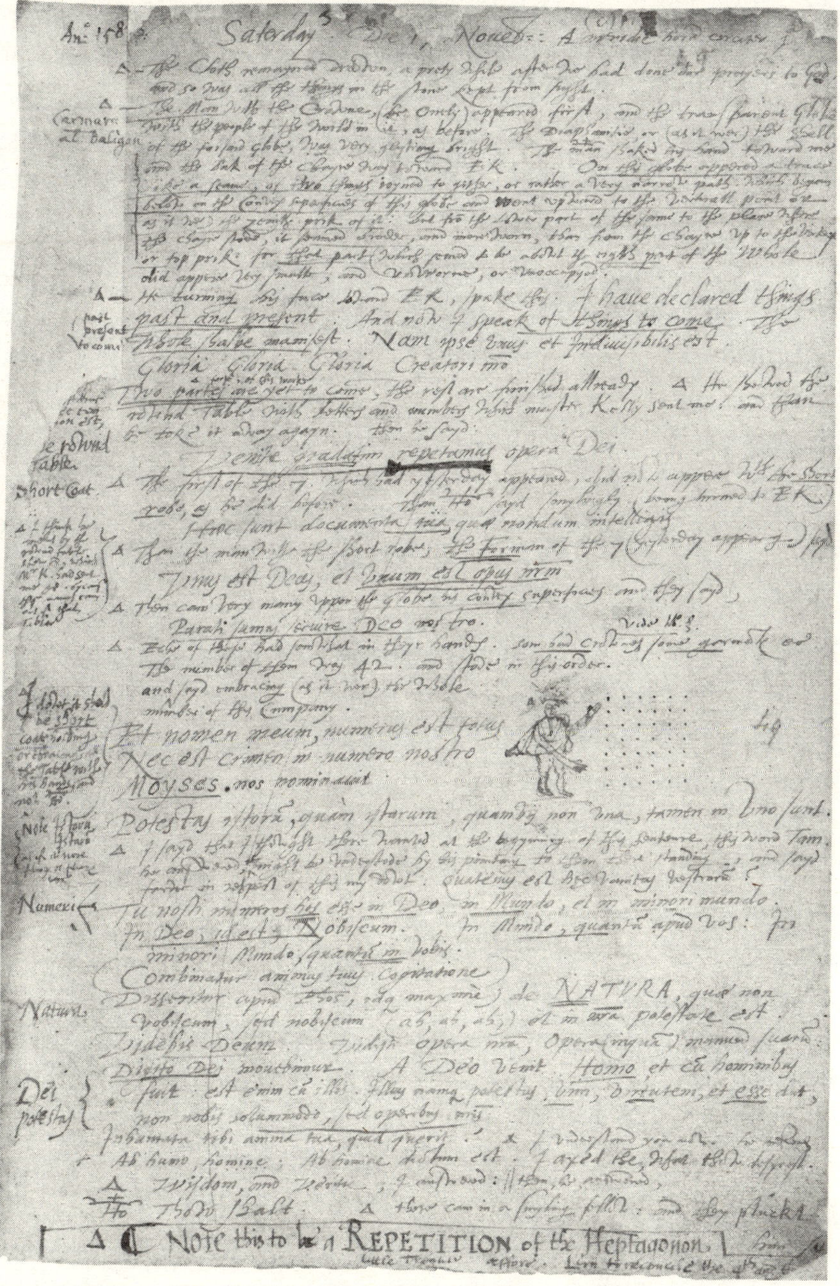

25. A page from one of John Dee's angel diaries, including a small drawing of the angel Carmara.

abbreviated the names of the angels, wrote only the initials of his scryer, and drew a small triangle – the Greek delta, symbol for 'D' – to stand for his own name. For the most part, Dee crammed his words tightly onto the pages, with his letters sporting curly flourishes, but he also drew diagrams and small illustrations, such as the angel Carmara and a particularly fearsome demon.[27] Like other writers of his time, he highlighted important content by drawing manicules – hands with long fingers that point at particularly relevant sections.

In between their conversations about divine books, mystical matters, equipment design, and complex number tables, Dee, Kelly, and the angels discussed a wide variety of topics. Running low on cash, Dee asked the angel Carmara if he knew the location of any hidden treasure that could help him pay the bills.[28] Kelly was more blunt, and directly asked the angel Madimi for £100.[29] On one occasion, perhaps after hearing his stomach rumble, Dee asked the voice he was conversing with if it was acceptable for him to go to supper.[30] Another time, he asked for the location of his Arabic book, only to be told that it was in Scotland.[31] Kelly complained that the angels wanted him to marry, and was later mocked by them for spending an afternoon fishing when Dee wanted his help.[32]

The diaries also record regular appearances by demonic forces, such as Lundrumguffa, who could only be removed with brimstone. This demon was later beaten up by the angel Uriel, dragged off, and thrown down a pit.[33] One day, while Dee was busy ruling lines on paper for their massive tables of squares, a group of demons armed with spades attacked Kelly and bit his arm. The panicking scryer put a stool between him and his invisible attackers, and Dee threatened them with a stick, furiously drawing a cross in the air (once Kelly had pointed out where they stood).[34] Bizarre predictions also came true. Kelly received a vision of a fleet of ships sailing to attack England, reminiscent of the Spanish Armada, and of a woman being beheaded, explained by Uriel as the imminent death of Mary, Queen of Scots.[35] Even stranger are a reference to the Antichrist being alive, and one that Adrian Gilbert, the half-brother of the explorer and royal favourite Sir Walter Raleigh, was going to spread the word of God to the people of Atlantis.[36] There are also insights into the world of the angels: these are declared to be neither men nor women, but simply taking these forms, and they have no physical voices, only spiritual ones that fill the universe.[37]

A particularly unusual episode in the angel diaries revolves around a mysterious treasure and a red powder. On 22 March 1583, Kelly arrived at Dee's house with a man called John Husey. They had been to Northwick Hill, where a 'spiritual creature' had led them to a buried book and scroll. The scroll bore drawings of ten places, each shown inside a circle with enciphered captions, and an equally enciphered message. There was also a red powder, which Kelly explained was related to the philosopher's stone. It did not take long for Dee to decipher the scroll, revealing it to be written in Latin. The places were associated with a hidden treasure that belonged to a Danish prince called Menabon (and possibly another prince too, called Gordanigus). The enciphered captions gave clues about where to find these places. The angel El suggested that Dee and Kelly should uncover these lost riches, but Dee was concerned: digging up treasure was illegal without royal permission, and this was hard to obtain. Helpfully, the angels suggested that, if he simply collected some soil from each location, the treasure would magically manifest for him. Kelly set off to get the soil; when he returned, Dee consulted the angels about what to do with the small piles of earth he now found in his possession. Their answers were not particularly helpful. A year later, when Dee asked the angels to make the promised riches materialize, they were equally unhelpful. Dee never received his treasure.[38]

THE ANGEL-CONJURER'S LIBRARY

By Dee's time, various books claimed to give readers the ability to communicate with angels, so he was not alone in his interest. The *Ars notoria*, a probably twelfth-century text from northern Italy, is filled with prayers and rituals in a variety of languages meant to enable the reader to gain information from celestial sources. It may have been primarily aimed at university students, given that the subjects discussed with the angels are suspiciously similar to those found in contemporary course curricula. This work turned out to be very popular over the years, despite warnings that its readers might summon demons rather than angels. The early fourteenth-century 'Book of the Flowers of Heavenly Teaching', by the Benedictine monk Jean de Morigny, built on the *Ars notoria*'s success. Morigny writes about his experiences using this earlier work, but then presents his own prayers that give readers access to knowledge. Again, this all appears geared towards students – Morigny no doubt hoped to replace the *Ars notoria* with his own writings. The 'Sworn Book of Honorius', probably composed in early fourteenth-century Spain, goes one step further than these other manuscripts by claiming to provide direct access to God.[39] Angelic alphabets have also long existed in different forms in Jewish magic. Notably, Jewish texts of Late Antiquity and the Middle Ages include mystical symbols, known as charaktêres, which magicians attempted to decipher to reveal angelic alphabets.[40]

Over the course of his life, Dee obsessively collected books that he believed would help him further his knowledge of angel communication. In Antwerp, Belgium, in February 1563, he tracked down a manuscript edition of Trithemius's *Steganographia*, which he copied by hand in a printing house and bookshop called the Golden Angel on Den Camer Straet, where he was also staying. It cost him £20 to gain access for ten days, which was all the money he had to cover his travels.[41] The manuscript's instructions on angel magic, and what it could achieve, intrigued him. Dee also owned a copy of Heinrich Cornelius Agrippa's three-volume *De occulta philosophia*, released from 1531 to 1533. He kept this beside the window in the room where he held his angel actions.[42] Another book that strongly influenced Dee's thinking was Pompilius Azalus's *De omnibus rebus naturalibus*, which, as we know from Chapter 3, was actually written by Giovanni

Fontana a century before its publication under the name Azalus in 1544. Dee was particularly interested in Azalus/Fontana's writings about angels, and scribbled his own comments in the margins. Indeed, this book was so important to him that he took it on his travels in Europe – the next phase in his intriguing life.[43]

DEE'S TRAVELS IN EUROPE: THE NEXT CELESTIAL WRITINGS

The Polish nobleman Olbracht Laski had arrived at England's royal court for uncertain reasons, but had managed to charm everyone he met – at least at first. To Queen Elizabeth's advisors, he was a source of information about current affairs in Poland and Bohemia, so it was worth keeping him around. Laski was already aware of Dee's actions with angels when he visited him at Mortlake – instantly recognizable at Dee's door thanks to his trademark huge white beard. It was a tense time to drop by. The angels had recently warned Dee of a coming apocalypse and urged him to leave England – not an easy task when weighed down by debt – but the nobleman had frequently been mentioned in Dee's angel actions, making his presence welcome. On 23 May 1583, the angels had predicted that Laski would become the ruler of a kingdom, and Dee had begun to believe that the nobleman could save him from his own troubles. Similar angelic prophecies were made on 2 June and 7 September, but by this time Laski's popularity in England had plummeted. He had foolishly promoted his ancestral ties to the noble Lacy family, which in turn made him a relative of the queen and a danger to the court. Dee's close relationship with Laski through his angel actions brought this danger on him too, leaving him in a desperate situation that required a dramatic response. Afraid of running into anyone he owed money to, as well as members of the royal court, Dee and his family left Mortlake under cover of darkness on 21 September 1583, met Laski in London, and sailed away. Five days later, they reached Holland and their new life on the continent began.[44]

Laski invited Dee to Poland, where he stayed from 1584 until the middle of 1585, initially spending around five weeks in Lask before moving to Krakow. Throughout this time, money continued to be a problem. On 22 February 1584, while still in Lask, Dee was sick with a fever and asked the angels for a cure. Knowing that, like himself, Laski suffered from financial troubles, he also asked the angels to 'very speedily' bring the Danish treasure, first discussed nearly a year earlier, and for advice on the function of Kelly's mysterious red powder.[45] This did not help. Dee was in Krakow by mid-March 1584, where he and his family rented a stone house on St Stephen's Street, today called Szczepańska, for 80 guilders – enough for a year.[46] It stood beside the Merchant's Hospital of the Fraternity of the Virgin Mary, close to the city wall, and in front of St Stephen's church. Dee set up his study on the house's first floor, and it was there, on 12 April 1584, that the angels started to dictate a new book to Dee and Kelly, one that would enable Dee to summon angels capable of revealing the secrets of nature.[47]

Over the next three months, the angels revealed their book by referring Dee and Kelly to individual letters and numbers in the tables of the *Liber Logaeth*.[48] As Kelly read each character aloud from the tables, he spelled out the angelic words backwards, apparently to prevent them from overpowering him and Dee. This meant that Dee had to reverse each word to find its correct pronunciation, adding an extra layer of complexity to an already difficult task.[49] Unlike the previous celestial language from their earlier actions at Mortlake, this time the angels provided translations for their mysterious words. The resulting book, named the *48 claves angelicae*, or the '48 Angelic Keys', was complete by 23 July 1584. Dee's official version, as usual extracted from his angel diary, is written in uncharacteristically neat handwriting, with each line of angelic words followed by its English translation on the line below. Other books soon followed. Among them was the *Liber scientiae auxilii et victoriae terrestris*, which contains tidily presented tables bearing the names of angels who oversee different locations, from Egypt to Mauritania, and their symbols. This book was associated with the *Tabula angelorum bonorum*, another work of mysterious tables filled with numbers, zigzagging lines or symbols, and letters.[50]

At the urging of the angels, after their time in Poland, Dee and Kelly packed their things and moved to Prague, to try to secure a place for themselves at the court of Emperor Rudolf II. There, they lived in the house of Tadeus Hajek, who served as the emperor's personal doctor and was renowned for his knowledge of a great many topics, including alchemy and astronomy. Hajek had been a friend of Dee's for some time, and provided a much-needed 'in' for his attempts to meet Rudolf. In the meantime, the angel actions continued, now from a study adorned with paintings of alchemical vessels. It was during one of these sessions that the angels told Dee the year of his death – 1601, incorrectly.

When Dee finally secured an audience with the emperor, he failed to make a good impression. Rudolf did not understand the *Monas hieroglyphica*, which he had received as a gift, and did not appreciate Dee telling him that the angels wanted him to repent of his sins. When Dee attempted to get Rudolf to look at his angel actions, he

26. The city of Prague in the early seventeenth century, during the reign of Emperor Rudolf II – home to John Dee, Johannes Heckius, and Michael Maier, as well as the Voynich Manuscript.

sent an underling in his place. After this latest failure, Dee spent a brief period in Hungary and Poland before returning to Prague. His finances continued to be a source of intense stress. To help, the angels provided a recipe for the philosopher's stone, though this only served to improve Kelly's reputation. Even the presence of King Stephen Bathory of Poland, during angel communications held in Krakow on 28 and 29 May 1585, achieved little to alleviate the gloom.[51]

BURNING BOOKS AND SWAPPING WIVES

On the morning of 10 April 1586, Dee, Kelly, and a Catholic priest called Francesco Pucci were holding a meeting with the angels in the tower of their rented home beside the Cattle Market of Prague's New Town.[52] An angel demanded to see all of the manuscripts that Dee had produced from his actions, which he duly brought in a white box. 'Destroy them', the angel said. Obediently, Dee tore up his notes and all of the manuscripts in which he had carefully copied out the angels' words. Then, as instructed, he put their remains in a bag, along with the book and red powder that Kelly had unearthed at Northwick Hill. The angel told Kelly to burn the bag in the house's large stove, and Pucci was instructed to watch until he had personally witnessed it all reduced to ashes. Dee prayed. Watching the papers go up in flames, Kelly saw an angel carefully collecting the items. Afterwards, the group burned any remaining papers in the stove too. Dee and Kelly removed the show stone from its position on the holy table, and hung the table itself on the wall in memory of the angel actions.[53] This was the end. Or so it seemed.

On 29 April 1586, Kelly peered down from an upstairs window of their Prague home and spotted a gardener in the vineyard below. The man approached the wall beneath Kelly and shouted up for Dee to come outside, then erupted into a huge pillar of fire. Dee and Kelly rushed to the garden (after first sending Kelly's wife to investigate). Fifteen minutes later, beside an almond tree, Dee spotted three of his destroyed books, now miraculously intact: the *48 Angelic Keys*, the *Liber scientiae auxilii et victoriae terrestris*, and the *Liber Logaeth*. Kelly left with the gardener (no longer aflame, we must presume), only to return soon after with more of the destroyed material. The supernatural gardener had discovered the manuscripts intact within the stove and handed them to Kelly before vanishing. Unusually for his interactions with angels, Dee reports seeing this mysterious gardener himself, whom he describes as floating a foot in the air.[54] Certain books were never found, however, including companion volumes to the *48 Angelic Keys* and a manuscript called 'The Mystery of Mysteries and the Holy of Holies', which Dee believed to be of particular importance.[55]

Although these events sound rather unusual – even in the lives of Dee and Kelly – it may have been Kelly's attempt to show the Catholic Church (through Pucci) that the angel books no longer existed. Over recent months, the Vatican had been taking an increasing interest in the angel actions, and had wanted to see Dee's documents, probably as the first step towards an accusation of heresy.[56] The destruction of this evidence would weaken the Church's case against them. But if this had indeed been Kelly's aim, his plan failed. Shortly after these events, the pope's representative in Prague accused Dee and Kelly of necromancy, put pressure on Rudolf II, and had them banished from the city. Dee's family made their new home in Třeboň, now in southern Czechia, where the angel actions became less frequent. Dee and Kelly turned their interests towards alchemy, a potentially more lucrative enterprise.[57] Yet even this was not the end, for there was one final, dramatic event.

On 18 April 1587, the angels told Kelly and Dee to share everything, including their wives. This shocking announcement shook Dee's faith – how could the angels have demanded something so offensive to God? He queried their request, and received a cipher in return, which, when decrypted, urged him to obey. He broke the news at supper that night, much to the confusion of his wife Jane and

Kelly's wife, Joanna. Dee and Jane argued into the early hours of the morning, and Jane cried, trembling, for fifteen minutes before agreeing to do as asked. Nonetheless, Jane and Joanna demanded that their husbands hold an extra angel action, to receive 'better information' from the divine messengers, but Kelly felt the issue was settled and no action was held. Eventually, the two couples signed a covenant together, read before the angels in a chapel. When Dee had slept with Joanna, and Kelly with Jane on 21 May, Dee recorded it in his personal diary in Latin – 'pactum factum'. Nine months later, Jane gave birth to a son. Was it Kelly's? We will probably never know.

With the exception of a few extra pages written years later, the final entry in Dee's angel diary is dated Saturday 23 May 1587, two days after the wife-swapping episode, when a horseman manifested in the show stone to ask each man if the other's wife had been 'obedient'. This entry, recording that each replied in the affirmative, can now barely be read. Someone, perhaps Dee, had tried to erase it. Dee held no further angel actions with Kelly, and the two men never saw each other again after 16 February 1589.[58]

INVENTING A CELESTIAL LANGUAGE AND SCRIPT

How did Kelly invent the angelic language and script that so entranced Dee? Although no known script exactly matches the designs of the celestial alphabet, it is probable that Kelly found inspiration by flicking through books in Dee's library at Mortlake. There, he would have found the 1530 work *Voarchadumia contra alchimiam* by Giovanni Pantheus, which includes an Enochian alphabet similar in appearance to Dee's angelic script. Other books that might have caught Kelly's eyes were Theseus Ambrosius's *Introductio in chaldaicam linguam, syriacum atque armenicam et decem alias linguas*, from 1539, which presents an intriguing selection of scripts; and certainly Agrippa's famous *De occulta philosophia*, with its various mystical alphabets and angelic *scriptura malachim*. In fact, many of the angels found in Dee's actions can also be found in Agrippa's volumes, where they are even described with the same titles and roles, suggesting that Kelly perused the books often. Kelly's angelic script also resembles Samaritan and Ethiopic.

As for the angelic language itself, there are quite significant differences between the first angelic words received in Mortlake and those delivered later, when Dee was on the continent. The early form is more pronounceable, like words spoken off the top of the head; the later angelic speech often includes repeated vowels and strange groups of consonants, reflective of letters selected at random from the tables of the *Liber Logaeth*. Over half of the later celestial words appear only once, adding to this sense of randomness. Kelly also made life easy for himself by letting one angelic word stand for many English words, giving him a lot of flexibility in his translations; and what exists of the sentence structure and pronunciation is very English, though, for the most part, the grammar makes little sense. The language had many variances and exceptions, which irritated the careful scholar Dee. Numbers, for example, were clear from one to nine, but the way Kelly formed larger numbers is impossible to explain unless they were spontaneously invented. Although it is possible that Kelly relayed the early angel communications in a trance – the sentence structure he uses is similar to that found in glossolalia, or speaking in tongues – it is more probable that he was consciously speaking gibberish.

Indeed, there are plenty of hints that Kelly consciously spoke for the angels, rather than taking part in the conversations deep in a trance. The angels identify Dee's library books by the colour of their spines, rather than their titles, just as Kelly might have recognized them from wandering around Dee's house. The cipher sent to confirm that the angels wanted Dee and Kelly to swap wives featured Latin errors when deciphered and mistakes in the cipher itself – careless mistakes. On one occasion, after Dee had received certain details from the angels, Kelly announced that this same information could be read in a book by Agrippa: perhaps he suspected that Dee would notice, and wanted to cover his back. The angels also knew that Dee had hidden records of his earlier spirit actions with Saul and other scryers in a capcase in the chimney. Did Kelly go snooping around when left alone, searching for secrets? He certainly read Dee's private diary, and even wrote comments within when he disagreed with something Dee had written, forcing Dee to compose some entries in English using Greek script.[59]

What happened to Kelly? After leaving Dee's employ, he became famous for his alchemical skills. Rudolf II even made him a baron, but he was later forced to flee when orders were sent out for his arrest. Had he been revealed as a fraud? Was it because of his debts? No one knows, but he was locked up in Krivoklat Castle, 40 kilometres west of Prague, until the autumn of 1593. He returned to Prague after being released, but was imprisoned again, this time in Hněvín Castle in the town of Most, in November 1596, apparently because a duel he had fought ended with his opponent – a courtier – lying dead on the floor. After this, his story becomes murky. He was last seen alive in 1598.[60]

DEE'S LATER LIFE

Dee returned with his family to England via a short stay in Bremen, Germany, at the end of 1589, with the intention of re-establishing himself at Queen Elizabeth's court. When he opened his front door at Mortlake, he was astonished to find his home ransacked and five hundred books stolen. It was a devastating loss for the bibliophile, but he soon returned to his old routine and hired a new scryer for his angel actions, a man called Bartholomew Hickman. These renewed celestial conversations led Dee to conclude that a great cosmic revelation would occur in 1600. He also had to contend with an additional occult force in his home when his children's nurse, Ann Frank, was thought to be possessed, requiring Dee to perform an exorcism.

Though she appeared to recover, Ann later threw herself down a well, only to be rescued from drowning, just in the nick of time, by Dee. Nonetheless, she committed suicide in August 1590 by slitting her own throat in the building next door to Dee's home.[61]

Money continued to be tight for Dee's family, so in 1592 he was forced to expand his freelancing offer to include exorcism (despite his failure with Ann Frank) and searching for buried treasure using occult means. It was not enough, and he had to let Hickman go in December 1594 because of his financial woes. Life only improved in 1596, when Dee accepted the position of Warden of Christ's College in Manchester (even though he still spent much of his time at Mortlake). Finally earning a steady income, he rehired Hickman and brought him to Manchester, while also occasionally receiving help from another scryer, Francis Nichols, who was one of Dee's students. When Hickman's predicted revelation failed to materialize in September 1600, Nichols told Dee to incinerate his rival's angel actions, leading to the loss of nine years' worth of records.[62]

At eighty years old, Dee was still contacting angels for advice. With Hickman serving as his scryer, these actions were held at various locations, including Mortlake, an inn called the Three Kings in Westminster, London, and the house of a woman named Goodman. He had left Manchester a few years earlier, following the death of his wife Jane from plague on 23 March 1605, and laying her to rest in Manchester Cathedral.[63] In an angel action from 20 March 1607, Dee was concerned about his own health. He suffered from kidney stones and intestinal bleeding, but was still trying to gain celestial advice on how to deal with the royal court and improve his financial situation. Nothing ever changes.

A few months later, the angels told Dee that he would receive the philosopher's stone, among other items, and he consulted them regarding a client's stolen money, showing that he was still free-lancing, even at his advanced age. Then, in September 1608, the angels told him that it was time to leave England again. To fund his trip, he would need to sell all of his belongings, including his beloved books. As trusting as ever, Dee sold his home at Mortlake and started making plans. He did not get far. At eighty-five, he was living in the home of his friend John Pontois on London's Bishopsgate Street, his precious angel diaries still with him. Dee died there on 26 March 1609, at 3 a.m., and was buried in the church at Mortlake. His last angel action records an appeal for alchemical advice and a search for buried treasure – his finances still on his mind to the very end.[64]

EXCAVATIONS AND PIE DISHES

After Dee's death, his manuscripts became widely dispersed and were highly desired by book collectors. Robert Cotton, a politician who had himself amassed a huge library, is said to have bought land that once formed part of Dee's Mortlake estate so that he could search for manuscripts rumoured to be buried there. In this, he was apparently successful, because one of Dee's angel diaries ended up in his possession.[65] Covering Dee's angel actions from 28 May 1583 through to 23 May 1587, with additional pages from 1607, the angel diary in Cotton's collection passed to his son Thomas upon his death in 1631, and was published in 1659 by the classical scholar Meric Casaubon, based on 'The Original Copy, written with Dr. Dees own Hand'. In his introduction, Casaubon relates that Robert Cotton had bought Dee's library, but adds that the manuscript had been 'buried in the Earth, how long, years or months, I know not'. It was covered in soil, had become mouldy, and had started to perish, warranting the need for its content to be copied out.[66] Casaubon declares the angel communications to be a 'work of darkness', and his purpose for publishing them is to warn readers about the dangers of summoning spirits and devils.[67] After reading it, the natural philosopher Robert Hooke argued that Dee's angel diaries hid secret messages, just like Trithemius's *Steganographia*. Others subsequently made similar arguments.[68]

From Thomas Cotton, the angel diary passed to John Cotton, who gave it to the country when he died in 1702. The Cotton Collection was stored at Cotton House in Westminster until 1722, when it was moved to Essex House on the Strand, London. It was then transferred to Ashburnham House in Little Dean's Yard, Westminster, in 1730. A huge fire tore through this building on 23 October 1731, damaging some of the diary's pages.[69] Today, the manuscript is stored in the British Library under catalogue entry Cotton MS Appendix XLVI.[70] The *Liber Logaeth* also found its way into the Cotton Collection and, like the other manuscripts, eventually to the British Library; apparently, it was sold for one guinea by a certain Dr Biggs at some point in its journey.[71]

Dee's other surviving angel diary, covering 22 December 1581 to 23 May 1583, had an equally eventful life after its owner's death. Dee had hidden this diary away in a secret drawer inside one of his cedarwood travel chests, which was sold after his death, probably as part of the sale of his household items. If so, this is probably when it entered the possession of a surgeon called John Woodall. From Woodall, the chest made its way into a joiner's shop on Adle Street, London, where it was spotted by the recently married Mr and Mrs Jones of Lombard Street. They were quite taken by the cedarwood chest, particularly its lovely lock and hinges, and immediately bought it for their home. Twenty years later, the couple decided to move the chest. Having picked a new spot for it to sit, they carefully lifted it, and were carrying it across the room when they heard a noise coming from inside. They shook it to confirm. It rattled again. Intrigued, Mr Jones took a piece of iron and, noticing a small crevice underneath the chest, shoved the iron inside. A secret drawer opened. It was filled with mysterious items – books and papers, beads, and a wooden cross. The angel diary had been revealed.

It was an astounding discovery, though no one conveyed this importance to the Jones's maid, who, seeing random old pieces of paper lying around, used around half of them to line her pie dishes when cooking. The family put a stop to this as soon as they discovered what was happening. Two years later, Mr Jones died, and the cedar-wood chest met its own end in the Great Fire of London in 1666. Luckily, the quick-thinking Mrs Jones saved Dee's papers and manuscripts from the flames, including the angel diary. Later, she married a warder of the Tower of London called Mr Wale, who brought Dee's documents to the attention of the politician, antiquarian, and founder of the Ashmolean Museum, Elias Ashmole. Mr Wale sent Ashmole the pages and manuscripts in a package, which Ashmole received on 20 August 1672, and on 5 September he visited Ashmole in his office at the Excise Office on Broad Street (today Old Broad Street), to explain that he would be happy to exchange the manuscripts and papers for one of Ashmole's own books. Five days later, on 10 September, the former Mrs Jones, along with her new husband, came to Ashmole to tell him the story of how they came to own the papers. This is how Dee's angel diary entered Ashmole's collection.[72] After Ashmole, the manuscript passed to William Shippen, and then to Hans Sloane, and onward to the British Museum.

This angel diary is now in the British Library under the catalogue entry Sloane MS 3188.[73] Four other manuscripts, extracted from Dee's angel diaries, found in the chest are also in the British Library, having taken the same route into the collection.[74] As some of these manuscripts were apparently burned in Prague, and later magically recovered, they are perhaps the only manuscripts in the British Library to claim to have been saved by the actions of angels. Whatever the truth may be, given their eventful history, the fact that they survive at all is surely a miracle.

We will next travel to Spain, where the discovery of a puzzling parchment in the ruins of a medieval minaret will spark nearly a century of religious debate – and reveal the power of a well-designed hoax.

6

THE TURPIANA TOWER PARCHMENT (1588)

Manuscripts and Secret Scripts as Hoaxes

Once part of the grand mosque at the centre of the city of Granada, the old minaret had stood as a symbol of Muslim rule in Spain, visible to all, for centuries; but since the return of Christian control in 1492, the authorities had converted it into a bell tower. Now, even that was not needed. The cathedral was being extended and the old minaret stood in its way. The sharp clink of mattocks striking stone had replaced the ringing of bells and the call to prayer, as sweating workmen dismantled the tower, block by block, from the top down. Careful not to let it fall and damage the growing cathedral, they hacked away at its peak and dumped the old stonework to ground level, where, each day, it was removed from the site. As the work continued on 19 March 1588, a worker spotted something unexpected among the growing pile of bricks and dust: a lead box, covered in bitumen. Curious, the man opened it and, to his surprise, the scent of flowers wafted up into his face. He peered inside and found a piece of bone, some triangular cloth, and an image of the Virgin Mary. There was also a folded parchment. This unusual find immediately caused a stir. Word spread among the workmen and onlookers. What did it all mean? The archdeacon, Luis de Pedraza, summoned the cathedral chapter, and that afternoon they sat together to discuss the bizarre events of the day.[1]

Eager to better understand the contents of the box, the archdeacon and his fellow dignitaries unfolded the parchment. Their eyes were met with a confusing mix of languages and symbols. There were

27. A view of Granada in the sixteenth century.

two paragraphs of Arabic at the top, followed below by two huge grids, one above the other. The uppermost grid was formed of twenty-nine horizontal rows and forty-eight vertical columns, space for a total of 1,392 characters. Each grid square contained a single Latin letter: one in brown, then one in red, one in brown, then one in red, and so on. Occasional Greek symbols and unreadable shapes were dotted among them. None of it made sense. To the left side of the grid was another set of Arabic writing. The lower grid was formed of 150 rectangles – fifteen columns and ten rows. Each rectangular space contained one or two Arabic words, with those in each box alternating in brown and red ink, just as above. Further below, there were more lines of Arabic, what appeared to be a signature, and then, at the bottom left, sentences in Latin written slanted across the page. Extra Latin and Greek letters flanked the grids. The clergymen were perplexed. What did it all mean?

The Arabic text, which should have been easy to read, was itself highly unusual. The script was overly cursive, and the dots that help readers to determine the meaning of the letters were frequently absent. Some letters took forms that were closer to Hebrew and Greek. These peculiarities, along with the lack of vowels, meant that it was possible to read the text in multiple different ways. Taken together, the unusual writing and the layout gave the document a feeling of antiquity and mysteriousness. The whole parchment appeared to be one large puzzle.[2]

As the clergymen ran their eyes over the parchment's mysterious mangle of texts and symbols, they could only read one of its languages with ease: the slanting Latin at the bottom. Perhaps this could shed some light on the mystery, they figured. It proved most helpful. These lines had been written by a priest called Patricius, who had been entrusted with a collection of holy relics by the martyr Saint Cecilius – according to tradition, the first Bishop of Granada during the first century. The parchment was one of these relics. The seemingly random selection of brown and red letters, spread out in the squares above, was said to be an apocalyptic prophecy written by the apostle John. Although the churchmen could not read that part yet, Patricius's statement appeared to be confirmed by the Arabic words in the signature. Drawing on their basic knowledge of Arabic, they managed to spell out the word 'Sisiliyu' – surely the name Cecilius, they decided – followed by 'Bishop of Granada'. Patricius's message went on to explain that the Virgin Mary had wiped away the tears she had wept at Jesus's crucifixion with the triangular cloth, while the bone in the box was a relic of Saint Stephen. Patricius himself had hidden the lead box of relics in the minaret, which he referred to as the Turpiana Tower. He did not want them to be seized by the Moors, a word used by Christians to describe Muslims from southern Spain and North Africa. It was clearly a find of unparalleled importance, the archdeacon recognized, one that could change Granada forever and prove the presence of early Christians in Spain. But, unable to decipher the grids of seemingly unconnected letters and words, or to comprehend the Arabic, he needed help.[3]

TRANSLATORS AND TRANSLATIONS

To understand the parchment's unusual Arabic, that same month the Archbishop of Granada contacted Miguel de Luna and Alonso del Castillo, two members of the city's Morisco community – Spanish Muslim converts to Christianity. Granada had fallen to the Christian reconquest in 1492; in the decades that followed, the Muslim population had been forced to convert or face exile. Some who refused were executed. The situation had become especially dire since the 1520s, when the Spanish kingdom banned Moriscos from having Arabic names, from speaking or writing the Arabic language, and even from wearing their traditional clothing. Despite such restrictions, many Moriscos remained in Granada, and Arabic continued to be used among translators. Those who converted – and especially members of old families who became Christian before the forced conversions – tried to connect themselves to a distant Spanish heritage, one in which their families had been Christians in Spain all along.[4] It was ironic, then, that a knowledge of Arabic would be key to unlocking the mystery of the Turpiana Tower parchment.

Luna had been born into a well-off Granada Morisco family around 1550. He studied to become a doctor at Granada University, and then built a career as a physician and Arabic translator. Castillo was thirty years older, born around 1520. Better established, he had also trained as a doctor, but had worked as an Arabic translator successively for the city of Granada, for the Inquisition, and then for the Spanish royals.[5] The archbishop instructed the two men to translate the parchment separately and in complete secrecy; any slip of information meant excommunication. Luna went first, working on the parchment in his home with two assistants from 26 to 30 March. Castillo likewise worked at home on the parchment, from 2 to 5

April.[6] Inspired by an Arabic clue at the side of the parchment, each man deciphered the upper grid by first reading only the letters in brown and then those in red. The same approach worked for the brown and red Arabic writing in the grid of rectangles below. They had cracked the code but, as quickly became apparent, this turned out to be the least of the text's complications. When the clergymen later compared the two Arabic translations – whether from the 'coded' section or not – Castillo's differed from Luna's in about 120 parts. Castillo had greater experience, that was certain, but Luna somehow better comprehended the Arabic's more unusual archaic elements. Castillo adapted his reading to fit standard Arabic, making it difficult to follow. Luna read the text as found, straight from the page.[7]

But what did the parchment say? Just as the Latin sentences had promised, the deciphered text revealed an apocalyptic prophecy by Jesus's disciple Saint John – one that had wide implications for the history of Spain, something not lost on the clergymen. Cecilius, the Bishop of Granada, had discovered this prophecy in Athens, Greece, after his blindness had been cured by the cloth held by the Virgin Mary at Jesus's crucifixion. The prophecy was originally penned in Hebrew, then in Greek, and now, Cecilius writes, he had translated it into Spanish and added an Arabic commentary; this made the text's secrets available to all Christians, he says, for each was a language spoken in Spain. The brown and red grid letters, when read in the correct order (and with a great deal of flexibility in the reconstruction), revealed Saint John's prophecy in Spanish. Speaking from the perspective of the first century, John predicts that the sun will dim after six hundred years and a temple will be oppressed. Once fifteen centuries have passed, a dragon will cause Christianity to break into sects. Three enemies will then threaten humanity and be the harbinger of the Antichrist, leading to the final judgement. The Arabic rectangles, when read correctly, presented Cecilius's explanation of this prophecy. Using an Andalusian form of Arabic, and including Spanish words, his commentary primarily speaks of a king arriving from the east, and is followed by an excerpt from the Gospel of Saint John.[8]

Scribes dutifully copied out Luna's and Castillo's decipherments and translations, and these were sent off to the Spanish king and the Vatican. It did not take long for experts to express concern about how genuine the parchment might be. Frankly, they complained, much of what was written did not add up. Its content implied that Spain's first-century population spoke Arabic, and that Patricius protected sacred artefacts from the Moors, even though the parchment claimed to predate the arrival of Muslims in Spain and the spread of Islam. The parchment's anachronistic use of sixteenth-century Spanish was even more confusing, for this language simply did not exist during the Roman era. One expert explained that the parchment's ink was inconsistent with first-century examples, and that its author had written with a quill, unknown in ancient times. Over the following years, further specialists added their voices to the chorus; some looked deeper at the parchment's handwriting and ink, and one compared it to famous fakes.[9] In the end, the academic consensus was clear: the Turpiana Tower parchment was a contemporary invention, a hoax, a deception. The story might have ended there, if not for another series of dramatic discoveries in Granada, seven years later.

THE LEAD BOOKS

In the winter of 1594, an eagle-eyed visitor staring eastwards from the ornate windows of the Alhambra Palace would have been entertained by the daily sight of two men digging on the hillside of nearby Mount Valparaíso. These men had come into possession of a diary, once owned by a prisoner, which gave tantalizing directions to an old gold mine. Somewhere on the hillside, they believed, was a cave filled with treasure. For months they followed the diary's instructions, digging fruitlessly and exploring every dark cavern they came across. This continued until one day in February 1595, when they happened

28. The text inscribed on two of the lead sheets found on the Sacromonte. This includes the first lead sheet (lower text) and the second one (upper text), each accompanied by translations in Latin and Spanish.

upon a boulder blocking the entrance to a cave. They made their way inside, poked around, and dug into the brown-grey earth. There was no gold, but on 21 February they did find a sheet of lead. It was inscribed with what appeared to be Latin characters, but which were similar in style to the Celtiberian script used by Spain's pre-Roman population. When translated by experts, the text described the martyrdom of a man named Mesiton, who had been buried nearby in AD 56. To everyone's surprise, the lead sheet was another relic of early Christianity in Spain. The discovery provoked a wave of religious fervour across Granada, and all eyes turned back to the Turpiana Tower artefacts.[10]

With the lead sheet now the talk of the city, the Archbishop of Granada, Pedro Vaca de Castro y Quiñones, not only took a personal interest in the hillside excavations but took control of them too. On 21

March, a month after the first discovery, his workmen unearthed a second lead sheet. It was inscribed with Latin, and its words added a further chapter to the unwinding story of the hill's bloody past. The text revealed that five martyrs had once been executed in the very cave that the lead sheets had been found. One of them was Hiscio, a follower of Saint James. The sheet also bore Valparaíso hill's ancient name: Sacromonte – the Sacred Mountain. Spurred on, the digging continued. Over time, the archbishop's men exhumed the ashes of the hill's five martyrs and excavated a third lead sheet inscribed with the tale of another martyr. They also found two 'books' made from round lead sheets, each inscribed with a form of Arabic. At the end of April, a fourth lead sheet made reference to Saint John's apocalyptic text from the Turpiana Tower parchment, and described how Cecilius had been executed in the Sacromonte caves. His remains were unearthed alongside it. As Archbishop Castro's men freed each discovery from the

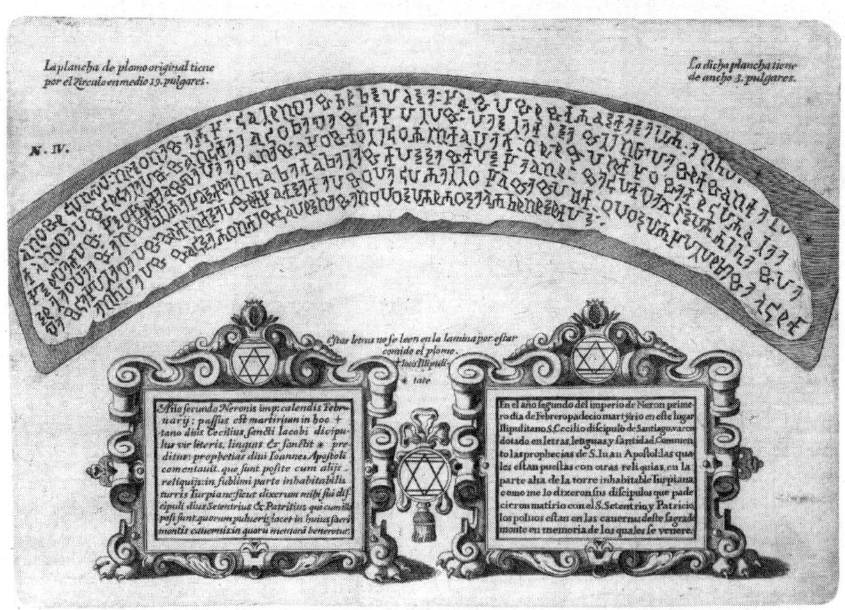

29. The text inscribed on the fourth lead sheet found on the Sacromonte. This sheet mentions the Turpiana Tower.

earth, people from all walks of life gathered at the newly holy site to help the excavation or simply to pray nearby. They erected hundreds of crosses on the hillside and experienced miracles in the caves.[11] Miguel de Luna even said that he had seen lights moving above the Sacromonte Hill, eight months before the discovery of the first lead book.[12]

By 1599, the excavations had unearthed twenty-one lead books, some only four leaves long, others with more than twenty. Each resembled Islamic amulets of the eighth to tenth centuries, was decorated with a six-pointed star called the Seal of Solomon, and bore unusual Arabic writing described as Solomonic – a form found on magical talismans and amulets.[13] The authorities once again approached Luna and Castillo for their expertise, and their resulting translations revealed a curious mix of Christian and Islamic belief. The lead books present a history in which Arabic speakers were the first converts to Christianity in southern Spain, proving that the region's original Christians were Moriscos. There are also references to the apostle James, who was believed to have visited Spain, the Virgin Mary, and the excellence of Arabic as a language.[14] Two lead books hide the meaning of certain words behind an unreadable script, while another is almost entirely written in this impenetrable manner; because this book cannot be translated, it became known as the *Libro Mudo*, or 'Silent Book'. Our only insights into its content are found in other lead books, which say that the *Libro Mudo* is a holy book that the Virgin Mary had been asked to reveal. As its unusual script has more symbols than exist in Arabic, it is possible that the *Libro Mudo*'s author wrote in cipher (that is, if it is not gibberish).[15]

Archbishop Castro proclaimed the human remains, found in the Sacromonte caves and within the box from the Turpiana Tower, as official saintly relics on 30 April 1600. A week later, he gave mass on the hillside spot where his men had unearthed Cecilius's remains, apparently to 40,000 people. It was in his power to make such proclamations, but the parchment and the lead books were a different matter. Critics in Spain already regarded them as fakes, and their authenticity could only be declared by the Vatican, which in 1596 had forbidden people from writing about the lead books.[16] The people of Granada paid little attention to this scepticism, and the archbishop continued to fight for their acceptance, backed by the Spanish royal court, under first King Philip II and then King Philip III. Over the years, experts argued for and against the authenticity of the texts. One supporter even said that the presence of contemporary Spanish in the Turpiana Tower parchment was a sign that God knew when it would be discovered and had ensured that it would be easily understood by those who found it. Other more sceptical specialists pointed out that its inclusion of words and phrases in Latin and Spanish that did not exist in ancient times was obvious evidence for a hoax.[17]

THE VATICAN'S DECISION ON THE SACROMONTE RELICS

The Vatican would not proclaim the authenticity of the Sacromonte finds and Turpiana Tower parchment until their experts had had the chance to properly investigate them in Rome. But the Spanish authorities refused to send the sacred artefacts, leading to years of uncertainty about their status. Meanwhile, Archbishop Castro dismissed Luna's and Castillo's translations of the lead books and tried to track down Arabic specialists who would be happy to produce translations to his liking. Such was his desire to control his precious relics that, when the king reassigned him to Seville, he packed up the lead books and brought them along for the ride, only to later be forced to send them back to Granada. They did not depart again until 1631, years after Castro's death, when King Philip IV decreed that the lead books should be examined in Madrid. This did not happen without a fight: when the canons of the recently founded Sacromonte Abbey withheld the key from the royal officials demanding the relics, an officer had to smash open the lock and take them. Despite such turbulence, the lead books eventually made their way to the Spanish capital and were kept at the Convent of San Jerónimo el Real from 1632.[18]

It was another decade before the Spanish authorities agreed to send the lead books to Vatican City. Even then, the sacred artefacts' time in Madrid only came to an end because Pope Urban VIII put his foot down and brought up the dreaded word 'excommunication' with King Philip IV. When the lead books left Spain, the Turpiana Tower parchment travelled with them. From 1643, within the opulent chambers of the Holy See, a team of specialists scrutinized and translated the controversial parchment and lead books. (Among them was the Jesuit scholar Athanasius Kircher, who would later own the Voynich Manuscript.) A representative from Sacromonte Abbey travelled to Rome as well, to fight on their sacred objects' behalf. Twenty-two years later, the Vatican's esteemed (yet slow-working) experts finally laid down their quills, their research over. But it took a further seventeen years – after delays caused by protests from Granada – for Pope Innocent XI to announce their conclusion. In 1682, a full six popes since the investigation began, he proclaimed that the lead books and Turpiana Tower parchment were forgeries. The Vatican ignored a petition from the Spanish royal family to rethink their conclusion.[19] To the Church, the matter was closed. The parchment and the lead books were nothing but fakes, and would remain somewhere in Vatican storage, to be ignored and forgotten.

A HISTORY OF HOAXES AND FRAUDS

There is a long history of people presenting fakes as genuine manuscripts bearing ciphers, codes, and mysterious scripts. Hoaxers produced these for a variety of reasons, but money, career progression, and fame were the most common. In the case of an enciphered manuscript called 'The Subtelty of Witches', now in the British Library, the readable text on the cover presents it as written in 1657 by a certain Ben Ezra Aseph. However, once the researchers Rian

Hagebeuk and Katherine Mueller cracked its cipher, the manuscript turned out to be filled with verbs copied from a Latin dictionary, probably around 1543. At some point in the manuscript's history, someone added the cover text, probably hoping that the reference to witches and its enciphered content would intrigue potential buyers and help to sell it for a higher price. Why the original author wrote a Latin verb list in cipher remains unknown.[20]

The *Lumen luminum*, a manuscript in Yale University's Beinecke Rare Book and Manuscript Library, written in Italian and Latin, but with certain parts in cipher, presents a similar case. Its cover bears a holy monogram; according to one page, its content – a collection of alchemical recipes – was written by Elias of Cortona, an early follower of Francis of Assisi, in 1315. Given that Elias lived from around 1180 to 1253, and so was long dead by that time, this seems rather unlikely. Indeed, the manuscript actually appears to have been produced in northern Italy, perhaps Venice, around 1525. An enterprising bookseller probably copied the text, including its intriguing use of cipher, invented its association with the famous early Franciscan, and added the holy symbol to its cover in order to deceive a customer, perhaps a Franciscan.[21]

One of the most successful early modern forgers was Giovanni Nanni, also known as Annius of Viterbo, Italy. He was born in 1438 and had a successful career as a Dominican friar. After retiring in around 1490, the fifty-something Nanni returned to Viterbo to lecture on the history of his city. His talks caused quite a stir, because his historical account drew from previously unknown evidence, in particular two old manuscripts and a variety of ancient artefacts, all of which he published in 1498. His book was a massive hit across Europe and led to his appointment as a theologian working directly for the pope, Alexander VI. Nanni became particularly famous for his ability to read Etruscan, the script used by an ancient people who controlled large parts of Italy in the first millennium BC, and he wrote a history of their civilization based on his translations. Of

1. Hildegard of Bingen experiences a vision, from *Scivias*.

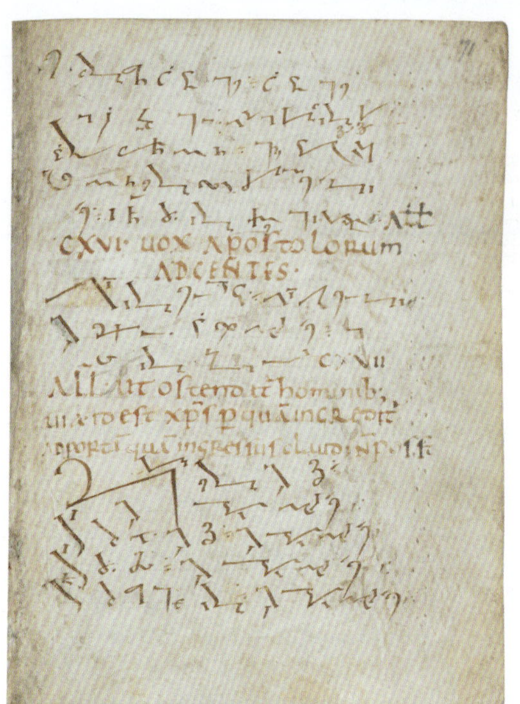

2. Tironian Notes in a ninth-century psalter. This shorthand system was used by medieval scribes to replace Latin words, parts of words, or letters.

3. The cover of Hildegard of Bingen's *Riesencodex*, a manuscript that contains both her *lingua ignota* and *litterae ignotae*, as well as many of her other writings. The manuscript weighs a massive 15 kilograms.

4. A plant with roots entangled with snakes or worms, from the Voynich Manuscript.

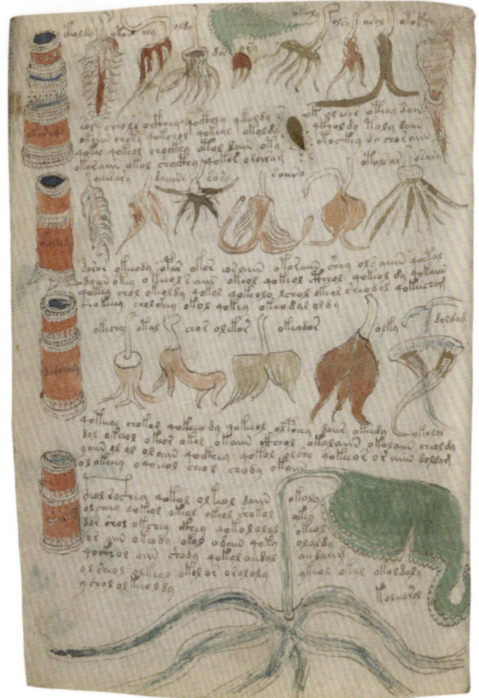

5. Plants and pots, perhaps for making herbal concoctions, from the Voynich Manuscript.

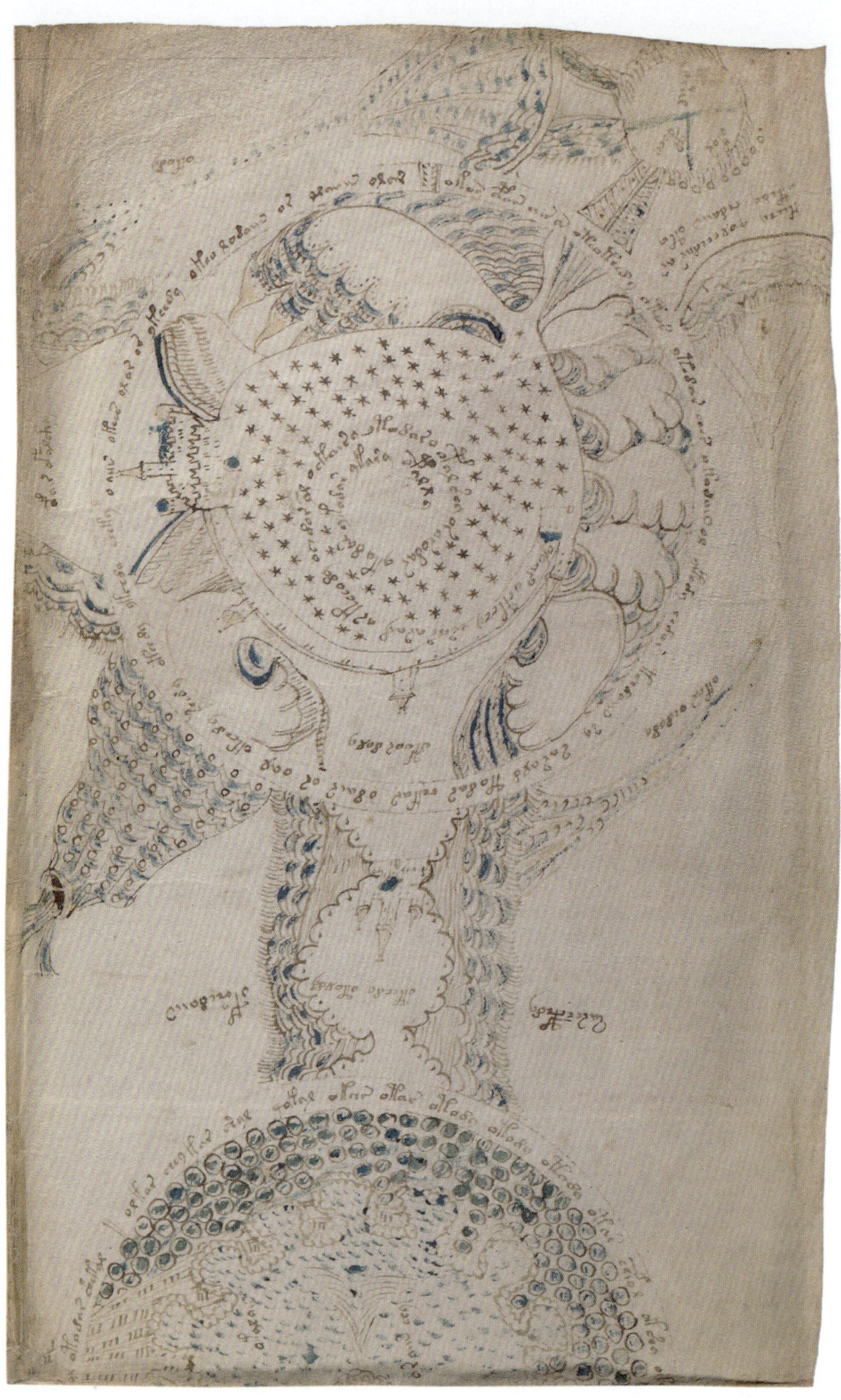

6. A castle with swallowtail merlons (left side of the upper circle), from the Voynich Manuscript. Castles with this architectural feature are often found in northern Italy.

7. A gigantic tower-shaped battering ram on wheels, from Giovanni Fontana's *Bellicorum instrumentorum liber*.

8. A fire-breathing witch, from Giovanni Fontana's *Bellicorum instrumentorum liber*. Fontana enjoyed designing creations that would amaze and scare people.

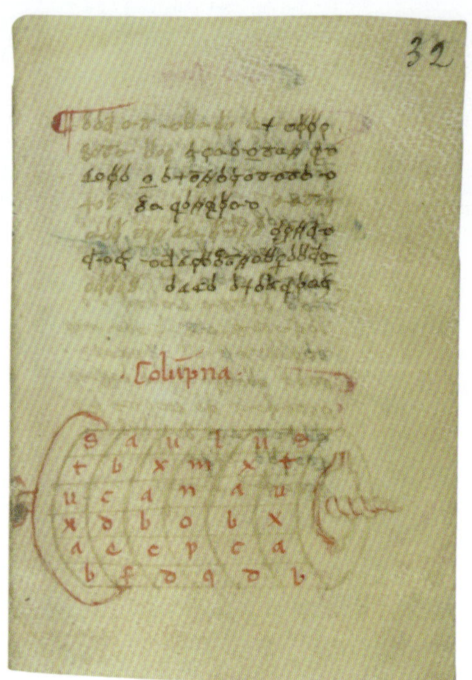

9. A memory device from Giovanni Fontana's *Secretum de thesauro experimentorum ymaginationis hominum*. Above the diagram, there is writing in his unique cipher.

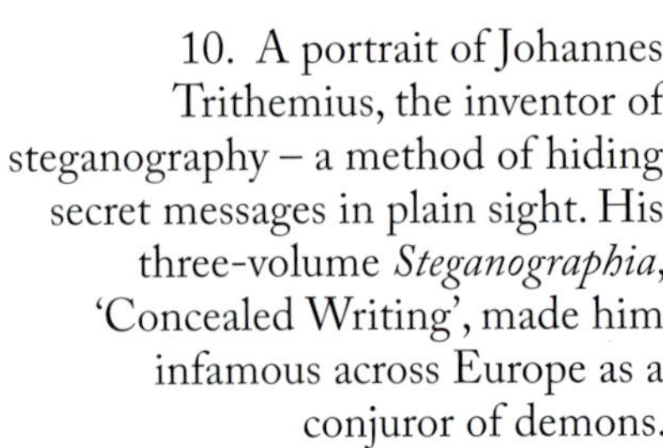

10. A portrait of Johannes Trithemius, the inventor of steganography – a method of hiding secret messages in plain sight. His three-volume *Steganographia*, 'Concealed Writing', made him infamous across Europe as a conjuror of demons.

212 *STEGANOGRAPHIA*

de præteritis quam futuris certitudo. Liceat itaque divinare & dicere, quaternarium librorum numerum fuiſſe duplicatum in octonarium, adeoque ſingulos libros in binos eſſe auctos, ut ita in primo & ſecundo Steganographiæ libro contineatur, quod primus quaternariæ diviſionis inſinuat, in tertio & quarto quod ſecundus, in quinto & ſexto quod tertius, in ſeptimo & octavo, quod quartus exhibet; atque ſecundum hanc diviſionem tertius hic liber deberet continere artem, quâ per ignem poſſum mentis meæ conceptum notum facere artem ſcienti, ſed quodnam hujus opinionis argumentum? non aliud quam cœci de coloribus. Attamen clavis libri hujus tertii non adeò fuit abſcondita & obſcuritatibus involuta, quin poſt inquiſitionem diligentiſſimam à me fuerit reperta, quam tamen, quia ſcio non defuturos, qui qualemcunque hanc meam induſtriam pro more carpant, & clavem horum omnium ante me ſe reperturos fuiſſe jactent, modo publicæ luci exponere non cogito, ſed ne ipſemet ignorare credat, placuit ſaltem ſub alphabeto per transpoſitionem literarum communium efficto in tenebris curioſo & induſtrio lectori oſtendere.

Clavis generalis.

Dzcpiz nmlb caoghzmas kuhppftelfkzh pl ftm ftxagxz nxzu kppoeqiill kqktsso xtcz psgkz bmdct gqmrc czfxzbl mzigxga holdpqh raotloep cxdlkcdg piusuclg atodxd ratlot qhqkq of ltxzprr dmpnzeq chadatfxus mk tlrbtrzdsd frz re kx zhsgtpp qbrx a qkslp afugtbe.

Clavis Saturni prima.

Fgh dmoxsze pcikoaazg kezraks kokcgd dmouce, cfeculq : cdfg fabmreui dzdznfi fsgtl rctkgt ku lrprhmhxi ; heutpp, blckpi xxxhtqha zltqd rmi kbs blpctg sflil opidn llamrfxe fch tst fbikgl iztn.

Clavis Saturni ſecunda.

Sukpgzurzxp xxtcz imip qdb kx ebhghgi afd rmchal cpkdcug clnf.

Clavis

11. Wolfgang Ernst Heidel enciphered his solution to the mystery of *Steganographia*'s third volume and published it in a book entitled *Steganographia vindicata*. This page is from the 1721 reprinted edition. His cipher would not be broken for three hundred years.

12. A portrait of John Dee by an anonymous artist. The famous Elizabethan polymath believed that he had received the language and celestial script of angels, and jotted down his findings in his angel diaries.

13. The cover of John Dee's *Monas hieroglyphica* showing his mystical symbol. This new symbol combined existing ones to create an ultimate symbol of power.

14. The *Ars notoria*, a probably twelfth-century text from northern Italy, is filled with prayers and rituals in a variety of languages. Readers believed that the book enabled them to gain information from celestial sources.

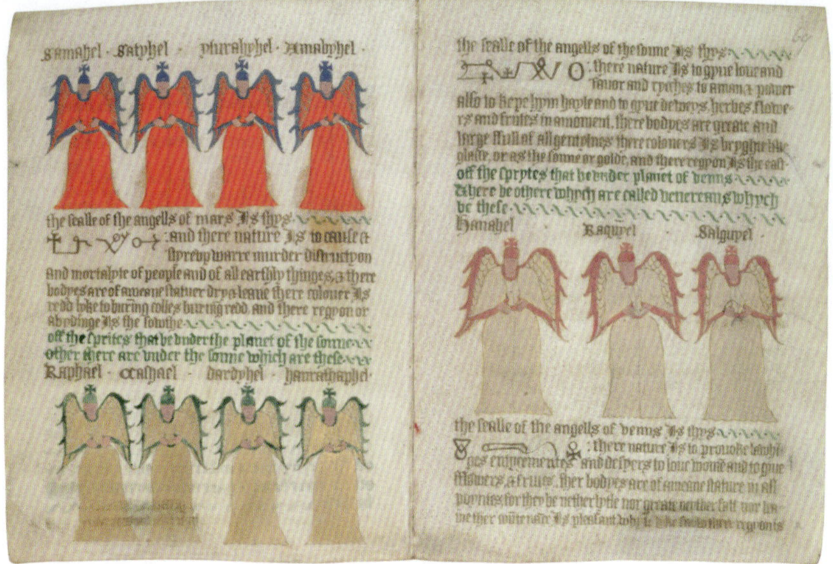

15. The 'Sworn Book of Honorius', a book of angel magic, was believed to give readers direct access to God.

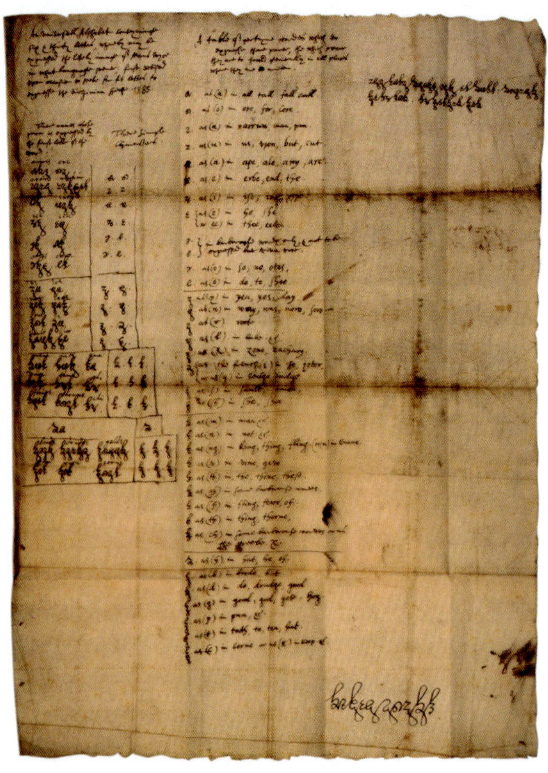

16. Thomas Harriot's 'An Universall Alphabet, conteyninge six-and-thirty letters, whereby may be expressed the lively image of Man's voyce in what language soever; first devised upon occasion to seeke for fit letters to expresse the Virginian speeche, 1585'.

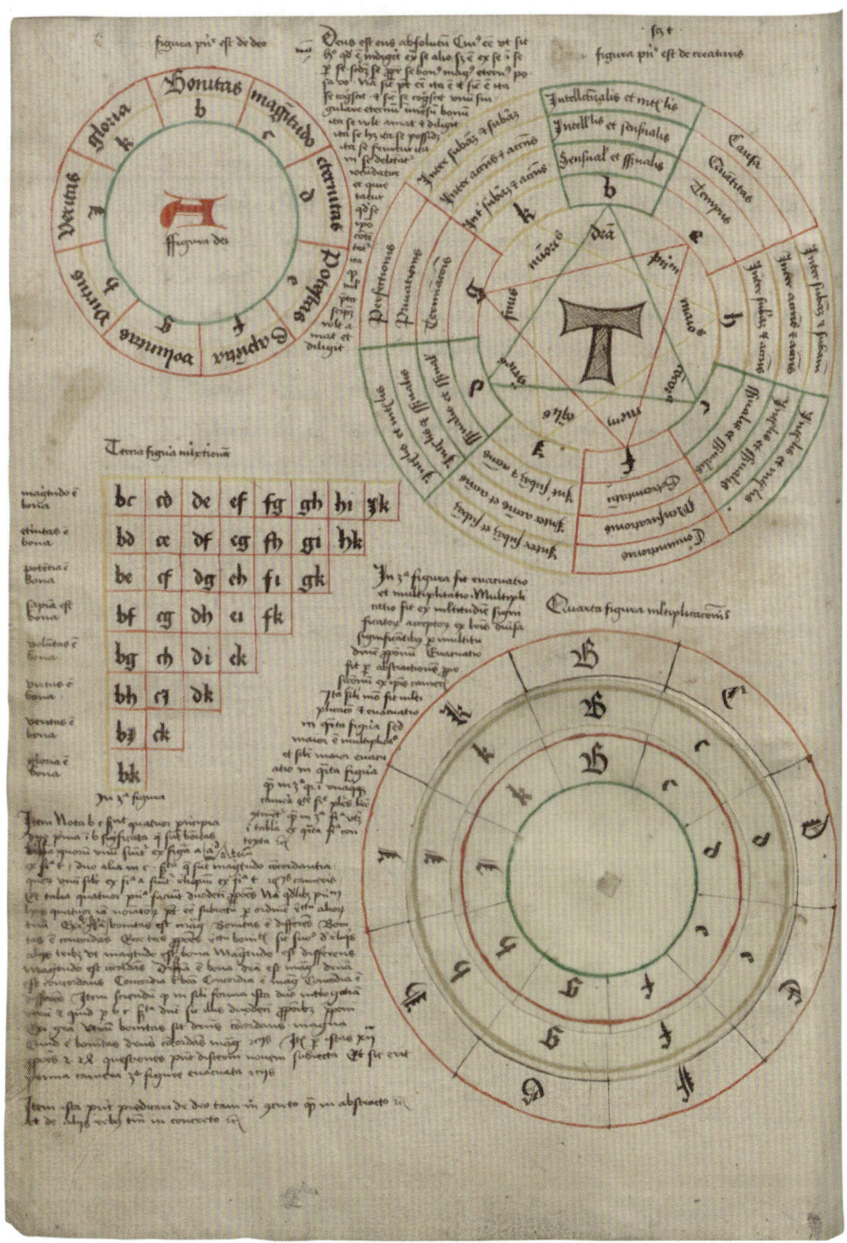

17. Raymond Lull developed diagrams to explain concepts in a way that people could understand irrespective of their language. The lower-right diagram was meant to have rotating sections.

18. A sketch of a snake made by Johannes van Heeck (Heckius) in one of his *Fructus itineris ad septentrionales* notebooks. His *Fructus* notebooks as a whole contain around six hundred illustrations.

EMBLEMA XI. *De secretis Naturæ.* 83

Dealbate Latonam & rumpite libros.

EPIGRAMMA XI.

Latonæ sobolem non novit nemo gemellam,
(Ceu fert fama vetus) quæ Jove nata fuit.
Hanc alii tradunt cum luna lumina solis
Mixta, nigræ cui sint in facie maculæ.
Latonam ergo pares albescere, damnáque dantes
Ambiguos, adsit nec mora, rumpe libros.

G 3 TANTA

19. Emblem 11 from *Atalanta fugiens* by Michael Maier. This has the title 'Dealbate Latonam & rumpite libros', which translates as 'Whiten Latona and tear up the books'.

20. A dragon eats a toad, perhaps representing a stage in the process of creating the philosopher's stone. Produced from the late fifteenth century to the early seventeenth century, the Ripley Scrolls, such as this one, bear alchemical poems and associated imagery.

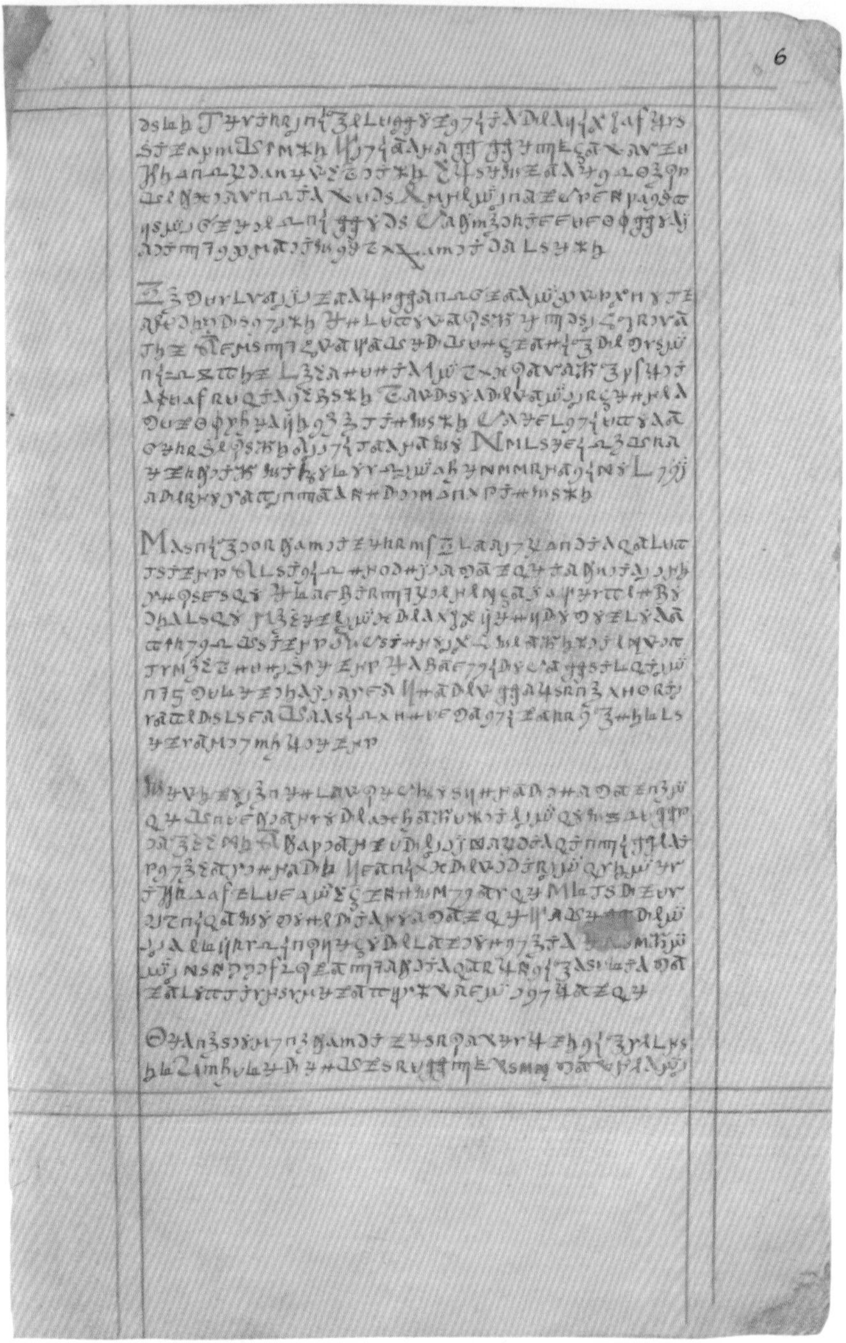

21. This fifteenth-century alchemical manuscript, entitled the *Libro del tesoro*, features enciphered text written in red ink, and was created to look as if it dated to the thirteenth century. It was possibly created by a group of alchemists hoping to sell it to Alonso Carrillo, an Archbishop of Toledo who had an interest in alchemy.

22. A page from an alchemical herbal showing a dragon and a plant. Alchemical herbals were produced in northern Italy in the fifteenth century and were perhaps made for physicians and pharmacists.

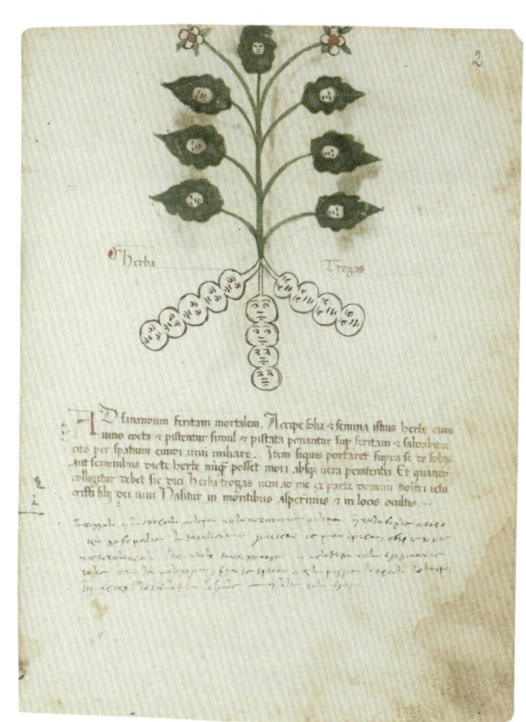

23. A page from an alchemical herbal showing roots and leaves with faces.

24. An astrological scene from a German *Volkskalender*. People consulted these manuscripts as reference works for practical astrological and medical advice, helpful in daily life.

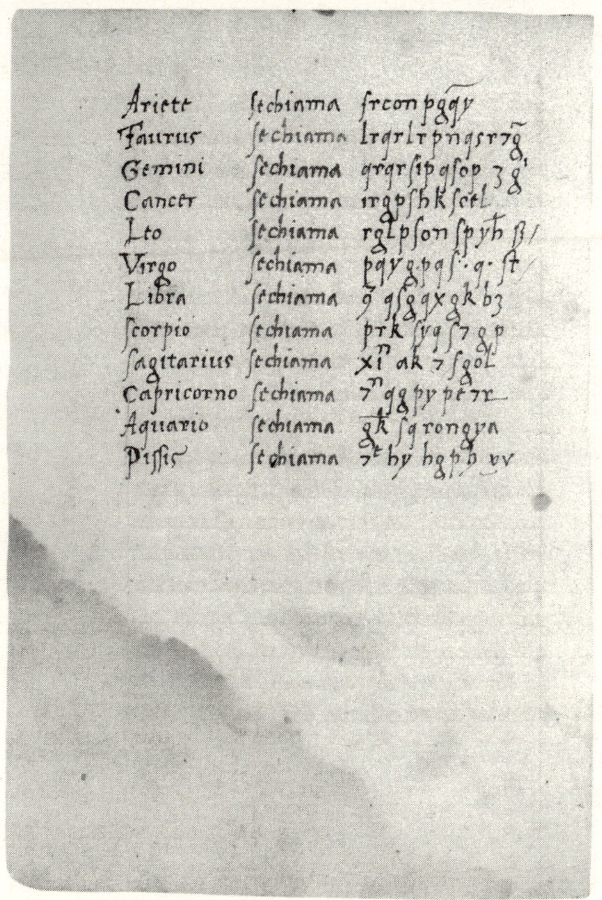

30. Enciphered text in the *Lumen luminum*.

course, all of his claims and discoveries turned out to be fake, but scholars only realized this following his death in 1502, when he was poisoned by the pope's son Cesare Borgia.[22]

Nanni's spiritual successor in faking Etruscan history was Curzio Inghirami. One day in 1634, the nineteen-year-old comedy writer was descending the steps from the Tuscan hilltop town of Volterra, Italy, to the river below. According to Inghirami, along the way he threw a lump of soil, which smashed into pieces to reveal a document hidden in the dirt. It was a prophecy in Latin. This was the first in a series of remarkable finds, including Etruscan texts, each (suspiciously) penned on paper. Critics immediately raised concerns, but the authorities advised them to tread cautiously. Volterra had recently emerged from a dark era of plague and misery, and Inghirami's discoveries had not only shone a light on the region's great heritage but renewed the town's vigour. Inghirami went on to write a history of Volterra in medieval times, citing – unsurprisingly – manuscripts that have never been identified.[23] Other early modern hoaxers faked Roman inscriptions, such as one anonymous sixteenth-century individual, who produced at least seventy-three forgeries, said to have been copied from monuments across Spain. He or she published these fake inscriptions alongside authentic examples, probably to give them a sense of legitimacy.[24]

Another famous forger was Alfonso Ceccarelli, who was born in 1532 in Bevagna, Italy, and trained as a doctor, but made a living inventing family trees for rich families. He connected his clients with important or famous people of the past, and backed up his inventions by writing fake historical manuscripts. He also offered his services as an astrologer, claiming to have developed a special knowledge of the subject by reading Chaldean, Arabic, and Greek sources, all of which he invented.[25] The authorities eventually arrested and tried Ceccarelli for his activities, and beheaded him in 1583 on Rome's Ponte Sant'Angelo.[26] Guglielmo Raimondo Moncada, better known as Flavius Mithridates, was another who created fake sources to make a name for himself. Born in Sicily in the second half of the fifteenth century, he translated existing texts into a mishmash of Hebrew and Aramaic and wrote them out in Ethiopic script, which virtually no one in Europe knew at the time. He passed off these writings as ancient Chaldean (Chaldea, a part of Babylonia), and taught the language to a student, the philosopher Giovanni Pico della Mirandola, who believed that he could use it to immerse himself in Zoroastrian knowledge. Pico was particularly excited because he believed that he could use the language to directly study the original sources, rather than read them filtered with errors through other languages, such as Greek. Mithridates made Pico promise not to share his new knowledge of Chaldean with anybody, helping him to hide his hoax.[27]

Perhaps the most high-profile case of early modern forgery centres on a man who went by the alias George Psalmanazar, who invented his entire life story. His origins are obscure, but he was probably born around 1680 in France. After completing his education under the Jesuits, he decided to travel, and almost immediately began to experiment with a different persona. Wearing a pilgrim's cloak that he had stolen from a church, Psalmanazar pretended to be Irish but spoke in Latin, and explained to everyone he met that he was travelling to Rome. There was one big problem, however: too many people in France had visited Ireland, making his ruse easy to spot. If he truly wanted to develop a successful con, he needed a more unusual identity, one from somewhere much further away and less well known. Somewhere mysterious. He settled on Formosa, the Portuguese

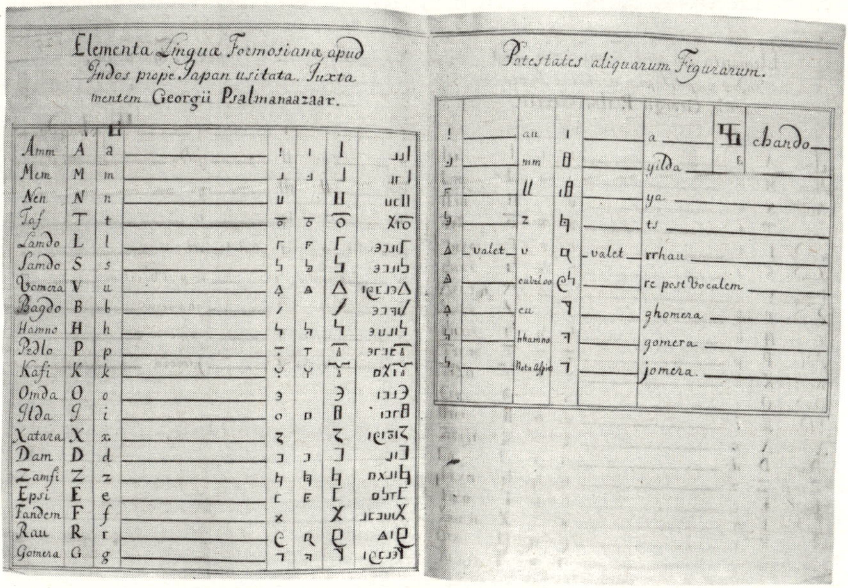

31. Psalmanazar's Formosan language and script.

name for Taiwan, which remained obscure in the West, despite the Dutch and Spanish having established settlements there in earlier decades.[28] To ensure that his act had authenticity, Psalmanazar invented his own Formosan language and script, creating twenty letters and writing it from right to left.

In his new guise, Psalmanazar joined the military in Cologne, Germany, and spoke only Latin with his fellow soldiers, often to make fun of their customs. They would watch him carrying a small book around camp, in which he had drawn astrological symbols, such as the moon and stars, and written out gibberish sentences in his invented script. He read aloud from this book, giving the impression to onlookers that he was reciting its words. News must have spread about the regiment's unusual foreigner because, in 1703, when the regiment was in the Dutch town of Sluis, Psalmanazar came to the attention of Alexander Innes, a chaplain for the Church of England. Innes listened with great interest when an English general spoke to the fake Formosan about religion and heathenism, and he recognized an opportunity for himself: by converting Psalmanazar, he could raise his own profile.[29]

Innes must have had doubts about Psalmanazar's story, because he decided to test him. When he asked his new acquaintance to translate a passage from the works of the Roman writer Cicero into Formosan, Psalmanazar put his pen to paper and did as requested. So far, so good. But when Innes removed the paper from view and asked him to repeat his work, he was stumped. Psalmanazar could not replicate his translation. It appeared the jig was up but, much to Psalmanazar's surprise, Innes's only response was to warn him to be more careful in future and to better develop his fake language. The crafty chaplain did not want to let this great opportunity for career advancement slip through his fingers. Afterwards, the two men travelled to England, where Psalmanazar was baptized and, as reward for his great work for the Church, Innes received a promotion (and was sent to sunny Portugal). Following Innes's advice, Psalmanazar copied out his Formosan alphabet, translated the Lord's Prayer into Formosan (using Latin characters, rather than his own symbols), and drew illustrations of Formosans from different roles in society. In a later published work, he translated additional religious texts and even went as far as adding a guide to his language's grammar. He cleverly included characters with similarities to Greek and Hebrew in his alphabet, playing on the widespread belief that connections existed between all ancient languages – even ones from as far away as Asia. This all added to his credibility. No one questioned his language or writing, even though, from surviving evidence, he never wrote Formosan in his invented alphabet.[30]

Despite Psalmanazar being blond, blue-eyed, and suspiciously good at French, Londoners took him seriously. It helped that Europeans lacked reliable information about the Far East, and that he enhanced his 'foreignness' by assuming unusual habits. He ate raw meat, left a candle burning while he slept to create the impression that he was always awake, and said that the Formosan calendar included only ten months. More dramatically, he told people that, as part of their religion, Formosans annually burned the hearts of 18,000 boys. He wrote such details, and much, much more, in a book about Formosa, which became extremely successful across Europe. Psalmanazar was also skilled at responding to his critics. He was questioned twice by London's Royal Society, first in 1703 and then in 1704, and chief among his detractors was the astronomer Edmond Halley – of comet fame – who went out of his way to reveal Psalmanazar's lies. Halley personally debated with Psalmanazar, and in 1704 brought a map of China and Formosa to the Royal Society that disproved details in the hoaxer's accounts. After an investigation, the Royal Society concluded that everything Psalmanazar had said was untrue, but they never published their results. Psalmanazar kept up his charade for some years afterwards, but eventually admitted the ruse and published a book about his experiences. He wrote that his main rule was never to contradict himself: if he said something, even just once, he ensured that it became part of his act forever. To this day, his true name and origin remain unknown.[31]

WHO FAKED THE LEAD BOOKS AND TURPIANA TOWER PARCHMENT?

If Granada's lead books and the Turpiana Tower parchment are fakes, who made them and why? What was the motivation behind this deception? Whoever produced these 'relics' must have had a good knowledge of Islamic and Christian thought and history, but they still made numerous errors. For the parchment especially, their attempts to make it appear ancient left the Arabic so incomprehensible that only someone who already knew what it was meant to say could read it. The lead books and sheets, meanwhile, employed the ancient Celtiberian script, which gave them a sense of antiquity. Their authors were well versed in magical talismans and amulets, and they knew that lead was commonly used in magical practice. As for setting the hoax in motion, someone must have hidden the lead box containing the Turpiana Tower parchment among the ruins of the old minaret during its demolition. It was probably that same person, or their associates, who discovered human remains on the Sacromonte and decided that it would be a good spot to bury the lead books. By pointing treasure hunters in that direction, they ensured that their 'ancient artefacts' would eventually be discovered. Afterwards, when it became too difficult to hide additional lead books in the caves, they simply buried them in the excavated soil dumped outside.[32]

On the question of 'who', for the past four centuries two names have frequently been raised as the hoax's perpetrators: the documents' earliest translators, Alonso del Castillo and Miguel de Luna, helped by other Morisco families.[33] Although the two men supposedly worked independently on the Turpiana Tower parchment, it is possible that Castillo received a copy of Luna's transcription, perhaps after spending days scratching his head over its incomprehensible text. He may have used this document to make corrections to Luna's reconstructions of the parchment's odd Arabic, and changed its content in the process. If correct, this suggests that Castillo did not understand the text as written, making it unlikely that he was involved in the hoax. Luna, on the other hand, made a clear translation, offered a believable interpretation, and was unfazed by the unusual words, even though the text itself is generally unreadable. Luna also had previous experience as a hoaxer, having written a historical forgery, *Historia verdadera del rey Don Rodrigo*, which he claimed to have copied from an original, true, Arabic text. Only later did he admit that it was a fiction. It is also possible that Luna was part of a wider group or movement dedicated to improving life in Spain for the Morisco community.[34] Another suspect is Francisco López Tamarid, a Morisco and Catholic priest who was involved in the translation work. He, too, might have wanted to help his community, while connecting famous Christian names to Spain and Granada.[35]

The whole hoax, spread across years, was designed to evoke antiquity and mystery – to confuse and intrigue. But if the ultimate goal was to save the Moriscos from expulsion, to emphasize their place in Spanish society, or to spread Islamic thought among the Catholics, it failed. From 1609 to 1611, the Spanish authorities exiled the Moriscos from Spain, with the exception of certain wealthy families. And after Pope Innocent XI declared the lead books and Turpiana Tower parchment to be fakes, only the authorities of Sacromonte Abbey continued to make the case for their authenticity.[36] The rest of the world moved on. When further lead tablets and pieces of marble bearing inscriptions were unearthed from 1754 to 1763 at Granada's Alcazaba – an old fortress and part of the Alhambra Palace – they were swiftly identified as fakes and little more was said about them. Nonetheless, over the centuries, the lead books and Turpiana Tower parchment continued to be venerated in absentia in Granada. They remained abroad until 17 June 2000, when the Vatican returned them to Spain, 359 years after they had left the country.[37]

The Turpiana Tower parchment and lead books – holy artefacts or daring hoaxes, depending on your perspective – remain in Spain today, kept within Granada's Sacromonte Abbey.

Our next destination is the east coast of what will become the United States, where, in England's first colony, a young mathematician is developing a unique script in the hope of improving communications between European settlers and Native Americans.

7

'AN UNIVERSALL ALPHABET' (1585)

Perfect Scripts and Universal Languages

One day in 1894, the classics teacher John Sargeaunt's footsteps echoed along the corridors of Westminster School, London, as he made his way to its library. Standing in the shadow of Westminster Abbey, holy place of royal coronations since William the Conqueror in 1066, and near the Houses of Parliament, the school's own history stretched back hundreds of years, more than enough time to assemble a collection of old manuscripts, documents, and rare books. Sargeaunt had kindly agreed to contribute a chapter to a memoir being written about Dr Richard Busby, the school's headmaster from 1638 until his death in 1695. The volume's author, G.F. Russell Barker, needed him to investigate one of Busby's account books, still stored in the library after two hundred years, and perhaps the only surviving example of what must have been many such manuscripts.

Holding the old account book in his hands, Sargeaunt noted that it was unbound and 168 pages long, and, as expected, was filled with payments, debts, receipts, and references to scholars known to Busby. He flicked through its pages from beginning to end, diligently making notes; but, to his surprise, it was the very first page that most caught his attention. It was a short essay on an unusual phonetic alphabet, filled with mysterious symbols and signs, not written in Busby's hand. Sargeaunt wrote down its title for Barker: 'An Universall Alphabet, conteyninge six-and-thirty letters, whereby may be expressed the lively image of Man's voyce in what language soever; first devised upon occasion to seeke for fit letters to expresse the Virginian speeche, 1585'.

Sargeaunt was already busy enough, and knew that this was not the time to deal with his cryptic discovery. He commented no further, except to write that the page must have escaped the notice of Alexander John Ellis, a famous phonetician who created two phonetic alphabets before his death in 1890. When Sargeaunt closed Busby's account book that day and returned it to the archive, the puzzling page remained inside, once again sealed away.[1]

Sixty years later, the English literature scholar Ethel Seaton, a lecturer at Oxford University, had become intrigued by a curious script she had found written in the papers of the Elizabethan natural philosopher and mathematician Thomas Harriot. Realizing that it had never been investigated and hoping that she could figure out the meaning of the symbols, she travelled to the British Museum in London, where most of Harriot's papers were stored. Seaton scoured the archive and discovered various examples of the unusual alphabet, often little more than a few words scribbled on a page. But two words stood out; they often appeared together and resembled a signature. Using this assumption, Seaton equated the symbols with letters from Harriot's name. This worked perfectly. From there, she also identified the names Walter Warner and N. Torporley – the N standing for Nathaniel – two people close to Harriot, adding extra letters to her growing decipherment.[2]

The next breakthrough came when the Shakespearean scholar Dover Wilson told Seaton that Sion College's library in London held manuscripts belonging to Harriot's friend Torporley. Once again, Seaton investigated, and she found two additional papers bearing the mysterious script, which helped her to decipher the sound values of the remaining symbols. Decrypted, each paper bore alchemical recipes in Torporley's hand. One gave details for producing 'spirit of wine'. The other taught readers how to make pewter. Armed with a better understanding of the script, Seaton returned her attention to the documents she had uncovered earlier. Harriot wrote the script better than Torporley, she notes. The words flow one into the other; some lack vowels and are misspelled; and they look similar whether they are upside down or right side up. On one page, Harriot had used his script to write the opening words of the Book of Genesis. When Seaton published her findings, she suggested that Harriot and Torporley invented the symbols to record their alchemical or scientific experiments.[3]

In the 1970s, the researcher Alec Wallace discovered a map of the Irish estates owned by Sir Walter Raleigh, the explorer and dashing favourite of Queen Elizabeth I. Harriot had drawn this map in 1589 and Wallace noticed that it bore the mathematician's unique alphabet. This led him to the British Library and to discover a paper that lists the consonants and vowels of Harriot's script – another piece in the puzzle. By the 1990s, scholars were aware of Harriot's invented alphabet and could read it, but its purpose remained obscure. However, when the historian Christopher Stray was conducting research in Westminster School's library, he came across Dr Busby's account book. He turned over its cover and his eyes were met with the mysterious symbols last seen by John Sargeaunt a century earlier. Stray passed news of his discovery to Vivian Salmon, a specialist in the history of linguistics, who recognized that this page was the solution to the mystery of Harriot's puzzling script. After studying the handwriting, Salmon concluded that it was indeed Harriot's, and that the page had been created for a goal that only now became clear: Harriot had been attempting to create a script that could accurately reflect the sound of any language and, in particular, that of the Algonquin Native Americans.[4]

After four hundred years, the purpose of Thomas Harriot's 'Universall Alphabet' had been revealed – but how did it come into being?

THOMAS HARRIOT'S EARLY LIFE

Born in 1560, Thomas Harriot studied at Oxford University, and moved to the bustling expanse of London after graduating in 1580. Although young, he quickly made a name for himself across the city for using his mathematical skills to improve sailors' navigation. This was something that Walter Raleigh desperately needed. Raleigh's recent attempt at sending an expedition to the New World had failed miserably: having wasted a few embarrassing days lost at sea, his ship had reversed course and sailed back to England, enraging the explorer. Any further delays could lead to the Spanish catching wind of his plans to found a settlement in North America – a place where his men could repair their ships and launch incessant strikes on Spanish interests in the region. Plus, his royal patent to found a settlement in North America was set to expire in 1591, giving him a firm deadline for success. Without it, Queen Elizabeth I would not allow him to exploit the resources of the New World and make himself even richer. So, in 1583, Raleigh gave the twenty-three-year-old Harriot a job teaching navigation to his men, and assigned him quarters on the top floor of Durham House, a royal manor that the queen let Raleigh use.[5]

Raleigh sent two ships to North America in April 1584 but did not personally accompany the voyage as Queen Elizabeth would not let him leave England. It is probable that Harriot joined the crew though; if he did, his new job for Raleigh was to learn the language of the Native American tribes that the Europeans expected to meet on their travels. This time, perhaps thanks to Harriot's navigational lessons, in July 1584 Raleigh's ships made it safely across the Atlantic and reached the line of sandy islands that lie just off the coast of what would soon be called Virginia, but today is North Carolina. After four days, they established friendly relations with Granganimeo, the brother of Chief Wingina, leader of the region's Algonquin tribe. Wingina himself was unavailable due to a recent battle injury. The English and Algonquin sat together on a mat and, although they could not understand one another's speech, they expressed their intentions for friendship and peace through gestures. After further gift exchanges and explorations of the local area, the crew visited Roanoke Island, Granganimeo's home. With green hills and plains, tall red cedar trees, and deer, rabbits, and fowl, plus excellent fishing,

The arriual of the Englishemen II.
in Virginia.

THe sea coasts of Virginia arre full of Ilãds, wehr by the entrance into the mayne lãd is hard to finde. For although they bee separated with diuers and sundrie large Diuision, which seeme to yeeld conuenient entrance, yet to our great perill we proued that they wear shallowe, and full of dangerous flatts, and could neuer perce opp into the mayne lãd, vntill wee made trialls in many places with or small pinness. At lengthe wee fownd an entrance vppon our mens diligent serche therof Affter that wee had passed opp, and sayled ther in for a short space we discouered a migthye riuer fallnige downe in to the sownde ouer against those Ilands, which neuertheless wee could not saile opp any thinge far by Reason of the shallewnes, the mouth ther of beinge annoyed with sands driuen in with the tyde therfore saylinge further, wee came vnto a Good bigg yland, the Inhabitante therof as soone as they saw vs began to make a great an horrible crye, as people which meuer befoer had seene men apparelled like vs, and camme a way makinge out crys like wild beasts or men out of their wyts. But beenge gentlye called backe, wee offred thẽ of our wares, as glasses, kniues, babies, and other trifles, which wee thougt they deligted in. Soe they stood still, and perceuinge our Good will and courtesie came fawninge vppon vs, and bade us welcome. Then they brougt vs to their village in the iland called, Roanoac, and vnto their Weroans or Prince, which entertained vs with Reasonable curtesie, althoug the wear amased at the first sight of vs. Suche was our arriuall into the parte of the world, which we call Virginia, the stature of bodee of wich people, theyr attire, and maneer of lyuinge, their feasts, and banketts, I will particullerlye declare vnto yow.

32. A map from Thomas Harriot's account of his time in the New World, showing the island of Roanoke.

they realized it would be the perfect location for their settlement. Six weeks after their arrival in the New World, the ships returned to England, now joined by two Algonquin men: Manteo, a commander from Croatan Island, and Wanchese from Roanoke. This may have been when Harriot first began his attempts to understand Algonquian and, in turn, to introduce the Algonquin to English.[6]

Manteo and Wanchese's arrival in England was an important part of Raleigh's long-term plan for his settlement. Unlike his predecessors, who brought people from the Americas as curiosities to display at court, he knew that communication was necessary to properly exploit these new lands. Indeed, Raleigh may have specifically asked his captains to bring Native Americans to England to learn each other's languages. Why the two Algonquin chose to accompany the English is not entirely clear, however.[7] Raleigh did not kidnap people to bring them to Europe, though coercion was certainly a possibility. It is likely that the two men's own leaders sent them as a way to gather information about the unusual foreigners.[8] The English made Manteo and Wanchese dress in European clothing after reaching London, and they lived at Durham House along with Harriot. This is perhaps when Harriot developed his 'Universall Alphabet' to help him better pronounce Algonquian words. As communication became easier, Harriot learned about the Roanoke area and its resources: information that Raleigh exploited to encourage backers to see Virginia as a future commercial centre.[9]

RETURNING TO THE NEW WORLD

When the fleet of five ships left port from Plymouth for North America on 9 April 1585, Manteo and Wanchese had learned enough English to serve as translators for the Europeans. They had spent eight months in England and were now sailing home aboard the flagship, the *Tiger*, accompanied by Harriot and John White, who would illustrate what they saw on the expedition. Six hundred men – settlers and soldiers – lived in close quarters aboard the ships, all under the command of Sir Richard Grenville.[10] The newly knighted Sir Walter Raleigh was again absent. Ten days after setting out, Harriot watched a solar eclipse from the swaying deck of the *Tiger*. It must have impressed and intrigued the young man, but his main role on this voyage was not as an astronomer, mathematician, or navigator – all areas in which he excelled – but as a geographer and linguist. His job was to interact with the original inhabitants of this New World, to improve the English's knowledge of the Algonquin language, and to chart where that language gave way to other languages or morphed into different dialects. He also planned to write an English–Algonquian dictionary.[11]

After spending some time threatening Spanish ports and ships around the Caribbean, the English fleet sailed north, but the *Tiger* drifted too close to the shore and was beached just over 60 kilometres south of Roanoke Island. Salt water flooded inside, ruining the majority of the ship's supplies. While sailors busily repaired the hull, Grenville sent a small boat to the island to tell Wingina that they had arrived in North America. Wanchese joined the voyage but, after reaching Roanoke, ditched the English to stay with Wingina's tribe. He wanted nothing more to do with the foreigners; perhaps, after his experiences in London, he already suspected the damage that they would inflict on his society. Unfazed, Grenville despatched a second boat, this time accompanied by Manteo, who interpreted for the English when they finally met Wingina at the village of Dasemunkepeuc. Despite what Wanchese might have told Wingina about the English, he did not turn them away, and Manteo sailed back to the *Tiger* with the good news.[12]

While the *Tiger* was beached, Harriot, White, and Manteo, along with others, spent their time visiting the nearby villages of Pomeiooc, Aquascogoc, and Secotan, where they attended a festival. Thanks to Manteo acting as their interpreter, the Europeans learned about the local people and their customs, and White drew everything they saw, from the wood and mat-lined houses to a small pet dog. But events took a dark turn when an English soldier noticed that a silver cup had gone missing at Aquascogoc. Not willing to let this perceived theft go unpunished, the English sent a boat of soldiers back to the village, led by the aggressive Admiral Philip Amadas and probably with Manteo, to demand the return of the cup. Nobody came forward, so the soldiers burned the village to the ground and set fire to its corn. The people fled in terror. These terrible events did not affect relations with Wingina. When the *Tiger* finally reached Roanoke Island, Manteo and the English met with Granganimeo, and Wingina offered them land at its northern end where they could build their settlement.[13]

Raleigh's plan was finally coming to fruition. For the first time, an English settlement – or military base, depending on your view – existed in the New World. On 25 August 1585, the *Tiger* vanished over the horizon, sailing east to England. The fleet's other ships followed over the coming weeks, leaving 108 men behind in the Roanoke settlement, all under the command of Governor Ralph Lane.[14] Harriot's house, once constructed, was big enough to give him privacy for his studies and to store his equipment, including the charts he had been making since arriving in the New World.[15] Chief Wingina, meanwhile, lived at Dasemunkepeuc, in a swampy region of the mainland to the north of Roanoke Island. He may have led the community on Croatoan Island too, south of Roanoke.[16]

CREATING A SECRET SCRIPT

Harriot wrote his 'Universall Alphabet' in 1585, the year he set out for Virginia. Although he may have devised the script before his departure, it is equally probable that he wrote the page's content while in the New World, drawing on his earlier experiences speaking with Manteo and Wanchese in London. From these conversations, Harriot must have quickly realized that the Latin alphabet could not record Algonquian with any level of accuracy. The sounds represented by English letters can be quite varied depending on the word – take, for instance, the 'a' in 'fall' compared to the 'a' in 'fan'. In addition, there were sounds in Algonquian that the Latin alphabet could not represent. As far as Harriot was concerned, a new, more accurate system was a necessity.

To address this problem, he created thirty-six characters, based on a mixture of Greek, Roman, algebraic, and invented symbols. The basic versions of these characters formed the twelve vowels of his system, while the differing position of loops attached to these letters signified the consonants. In columns on his page, Harriot used his innovative script to write out English words, along with their vocalization in the Latin alphabet, and, in a column beside them, the first letter of each of these words alone, again in his script. He jotted down his symbols in the page's central column, and beside them provided explanations for the sound values they represented, adding examples of words in English, French, or Greek that have these pronunciations. In some cases, when there were no similar pronunciations, he simply remarked that these were 'barbarouse wordes'. At the top right of the page, he wrote out the start of the Lord's Prayer in his script, and at the bottom right, the name of the poet Matthew Royden, again using his symbols. Taken together, all of this ensured that any reader would understand the sounds represented by his new script; intriguingly, however, he did not write any Algonquian words as examples.[17]

Harriot's interest in alphabet creation might have been inspired to some extent by reading the works of Trithemius and by his interactions with John Dee. He copied parts of Trithemius's *Steganographia* from a manuscript edition, so he was well versed in secret writing and mysterious symbols. It is even possible that he consulted one of the copies made by Dee, a friend since Harriot's Oxford days. Both studied mathematics and they had a mutual interest in navigation and New World exploration, so they had much in common, and may have been introduced to each other by Walter Raleigh. When Dee returned from his seven years living in Europe, Harriot gave him a book as a present; in the 1590s, he twice visited Dee at his house in Mortlake. Harriot also presented an alchemical manuscript to John's son Arthur, on 6 June 1602.[18]

HARRIOT AND THE ALGONQUIN

Thanks to the help of Manteo and Wanchese, Harriot learned enough Algonquian to communicate at a basic level with the people he met in Virginia. Although, as he later wrote, he had 'want of perfect vtterance in their language', he could ask questions about food, fish, trees, and products like alum and resin, and he jotted down the Algonquian words for them, particularly when he could not find an English equivalent. 'Wapeih', he notes, was a type of earth that healed wounds, whereas 'winauk' was a sweet-smelling type of wood. Noticing that one leader wore silver earrings, he asked about the source of the metal. He heard the differences in the language among the tribes he met, and how these differences amplified the further he travelled. Harriot wrote about the daily lives of the people he encountered too, and about their technology and clothing, and he spoke with priests to learn about Algonquian deities, rituals, creation myths, and afterlife beliefs. He even records two stories about men who returned from the dead. One died and met his deceased father, Harriot says, while the other had been close to entering a hellish place called Popogusso, but was saved by the gods.[19]

In turn, Harriot used his knowledge of the Algonquin language to talk with people about European technology and religion. When Harriot taught the Bible in Algonquian, he found that Wingina and others joined him in prayer. People touched the Bible, he says, and they held it close to their chests and kissed it. As conversion to Christianity was one of Raleigh's goals with his new settlement, he must have been pleased to hear about such developments. On two occasions when Wingina fell ill, and traditional remedies failed to help, he asked the English to send people to pray for him. Nevertheless, the Algonquin began to notice that illness spread like wildfire wherever the Europeans travelled. Some thought that the deaths were caused by invisible bullets, fired by the English from great distances. Some believed it was the work of their foreign god. Through all of this, Wingina tried to help his foreign guests, providing food even during times of drought, and putting pressure on his own resources; he wanted to better understand the cause of the deaths and the power that the English held. In reality, it was probably influenza, and it had a devastating mortality rate.[20]

INVENTING SCRIPTS FOR EXISTING LANGUAGES

In ancient times, writing developed to serve specific needs. In Mesopotamia, people created cuneiform for commerce. The first-known ancient Egyptian hieroglyphs were inscribed on labels detailing the origins of goods put in a royal tomb. The earliest Chinese characters record oracular consultations: information that needed to be read and reread over time.[21] But most of the world's population remained illiterate. Literacy was reserved for the elite and those whose work required it: for a scribe, reading and writing was a trade skill, like metal-working or stone carving. All over the planet, in societies with and without scripts, families, experts, and leaders continued to pass on their knowledge, history, and traditions through oral transmission. Writing is taken for granted in our modern world, but in the past, and for some communities today, it was not and is not a necessity. Thomas Harriot created his 'secret script', as Seaton dubbed it, to accurately record Algonquian pronunciation. It was not his attempt to bring writing to the tribe or because they needed or even wanted a script, but rather a tool for his own academic use and linguistic curiosity. Nonetheless, there are many historical cases of people developing scripts to write a language, either for a community or by the community themselves.

Most often in history, the need to read sacred writings is the prime motivation for the spread of scripts. The Arabic alphabet travelled through Islam, while Christian missionaries wanted people to read the Bible. In most cases, people adopted existing scripts – usually Latin, Arabic, or Greek – but sometimes they created new ones or adapted others to better suit their needs. In the fifth century, Bishop

Mesrop Mashtots developed a script for writing Armenian, so that its speakers could read the Bible. The Georgian alphabet was also created in the fifth century, shortly after the country's conversion to Christianity. And, as we saw in Chapter 1, Greek missionaries produced the Slavic script Glagolitic. The same process can be seen all over the planet in more recent centuries.[22]

At other times, members of communities developed their own scripts, often inspired by seeing others using writing and deciding to create a system for themselves. In Liberia, West Africa, in the early nineteenth century, Momolu Duwalu Bukele created a syllabary called Vai after it appeared to him in a dream; in 1948, Soulemayne Kante developed the N'ko alphabet for speakers of the Mandekan languages in Guinea. On the other side of the world, in North America, from 1819 to 1820, a Cherokee named Sequoyah invented the Cherokee syllabary, which was quickly adopted and led to a newspaper being produced in the script.[23]

As we have seen in earlier chapters, people also created and copied many mystical and 'exotic' scripts over time. They used these symbols in magical practice, rather than to write lengthy texts in a specific language. The eleventh-century astrological work *Picatrix*, for instance, includes various magical alphabets, but its author only used them to write out short segments of text. Others copied magical sigils and signs for centuries from *The Key of Solomon*, a thirteenth- or fourteenth-century work; this popular grimoire claimed to be written by King Solomon to give it ancient authority. The invented script of Aethicus Ister was reproduced repeatedly too, but it was rarely employed to write out a true language. Medieval and early modern writers preserved alphabets of this kind for their believed power, not for communication. Similarly, the presence of 'exotic' or unusual alphabets, whether real or invented, lent credibility to early travel accounts, such as the twelfth-century John Mandeville's *Travels*. Such scripts intrigued European readers, who were unaware of the vast majority of the world's various writing systems, even into the late fifteenth century.[24]

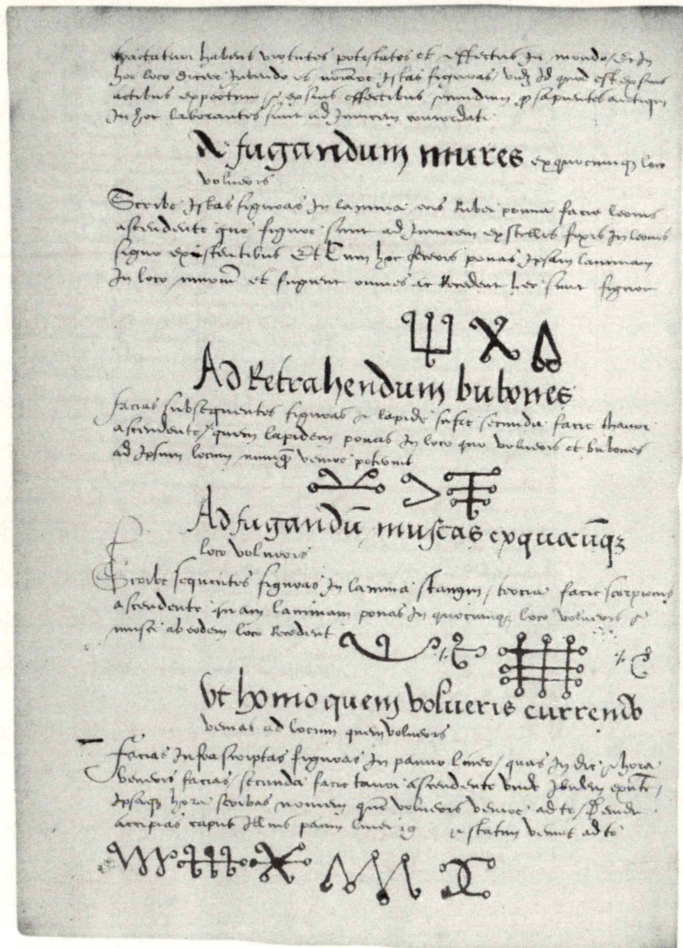

33. Magical symbols, from an early sixteenth-century copy of *Picatrix*.

MASSACRE

As the months of 1586 passed, Chief Wingina became Pemisapan – his change of name reflecting a change in his attitude – and warned Governor Lane of a suspected coalition of tribes planning to attack the Europeans. It is possible that Pemisapan did this expecting the English to be killed in battle, or maybe he wanted to use them to harm an enemy tribe. Whatever the case may be, Lane and his soldiers sailed deep into hostile territory, found the supposed coalition, and took Menatonon, an elderly chief, hostage. Menatonon was surprised by all of this. He had no quarrel with the foreigners. Perhaps Pemisapan is your true enemy, he helpfully suggested – after all, he tipped us off that you were coming.[25]

The situation was getting increasingly unpredictable for Lane and his men. On a subsequent journey, while sailing along a turbulent river far to the west of Roanoke Island, over the sound of the roaring water and splashing oars, Lane heard the Moratuc tribe singing among the trees. 'They are welcoming our expedition,' Lane said. Manteo corrected him: 'This is a war chant – the prelude to a fight.' Suddenly, arrows flew from the darkness between the trees, narrowly missing their targets. The English were lucky to be alive. The increasingly paranoid Lane assumed that Pemisapan had told the Moratucs to attack him. By the time that he and his men returned to Roanoke Island, their collective mood was an explosive cocktail of exhaustion, suspicion, and rage. At their settlement, they learned that Pemisapan's brother, their supporter Granganimeo, had died, and that Pemisapan and his people had deserted Roanoke for their village at Dasemunkepeuc on the mainland. As the English needed food from the Algonquins to survive, this effectively left them to starve. Convinced that Pemisapan was gathering a coalition of tribes to kill the Europeans, Lane decided to act first.[26]

On 31 May 1586, the English shot or beheaded every Algonquin they could find on Roanoke Island. Lane wanted there to be no chance of anyone spreading details of his movements to Pemisapan at Dasemunkepeuc. The next day, he and his men sailed to visit the chief, who was unaware of the blood on his visitors' hands. Pemisapan welcomed the foreigners into his village and, accompanied by his advisors, sat with his guests, wondering what had prompted their unexpected visit. Suddenly, Lane shouted a signal. Gunshots were fired. Algonquins fell dead. Pemisapan was hit and dropped to the ground, but picked himself up and ran. A second bullet struck him from behind. The injured chief fled, hoping to find safety in the nearby woods. He was chased by Edward Nugent, one of Lane's soldiers. Out of sight among the trees, Nugent caught and decapitated Pemisapan.

Thomas Harriot's account is silent on this massacre, beyond a passing mention that the English killed local people and were too fierce – a hint of whom he truly blamed for the blood-soaked carnage. This disaster marked the end of his time in the New World. Soon after, Wanchese became the new leader of the Roanoke Algonquins and Sir Francis Drake's fleet sailed along the coast of Virginia, offering the Europeans a chance to return home.[27]

THE SEARCH FOR A UNIVERSAL CHARACTER AND LANGUAGE

Thomas Harriot was not alone in wanting to create a universal alphabet. In the thirteenth century, as a means to help him convert people to Christianity, the Spanish philosopher Raymond Lull developed a system of combining letters and figures to present concepts to anyone, irrespective of their language, and wrote about his invention in his influential work *Ars magna*. But it was mainly in the mid-seventeenth century that a widespread interest in creating a universal language or alphabet – or both combined – emerged. This was spurred on by the scientific community. Faced with the inevitable loss of Latin as the main way of communicating their research across language barriers, and by the realization that their own languages were not equipped with the words necessary to properly express their discoveries, they wondered if a new script could be devised that everyone could understand. After all, mathematicians could read mathematical formulas, no matter the language they spoke, and musicians from different countries could read the same musical notation. They were also inspired by Chinese characters, which Europeans had recently learned could be read by different cultures across Asia without affecting the meaning. Could a similar system, one employing ideograms, be invented for their own use? In the second half of the seventeenth century, the German polymath Gottfried Wilhelm Leibniz developed a system of symbols that represented concepts, which could be combined to express complex ideas. Others, meanwhile, considered creating a universal language from scratch – a new, better language, suited for the needs of the day, that everyone could understand.[28]

In 1661, the Scottish teacher George Dalgarno published his *Ars signorum vulgo character universalis et lingua philosophica*. Within, he places words into various categories, each designated by its own Latin letter. Every word begins with the letter of its category, followed by extra letters marking subdivisions. 'Bee' is 'snapgnm', which combines the category of flying insect with 'sweet'. 'Eagle' is 'napsuf', meaning a carnivorous bird, but the largest among them. Dalgarno argues that his system can help young people learn science and logic more easily, aid the deaf, and serve as a form of shorthand. On the cover of his book, he boldly claims that, by using his method, readers of different languages will be able to communicate with each other in just two weeks.[29] Similarly, in 1668, the English polymath and clergyman John Wilkins published his *Essay Towards a Real Character, and a Philosophical Language*. His manuscript had been ready for publication two years earlier, in 1666, but much of his draft had burned in the Great Fire of London. Across 270 pages, Wilkins lists and categorizes nature, building new words according to how similar one feature is to another; his words for 'comet' and 'flame' are one character different, for example. If something is similar in nature, then the word should be similar too, he argues. He also presents a script for reading his system – one formed of lines with dashes, triangles, curls, or circles emanating from them – and uses it to write out the Lord's Prayer.[30]

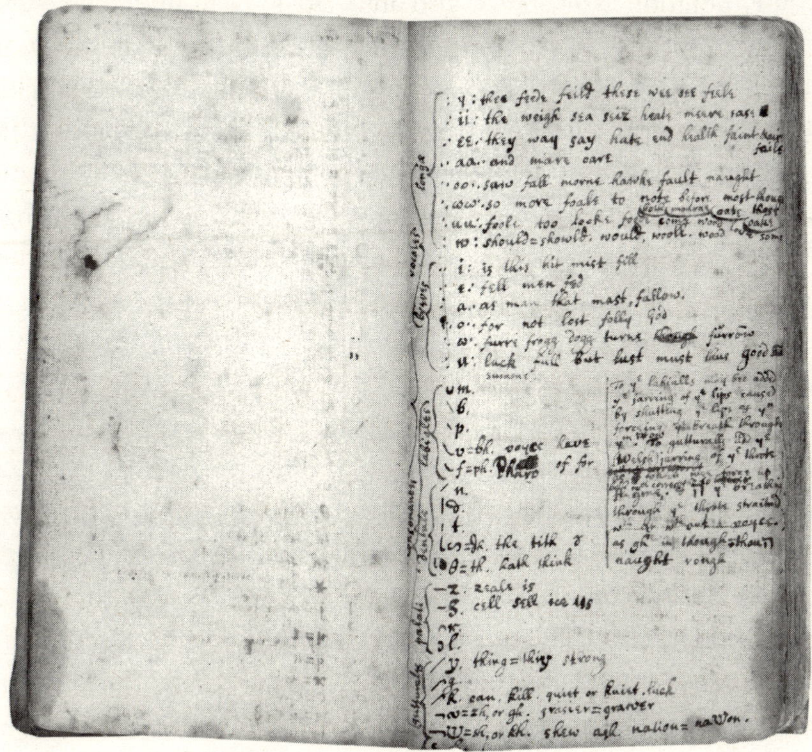

34. Isaac Newton's universal language.

Years before developing the mathematical and scientific theories that made his name, the young Isaac Newton also attempted to create a universal language. Probably inspired by the work of Dalgarno, he divided nature into categories, and assigned the first letter of each word according to this categorization. All 'beasts', for example, begin with the letter 'T'. He developed this scheme in about 1661, either before or just after entering Trinity College at Cambridge University, and appears to have abandoned his plan soon after.[31]

Other scholars, such as the English schoolmaster Cave Beck, proposed systems that use numbers to express words. Beck published his thoughts in his 1657 book *The Universal Character*. In the introduction, he writes that he wants to remove ambiguity from communication; to create a method of sending secret messages; to have a useful means of sharing knowledge; and to help teach the Bible. He compiled a list of 3,996 words, each with its own number. A writer could then add standardized letters to these numbers to express his or her meaning, transforming them into adjectives or adverbs for example, or to convey gender or tense.[32] By replacing English words with their equivalents in another language, but keeping Beck's associated numbers, theoretically, anyone could read the same sentence.

The Jesuit polymath – and one-time owner of the Voynich Manuscript – Athanasius Kircher also wrote a book on this subject: *Polygraphia*, published in 1663. Apparently, the Holy Roman Emperor Ferdinand III wondered whether Trithemius's cryptographic ideas could be used to communicate internationally, but doubted that it was possible; so he did what anyone with a language-centric question did in the seventeenth century and asked the famous Jesuit to solve the problem. Kircher's solution was similar to Beck's system. At its most basic level, he simply associates words in multiple European languages with numbers, enabling people who speak different languages to read the same message.[33]

HARRIOT'S LATER YEARS

In June 1586, when Sir Francis Drake's fleet arrived off the coast of Virginia, the plan was simply to provide the Roanoke settlers with supplies. But within a few days, a hurricane swept in and battered the coast. Under pressure, Lane took the decision to abandon the settlement and for the colonists and Manteo to return to England with Drake. Pelted with hailstones and rain, beneath thunder and lightning, thrown around by the wind, the men packed whatever they could find and loaded their chests on to pinnaces – small boats that ferried people and goods between ships at sea and the land. But the

35. Thomas Harriot's script, from a map of the area surrounding Molana Abbey, Ireland.

water was rough. To steady the pinnaces, Drake's sailors threw many of the passengers' belongings overboard, including Harriot's notes, sketches by John White, and various items collected during the year. If Harriot took the page bearing his 'Universall Alphabet' to the New World, or had written it there, it was important enough that he managed to keep it safe during this great loss.[34]

After July 1586, Harriot moved to Ireland to continue working for Raleigh, where he helped to produce a map of the area surrounding Molana Abbey and, for unclear reasons, wrote his name and source at its bottom-right margin in his secret script. A year later, however, he returned to England to enter the service of Henry Percy, the Earl of Northumberland. He later lived at Syon House – one of the earl's properties – in Isleworth.[35] Over the years, Harriot completed a short account of his time in North America, and may have completed his Algonquian–English dictionary. Meanwhile, in 1587, the Roanoke expedition's illustrator, John White, returned to the island to found a new settlement, one that vanished and became known as 'the lost colony'. Manteo accompanied this expedition, travelling to his homeland after helping Harriot and Raleigh in Ireland. Before vanishing, the colonists carved the letters 'CRO' into a tree, and the word 'Croatoan' at their settlement, indicating that they had moved to Croatoan Island – Manteo's birthplace. Manteo's fate, like that of the other colonists, is unknown, though they perhaps integrated with a local tribe.[36]

Although Harriot's life moved on from the New World – his career now focused more on mathematics, optics, and astronomy – the New World did not leave him. In 1602, he scribbled notes on a piece of paper, listing the types of equipment that an expedition to North America might need to bring along. Below, in Latin characters, he wrote in Algonquian, 'Kecow hit tamen', which he translated as 'what is this'.[37] Elsewhere, he wrote the opening line of Genesis in his script, and, in 1609, the royal court asked for his advice about what gifts might be suitable for a visiting chief's son, and about a planned voyage to North America.[38] Harriot and White also began to write a book dedicated to the ethnology and natural history of North America, but their unfinished manuscript is now lost.[39]

In July 1603, Walter Raleigh was arrested on suspicion of plotting to remove King James I from the throne. Suspicion fell on Harriot too, and both men were accused of atheism. Harriot remained free, but Raleigh received a death sentence, fortunately commuted, but he still ended up imprisoned in the Tower of London. Then, in 1605, the Earl of Northumberland's cousin was involved in the Gunpowder Plot, a grand plan to blow up England's Parliament. Although innocent of any involvement, the earl was sent to the Tower, and those working for him were arrested. Harriot spent a few weeks in the Gatehouse Prison, which stood in front of the entrance to Westminster Abbey, but continued working at Syon House afterwards.[40] With his patrons past and present locked away in the Tower of London, he repeatedly visited them over the years that followed.

Raleigh was released from the Tower in 1616, after thirteen years of incarceration, and almost immediately set out on an expedition to South America. This was a major disaster: he was meant to be searching for El Dorado, with royal orders to avoid any conflict with the Spanish or their territories, but ended up looting a Spanish town. His son was shot and died during the battle. Having acted against the king's wishes, the moment Raleigh set foot on English soil, he was arrested and his death sentence reinstated.

On the morning of 29 October 1618, Harriot made his way to London's Old Palace Yard, beside the Palace of Westminster and Westminster Abbey, to attend his old patron's execution. Raleigh ascended the scaffold and captured the crowd's attention. He spoke on his innocence for around thirty to forty-five minutes, and urged everyone to gather closely; he was sick, he said, and his voice weaker than usual. Somewhere in the crowd, Harriot stood within earshot, holding a thin scrap of paper on which he jotted down Raleigh's final words. He crossed out and corrected as he did so, and numbered each major point. Beneath the twelfth point, Harriot drew a line, then decided to add an extra sentence. Raleigh asked the crowd to pray with him, Harriot wrote. He then scribbled an '&c' – et cetera. Nothing follows.

From other accounts, Raleigh inspected the executioner's blade immediately before his death. He turned down the offer of a blindfold and to warm himself, then arranged himself on the block – twice, because a spectator urged him to switch facing west for east, the direction of resurrection. Raleigh then signalled to his executioner. It took two blows to sever his head.[41] Harriot must have watched as the axe came down.

THE FATE OF HARRIOT'S PAPERS

Harriot himself was dead within a few years of Raleigh. During his time in North America, he had picked up a fondness for smoking tobacco, and back in England may have been the one who convinced Raleigh to promote the addictive plant at Queen Elizabeth's court.[42] Over the years, he developed a cancerous growth on his nose, no doubt as a result of his smoking, and passed away on 2 July 1621 in the house of a friend, Thomas Buckner, in the parish of Saint Christopher-le-Stocks, London.[43]

Harriot left the executors of his will with rather a mess. His writings, covering around seven thousand manuscript pages, were a disorganized jumble of ideas. He left these to the Earl of Northumberland at Petworth House in Sussex, but with the understanding that his mathematical papers could be used by his friend

Nathaniel Torporley. He wanted Torporley to go through his notes and publish anything of worth. Torporley made a start, working from Sion College, London, but little came from his efforts because of his own death in 1632. Afterwards, Torporley's archive, now mixed with some of Harriot's papers, remained at Sion College. Among the College's collection was a work called 'Virginia: A Vocabulary with Severall Phrases of Speech in Virginia'. Harriot was most likely its author; it may even have been his planned Algonquian–English dictionary, but, sadly, this manuscript perished in the Great Fire of London in 1666. Scholars came across the rest of Harriot's papers at Petworth House in 1784, bringing his work to light once again. Most of these were given to the British Museum and, in turn, to the British Library, but a few remained at Petworth House.[44]

The paper bearing the final version of Harriot's 'Universall Alphabet' appears to have followed a different route to the present day than the rest of his jumbled manuscript pages. It was once owned by the mathematician John Pell, who lived from 1611 to 1685. On 31 March 1680, the elderly Pell told John Aubrey, who was busy writing short biographies of notable people, that among his papers was, as Aubrey records, 'an alphabet that he [Harriot] had contrived for the American language, like Devills'.[45] It is unclear how this paper ended up in Pell's possession, for he would have been only ten years old when Harriot died, but, as Harriot's work influenced Pell, he may have found an opportunity to investigate Harriot's papers – after all, Pell was one of a group of scholars who unsuccessfully tried to locate works by Harriot once kept by Thomas Aylesbury, an executor of his will.

There is another possibility, however. The mathematician and natural philosopher Walter Warner (along with Aylesbury) was behind Harriot's single posthumous publication, *Artis analyticae praxis*, in 1631. To edit this work, he must have explored the Harriot archive kept by the Earl of Northumberland. As Warner and Pell were both mathematicians living in Westminster, and knew each other, this could be the connection that brought the paper to Pell. Whatever the case may be, by 1684 the 'Universall Alphabet' had passed to Dr Busby, who enjoyed studying languages, and from there into one of his Westminster School account books.[46]

Today, 'An Universall Alphabet' remains in Westminster School, London, under the reference code GB 2014 WS-05-HAR-01.

In our next chapter, we return to Italy, where the inquisitive Doctor Heckius is exploring the secrets of nature and enciphering his thoughts in a series of travel notebooks – but his experiences in exile, his angry temperament, and the weight of his work take a heavy toll on his mental health.

8

FRUCTUS ITINERIS AD SEPTENTRIONALES (1603–5)

Hiding the Secrets of Science and Medicine

In the autumn of 1605, the twenty-six-year-old Doctor Johannes van Heeck, better known as Heckius, had left Prague, in Czechia, for Italy, ending nearly two years of forced absence from his adopted country – an exile in all but name. As the leaves fell, while riding on horseback with a group of companions in the Alps, he spotted an intriguing beetle on the ground below. His friends knew what to expect from the eccentric doctor and chuckled to themselves. Heckius pulled his reins and brought his horse to a halt, holding up the whole group. He leapt to the ground and chased the beetle, trying to get a closer look. Once it was caught, he jotted down his thoughts on its appearance and characteristics, and sketched it in his notebook.

It was the same each time he saw an insect or animal, from butterflies to snakes, but also for plants and herbs.[1] Heckius had a tireless dedication to study, from the earth, plants, and fungi, to the skies above and the movement of the heavenly bodies. He wanted to better understand nature, to cast aside the received wisdom of the past and observe the world anew, making meticulous observations of everything around. As a founding member of one of the world's first scientific societies, the Accademia dei Lincei (Academy of the Lynxes or Lincean Academy), it was his duty and passion. Some might call it an obsession.

But such devotion often comes at a price. Heckius was quick to anger, frequently out of money, and slowly descended into a state of confusion. To keep his research away from prying eyes, he wrote down his observations in a series of notebooks in a cipher devised by himself and his fellow Linceans. Whenever he filled a notebook, he posted it to the society's leader, a young noble called Federico Cesi. This use of cipher generated suspicion about their activities, and in particular from Cesi's father, who wanted his son to focus on his noble duties rather than scientific discovery. Such problems and machinations led to Heckius being exiled from Italy, an event from which he never truly recovered. Many years after his death, when French revolutionaries were looting collections of art and manuscripts across Rome, Heckius's enciphered notebooks became separated. Some made their way to Montpellier, another to Florence. One cryptic notebook, later identified in the Vatican Library, lost its association with its author and remained anonymous and unread for two centuries. It was only in 1822, when the Lincean cipher was cracked, that extra details about this most unusual scholar's life became known, and only through reading Heckius's notebooks in the centuries since that his wide research interests have become clear. These notebooks had the overarching title *Fructus itineris ad septentrionales* – 'Fruits of My Journey to the Countries of the North'.

DOCTOR HECKIUS GOES TO PRISON

Heckius was born into a Catholic family in Deventer, Netherlands, in February 1579, and moved to Italy at the age of fourteen, crossing Europe with a group of Flemish merchants to escape the danger of persecution by Protestants. He trained as a doctor at the University of Perugia, Italy, starting in 1596, and wrote profusely on medicine, as expected, but also on astrology and alchemy, subjects that had recently been condemned by the Catholic Church.[2] At the same time, he filled notebooks with drawings of legendary creatures and quotations from classical authors about them.[3] From the beginning, then, Heckius trod a different path from his contemporaries – his interests went far beyond those permitted by his university, where the chair of astrology had been removed. As the years passed, his approach to medicine fused the novel ideas of Paracelsus, Marsilio Ficino, and Jean Fernel, and his fascination with alchemy grew.[4] His dedication to learning was emphatic, obsessive, devout. To Heckius, such mental rigour demanded an equal level of physical perfection, so he developed a special diet and fitness regime to enable both him and fellow academics to best achieve their goals.[5]

In August 1601, the twenty-two-year-old Heckius gained his doctorate in medicine.[6] He stayed in Italy, basing himself in Maenza, where he specialized in healing the sick with local herbs. He collected recipes for 'simples' – herbal remedies – and made notes on the illnesses he encountered, from skin problems to the plague, from a boy with intestinal worms to a patient with dysentery. If one of his remedies worked, he jotted that down too.[7] Thanks to his success as a healer, his fame swiftly spread, bolstered by the many books he wrote.[8] In 1602, he started practising medicine in Scandriglia at the request of Duke Giovanni Antonio Orsini. This was a fabulous opportunity but it created a feud with the local apothecary, Raniero Casolino, who prepared the remedies that Heckius prescribed for his patients. According to Heckius, Raniero omitted some of the substances needed for his remedies to succeed, and added low-quality ingredients. In turn, Raniero hated Heckius because the doctor's methods meant that he lost income. Heckius was strongly against using exotic herbs – an excellent source of money for apothecaries – and insisted on developing remedies from cheaply available local ingredients. Their disagreement turned violent when one of Heckius's prescriptions failed to cure a sick man. Heckius suspected that the useless apothecary had not properly prepared his remedy, and the two men had to be held back from exchanging blows.[9]

On 1 June 1603, Heckius was in the green hills of Scandriglia visiting the sick. Having tended to the ill, he mounted his horse to continue on his journey to the monastery of San Salvatore. The horse had hardly trotted a few steps when Heckius felt a sudden sharp pain at the back of his head. Shocked and stunned, he did not know what was happening. Further blows struck his back. Someone was throwing rocks. Heckius turned his horse to find two men: one of them was Raniero Casolino. Blood dribbled down the side of Heckius's head as Raniero threw more stones and shouted, but the disorientated Heckius could not understand what he was saying. He felt weak, but needed to act. Heckius reached for his scimitar, which hung from the side of his horse, and was dismounting when his foot slipped from the stirrup. He steadied himself and got down. Raniero ran to gather more stones and Heckius chased him. One of Raniero's stones hit Heckius's right arm with such force that he dropped his scimitar and felt his hand go numb. The injured doctor raised the scimitar with his left hand and struck Raniero on the head. Raniero bent over, then fell to the ground. Heckius stood on his adversary's stomach with one foot. The fallen apothecary screamed for help, grabbing and grasping at Heckius's foot. The fight was over. Covered in blood, Heckius turned himself in to the local vicar. The authorities interrogated him on what had happened, then tended to his wounds, doing likewise for Raniero and his friend. Witnesses were interviewed, and Heckius was imprisoned at the Castle of Nerola, five kilometres to the west of Scandriglia, before being taken to the Corte Savella, a prison in Rome.

Fifteen days later, Raniero died from his wounds.[10]

THE SECRETS OF THE LINCEAN ACADEMY

This would have been the end for Heckius, if not for the intervention of an influential young fan, Federico Cesi, the son of the Duke of Acquasparta. Obsessed with science, the eighteen-year-old Cesi secured Heckius's release by vouching for his learning, piety, and good character on 26 June 1603. He then invited the doctor to stay at his family home in Rome, Palazzo Cesi on Via Maschera d'Oro, as his resident scholar.[11] Six weeks later, on 17 August 1603, Cesi,

Heckius, and two of Cesi's friends, Anastasio de Filiis and Francesco Stelluti, signed an agreement to found a new academy dedicated to the study of science and nature. Because they needed sharp eyesight for their observations, they named it in honour of the lynx – Accademia dei Lincei – and to mark this new beginning each took a secret name and a focus of study. Heckius was to research astronomy, philosophy, natural history, and cures for illnesses, and he took the name 'Illuminatus'. They immediately got to work, devising a schedule of research and teaching. They gave names to every new species they discovered, designed their own equipment, and learned Arabic to give them access to medieval Arab writings. Outside Rome, they conducted some of their investigations in Acquasparta, southern Umbria, where they wandered the hills and fields and took a particular interest in fossils.[12]

The academy held their meetings in private, and the members communicated with each other through a cipher of their own creation, guided by examples they had studied in the 1602 edition of *De furtivis literarum notis, vulgo de ziferis libri* by Giambattista Della Porta (who would join the Lincean Academy in 1610 at the age of seventy-five). Their cipher was relatively simple. They switched consonants for planetary and zodiacal symbols: the symbol for Mars stood for 'm', Mercury was 'r', and Libra was 's'. Symbols for the planets' aspects – representing the angles between the planets, used when making horoscopes – replaced vowels. A triangle stood for 'u' and 'v', while a square was 'o'. To put additional obstacles in the way of codebreakers, they wrote their cipher from right to left, and sometimes from the bottom of the page to the top. Symbols with two or three dots were not to be read, whereas a symbol with a single dot meant that the letter was doubled. To make his writing even more obscure, Heckius wrote Latin in Arabic script. This cipher created an extra level of bond between the academy's brothers; they could keep their discoveries to themselves while collecting information and building networks of like-minded thinkers across Europe.[13]

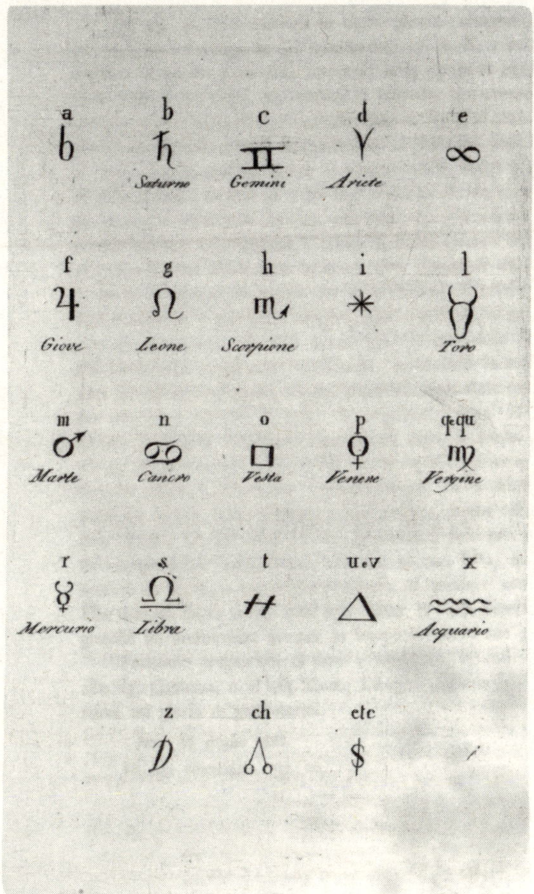

36. The Lincean cipher, from Morosini's *Lettere del conte Domenico Morosini, nobile veneziano, al signor abate Francesco Cancellieri di Roma, e di questo a quello intorno ad alcune cifre spettanti all'Accademia de' Lincei, e per la seconda volta pubblicate*, 1865.

Not only did members of the Lincean Academy use ciphers and special names, but each also received an emerald ring engraved with a lynx, and each had their own secret symbol and motto. They had the right to add the word Lincei after their names when writing as members too. There was also an initiation ceremony, in which attendees wore silk cloaks with fur borders. During the initiation of

Heckius and the first members, Cesi sat on a chair and asked each if they would follow the academy's rules. Heckius held his right hand to his chest and swore that he would. Cesi gave him a golden necklace hung with a lynx pendant, and did likewise for the other founding members, and they sang a hymn together. According to the rules, each Lincean had to make a vow of chastity, dedicating himself solely to learning. Heckius chose their patron saint, John the Evangelist, protector of virgins; each day, they had to say a prayer to him. It would not be going too far to see this early scientific academy as a secret society dedicated to learning, organized like a religious order. Certainly, Heckius had an intense approach to study and, like a monk of science, he lived with rules dictating what he could eat and how he behaved. Yet, one of the Linceans' founding principles was to publish their findings, making public their discoveries.[14]

This high level of secrecy generated suspicion. Cesi's family worried about the impact that their son's close friends were having on him; he was a noble, after all, and had duties to fulfil, particularly in the future. Would Heckius take Cesi away to the Netherlands? Was the Dutch doctor a bad influence, or perhaps even an undercover Protestant? Why were these young men communicating in cipher? With such thoughts swirling in his mind, Cesi's father made plans to rid himself of the disruptive doctor. His chance came in April 1604. Heckius's father had died, so the doctor set off for the Netherlands to receive his inheritance, leaving most of his possessions with Cesi, because he expected to return soon after. On the first leg of Heckius's journey, soldiers loyal to Cesi's father accompanied him to Turin. The doctor might have regarded this as a friendly gesture, but in reality it was meant to ensure that he left. Once he was absent from the family's lives, Heckius's influence over Cesi was expected to vanish too, for Cesi's father got to work ensuring that his unwelcome guest would never set foot on Italian soil again: without delay, he slandered Heckius's name, making accusations against him to the governor of Rome and to the Holy Office.[15] This would not be a return journey.

SCIENTIFIC ACADEMIES AND SECRET SOCIETIES

Academies dedicated to a variety of subjects in the arts and sciences sprang up across Italy in the seventeenth century – indeed, from 1525 to 1700, 496 have been counted across the country. Many had unusual names, such as Oziosi ('idle'), Gelati ('frozen'), or Timidi ('shy'), and could be dedicated to wider knowledge or a specific goal, such as the Florentine academy's attempt to popularize Tuscan. Often, they met in members' houses. As with Cesi and the Linceans, other academies were founded by young men. The three brothers who founded the Gelati in Bologna were all younger than twenty-four, while Scipione Gonzaga, who founded the Accademia degli Eterei in Padua was twenty-one. One academy, based in Siena, was created and run by women.[16]

A short-lived predecessor to the Lincean Academy was established in Naples by Giambattista Della Porta in the early 1560s. This was the Academia Secretorum Naturae, also called the Accademia dei Segreti. Its members dedicated themselves to exploring the secrets of nature and, like the Linceans, communicated in cipher. In 1558, Della Porta had published his *Magia naturalis* ('Natural Magic'), which covers many fascinating topics, from illusions to growing plants and alchemical recipes. In one section, he discusses a salve that sends sleeping witches to a sabbat (even if he explains this as a natural result of certain ingredients causing powerful dreams). He also notes that a particular magnetic stone can ascertain whether a woman is faithful. With the stone under her pillow, she will fall out of bed if she has been unfaithful, but if all is well, she will hug her husband. In 1574, suspecting necromancy, the Inquisition arrested Della Porta, closed his academy, and dragged him off to Rome. Though his inquisitors could not prove that he practised demonic magic, Della Porta could not show that he was innocent either. This meant that, if he were to be rearrested for heresy, he could be executed.[17]

Unfortunately for Della Porta, he had been caught up in a new movement of Church censorship that had begun in 1543, spearheaded by the Inquisition. Inquisitors had a particular interest in defining what was demon magic, what was natural magic, and what was acceptable reading for Catholics. Nearly twenty years after his trial, in 1592, Della Porta still had to obtain the Church's approval before publishing anything, and his *Magia naturalis* remained on a prohibited list. This did not stop him from bringing out a second edition, however. Surprisingly, this was not banned, because Della Porta removed the sections that troubled the Church.[18] He also wrote the first European book on cryptography and invisible writing, published in 1558, as well as many other works on scientific subjects, from mathematics to agriculture, and he even found time to write seventeen plays. Wearing his black hat and black cape, he fulfilled the stereotype of a magician – perfect for the author of 'Natural Magic'.[19]

Given the experiences of people like Della Porta, it is no surprise that secret societies emerged during the Renaissance and, like the natural philosophers of their day, hid their thoughts and activities behind enciphered writing. While the Lincean Academy was growing, a new movement called Rosicrucianism spread across Europe, thanks to the wide dispersal of manifestos attributed to the legendary German noble Christian Rosenkreuz. These were even read by Cesi and may have influenced his writings.[20] Although the manifestos came to be regarded as a hoax, manuscripts and books associated with the Rosicrucians continued to be produced over the following centuries. A collection of Rosicrucian secret symbols existed in manuscript form in the seventeenth century and was later published.[21] One enciphered manuscript, tentatively assigned to the Rosicrucians or possibly the Freemasons, is the ninety-page 'Kassel Magic Manuscript', dated to the late eighteenth century, which includes spells for invoking spirits that will lead the conjuror to treasure.[22]

Equally mysterious is an eighty-four-page enciphered manuscript that, when cracked, turned out to be connected to the Freemasons. It

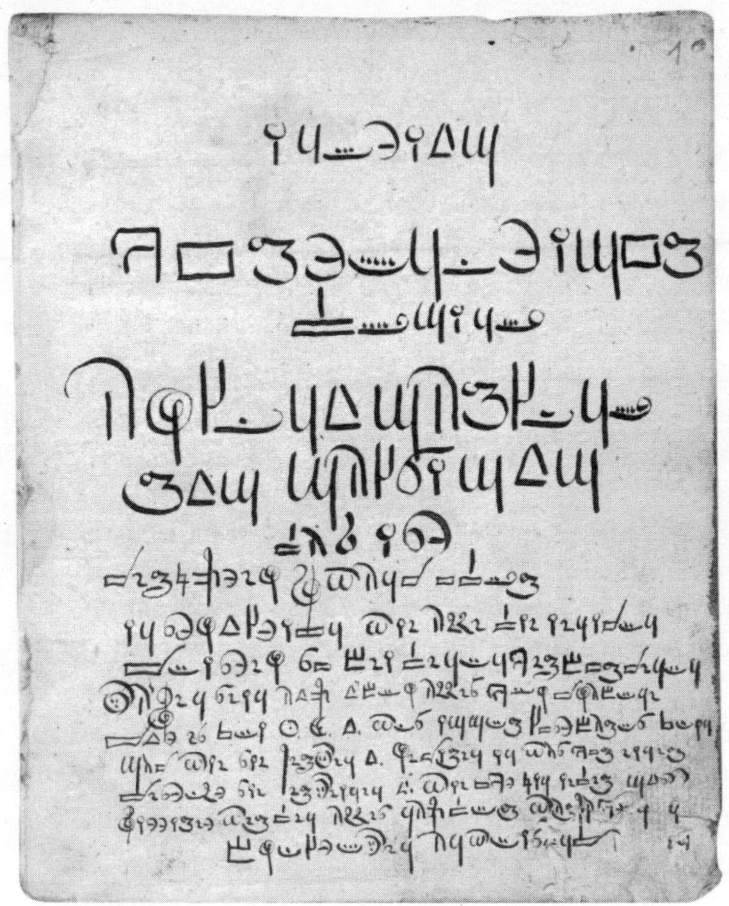

37. A page from the 'Kassel Magic Manuscript'.

lists Masonic grand masters back to the time of Adam and Noah, people from Greek mythology, Romans, and even includes the Dominican theologian Thomas Aquinas. This copy was made by Ádám Pálóczi Horváth between 1783 and 1795, from an original book apparently owned by a German lieutenant. Horváth did not understand the cipher, so made mistakes in his transcription.[23]

Another intriguing secret society that produced enciphered content was the Highly Illuminated Order of the Oculists, a rather obscure group based in Wolfenbüttel, Germany, in the eighteenth century, who only existed for around twenty years. Members received a variety of eye-related paraphernalia, including eye medallions, a magnifying glass, a scalpel for eye surgery, tweezers, and a pair of glasses. In the 1740s, they produced a 105-page cipher manuscript, which is divided into two major parts. Enciphered by a mix of abstract symbols and Greek and Roman letters, the first section presents the society's initiation ceremony, themed around a fake eye operation (including testing the person's eyesight and, more oddly, plucking a hair from an eyebrow), and rules for its lodges. The second part describes the different levels of membership of the Freemasons because the Oculists wanted to expose their secrets. There is also a short section on alchemy.[24]

FIGHTS, FUNGI, AND FRUSTRATION

Heckius did not realize it at the time but, when he left Italy, he would not return for eighteen months. He made the most of this unexpected period of travel, building connections with scholars, collecting books, and continuing his observations of nature, all the while reporting back to the Linceans. He passed through various Italian cities and entered France, where he spent time in Lyon, Paris, and Rouen, before heading to Dieppe. There, a heated debate about religion culminated with 'heretics' trying to kill him; Heckius had to fight them off with a sword.[25] He next travelled through England but, without any money, he only found a place to stay thanks to the kindness of a stranger who paid a tavern owner for a room until he could pay for it himself. Eventually, Heckius's brother had to meet him and escort him back home to Deventer in the Netherlands. This did not go well for Heckius either. After he was found fighting with local Protestants, the authorities kicked him out of the city and took his inheritance money. Forced back on to the road, he went to Sweden and Denmark, and back around to Brussels.[26]

Through it all, Heckius longed to return to Italy, and believed it would still be possible. This all changed in Brussels, when the papal nuncio, the pope's ambassador, told him of certain accusations made against him in Rome. The nuncio in Cologne, his next stop, relayed the same message. Since Heckius had left Italy, his name had been smeared across the country, the Inquisition were on the lookout for him, and he was in danger of being arrested. Italy was no longer an option for him. What had happened, he wondered. While Heckius was away, Cesi's father, afraid that the Dutchman was trying to convert his son to Protestantism (even though Heckius was Catholic), had exploited his connections to have him labelled a heretic and exiled.

Dismayed, Heckius threw himself into his studies and experiments – many involving mushrooms. In Germany, he came across a mushroom which, even when held at arm's length, caused a headache by its smell alone. His self-made plague remedy helped him to recover swiftly, but his servant, who smelled it too, was not as lucky; he fell sick and his headache lasted for days. In Norway, Heckius held a mushroom out in front of a dog, which collapsed in intense pain, despite not touching the dangerous fungus. As time passed, Heckius sent letters to Cesi in Rome, but many failed to arrive. Nonetheless, his travels were good for the Linceans, spreading word of their goals, and drawing intellectuals across the continent into their circle of correspondence.[27]

Eventually, just like many job-seeking scholars of his day, Heckius settled in Prague. With money from Cesi, and possibly a recommendation to help him gain access to the court, he hoped to find work under Emperor Rudolf II. He got lucky. In the emperor's gardens, he examined Asian and American plants, and explored the wonders of Rudolf's 'Kunstkammer' (Art Chamber). He also spoke with followers of Paracelsian medicine, deepening his interest in this controversial approach to healing.[28] In October 1604, he was among the many scholars in Prague transfixed by a supernova that had suddenly appeared in the night sky, and was inspired to write the Linceans' first published work about it. When Cesi received the manuscript, he heavily edited it, removing Heckius's aggressive comments towards Protestants and his various attacks on astronomers and anyone arguing against the Aristotelian view of the cosmos. There was valuable information in the manuscript, Cesi recognized, but he himself was now challenging Aristotelian views and wanted the academy to take a similar approach. Knowing how hurt Heckius would be by his edits, Cesi published the book without sending advance warning about his changes. Heckius first saw them in the published work and, understandably, fell apart. His writing no longer represented his own thoughts, he lamented.[29] But he continued to research and, in 1605, he published *Disputatio unica de peste*, in which he argued that a plague rampant in the Low Countries was caused by celestial phenomena attracting poisonous air from underground.[30]

Despite finding a stable life in Prague, with time to research and write, Heckius sent letters to Cesi expressing his unhappiness and his desire to return to Rome. Cesi listened to his pleas and proposed a solution: Cesi would cover the cost of Heckius's travels, but he would need to move cautiously and anonymously, and, rather than return to Rome, he would have to settle in Naples, beyond the reach of the pope. Heckius refused the offer – he was too proud to hide his name and live like a ghost in Naples.[31]

THE FRUITS OF HECKIUS'S TRAVELS

During his travelling years from 1603 to 1605, Heckius wrote down his exploration of science, technology, and nature in a series of illustrated notebooks, each dedicated to different phenomena, but with the overarching title *Fructus itineris ad septentrionales*. Across these notebooks, there are around six hundred illustrations, often in colour, and with descriptions in Latin, Dutch, or Italian. At different locations in autumn 1605, he posted them off to his Lincean brothers in Rome to add to their ever-expanding library of research. He appears to have sent at least one of them in haste, because certain pages only bear the names of species, without the illustrations. Heckius owned more notebooks than have apparently survived, including one on animals that live in water, and one covering the histories of different regions between Italy and the north, which he had been told about on his travels.[32]

Heckius dedicated one notebook, subtitled *De annulosis*, to species he observed in places like Poland, Bohemia, Bavaria, and Austria; it is filled with drawings of butterflies, crickets, beetles, spiders, and snakes.[33] Another, subtitled *De vegetabilibus*, covers plants and their roots, and other things that grow on the Earth that he spotted while travelling in England, Scotland, Denmark, and Norway, among others. Here, he made his notes after the drawings, filling the space

38. Heckius's drawing of a basilisk in one of his *Fructus itineris ad septentrionales* notebooks.

around them.[34] Heckius dedicated a third notebook to insects and reptiles, including a lovely drawing of the legendary basilisk – a lizard with cockerel-like features.[35] It seems likely that Cesi wanted to use the content of some of Heckius's notebooks as the basis for a zoological publication.[36]

The most unusual of Heckius's notebooks are two filled with mysterious Lincean symbols and Arabic and Syriac letters. He may have written these in cipher to keep their content out of the hands of ordinary people, or away from the Inquisition, or he may simply have done so for his own enjoyment. One of these notebooks bears the subtitle *Mechanica et naturalia Ioannis Ecchi Lincaei* – a title that Heckius wrote twice, first in Arabic script and then in Syriac letters, though the language itself is Latin. Within, he writes in both Lincean cipher and Arabic script, and includes a message to potential thieves, saying that his notebook has nothing to do with them (folio 3v). The notebook begins with an elegy to the Virgin Mary in Latin couplets. In the prayer, he describes being exiled from Deventer in his youth because of his Catholic faith, and how he is now once again in danger and exiled, this time from his home in Italy. He follows the elegy with various notes on alchemy (with the goal of identifying its medical uses rather than finding the philosopher's stone), astrology, natural sciences, and mechanisms; a brief thought on animal communication; and a list of places that he visited on his travels. All of this is accompanied by his drawings of intriguing devices, including apparently alchemical equipment, and an unrelated sketch of two birds fighting.[37]

Another of Heckius's enciphered *Fructus itineris* notebooks mainly contains medical notes for natural remedies without illustrations.[38] It has the subtitle *De naturalium mixturis et operationibus in humani corporis affectibus in septentrione consuetis* – 'Of Natural Mixtures and Operations on the Affections of the Human Body Customary in the North'.[39] He filled the notebook's nearly four hundred pages with cures for a variety of ailments, often with the names of the people who developed or first recorded the cures, and those on whom the

39. A page from *Mechanica et naturalia Ioannis Ecchi Lincaei*, one of Heckius's enciphered *Fructus itineris ad septentrionales* notebooks, showing a medical device for a leg, and Latin writing in Arabic script and Lincean cipher.

medications worked. He took his content from a variety of sources, such as Marcus Graecus's *Liber ignium*, Valerius Cordus's *Novum dispensatorium*, and Caesar Longinus's *Trinum magicum, sive secretorum magicorum opus.*[40] Within, Heckius jotted down solutions for people suffering from dysentery, painful breasts, and constipation; cures for hernias devised by a monk called Blauius; a method to treat haemorrhoids; and the intriguingly titled, 'Leonhard's great secret for gout'.

40. An illustrated page from *Mechanica et naturalia Ioannis Ecchi Lincaei*, one of Heckius's *Fructus itineris ad septentrionales* notebooks, showing alchemical equipment.

There are pills to take for those with syphilis; powder for cases of plague; ointment to help reduce pain during childbirth; and help for excessive menstruation. There is also relief from inflammation pains using the oil of a frog. (Heckius notes that, during the plague of 1450, some peasants used frogs to draw out the venom from boils – all apparently survived.) There is a cure for blindness; a remedy that, if given to babies, stops them developing epilepsy; a cure for fainting donkeys; a method for making writing turn invisible and for revealing it again; a way to make gluttonous servants throw up; and a means for curing toothache within half an hour. Among all of this, and a little out of place, is a method for keeping swords and weapons from rusting.[41]

Perhaps also from the *Fructus itineris* series is an enciphered manuscript from 1605, *Magna mechanica*, which he dedicated to Cesi and which covers herbs, genealogies, machines, fish, and geography.[42] This notebook is filled with drawings, among them war machines and a chair on wheels that Heckius designed for the disabled – it includes a device that would enable the driver to move the chair by hand. He may have written up these observations while in Deventer.[43]

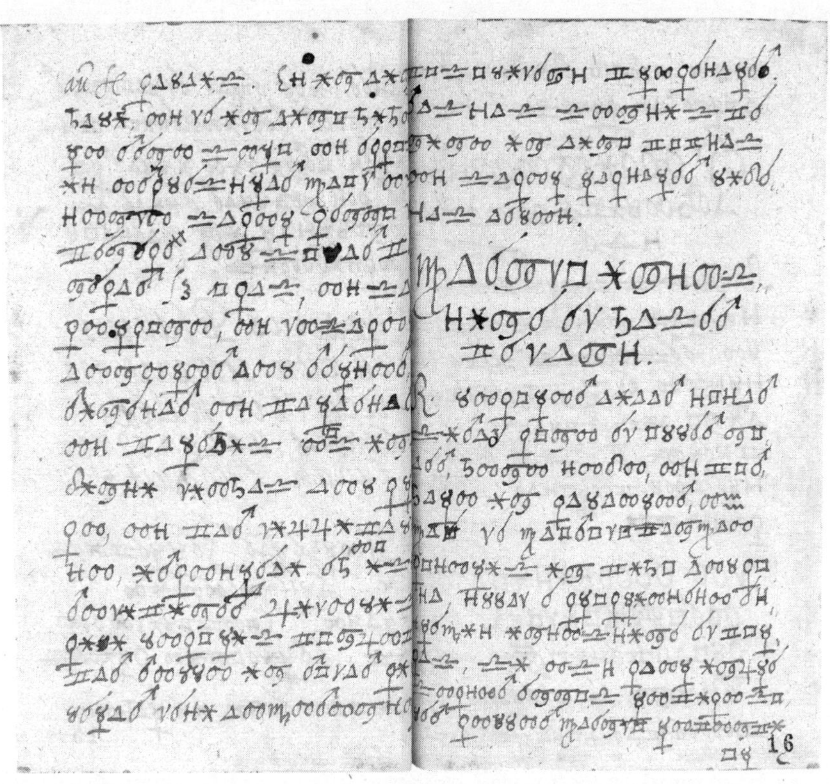

41. The Lincean cipher, from *De naturalium mixturis*, one of Heckius's *Fructus itineris ad septentrionales* notebooks.

SCIENCE AND SECRECY

Despite one of the main tenets of modern science being openness – making data available to all so that it can be replicated and verified – early modern investigators of the natural sciences often indulged in secrecy, and hid or protected their findings behind codes and anagrams. During the seventeenth century, the president of England's Royal Society received information about new discoveries and could choose to keep them secret from the public. Sometimes a member would present his findings but ask that they not be shared until publication; this ensured that a restricted few knew exactly who had made the breakthrough, just in case someone tried to pass it off as their own. The natural philosopher Robert Boyle, one of the founders of the Royal Society, used ciphers and anagrams to hide key aspects of his work too, but purposely did not reveal certain findings because he liked to swap his ideas for those of others, who equally would not share their findings without a good secret to exchange.[44]

The publication of anagrams was another method of secrecy. The anagram hid a message about the discovery, and its content could be decrypted by the writer if someone else claimed to have made the breakthrough first. Galileo Galilei, a member of the Lincean Academy from 1611, employed such methods when he first observed Venus's phases and Saturn's unusual shape; for the first case, his anagram was an unusual sentence, while for the latter it was a jumble of letters. Galileo also enciphered content in his letters to friends and family. In 1633, he asked friends to remove incriminating manuscripts and papers from his Florence villa before the arrival of the Inquisition. Earlier, he had hired a bricklayer to build a secret compartment under the stairs in a second villa, north-west of Florence near the city of Prato, and wanted them to hide everything there. He never went back for them. The manuscripts and papers were discovered in 1753, still hidden, untouched for over a century, after a librarian found a reference to the hiding place's construction in one of Galileo's account books. Even Galileo's death was communicated in cipher to Cardinal Francesco Barberini, a fellow Lincean, in Rome, who was involved in decisions regarding where he would be buried.[45]

Though secrets and ciphers were part of the Lincean way of doing things, demarcating 'insiders' from 'outsiders', for a doctor like Heckius, writing his medical notes in cipher was also a way of protecting his trade secrets and evading accusations of practising the

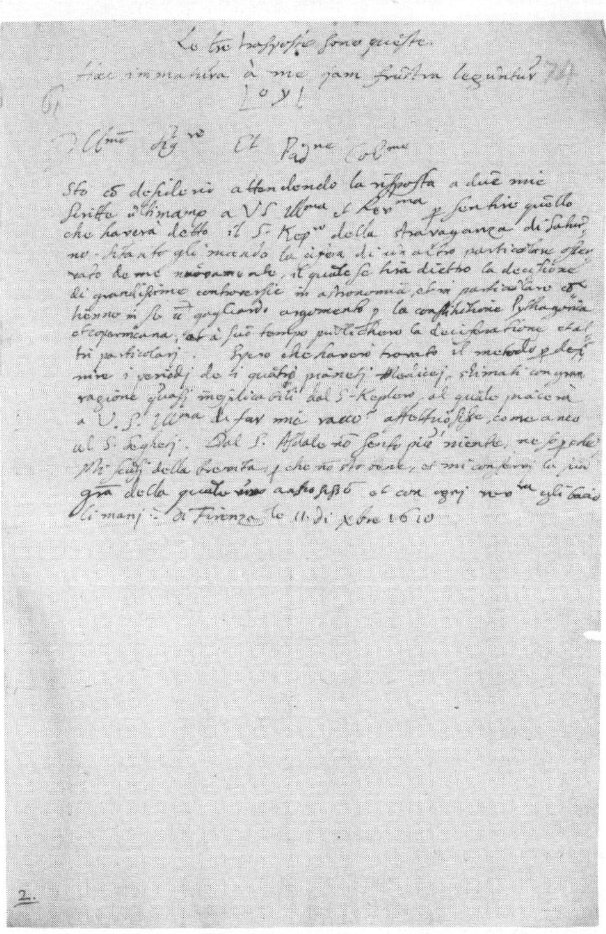

42. A page bearing Galileo Galilei's anagram about Venus.

dark arts by the Church.[46] Physicians enciphered content when writing about practices that they did not want the untrained to try for themselves or misuse, or when covering taboo subjects, especially those related to women, such as gynaecological matters. A late fourteenth-century manuscript in the British Library enciphers recipes for contraceptives, for example, while one from 1389 in the Bayerische Staatsbibliothek hides words for breast pain and the pains of childbirth. A manuscript from the late fourteenth or early fifteenth century in the Staatsbibliothek zu Berlin enciphers lines related to menstruation, and recipes for the womb and foetus.[47] In the early fourteenth century, John de Foxton wrote the encyclopaedia *Liber cosmographiae*, in which he enciphered words that he did not want casual readers to understand. These only appear in certain chapters, such as one dedicated to reading palms. Here, the reader is told how to know from a woman's palm if she has slept with many partners or none at all, or even if she will suffer an unpleasant death. Nonetheless, the majority of the enciphered words do not relate to sexual matters, but are obscured to stop people misusing John's instructions – for example, 39 of the 135 enciphered words relate to the position of veins.[48]

One 208-page manuscript containing technical and medicinal texts, its earliest entry dated to 1489, includes enciphered content related to horse and human medicine, but also on creating dyes and making wine.[49] Later, during the seventeenth century, Sir Peter Temple encrypted key words in a notebook of medical remedies that he gave to his daughter Eleanor. He wrote in cipher in case his enemies stole the notebook, but also to hide the information from friends, and to stop the uneducated from abusing the remedies in ways that might harm patients. Although some of the remedies were passed on to Temple by people he knew, others were taken from books available in shops. These sources were publicly available, so why encipher them? What mattered here was that the notebook contained a curated selection of remedies – ones of importance to Temple. Only a restricted circle would have access to this knowledge; using ciphers also added to the secrecy, and therefore to its value.[50]

HECKIUS'S DEATH AND THE MANUSCRIPTS' MOVEMENTS

During the second half of 1605, everything changed for Heckius. Through his connections, Cesi managed to secure him Roman citizenship and, six months later, he finally re-entered the Eternal City. His dream had come true, but in his absence Italy had changed. Cesi had become more involved in wider society, playing the role expected of a man of his rank and position. This created a gulf between the two friends; and so, despite only recently pining to return to Cesi and Rome, Heckius left again. In 1608, he moved to Madrid, Spain, where he set up a practice healing the poor. He collected Iberian plants and found time to visit the Royal Library's collection of dried plants from Mexico. He also fell in love. Then he vanished for six years.[51]

When Heckius resurfaced, living at the Botte d'oro (Golden Barrel) near Cesi's home in Rome, he was a changed man. Gone was the voracious researcher, obsessed with details, ready to argue with anyone he met. This new Heckius found it hard to focus and was often seen lost in prayer. His mind was faltering. In 1615, while visiting the Abbey of Sant'Angelo in Capoccia, he told his fellow Lincean Teofilo Müller that the King of Spain was trying to get him to marry his daughter. Fantasy had overtaken reality. The last mention of Heckius is dated 24 March 1616, shortly after his thirty-seventh birthday, when the Lincei suspended his membership because of his mental illness. The date of his death is unknown.[52]

After his death, Heckius's *Fructus itineris* notebooks remained in Cesi's library on the first floor of the ducal palace in Acquasparta, among around three thousand other volumes.[53] When Cesi himself died on 1 August 1630, unexpectedly, at the age of forty-five, he had left no instructions on what should be done with the Lincean books, which were intermingled with his own private collection. As a result, they passed to his wife and daughters, who later sold them to the bibliophile and Lincean Cassiano Dal Pozzo, to become part of the Puteana collection at his home, the Palazzo di Sant'Andrea della Valle. In turn, Dal Pozzo's descendants found it too expensive to maintain such a large library and sold the collection to Abbot Zacagni of the Vatican Library for 4,500 scudi. Zacagni bought the lot with money loaned from the Apostolic Camera (the pope's treasury), but he could not afford the repayments, so in 1714 his successor sold the books and manuscripts to Cardinal Alessandro Albani, a nephew of Pope Clement XI. They were absorbed into Albani's collection at the Quirinal Palace in Rome, and were later moved to the Palazzo degli Albani alle Quatro Fontane, also in Rome.[54]

Heckius's enciphered *Fructus itineris* notebooks were among the Lincean manuscripts accessioned into the Albani library.[55] They remained there until 1798, when French revolutionaries, dedicated to spreading the ideals of their movement beyond the borders of France, seized Rome. Cardinal Giovanni Francesco Albani led the fight against these invaders, but fled south to Naples in February 1798. With the cardinal out of their reach, the French could not arrest him, but they could loot his famous collection of art and manuscripts, justifying this as an act of retaliation for the killing of the French General Duphot in December 1797. In reality, the revolutionaries wanted to take such Italian wonders back to Paris, to be investigated and serve as a foundation for their new glorious era. Over the decades that followed, the Albani family tried to recover their lost artworks, books, and manuscripts. Sometimes they were lucky. Many people were appalled by what had happened; if they discovered that a book they had bought had been looted from the Albani collection, they sent it back to the family. In other cases, the family had to buy back their own manuscripts. By 1839, they had recovered 10,000 manuscripts, but it was all for nothing. The Albani family line came to an end in 1852 and, shortly afterwards, their restored collection was again dispersed.[56]

In the meantime, the Lincean cipher had been broken in 1822 by Domenico Morosini, at the request of the Albani librarian Francesco Cancellieri. This helped to exonerate the Linceans of accusations, which had arisen by the early nineteenth century, that they had tried to hide anti-religious, or immoral, behaviour or thoughts in the enciphered letters sent between them. When decrypted, these letters revealed no such activity – indeed, quite the opposite. The letters showed them to be concerned with good Catholicism, piety, and behaviour, and that they spoke well of kings and rulers.[57] This breakthrough opened a new window onto the lives of the founding Linceans, and especially that of Heckius.

The various disruptive events that befell the Albani collection in the late eighteenth and nineteenth centuries caused Heckius's enciphered notebooks to be separated from one another. In 1798, after the arrival of the French revolutionaries, his *Mechanica et naturalia Ioannis Ecchi Lincaei*, along with three other *Fructus itineris* notebooks, was taken from Rome to France by a contributions and finance agent called Henri Paul Reboul. Doctor Clement Francois Prunelle then asked the French government to buy them for the Montpellier medical school collection.[58] Father Tito Cicconi, the Albani collection librarian in the first half of the nineteenth century, tried to have them returned to Rome, but failed, and they remain in Montpellier today.[59] The *Magna mechanica*, meanwhile, another enciphered manuscript that may have been part of Heckius's *Fructus itineris* series, was bought in a public sale sometime in or before 1841, and is now in the Biblioteca Medicea Laurenziana in Florence.[60]

The movements of the enciphered *De naturalium mixturis* are more obscure. At some point after Cancellieri made a list of the Albani collection's holdings in the eighteenth century, the notebook found its way into the library of the Sacred Congregation for the Propagation of the Faith (Propaganda Fide) in Rome, which was dedicated to promoting Catholicism around the world. Intriguingly, before it entered this collection, someone tore out the first page of the notebook, leaving a scattering of symbols along the broken edge of the page.[61] It is not clear when or how the notebook arrived in this collection, as donations, bequests, and acquisitions were frequent, but it was most likely after 1798, through one of the dispersions of the Albani collection. The Propaganda Fide manuscript collection as a whole then entered the Vatican Library in 1902.[62]

During this time, the notebook's association with Heckius and the Linceans was forgotten and its enciphered content remained unread. A later list of Heckius's known or lost works did not even include it.[63] It was only in 2016, when the manuscript's content was studied by the DECODE project, that its content was fully decrypted, though the team did not connect it to Heckius or the Linceans, because neither are mentioned explicitly in the text. That same year, however, the researcher Nick Pelling independently broke the cipher and published the results on his website, linking the content with Heckius because of its title, but believing it to be a copy of the enciphered notebook in Montpellier.[64] The final piece in the puzzle came years later, while I was researching this chapter. Building on the valuable work of Pelling and the DECODE project, I investigated the notebook's subtitle, *De naturalium mixturis*, and found that the manuscript was mentioned in Cancellieri's eighteenth-century catalogue, listed as a work by Heckius. Thereafter, it vanished. When I pulled all of this research together, it became clear that the Vatican manuscript is this lost *Fructus itineris* notebook. Although its pages do not mention Heckius by name, his secret name, Illuminatus, is written in Arabic characters on the cover – just as you would expect from the mysterious Lincean doctor. Perhaps, then, Heckius's other lost *Fructus itineris* manuscripts are still out there somewhere, held in a library or private collection, just waiting to be discovered.

Mechanica et naturalia Ioannis Ecchi Lincaei is H 505 in the Bibliothèque universitaire historique de médecine of the University of Montpellier, France. *De naturalium mixturis* is Borg.lat.898 in the Biblioteca Apostolica Vaticana, Vatican City.

In our next chapter, we return to Germany, where a young doctor embarks on a quest to decipher the alchemical secrets hidden in ancient myths, but struggles to find the support of a noble patron.

9

DE THEOSOPHIA AEGYPTIORUM AND *ATALANTA FUGIENS* (*c.* 1610 AND 1617)

Alchemy and Hidden Knowledge

The summer sun beat down on a peaceful countryside field in Germany. It was 1568, and the pregnant Mrs Maier and a relative, her travelling companion, had decided to stop in the field to rest. Left alone for a few moments, sitting on the grass, Mrs Maier was enjoying the scenery around her and trying to relax when a dove gently descended from the sky to settle on her lap. It was beautiful, she thought, and surprisingly calm. She reached out to hold it, but the dove retreated from her hands and took flight. Three days later, in the region of Holstein in northern Germany, Mrs Maier gave birth to a son, whom she called Michael. Years after these events, thinking about this story, Michael wondered whether the inquisitive dove had been a sign, perhaps representing his future, as others already believed, or if its arrival had simply been a random occurrence. He would later write that he felt apathetic about the event – but perhaps he should not have been so dismissive. The dove was associated with the Holy Spirit, reflecting his deep religious devotion; just as importantly for Maier, it had alchemical significance, standing for the rising and falling of a liquid during distillation. There could not have been a better symbol for the themes of his turbulent life.[1]

Maier's search for alchemical knowledge and a medicine that could cure all sickness – the true philosopher's stone – was his life's mission. Across his decades of study and travel, of failures and setbacks and minor triumphs, he tried to heal the sick wherever he lived, longed for the support of a wealthy patron to support his experiments, and published many books. He was a master of the obscure symbols, allegories, and imagery that alchemists employed to shield their 'divine art' from the wider public. One of Maier's greatest obsessions was revealing the alchemical secrets hidden in ancient myths. He first developed his thoughts on this subject in a manuscript written at the magic-soaked court of the Holy Roman Emperor Rudolf II in Prague, *De theosophia aegyptiorum* – 'On the Theosophy of the Egyptians' – which he later published under the title *Arcana arcanissima* – 'The Most Secret of Secrets'. In turn, this led to Maier's greatest alchemical achievement: a book of many layers, into which he poured his deep knowledge of mythology, alchemy, and music; a book that was meant to be read and looked at, mulled over and debated, sung and listened to; a book that is still being dissected and revealed today: *Atalanta fugiens* – 'Atalanta Fleeing'.

THE SEEKER

Michael Maier grew up as a follower of the teachings of Martin Luther, the German priest who, according to the famous story, nailed his ninety-five theses to the church doors of Wittenberg just over fifty years before Maier's birth, sparking the Protestant Reformation and upturning Christianity. Michael's father, Peter, worked as an embroiderer of gold for the Danish royal family and other aristocrats, so, although his family were not rich, they were well off compared to most people. Michael was thirteen when his father died, leaving the cost of his education to fall on his mother. It can't have been easy for her, for Maier had to abandon the degree course he enrolled on at the University of Rostock in 1587 for lack of funds. Luckily, this did not hold the budding scholar back for long. In 1592, Maier continued his studies at the University of Frankfurt-an-der-Oder, gaining a master of arts degree. After visiting the court of the King of Denmark, Christian IV, from the age of twenty-three, he studied medicine for three years. Such travels would be a constant part of Maier's life, and his Lutheran upbringing taught him that his earthly existence was a journey for the soul, during which he would face many challenges.[2]

Maier next spent a year on the road, taking time in the spring of 1595 to explore what are today Latvia, Lithuania, and Estonia, and part of Russia. In the autumn, he crossed into Italy to continue his studies in medicine at the University of Padua, a major centre of medical learning, where he researched epilepsy.[3] As a medical student, Maier would have been among the first to use the world's earliest permanent anatomy theatre, constructed at the heart of the university in Palazzo Bo in 1594. Within its cone-shaped wooden chamber, staring down at the dissected body below, he would have stood shoulder to shoulder with his fellow students and local dignitaries, the only light cast from two candelabras on the operating table and the candles held in students' hands. Between autopsies, musicians played string instruments to ease the tense atmosphere.[4] As he entered the palazzo for his lessons, passing beneath hundreds of crests on the walls representing past rectors (perhaps including Giovanni Fontana), Maier might have run into Galileo, who taught in the building's Great Hall. The university also had its own botanical garden, founded fifty years before Maier's arrival, where scholars studied plants brought from across the world and used them to create remedies for all sorts of illnesses; it was such an important resource that plant thefts were treated harshly – punishments included exile. With his fellow students, Maier would have taken lessons in the garden and its pharmacy.[5]

At Padua, Maier was celebrated for his Latin poetry and was proclaimed Poet Laureate, but disaster soon struck for the promising wordsmith. In July 1596, he got into a heated dispute with Heino Lambechius, another student at the university. They shouted abuse at each other until Maier's temper got the better of him. A fight broke out. Fists slammed against flesh. Swords may have clashed. He severely injured his opponent. Repercussions were inevitable. Soon after, Maier found himself on trial before the university's representatives for German students (each nationality at the university had their own body of representatives). Maier was guilty, they declared, and he was sentenced to make a payment to Lambechius. In a twist, Lambechius refused Maier's money, so, the next day, Maier made a run for it. He escaped north across Italy's mountains and ended up in Basel, Switzerland, where he continued his doctorate. Though Padua's German representatives tried to block his graduation, he gained his degree two months later, on 4 November 1596.[6] He could now begin his career as a doctor but, before long, it would take an unexpected turn.

DE THEOSOPHIA AEGYPTIORUM AND *ARCANA ARCANISSIMA*

While working as a doctor in either Königsberg or Danzig, Maier watched, engrossed, as a man used a mysterious yellow powder from England to cure a patient suffering from serious asthma. Without this intervention, the man would surely have died. This sparked an interest in alchemy and its application for healing the sick that remained with Maier for the rest of his life. He devoured every book he could find on the subject, and became so engrossed that he suffered from insomnia.[7] He built his own laboratory and sourced materials for his experiments, all with the goal of discovering a universal medicine that could cure every illness. This powerful cure would be as good for the soul as it was for the body, he decided, and all in the honour of God.[8] He began his experiments in earnest in 1604. Over the following years, although he failed to create the philosopher's stone, he did develop a universal cure, which he took himself and gave to his three nephews, as well as others.[9] This was his *medicina regia*, or 'royal medicine', and he penned an account of his work called *De medicina regia et vere heroica, Coelidonia*, published in 1609.[10]

As Maier's alchemical interests deepened, he hoped to secure a rich patron to fund his research and experiments. Once these thoughts had nested in his mind, his next move was inevitable. In 1608, he entered Czechia, his heart set on making his name at the centre of all things mystical and magical: Prague, and the court of the Holy Roman Emperor Rudolf II. He was surprisingly successful. Rudolf read Maier's *De medicina regia*, proclaimed him a hereditary noble and Count Palatine, and appointed him his personal doctor. He may also have let Maier use the royal alchemical laboratories, which stood beside Rudolf's castle.[11] It was there, around 1610, that Maier started to investigate a subject that would come to define his work: ancient mythology and the alchemical secrets he believed to be locked within.

Sitting in Prague, Maier began to pen a manuscript that he entitled *De theosophia aegyptiorum* – 'On the Theosophy of the Egyptians'. Across its 260 pages, he investigates and discusses how the ancient priests of Greece and Egypt hid alchemical knowledge in their myths, images, and symbols, keeping them accessible to initiates and shrouding them from the unworthy. To Maier, myths were codes to be deciphered. Alchemy had first passed from God to Adam, and, from him, had spread through the ancient and classical world. By understanding this hidden alchemical knowledge – which had survived the centuries to his day thanks to the efforts of secret societies – physicians could concoct the most powerful medicine possible. In his manuscript, Maier explores these themes over six chapters, moving from hieroglyphs and Egyptian deities to the Greek myths of Jason and the golden fleece, the huntress Atalanta, the hero Hercules, and the Trojans through the *Iliad* and the *Odyssey*.

In the classical account of the myth of Osiris, the Egyptian god is murdered by his brother Seth, cut into pieces, and later restored by his sister-wife, Isis. But in *De theosophia aegyptiorum*, Maier sees Osiris as philosophic sulphur, burned and broken down by Seth as fire, and reformed by Isis as mercury. Jason's quest for the golden fleece is, in reality, none other than the quest for the philosopher's stone in its guise as the perfect medicine; while the Hydra fought by Hercules actually represents an alchemical process involving mercury. Maier also compares the stages of producing the philosopher's stone

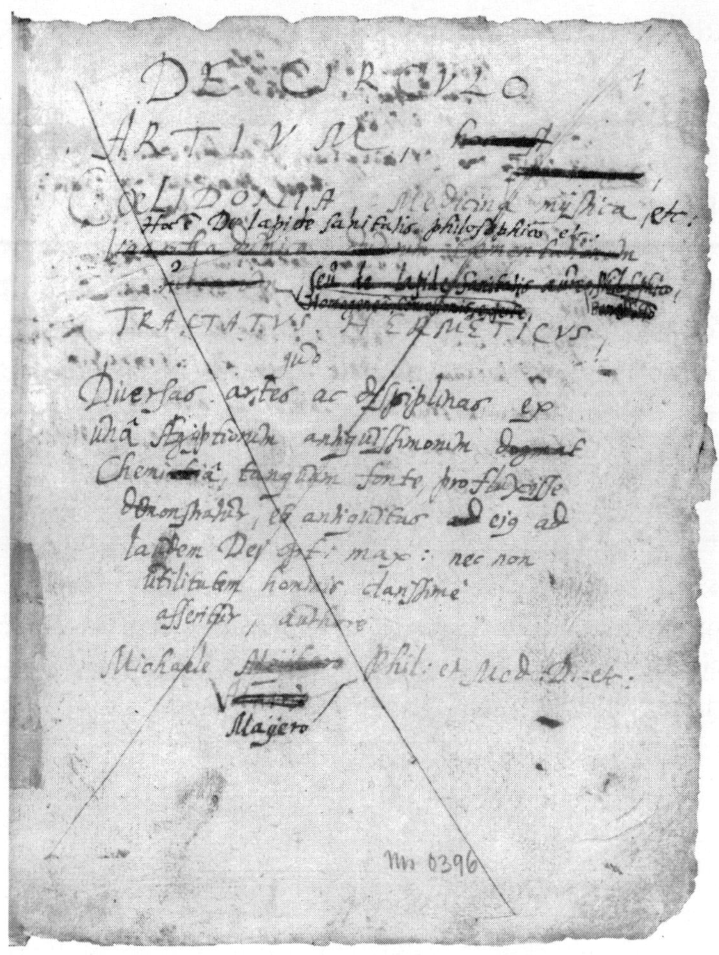

43. The crossed-out first page of Michael Maier's *De theosophia aegyptiorum*.

to the challenges of passing through three interlocked labyrinths. The alchemist must slay the Minotaur at their centre, before striving to find his way back out. Maier's manuscript is filled with scribbled-out text and replaced ideas, including a fully crossed-out title page. He even changed his mind on how to spell his own surname three times. The manuscript reveals a mind that was constantly adapting his thoughts, switching and refining his words as he progressed, never satisfied with what he produced.[12]

Although life was good in Prague, the one thing Emperor Rudolf did not give Maier was funding for his experiments, so, despite everything he had gained, he moved on. In 1611, he travelled to England, the origin of the magic powder that had inspired his interest in alchemy. He stayed there for four years, continuing his experiments and interacting with the royal court of King James I. He joined the funerary procession of the Prince of Wales in 1612 as it made its way to Westminster Abbey, and attended the public wedding ceremony of Friedrich V of the Palatinate and Princess Elizabeth in 1613. But, as usual for the unfortunate Maier, he made little headway into England's elite circles. His wealthy patron still eluded him, so he travelled the country studying English alchemy.[13] In 1614, he slightly updated his *De theosophia aegyptiorum*, and had it published in London as *Arcana arcanissima*, 'The Most Secret of Secrets', filling its title page with ancient Egyptian iconography. It was very likely also in England that Maier began writing his mysterious alchemical masterpiece, *Atalanta fugiens*.

THE PHILOSOPHER'S STONE

Alchemists believed that the seven metals – gold, silver, copper, iron, tin, lead, and mercury – were compounds created from the same basic ingredients. Underground, deep within the Earth, these went through natural processes over thousands of years. The water purified them and the heat of the Earth cooked them; as time passed, the various metals slowly transformed into silver and gold, regarded as noble metals (the rest were ignoble). Nobody agreed on what ingredients formed all metals, but mercury and sulphur were popular options, and the sixteenth-century physician and natural philosopher Paracelsus argued that salt should be added to that list. With this basic knowledge of metals, said the alchemists, it should be possible to figure out a way to artificially turn any metal into gold or silver by replicating natural processes in a laboratory. But to do this faster than happened in nature, they needed to determine what materials should be used, the correct level of heat, the necessary quantities, and the relevant time frame.[14] When the work was carried out correctly, usually following a lengthy process of many stages, the substance created could be mixed with cheap, readily available metals to forge huge quantities of gold. This substance was the legendary philosopher's stone. Any alchemist who achieved it would be handsomely rewarded by wealthy patrons, who were always on the lookout for more resources – and particularly gold.

By Maier's time, alchemists had been searching for the key to the philosopher's stone for centuries; the history of alchemy stretched back through Arab philosophers all the way to the ancient world. But although one aim of 'the art', as it was often termed, was to transform cheap metals into gold, there were other goals too. Chief among them was developing a cure for all illness – a universal medicine. As a doctor, this was something that particularly interested Maier. In the early modern era, the medical world was divided between those who healed following traditional, Galenic methods – based on the work of the second-century Greek physician Galen and the four humours he identified as crucial to health – and those who used alchemical methods to prepare cures. The best known, and most outspoken, of those who followed the alchemical method was Paracelsus (1493/4–1541), who spent his life lambasting the traditional ways and promoting the use of pharmaceuticals. To Paracelsus, all things consisted of mercury, sulphur, and salt. Any substance, even poisonous ones, could be broken down into these useful aspects and, in this purified state, be reunited and used for medical purposes. Paracelsian ideas stretched to the belief that living creatures called homunculi could be created from semen and blood, using their methods, and that even birds and plants could be brought back from the dead, in a process called palingenesis.[15]

To begin their alchemical journeys, students usually studied under accomplished alchemists, shared alchemical recipes, or performed their own experiments. Some, such as the polymath John Dee, asked angels for help. But the most accessible way to success was to read the many books published on the subject since the advent of the printing press.[16] Thanks to this technology, alchemists could share their knowledge widely, but this came with a downside: those unworthy of the knowledge, a sacred and divine thing, could learn their secrets too. Some of these books were written by charlatans – Maier himself wrote a book explaining the ways in which they duped people – but others were believed to truly hold the keys to the philosopher's stone. The problem was: how could real alchemists ensure that only the right people learned their secrets? The answer was to hide the true meaning of their words behind some very complex barriers. In *Atalanta fugiens*, Maier employed many of these techniques, building on his earlier work in *De theosophia aegyptiorum*.

DECIPHERING *ATALANTA FUGIENS*

From its title, Maier's *Atalanta fugiens* appears to be about the myth of Atalanta, which, as told in Ovid's *Metamorphoses*, concerns the speedy huntress Atalanta, who would only marry a man who could defeat her in a race; to add some extra spice, losing meant death for the suitor. Ignoring such danger, Hippomenes fell in love with Atalanta and asked the goddess Venus to help him win the impossible race. She gave him three golden apples that no one could resist – not even Atalanta. During the race, Hippomenes threw these apples to the ground as he ran, distracting Atalanta, who stopped to pick each one up. Because of this divine trick, he darted ahead and won the race and, with it, the hand of Atalanta in marriage. But Hippomenes did not thank Venus for her help, so out of revenge the goddess made the couple develop a sudden unbearable passion while visiting a divine sanctuary. Losing control, they slept together in this holy place, a forbidden act, and were transformed into lions as a punishment from the gods. In Maier's book, this story is told on the

ATALANTA
FUGIENS,
hoc est,
EMBLEMATA
NOVA
DE SECRETIS NATURÆ
CHYMICA,
Accommodata partim oculis & intellectui, figuris cupro incisis, adjectisque sententiis, Epigrammatis & notis, partim auribus & recreationi animi plus minus 50 Fugis Musicalibus trium Vocum, quarum duæ ad unam simplicem melodiam distichis canendis peraptam, correspondeant, non absq; singulari jucunditate videnda, legenda, meditanda, intelligenda, dijudicanda, canenda & audienda:
Authore
MICHAELE MAJERO Imperial. Consistorii Comite, Med.D. Eq. ex. &c.
OPPENHEIMII
Ex typographia HIERONYMI GALLERI,
Sumptibus JOH. THEODORI de BRY,
M DC XVIII.

44. The cover of the 1618 edition of *Atalanta fugiens* by Michael Maier.

cover through etchings. He explains his alchemical reading of the myth in the author's epigram that follows. In his interpretation, Atalanta is mercury and Hippomenes is sulphur, which transform when united, just like the characters in the myth. He thus used this ancient story as an explanation for the process of creating the philosopher's stone.[17]

Surprisingly, despite the prominence of the myth in the title, the book's main content is unrelated to Atalanta, beyond the occasional appearance of Venus, apples, and lions. Instead, after the dedication and preface, the reader finds fifty complex alchemical emblems created by the artist Matthäus Merian. Each is accompanied by a short epigram in Latin and German; a musical fugue with notation and lyrics, sung by Atalanta, Hippomenes, and a golden apple (though the words do not mention the myth); and a couple of pages of discourse on the topic of the illustration. The main content is arranged as an emblem book, a popular genre in Maier's day, combining images and short texts that usually lack a storyline. With *Atalanta fugiens*, the reader could progress from page to page as usual, or they could search for connections between the emblems and find other routes through its content. There were multiple ways in which the book could be approached, and multiple levels of comprehension, which, in turn, required a knowledge of multiple fields. By writing such a complex work, Maier was showing off his learning and skills, and engaging the eyes and ears of his elite readers, perhaps in the hope of impressing a wealthy patron.[18]

Maier's layers of meaning can best be understood by describing one of the emblems. Emblem 11 has the title 'Dealbate Latonam & rumpite libros', which translates as 'Whiten Latona and tear up the books'. The emblem shows a crouching woman, flanked by two men, one of whom is tearing up a book, and two children beside her. The boy on the left has the sun for his face; the girl on the right has a crescent moon balancing on top of her head. The woman is Latona, mother of Apollo, the Sun, and Diana, the Moon. But Latona is itself a play on Laton, a gold and silver alloy. An alchemist could separate Laton to create sun (gold) and moon (silver), but impurities would remain. The image and text therefore refer to an alchemical process. Maier was aware that there were a great many useless books on alchemy, and he urges his readers to tear up those without value. At the same time, he wants readers not just to read but to experiment (as the man on the left is doing) in their own laboratories, all in the quest for the philosopher's stone.[19]

Many of the book's emblems use animals to represent aspects of the alchemical process. In Emblem 29, the salamander, believed by classical authors to be able to live in fire, is likened to the philosopher's stone, as both can withstand great heat.[20] In Emblem 46, two eagles, one from the east, the other from the west, travel around the planet; these represent sulphur and mercury, which are also masculine and feminine respectively, and together must be used by the alchemist in the process of his work.[21] Other emblems return to Maier's interest in decoding myths. Emblem 44 shows the myth of the death of the ancient Egyptian god Osiris, in which Osiris is sealed in a chest and killed by his brother, and later cut up into pieces, before being restored. The emblem shows these dramatic scenes, with the god lying in a chest, a crown on his head, arms behind his back, while in the background a knife is raised over his sliced-off body parts. As in *De theosophia aegyptiorum*, Maier sees alchemical materials and processes in the actions of these gods (and here, for the sole time in the book's main chapters, mentions Atalanta and Hippomenes). Emblem 23 shows Minerva's birth, the goddess emerging, one arm raised, from Jupiter's head, as the god nonchalantly leans on one arm. Here, Maier compares the great work of the alchemist to Jason's quest for the golden fleece and Hercules' labours. In Emblem 35, he mentions Achilles, who had his mortality burned away by fire, as another reference to alchemy.[22]

Until recently, the various layers of *Atalanta fugiens* were believed to be well understood. But an extra layer may now have been revealed by the researcher Donna Bilak, hundreds of years after the book's first publication. If correct, it appears that Maier intended *Atalanta fugiens* to be a magic square, revealing a new route through its content. Clues spread throughout its pages suggest that certain emblems are connected. There are fifty emblems in the book, but the first two should actually be treated as one – something Maier shows his readers by splitting a quote from *Tabula smaragdina* ('The Emerald Tablet') by Hermes Trismegistus in two. When these two emblems are united, forty-nine are left, the number required for a seven-by-seven Venus

EMBLEMA XXIII. *De ſecretis Naturæ.* 101

Aurum pluit, dum naſcitur Pallas Rhodi, & Sol concumbit Veneri.

EPIGRAMMA XXIII.

Res eſt mira, fidem fecit ſed Græcia nobis
Ejus, apud Rhodios quæ celebrata fuit.
Nubibus Aureolus, referunt, quòd decidit imber,
Sol ubi erat Cypriæ junctus amore Deæ:
Tum quoque, cùm Pallas cerebro Jovis excidit, aurum
Vaſe ſuo pluviæ ſic cadat inſtar aquæ.

N 3 AURUM

45. Emblem 23 from Michael Maier's *Atalanta fugiens*, 1618, showing the birth of Minerva.

magic square, as recreated from earlier examples and popularized by Heinrich Cornelius Agrippa (who, as we saw in Chapter 4, was a friend and student of Johannes Trithemius). By combining the first two emblems, each subsequent emblem's number is reduced by one. This causes Emblem 26 – a woman wearing a crown, with the theme of seeking wisdom – to become Emblem 25 and stand at the centre of the square. In Agrippa's square, this spot is taken by Venus, a central character in *Atalanta fugiens*, who was also the wife of Vulcan, god of fire and the forge – apt for an alchemical work.[23] Using this method, many more secrets may still await discovery.

THE ALCHEMICAL CODE

What other methods did alchemists use to hide their secrets? Most commonly, alchemical writers swapped references to metals with the planet or planetary symbol that they were associated with. There were seven metals and, to early modern writers, there were seven planets – the Sun and Moon counted among them. The Sun was gold, the Moon was silver, Mars was iron, and Venus was copper, for example.[24] Any reader wanting to understand alchemical secrets first had to learn this system and the associated symbols for each planet/metal. This method of using one word to refer to something else is called Decknamen, meaning 'cover words'. Over time, the switching of words and phrases for others progressed far beyond just metals, to cover a vast array of alchemical practices and processes. Sometimes, multiple words could be used for the same material: the Sun, the god Apollo, rooster, and sulphur all stand for gold in Basil Valentine's 1602 work *Von dem grossen Stein der Uhralten* (a book that Maier later published in Latin).[25] The natural philosopher Robert Boyle chose from a selection of eleven words for gold in his alchemical writings, including ones in Latin, Greek, and Hebrew.[26] Such methods hid the secrets from the unworthy and outsiders, but were clear to the initiated, who had no problem deciphering their true meaning.[27]

Communicating alchemical secrets through allegorical descriptions and imagery was also popular among alchemists, who used them in much the same way as Decknamen.[28] Sexual imagery, for example, represented the uniting of two substances to create something new. Depictions of hermaphrodites served the same purpose.[29] The Ripley Scrolls, produced from the late fifteenth century to the early seventeenth century, are perhaps the most famous examples of alchemical messages hidden in art. Fifteen of these scrolls, which were associated with the fifteenth-century alchemist and Augustinian canon George Ripley, survive; though there are variations, each bears alchemical poems and associated imagery. Their origins and function remain

CHYMICALL CHARACTERS

Notes of Metalls

- Saturne, Lead ♄
- Iupiter, Tinne ♃
- Mars, Iron ♂
- Sol, the Sun, Gould ☉
- Venus, Copper, Brasse ♀
- Mercury, Quicksilver ☿
- Luna, the Moon, Silver ☾

Notes of Minerall and other Chymicall things

- Antimony
- Arsenick
- Auripigment
- Allum
- Aurichalcum
- Inke
- Vinegar
- Distilld Vinegar
- Amalgama
- Aqua Vitæ
- Aqua fortis, or separatory water
- Aqua Regis or Stigian water
- Alembeck
- Borax
- Crocus Martis
- Cinnabar
- Wax
- Crocus of Copper or burnt Brass
- Ashes
- Ashes of Harts ease
- Calx
- Caput Mortuum
- Gumme
- Sifted Tiles or Flower of Tiles
- Lutum sapientiæ
- Marcasite
- Sublimate Mercury

Notes of Minerall and other Chymicall things

- Mercury of Saturne
- Balneum Mariæ
- Magnet
- Oyle
- To purifye
- Realgar
- Salt Peter
- Common Salt
- Salt Gemme
- Salt Armoniack
- Salt of Kali
- Sulphur
- Sulphur of Philosphers
- Black Sulphur
- Soape
- Spirit
- Spirit of wine
- To sublime
- Stratum super Stratum or Lay upon lay
- Tartar
- Tutia
- Talck
- A Covered pot
- Vitriol
- Glas
- Urine

Notes of the foure Elements

- Fire
- Aire
- Water
- Earth
- Day
- Night

FINIS.

46. A page of alchemical symbols, seventeenth century.

unclear, but they were probably produced in England using existing poems that had circulated without illustrations, before they were combined with the art on the scrolls.[30] Among these images are a green toad, perhaps representing poison or 'philosophic sulphur', a form of the element lacking moisture; a red lion, which can symbolize normal sulphur; a green lion as the metallic element mercury; and snakes, which represent the god Mercury. A green dragon is shown eating a black toad, the doomed amphibian's leg already in its mouth; the meaning here is unclear, but it might relate to producing the 'black stone', a stage in the process of creating the philosopher's stone.[31]

Another method that alchemists used to hide their knowledge is called dispersion. In this technique, the writer separates the description of an alchemical process into pieces and spreads them throughout a book, or sometimes multiple books. Only those with the correct knowledge, who understand the clues and read the works in detail, can reconnect these pieces. Robert Boyle, for example, in his book, *Usefulnesse of Experimental Naturall Philosophy*, describes an alchemical experiment, but only reveals certain key details to understanding it three hundred pages later; even then, extra clues are given forty pages further on.[32]

ENCIPHERED ALCHEMICAL NOTEBOOKS AND MANUSCRIPTS

Alchemists used codes and ciphers too. Maier himself sometimes wrote in cipher when he wanted certain content hidden from his readers. Seven enciphered lines in his *Themis aurea* were first decrypted by Petro Borelli in 1656,[33] and then independently by Isaac Newton, who owned a copy of the book and wrote the cipher alphabet's key in the margin.[34] Maier also wrote an enciphered message in his *De medicina regia*, using the same cipher. When decrypted, this simply explains that the book was published in Prague in 1609; Maier's decision to write in cipher here might be associated with a strange comment that he makes elsewhere in the book: namely that it was published as if it had never been published.[35] He used his cipher again when writing to Count Moritz of Hessen-Kessel; here the word 'Tusalmat' decrypts to become 'Saturnus'.[36] Maier constructed anagrams in his writings too, in particular referring to himself as Hermes Malavici (from Michael Maierus) or when hiding his name in a poem. All of this can be seen as a form of performative secrecy, in which Maier and writers like him used ciphers and similar techniques to bring attention to the hidden knowledge in their works. The author knew something the reader did not, which made the book more desirable and valuable.[37]

In 1426, four alchemists in Germany devised a cipher to record their alchemical experiments, and wrote their results in a notebook entitled *Alchymey teuczsch*.[38] Leading the team was Niklas Jankowitz, who was helped by Michael von Prapach, Michael Wülfling, and a man simply named Friedrich. They filled the ninety-four pages of their notebook with enciphered alchemical recipes, using three sets of symbols to add to the complexity, as well as cover words: 'yellow earth' was gold, for example; 'white earth' was silver. Although not difficult to break, the cipher and cover words would have been complex enough to stop any outsiders with limited time from understanding the notebook's content. The alchemists also wrote unenciphered sections on medicine – help for flatulence, a spell for relieving fever, a love spell, and a way to force a poisoned person to vomit, as well as many more – and astrology, such as the best days and times to undertake their work. Among the pages are magic squares (some cut out) and, in two places, drawings, including one of a dog chasing a rabbit.[39]

Another enciphered fifteenth-century alchemical manuscript was produced in Spain: the *Libro del tesoro*.[40] A scribe wrote much of this manuscript in a cipher that obscures alchemical recipes for the philosopher's stone, along with instructions for the transmutation of metals, and medicinal help.[41] The cipher consists of 145 characters, written in red ink, each with roughly five different sound values.

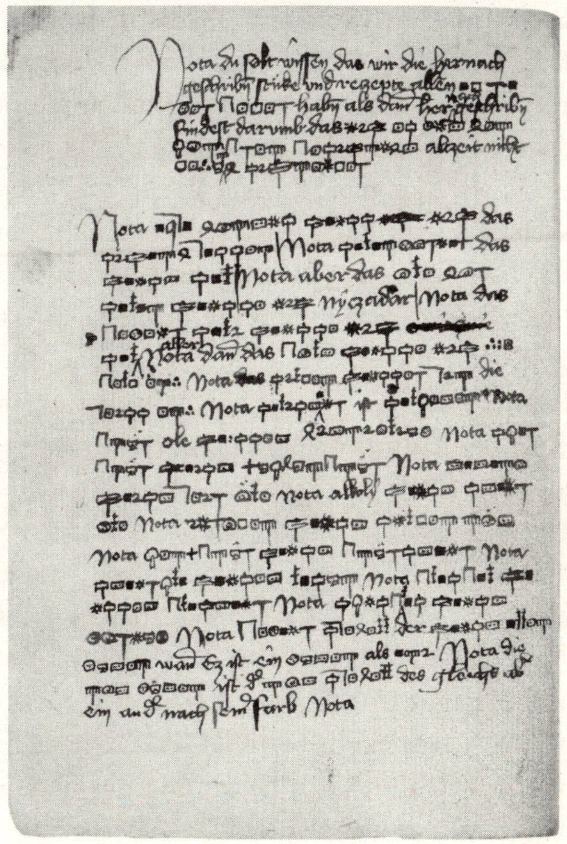

47. A page from the enciphered notebook *Alchymey teuczsch*.

There are also nulls – meaningless characters, meant to throw off would-be decipherers. Apparently, the scribe got tired of writing the nulls, because there are far more at the start of the text than at the end.[42] The cipher characters take a wide variety of forms, comprising symbols used by Christian Kabbalists, characters from the alphabet of Enoch, and symbols referred to by later writers as Egyptian and Phoenician.[43]

Everything about the *Libro del tesoro*'s presentation – its writing style, layout, and colours – show that it was meant to be taken as a thirteenth-century codex, made for King Alfonso X of Castile, León, and Galicia. Its wooden covers and the iron plates at its corners, perhaps to hold padlocks, add to the manuscript's air of mystery. But various clues, such as the system of dating and anachronisms in its use of language and style, scream that it was written in the fifteenth century. This is made even more obvious thanks to a 'later' note in the manuscript, which relates that it was discovered in the library of Don Enrique, marquis de Villena, a famed necromancer, who is described as the one tasked with deciphering the text. Sloppily, the ink and handwriting here are the same as that found in the 'earlier' parts of the manuscript. The book's true author remains unknown. Alonso Carrillo, a fifteenth-century Archbishop of Toledo, was interested in alchemy and had alchemists in his circle. It is possible that among them were the alchemists who made the *Libro del tesoro*, probably in the hope of selling it to the archbishop. Indeed, one alchemist in Toledo, Alarcón, a man who also worked for the archbishop as a butler, was beheaded in Toledo's Plaza de Zocodover, apparently for deception. Although the cipher of the *Libro del tesoro* was not cracked until the twentieth century, there are at least four additional deciphered copies of this manuscript held in various libraries, showing that its content was once understood.[44]

Other alchemical notebooks have individual enciphered words, rather than whole sections. One such notebook belonged to the Regent of Forli and Imola in Italy, Caterina Sforza, who lived from 1463 to 1509. Throughout her life, she collected recipes in a 553-page notebook with the title *Experimenti*. These cover a wide range of topics, from medical help, alchemy, and the philosopher's stone to cosmetics. Sforza wrote in cipher when noting down alchemical experiments, but also for treatments related to the loss of sexual interest and impotence. It was not a complex cipher: she simply substituted vowels for other letters. In some places, perhaps as another method to hide her content, she used Latin instead of Italian.[45]

During Maier's time, the alchemist and physician Arthur Dee (1579–1651) wrote his thoughts in a medical notebook, created by binding together earlier writings by his father, the famous polymath John Dee.[46] Most of its content is unenciphered, with sections covering astrology, alchemy, and medical treatments, alongside drawings, symbols, horoscopes, and notes scribbled in the margins. One page (folio 28r) bears John Dee's horoscope for Arthur, cast on the day of his birth in 1579, which predicts that his son will die an abrupt and awful death in a foreign country (he actually died in Norwich, England, during his seventies).[47] On both sides of another page, inserted the wrong way up in a section entitled 'Hermeticae philosophiae medulla', Arthur wrote a long enciphered text. This was associated with a cipher table and a key phrase in Latin, each written on other pages of the notebook, which together were meant to help the reader decrypt the text (except that there is an error in the table, making it difficult – Arthur had copied all of this content from another source). The deciphered text reveals 177 words of Latin and presents an alchemical recipe for the philosopher's stone; this is significant, given that Arthur later claimed to have produced this much-desired, yet legendary substance, in his 1634 book *Arca arcanorum*.[48]

THE JOURNEY ENDS

In 1616, Maier moved to Frankfurt am Main, forced to settle down by a mystery illness. It is unclear what he suffered from, but it may have been caused by the chemicals he touched and inhaled during his experiments, as was so often the case for alchemists. If so, his situation would only have worsened as he continued to experiment in search of a cure. Given his ongoing lack of success finding a patron, he may have suffered from depression too.[49] Still, for a man wanting to make a name for himself as a writer and thinker, there were worse places to be. At the famous biannual Frankfurt Fair, people could buy books ranging from the most serious Latin tomes to volumes on medicine, and smaller works on all manner of subjects. Although aimed at an international market, 70 per cent of the books sold were

48. An engraving of Frankfurt am Main in the 1600s, by Matthäus Merian, who illustrated Michael Maier's *Atalanta fugiens*.

printed in Germany.[50] Taking advantage of this situation, Maier published volumes of his writings in quick succession, including *Atalanta fugiens*, first released in 1617, with another edition in 1618. Thanks to the small payments he received for his books – income he desperately needed – he could focus on his writing. Sick, and sleeping little, he read and wrote mainly at night, surrounded by his glass bottles and chemicals, while his alchemical experiments bubbled away in the background. Much of his money went towards oil to keep his lights burning.[51]

An official portrait of Maier, aged forty-nine, was included in some copies of *Atalanta fugiens* in 1617. It shows him looking well: his short, combed-back hair rests above a furrowed forehead. His face sports a wide moustache and long goatee beard. His left hand rests on the hilt of a sabre, while his right hand holds a book, kept open at its centre by his fingers. A broad collar hides his neck, and a

49. A portrait of Michael Maier.

cloak is draped over one shoulder. A medallion bears a portrait that can barely be seen. Only his tired eyes, staring off into the distance, hint at his chronic illness.[52] For a man with only five years left to live, he seems in good health.

During these final years of his life, Maier continued to write books and served as a doctor in Stockhausen, not far from Frankfurt, to a noble named Von Riedesel. He also married, but little is known about his wife, other than that they had children together and she outlived him. In 1618, Maier sent a selection of his books to Count Moritz the Learned of Hesse-Kassel; the count must have been impressed because, in return, he brought Maier into his circle. Working from home in Frankfurt, Maier served as a physician and alchemist, searching for new cures to illnesses, but he also had to write to Moritz regarding events he learned of or witnessed that might interest the count. In short, he had become a spy. This role provided Maier with a much-needed regular income, but by 1621 he appears to have lost his job and was again earning money as a private doctor. He particularly helped people suffering from gout and arthritis, each brought on by a lack of piety and immoderation in Maier's view. His ongoing failures perhaps stemmed from his reliance on treatments based on golden powder and yellow quicksilver (a mixture of mercury and sulphur), which he developed to cure all manner of illnesses, but which mainly resulted in his patients vomiting and suffering from intense stomach pains.[53]

Around 1620, Maier moved 300 kilometres north-east of Frankfurt to Magdeburg, Germany, where he worked as a doctor and, as usual, sought patronage from local dignitaries, even if this meant bending his ideals. Writing to the Magdeburg nobleman Gebhardt Johann von Alvensleben, he praises astrology – an interest of the nobleman's, but something that Maier had previously been against. Maier talks of his proficiency in a true version of astrology, unlike that practised by others; he celebrates divination through geomancy; and he says that he employs talismanic magic as part of his medical practices. Given the difficult times brought on by the Thirty Years' War, it is perhaps not surprising that Maier was willing to adapt to make an income; he had even been forced to pawn his wife's golden bracelets and a silver girdle as a way to raise some much-needed cash.[54]

After years of failing health, Maier passed away under the golden summer sun of 1622. The only reference to his death is found in the printed edition of his final, posthumous book, in a foreword written by the publisher. His view of life as a journey might have given him solace in these final days. It was certainly on his mind as he neared death, for his last book was on the subject of Ulysses, the ancient

Greek hero famous for his travels, interpreted, of course, through an alchemical lens. As Maier's life slipped away, and as he pondered the secrets that permeate Homer's epic poems, perhaps his mind wandered back to his days in Prague and his first scribbled thoughts on myths and alchemy in *De theosophia aegyptiorum*, twelve years earlier.

There would be one final twist. Unaware of Maier's death, within the next twelve months, the alchemist Johann Staricius knocked on the door of his friend's Magdeburg home with a letter in his pocket. It was addressed to Maier from King Gustav II of Sweden, who wanted him to serve at his court. The job came with a large annual salary, and the deal was sweetened with free accommodation and food. It would have been a transformative event for Maier but, sadly, he had already moved on to the next destination in his alchemical journey.[55]

A BRIEF EXCURSUS: ALCHEMY AND THE VOYNICH MANUSCRIPT

Although the famous Voynich Manuscript (subject of Chapter 2) as a whole may not be entirely dedicated to alchemy, it could take some inspiration from contemporary alchemical imagery or perhaps have sections dedicated to this 'noble art'.[56] Among its herbal illustrations, a dragon inhales or exhales a plant; these mythical creatures have various alchemical meanings, including metals in their imperfect state, and solidified mercury.[57] There are pots, drums, and tubes – all typical of alchemists' equipment – while the frog or toad, drawn on one Voynich folio, was a symbol of poison and death to most people, or philosophic sulphur to alchemists.

But what is most significant is the Voynich Manuscript's bathing section. Bathing is often found in alchemical illustrations as an allegory for metals, usually gold and silver, dissolving in a liquid, such as mercury. This process united them. One fifteenth-century work, *Das Buch der heiligen Dreifaltigkeit*, includes an illustration of four nude women bathing in blue water beneath a moon-faced fountain, while four naked men bathe in a separate pool of red water, flowing from a sun-faced fountain. Here, the moon represents silver and the sun is gold.[58] Alchemical distilling scenes, in which liquid pours from one container to another, might also have served as an inspiration to the Voynich artist, but these do not usually include nude figures.[59] Another possibility is that the Voynich Manuscript's naked women are personifications of processes, materials, or bodies that play a role in the alchemical experiments – stars, for example, are personified in alchemical texts.[60] Given the wide range of ways in which alchemists hid the meaning of their words – including encipherment – the Voynich Manuscript's unusual script might fit an alchemical theme too, particularly as some of its characters resemble those found in alchemical writings.

Nonetheless, it must be stressed that, unlike the illustrations in the Voynich Manuscript's balneological section, which predominantly depict nude women, alchemical images of baths normally show both men and women. As noted above, this is because these scenes are allegories for separate elements dissolving and uniting – the inclusion of both sexes is key to the illustrations' function.[61] Meanwhile, potentially alchemical motifs like the dragon and frog/toad could simply be decorative flourishes, drawing from well-known late medieval imagery. In medieval Europe, dragons represented creatures from exotic lands, obstacles to be overcome, or the devil.[62] The Voynich Manuscript's various pots, drums, and tubes almost certainly show the production of recipes, but these might be medical, rather than alchemical. Furthermore, no known alchemical manuscript is entirely enciphered. Usually, only certain words or lines are hidden.[63]

DE THEOSOPHIA AEGYPTIORUM AND *ATALANTA FUGIENS* THROUGH THE CENTURIES

Over the years following its release in 1617, publishers reprinted *Atalanta fugiens* in different editions, including volumes that reorganized the all-important illustrations. During the seventeenth century, people adapted copies by adding colour to the emblems,[64] or made their own translations into French and English, while omitting the music, further impacting Maier's complex plan. Some copied the book by hand, creating manuscript editions.[65] A later edition, published in 1687, was retitled *Secretioris naturae secretorum scrutinium chymicum*; it excluded the imagery from Ovid on the title page, the fugues, and the German text. On the plus side, people took inspiration from *Atalanta fugiens*'s emblems, using figures from them in their paintings, including three paintings in Amsterdam's Bibliotheca Hermetica Philosophica.[66] Maier's name continued to be known too, though not always in the best light; later commentators, Isaac Newton among them, saw him as a man who wasted his time on alchemy.[67]

Maier's *De theosophia aegyptiorum* is the only one of his works to survive in manuscript form. That manuscript has been kept in the University of Leipzig's library since at least 1687, but may have spent some time in Kassel beforehand.[68] We can only imagine what the original manuscript for *Atalanta fugiens* looked like. To create such a complex work would have demanded months of focus, anguish, and a great many crossed-out words and pages. But it was worth the pain. The *Atalanta fugiens* remains one of the most famous works of alchemy ever produced, bringing together influences and diverse strands from its author's decades of reading and study. Perhaps Maier's greatest achievement, however, is that *Atalanta fugiens* is still being discussed and dissected today.

De theosophia aegyptiorum is in the Leipzig University Library under call number MS 0396.[69] Copies of the 1617 edition of *Atalanta fugiens* are extremely rare, but can be found in some libraries and private collections. Still rare, but more available, is the 1618 edition.[70]

In our final chapter, we will bring together what we have learned about how people in late medieval and early modern Europe hid knowledge, and explore whether a better understanding of cryptic writings can shed light on whether the Voynich Manuscript is an enciphered or encoded text, an artificial language and script, or a hoax.

10

CRYPTIC WRITINGS AND THE VOYNICH MYSTERY

Returning to the World's Most Mysterious Manuscript

Many of the manuscripts we have investigated over the previous chapters were, for the most part, produced by people who wanted to achieve something paradoxical: they set out to keep their knowledge hidden, while ensuring that it remained accessible. In the case of alchemical manuscripts, authors like Michael Maier wanted to hide information from the unworthy, while keeping it accessible to the alchemical community. If a reader understood how alchemists encoded information, their 'mysteries' were perfectly clear. You can see their complex use of imagery, allegory, cover words, dispersion, and ciphers as a form of performative secrecy: Maier's secrets drew attention to themselves and his knowledge, while not directly revealing them.[1] Such practices brought legitimacy and acceptance among the alchemical community, and helped alchemists to intrigue wealthy patrons. More tangible than someone simply saying that they knew a secret, an enciphered alchemical recipe hinted at something worth knowing. A potential apprentice, patron, or buyer could hold the enciphered page in their hands, see the masked words, and, for the right price, unlock it.

For those working in science, medicine, and engineering, like Giovanni Fontana and Johannes Heckius, hidden knowledge was of a similar kind. Fontana's extensive use of his own cipher was almost certainly him showing off in an era when ciphers were starting to become more complex and common in elite life. It was perhaps employed to advertise his skill to potential patrons – to prove his unique creativity and ingenuity. The illustrations and Latin content would have intrigued such clients, while the enciphered text suggested that there was more to learn. Rather than being a serious attempt at keeping his writings secret, it can be seen as another example of performative secrecy. After all, in Fontana's *Bellicorum instrumentorum liber*, the enciphered writing sometimes adds little or even nothing to what people could read in the plain Latin text. Fontana may also have experimented with encipherment simply for the intellectual challenge, or perhaps he saw it as a form of game to be played by the reader. For Heckius and his enciphered notebooks, his need for secrecy was more a case of keeping information exclusively for a select group: it highlighted his membership of a specific community, the Linceans – something he dearly cherished. Because he posted his notebooks to Rome, his enciphered writing also kept his words hidden from thieves, curious couriers, and – particularly important for medical texts – untrained hands. Secret societies like the Oculists used ciphers and codes in a similar way.

In all cases here, it is important to note that these ciphers are simple and easy to break. Complicated ciphers developed for military and diplomatic correspondence are not sensible options for longer works, simply because the more complex the cipher, the more difficult it becomes to read and write the text. If you only want to hide content from prying or unworthy eyes, entice a client, show off your skill (particularly if just for fun), or share information among a select community, a complex cipher used at length is a hindrance; obscuring certain words and sentences, or the odd paragraph, does the job just as effectively.

Trithemius's invention of steganography can perhaps be seen in a similar light to Fontana's cipher. It was an intellectual challenge and showed off the monk's inventiveness; after all, he originally hoped it would be useful to the Holy Roman Empire, to kings and emperors, revealing his intended audience. The true meaning of his writings was hidden behind a veneer of demon magic, rather than a cipher, and, as we have seen, such overtly mysterious content usually intrigues readers and brings extra attention to a text.

Other individuals we have met in this book invented their own scripts and languages. The reasons for Hildegard of Bingen's language creation remains unclear – it is virtually unique for her time. The suspicion that it was an attempt to reproduce a divine language or that it was an ornamentation to her songs is compelling, as is the suggestion that it was a form of secret communication among her community. Intriguingly, although Hildegard developed a unique script, she appears not to have used it to write her invented language, which, from surviving examples, was still composed using the Latin alphabet. Indeed, Hildegard's Unknown Letters basically act like a simple substitution cipher, and she used them only in a limited way, such as to name addressees in correspondence.

Centuries later, John Dee received his celestial alphabet and language from Edward Kelly, who claimed to be in contact with angels. Yet, like Hildegard's script, this alphabet was rarely used. It was much simpler to convey the sounds of the angelic speech and write them out in Latin script. The alphabet's purpose was to add a layer of complexity and legitimacy to Kelly's deception: it gave Dee exactly what he wanted and expected, and, like most magical scripts, was not designed to serve a practical function. The angel diaries are thus an interesting example of an artificial language and script being employed in a hoax that unfolded over years to generate an air of mystery and mysticism.

Thomas Harriot devised his script to record the spoken language of the Algonquin. He designed it to be efficient, sensible, and ordered, rather than an indecipherable mystery, and the language he wanted to write already existed. However, in his sole publication about his time in North America, he neither uses the script nor mentions it. He writes Algonquian words in English, despite knowing that this was an imperfect rendering. Even in his own notes, he almost never wrote anything in Algonquian. Most examples of his 'secret script' mask English words and act as a simple substitution cipher. The air of mystery that surrounds unusual scripts is highlighted by how one later writer saw Harriot's letters as 'like Devills'.

From these cases, we can see that a person requires great focus and dedication to learn, read, and write an invented script, and especially to use one to write an invented language at any length. Keeping track of an invented language that is consistent in its rules and vocabulary is hard enough work without the extra complication of an invented script. In the centuries covered by this book, invented or even existing scripts were usually only adopted by communities who needed to read religious texts as part of their faith – a strong motivation. At other times, they appear in works of fiction; even then, they are normally only deployed in a limited way. Although such methods sound like a good solution for hiding and transmitting knowledge, in reality, there are simpler and more efficient ways. They do, however, add a sense of mystery.

Other people created mysterious manuscripts as hoaxes. They produced these to dupe buyers, to create fame for themselves, and even to fight for a cause. In many cases, they included ciphers or other cryptic content specifically to intrigue and generate interest. Fraudsters were well aware that manuscripts with apparently mysterious content received extra attention from buyers. Sometimes, the people behind these frauds provided the reader with a 'way in' to the mystery – a hook. The creators of the Turpiana Tower parchment wrote Arabic clues explaining how to read the letters and words scattered across their grids, for example, while the Latin text gave the Church a reason to investigate further. Deliberate clues unlocked its revelations, further investing the religious authorities in its content, who, it was hoped, would then help to spread the cause of its creators. The parchment's archaic appearance and references to holy figures also contributed to the sense of mystery.

Other hoax manuscripts play similar tricks, but with no goal other than to earn money, their creators did not need to provide clues into a deeper mystery. These hoaxers invented hooks to lure people into buying existing, duller manuscripts. Whoever was behind 'The Subtelty of Witches' added a tantalizing fake title and author to an already enciphered manuscript to generate interest when selling it, tempting readers with hidden mystical knowledge. The creator of the *Lumen luminum*, attributed to Elias of Cortona, generated interest by adding this famous name from the past, as well as a holy monogram, combined with the extra spice of ciphers and alchemy. The enciphered *Libro del tesoro* was also associated with a famous name, and pretended to be much older – again, probably to help make it attractive to a buyer.

All of these hoax manuscripts use encipherment in a performance of secrecy. They appear to hide grand mysteries, locked away from prying eyes, but are designed to bring attention to themselves. When decrypted, often easily, their content is of little value, and sometimes completely unconnected to what made them intriguing in the first place. In other cases, the content is simply an extension of the fraud.

How, then, does the Voynich Manuscript fit into all of this? Is it an enciphered text, an artificial language and script, or a late medieval hoax? And why might someone have created it? Before attempting to answer these questions, it is crucial to gain a greater understanding of the manuscript's most probable context. Could this shed light on why it bears such an obscure script and intriguing illustrations? After all, context is key. With this in mind, over the following pages, I want to sketch out several areas of interest, related to context and content, that can only be dealt with briefly here, but which contribute to our understanding of the overall mystery.

THE VOYNICH MANUSCRIPT THROUGH FIFTEENTH-CENTURY EYES

On the weight of current evidence, the Voynich Manuscript was most probably produced in northern Italy during the early fifteenth century (with some southern Germanic influence on its content).[2]

So, it is important to explore what an educated and literate north Italian of that era would have understood or recognized when flicking through its folio pages. For certain, on first inspection of the manuscript, our reader would have identified obvious themed sections, just as we do today. These are herbal; bathing; astrological, astronomical, and cosmological; and pharmaceutical and recipes. As an avid book collector with a good knowledge of these various categories of texts and how people used them, what would our reader have found familiar or unusual about them? And in the end, when they turned its final page, would they have regarded the Voynich Manuscript as the world's most mysterious manuscript?

ILLUSTRATED HERBAL MANUSCRIPTS

If sufficiently well read – and let's assume that our reader is – they would see that the Voynich Manuscript's herbal section takes its inspiration from contemporary botanical works. The earliest reference to manuscripts of this kind was made by the Roman writer and philosopher Pliny the Elder in the first century AD, while an early example is Dioscorides' *De materia medica*, from the same period. This latter work was recopied for centuries across Europe and the Middle East, and was rarely illustrated. In the Middle Ages, people read it to learn which plants they could use for healing or their medical properties, and for knowing the names of plants in different languages. Another popular work was the Latin *Herbarium* of Pseudo-Apuleius, supposedly from the fourth century. This too was copied frequently but, unlike *De materia medica*, it was usually illustrated, even though its plant drawings do not often correspond to reality. By the late thirteenth century, a new form of herbal manuscript, known as the *tractatus de herbis*, brought together knowledge from different medical traditions – mainly Latin, Arabic, and Greek sources. The oldest-known example was produced in Salerno, in southern Italy, and contains illustrations that more closely resemble plants in nature.[3]

But it was only in the final decades of the fourteenth century and into the fifteenth century that illustrated herbal manuscripts became especially popular. The new naturalism in Italian art influenced the artists who produced illustrations for these manuscripts, while others continued to follow earlier traditions, taking a more schematic approach to presenting plants.[4] An offshoot of these new botanical works were the alchemical herbals, produced in northern Italy in the fifteenth century and perhaps made for physicians and pharmacists.[5] Twenty-four are known, and each contains the same text, broken into ninety-eight chapters, with illustrations produced to differing levels of quality. Although scribes usually wrote these alchemical herbals in Latin, a Hebrew edition is also known. As they were primarily medical works (with some application to alchemy), the illustrations focus particularly on the plants' roots, which people used in recipes for healing. Some of these bear human faces, or are combined with animals. Various animals can also be seen beside the plants, such as dragons and snakes, and even winged demons.[6] The *Erbario*, another early fifteenth-century Italian herbal manuscript that similarly features faces and other unusual elements in its illustrations, also provides instructions on how to prepare and use plants to heal people.[7]

Doctors and pharmacists did not usually consult the illustrations in herbal manuscripts to identify the plants they encountered; instead, the drawings helped them to remember the plants' uses, or functioned like an index to help the reader quickly navigate the book's content to find a particular cure. Indeed, drawings of roots intertwined with animals or bearing animal feet, as seen in the Voynich Manuscript and the alchemical herbals, highlighted which creatures these roots protected people from.[8] At the same time, the increasing access to classical medical texts in the fifteenth century led scholars to spot errors in earlier copies of herbal manuscripts. This spurred an interest in wanting to better identify the plants used in medicine, for a misidentified plant, created by an earlier copying error, could be a matter of life and death.[9] The Voynich Manuscript, then, would be useless to a physician who could not understand its text.

The *Herbal* of Manfred de Monte Imperiale, also called *Tractatus liber de herbis et plantis*, produced in the early fourteenth century in southern Italy, was inspired by the *tractatus de herbis* tradition.[10] It appears to have been a model for herbals produced in northern Italy after 1350: one manuscript based on it was likely made in Padua between 1376 and 1379. As with the alchemical herbals, scribes produced such books for physicians and pharmacists, but also for noble book collectors, who wished to show themselves as educated lovers of the most important forms of knowledge. Among this latter group, illustrated medical manuscripts were status symbols, such as the large *Carrara Herbal*, written in the Paduan dialect and produced for Francesco Novello II da Carrara, who ruled Padua until it was taken by Venice in 1405. Although this work is very different in size and artistry from the Voynich Manuscript, it illustrates how this subject matter could appeal to the most elite in society, at a time just before the Voynich Manuscript's creation. As an illustrated translation of an Arabic herbal treatise by Serapion, the *Carrara Herbal* was also unique, making it all the more valuable.[11]

Taking all of this into consideration, the Voynich Manuscript's herbal section would have intrigued our imagined reader because of the medical knowledge they would have expected to learn from it. But given that they would presume its content to be largely similar to other herbal manuscripts that they had read or owned, they would have been perplexed as to why its content was apparently enciphered. None of the other herbal scribes had felt the need to hide their work in this manner. Did this mean it bore secrets? Could something be learned from it that others did not know? Irrespective, one thing is clear: the Voynich Manuscript was produced in exactly the same place and at exactly the same time as when unique illustrated herbal manuscripts – ones that broke away from earlier traditions – were in vogue.

CRYPTIC MANUSCRIPTS ON BATHING

People visited bath houses for health reasons – our imagined Italian reader might even have frequented one – but illustrations in medieval manuscripts tend to focus on their recreational and sexual aspect. Near Naples, in the twelfth century, Petrus de Ebulo (*c.* 1160–1220) wrote an illustrated poem called *De balneis puteolanis*, which features images of male and female nude bathers, mixing together, in the baths at Puteoli (today's Pozzuoli). Such bathing resorts appalled early medieval Christians, because they were places of sex and inhibition, rather than being used for their intended medical purposes. Nonetheless, they became increasingly popular over the centuries.[12] Hundreds of years after Petrus de Ebulo, for example, the great fifteenth-century Italian manuscript hunter Poggio Bracciolini visited the baths at Baden, Germany, in the hope that it would ease the pains in his hand – perhaps arthritis – and noted female nudity.[13] Mixed bathing was not always the norm, however; certain baths in Italy were kept exclusively for women.[14]

Italy was Europe's major centre for balneological writings from the mid-fourteenth century and into the fifteenth century, primarily because of medical research at the universities of Padua and Bologna, and the popularity of mineral springs among both the rich and poor as places of healing. The Italian authors behind this new genre of writing – one dedicated to exploring the health benefits of baths – were usually physicians.[15] Roughly around the time of the Voynich Manuscript's production, our imagined reader would have been aware of Franciscus de Senis's *De balneis*; Petrus de Tussignano's *Liber de balneis Burmi*; Ugolino da Montecatini's *De balneorum italiae proprietatibus et virtutibus*; and Michele Savonarola's *De balneis et thermis naturalibus*, to name just four examples. The most popular bathing manuscripts, given the number of surviving editions, were slightly earlier in date; these were the *Tractatus primus et tractatus secundus de balneis* by Gentile da Foligno, from around 1348, and *De balneis Porrettae* by Tura de Castello, produced around 1353. Italian princes commissioned certain medicinal bathing treatises too.[16] In addition to prescribing bathing treatments to their patients (and writing treatises), physicians spent time advising authorities on their baths' infrastructures, and developing – or at least giving medical explanations for – new therapies, such as thermal showers meant to dispel humours from the brain, a practice that began in Tuscany at the end of the fourteenth century.[17]

In Germany, when Felix Hemmerli wrote his *Tractatus de balneis naturalibus* around 1450, he drew from earlier Italian works for its content.[18] German students, often after studying at Padua, copied such texts and brought them back to Germany across the fifteenth century, kickstarting an interest in medical spas in the second half of that century. Indeed, one copy of Gentile's *De balneis*, now in the Vatican Library, made around 1464 by a German medical student in Padua called Konrad Schelling, includes two slightly 'Voynich-esque' doodles of nude women in its margin, one with water pouring over her head from the spout of a barrel.[19] Copies of these medical texts are usually found in collective volumes, bringing together a variety of scientific knowledge.[20] They also tend to be unillustrated, being simple copies of the texts. Indeed, illustrations in any form showing bathing for medicinal purposes are rare.[21]

Our imagined reader, then, would not find a section on bathing in the Voynich Manuscript out of place for a northern Italian manuscript of the early fifteenth century, given the interest and specialization in this subject in that region and time. In fact, once again, it was a fashionable topic. Manuscripts dedicated to health, such as the illuminated *Tacuinum sanitatis*, had also become popular among elite collectors by the late fourteenth century.[22] Given that manuscripts on medicinal bathing usually lacked illustrations, the Voynich Manuscript's array of nude bathing women and their unusual positions might have piqued our reader's interest, enticing them to learn more about its content. They might have thought that it was

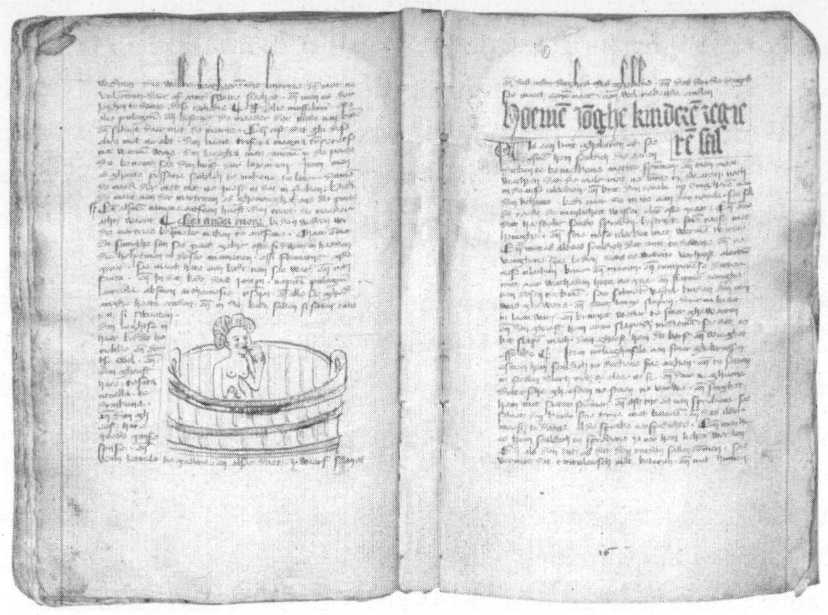

50. A therapeutic bathing scene from a 1399 Dutch manuscript edition of the *Trotula*.

dedicated to women's health, like the *Trotula*, a late twelfth-century compilation of three treatises on illnesses, treatments, and cosmetics for women, first produced in Salerno, near Naples. Popular for centuries, the *Trotula* prescribes herbal baths as a treatment for various health problems.[23] Nonetheless, our reader would still have been confused as to why the text was fully enciphered. If the content related to sexual or taboo matters, or women's health, would not only key words and sentences need to be hidden?

MANUSCRIPTS ON ASTROLOGY, ASTRONOMY, AND COSMOLOGY

Astrology played an important role in fifteenth-century Europe. People like our imagined reader believed that the movements of the heavenly bodies had a direct influence on every aspect of their lives.

Kings, princes, and lords consulted astrologers on the best time to travel or go to war, for predicting the weather and when their enemies might die, and also for medical help. To answer their clients' questions, astrologers made complex calculations based on the movements of planets and stars to produce horoscopes, which sometimes included simple ciphers. Many physicians used astrology in the course of their work too, and believed that the heavenly bodies impacted their patients' health by unbalancing the Galenic four humours – blood, phlegm, black bile, and yellow bile – causing sickness. Knowing the Moon's movement through the signs of the zodiac, for example, could help an astrologer predict how an illness might develop. To expand their knowledge, physician-astrologers copied out classical medical texts dedicated to health and healing, and compiled treatises for the elite. Although most physician-astrologers had studied at university, there were many others who were self-taught or out to con people. In the eyes of esteemed court astrologers, anyone who had not studied at university was basically a quack – in the sixteenth century, the physician Girolamo Cardano even complained about the complex and obscure works produced by such frauds.[24]

Across Europe, astrology was a major component of the arts and medical degrees taken by university students.[25] At the University of Bologna, during their four years of study, students read a wide range of astrological and astronomical textbooks, including Gerard of Cremona's *Theorica planetarum*, Johannes de Sacrobosco's *De sphaera*, Messahalla's *De astrolabio*, and various classical works by Euclid and Ptolemy.[26] The presence of sections on astrology and cosmology in the Voynich Manuscript would therefore not have surprised our imagined reader, given its wider medical theme. They might even have spotted diagrams and illustrations that reminded them of other books they had read. Circular diagrams or rotae, for example, are not unusual in medieval manuscripts. Inspired by the works of Isidore of Seville, who lived in the sixth and seventh centuries, writers used rotae to present information of many kinds, from the movement of winds to the ages of man.[27] Indeed, a Voynich illustration of what might be the four ages of man, all set within a crenellated ring around a sun (foldout folio 85r–86v), may have been inspired by older manuscripts, such as the four ages of women shown in the twelfth century *Tractatus de quaternario*. Equally, it may be a representation of the four humours.[28]

Illustrations similar to the Voynich Manuscript's zodiacs surrounded by concentric circles can be seen in other manuscripts, where they concern the position of stars in relation to constellations.[29] For example, one Greek copy of Ptolemy's *Handy Tables* – from the ninth century, but located in Italy during the fifteenth century – presents naked women in a ring around Helios, god of the Sun, and represents the movement of the Sun in zodiac signs.[30] Certain astrological motifs appear to have been inspired by other works. The Voynich Sagittarius, though shown wearing a Florentine archer's hat, carries a crossbow, following an art trend mainly known from manuscripts produced in German-speaking territories.[31] Meanwhile, at the bottom left of the manuscript's large foldout cosmological folio (85v and 86r), the artist drew a circle containing three further circles, two connected by lines. Resembling an off-centre clock face, this design might have been inspired by a work called *Picatrix* – an originally Arabic text on astrology and magic called *Ghāyat al-Ḥakīm*, translated into Latin by 1300.[32] Here, the symbol is associated with star spells, but it is also an alchemical symbol for potash, orpiment, or arsenic.[33]

In the early fifteenth century, people in Germanic-speaking territories owned manuscripts called *Volkskalender* ('people's calendars') and consulted them as reference works for practical astrological and medical advice, helpful in daily life. These manuscripts may have been another inspiration for the creator of the Voynich Manuscript. The earliest editions feature sections on measuring time, cosmology, tables for calculating the Moon's position and determining the date of Easter, and treatises on the planets and the signs of the zodiac. During the 1430s, expanded versions added medical advice, particularly on therapeutic bathing, unlucky days, and the four temperaments. *Volkskalender* manuscripts were mainly bought by the upper middle class – especially by travelling physicians, who consulted them to help diagnose and predict the fate of patients – as well as the aristocracy. But, due to their generally useful content, they appealed to anyone literate and with enough money to buy a copy. The *Volkskalender* could also be bound with other works, including unillustrated herbal texts; such editions may have been owned by apothecaries.[34]

In this section of the Voynich Manuscript, then, our imagined reader would have seen illustrations that were familiar in general style from contemporary astrological works produced in Italy and Germany, though their extremely unusual execution would have been puzzling. From the apparently enciphered text, the reader would have expected to learn about the movement of the Sun and Moon through the signs of the zodiac and how these affected their health, or perhaps how the stars impacted their life.

PHARMACEUTICAL AND RECIPE BOOKS

There was a tradition in medieval and early modern Italy for people to keep 'books of secrets', or recipe books, which families often passed down and added to for generations. The family of our imagined reader might even have had one. Mixing text in Latin and Italian, the contents of such books were usually eclectic. They covered topics like medicine (indeed, medical recipes were particularly popular), dyes, pharmaceuticals, cosmetics, and alchemy. Although people usually kept such recipe collections for personal use, they also drew from them to make concoctions for sale. One volume of medical recipes, written in the Venetian dialect, was produced by a scribe of the Benedictine Abbey of Santa Giustina in Padua towards the end of the fifteenth century; it covers recipes for eye problems, how to make plasters and bandages, drugs to take for a number of ailments, and the creation of unguents. Where it is possible to identify their owners, books of secrets often turn out to have been made by doctors, other health professionals, and members of the clergy.[35]

THE SCRIPT

Flicking through the Voynich Manuscript, our fifteenth-century Italian would have seen writing that, although unique, has similarities in its general appearance to *mercantesca*. North Italian merchants, artisans, and bankers chose this script when writing in the vernacular rather than Latin, and usually on paper instead of parchment. It is the script of account ledgers, diaries, treatises, and cookbooks, but was also used by people when copying out works of literature or writing in their notebooks to create miscellanies with drawings.[36] From a quick glance at the general appearance of the text, then, our imagined reader might have expected the Voynich Manuscript's content to be a miscellany of intriguing subjects, copied from other treatises.

Looking more closely, they would have recognized among its characters Latin shorthand symbols, which had already been in use for centuries. The Romans abbreviated Latin with symbols or letters – a system in which one letter could represent a whole word, while another could be a syllable. Other words were shortened and given a mark to show what the writer had done. The Voynich character that appears like a '9' at an angle is the same as the Latin abbreviation for 'con', 'cum', and 'com'. One that looks like two 'c's connected by a horizontal line can mean 'ra', 'ci', and 'cri'. In total, more than ten Voynich characters have similarities to Latin abbreviations.[37] Our reader might also have recognized certain characters as alchemical symbols. The Voynich character that looks like a '4' was used as 'Jupiter' and 'tin'; the '8' was white arsenic; while both '8' and '89', could represent 'salt'. One symbol – a vertical line attached to a 'P' (Currier symbol F) – looks like the alchemical symbol for 'to prepare', while a symbol that looks like a '9' and 'P' standing back to back

(Currier symbol P) is the alchemical symbol for urine.[38] It is possible, then, that, in addition to a knowledge of Latin shorthand, the author(s) of the Voynich script was aware of alchemical symbols.

A reader with experience in diplomatic or military circles would have known that the numbers and symbols that appear in Latin shorthand and alchemy also appear in fifteenth-century ciphers. In one Italian codebook, now in the Vatican Library, numbers stand for letters, and there is a large variety of symbols that, although never quite matching Voynich characters, certainly share similarities. Among them, there are the frequently used ligatures leading to symbols that appear like a 'P', while, on one occasion, the Voynich symbol that resembles a '9' and a 'P' standing back to back is present. There is also an example of three 'o's linked by a ligature standing for 'mm', reminiscent of the three 'c's linked by ligature in the Voynich Manuscript. Three linked 'c's stand for 'orator' in one Italian cipher; above this symbol on the same page, two linked 'c's represent the word 'legatus' – ambassador.[39]

So, although unique, certain Voynichese characters fit into the wider stylistic world of fifteenth-century Italian symbols used for shorthand, alchemy, and ciphers. Our educated reader, upon seeing these familiar characters, would probably have regarded the text as easily crackable, revealing the secrets behind the illustrations. But they would have been surprised by the extent of the apparently enciphered text. Enciphered correspondence was common and, as we have seen, people used ciphers to hide the odd sentence or words in manuscripts (particularly taboo words), but fully enciphered manuscripts were almost totally non-existent. If the reader searched hard enough, the only ones they might have encountered would have been the works of Giovanni Fontana – and, in Fontana's case, he invented his script from scratch, rather than using existing symbols (where would be the fun in that, Fontana might have said).

On the wider topic here, it must be remembered that writing – plain ordinary, unencoded, unenciphered writing in any popular

51. A fifteenth-century Italian cipher.

script – was, for much of history, a real mystery and 'cipher' to most people. In the late medieval and early modern eras, the widespread lack of literacy was a barrier to texts being read. Scholars estimate that the literacy rate in Italy from 1400 to 1500 was roughly 9–15 per cent, and for Germany, 6–9 per cent (though, as can be demonstrated for later centuries, literacy in the cities and towns was usually higher than in the countryside).[40] This means that writing in Greek, Hebrew, and Arabic, or indeed any script beyond the ones widely recognized in Europe, would have been an extremely secure way of transmitting information without the need for encipherment in an invented script. Heckius, for example, often wrote in Arabic script to 'encipher' his writings. This is an important point, given that some researchers see Voynichese as enciphered Hebrew or another language that uses a non-Latin script. There really was no need.

MATERIALS AND COST

The creator's (or scribes') decision to use parchment was an interesting choice, our reader might have thought. In around 1400, a sheet of parchment cost about the same as twenty-five sheets of paper; by 1450 it was the equivalent of fifty sheets of paper. In the 1410s, 90 per cent of all manuscripts in Austria and Switzerland were made from paper; in Germany it was 75 per cent. Parchment did remain in use – for example, in Florence – but mainly by booksellers who produced illuminated manuscripts for the rich. In the 1450s, a buyer in Florence could pick up a paper book on humanistic subjects for as little as 2 or 3 florins, while a noble had the option to commission a sumptuous humanistic text on parchment for around 50 florins.[41] Choosing parchment, in an era when paper was increasingly ubiquitous, would have brought attention to a manuscript as something special, and given it a sense of antiquity.[42] The *Erbario*, a herbal manuscript produced in fifteenth-century Italy with a roughly similar style of illustrations to the Voynich Manuscript, was made from paper, for example.[43]

It is difficult to estimate how much it would have cost to produce the Voynich Manuscript, as manuscripts were each unique, usually made according to a buyer's needs. Materials, labour, bindings, quality of the illustrations, and budget all made a difference. Examples of manuscripts produced in England reveal that paying for labour (including covering the scribes' food and drink) was roughly 74 per cent of the total cost. A scribe's ink and quill were reasonably cheap, while bindings of wood and leather were not overly expensive either.[44] In 1450s Florence, an expensive illuminated liturgical manuscript on parchment cost around 50 florins; Cosimo de Medici bought over one hundred manuscripts, their cost averaging out at about 14 florins per volume. To put all of this in context, the annual salary of a school teacher or banker was 40 to 60 florins; so, if you were on the lower end of that spectrum, a 20-florin parchment manuscript would have set you back half a year's wages.[45] Manuscripts, at least on parchment, were therefore out of reach for the vast majority of people in the era when the Voynich Manuscript was produced.

THE MANUSCRIPT AS A WHOLE

Overall, the presence in the Voynich Manuscript of sections dedicated to astrology/astronomy/cosmology, herbal medicine, and bathing, along with presumed recipes, would not have surprised an educated early fifteenth-century reader in northern Italy. The book's theme would have appeared medical, its content perhaps dedicated to women's health, and the herbal and bathing sections were particularly fashionable. It might not have been viewed as the world's most mysterious manuscript, but the illustrations were certainly unusual, while the apparently fully enciphered text implied that there was more to learn – perhaps something valuable. Given the presence of Latin shorthand and alchemical symbols, the reader would probably have felt able to decrypt its text, given enough time.

What might have bothered our reader, however, was that no scribe writing on these same topics had previously felt the need to fully encipher their work. There was no reason, or precedent, to do this. In fact, if a physician had produced something new, worthy of making an impact, you would expect them to want their writings and name to be known. In this era, there was a lot of competition among medical practitioners, and employment opportunities often came about because of a physician's prestige and word of mouth among clients, or because they held an influential university position.[46] If someone wanted to keep their writings secret, there had to be a reason. For this then, we need to look at the bigger picture: Italian manuscript culture in the early fifteenth century.

ITALIAN MANUSCRIPT COPYING AND COLLECTING

The fifteenth century was a time of great interest in Italy in manuscript collecting. Manuscript hunters travelled large distances across Europe in the hope of discovering the lost works of antiquity among the dusty shelves of old monasteries, copied from ancient scrolls during the first millennium and since forgotten. This craze began in earnest in 1416, when Poggio Bracciolini visited the Abbey of Saint Gall in Switzerland and discovered a complete copy of the twelve-volume *Institutio oratoria*, written by the Roman author Quintilian around AD 90. Although parts of this text were known, and highly prized due to its advice on rhetoric, the whole work had long been missing. After making this major discovery, Poggio travelled widely, seeking out further forgotten manuscripts. Whenever successful in his hunt, he bought the manuscript or made a copy, and sent his prize back to Florence. This was a major transformative event, opening up the wisdom of the ancients in a time when people believed it could not be recovered.[47]

Over the course of the fifteenth century, it became increasingly normal for merchants, artisans, and nobles to own a collection of books. It was also popular among students to collect textbooks for their professions, particularly in law, medicine, and theology. Humanists, meanwhile, collected manuscripts in various languages, mainly Latin and Greek, and compared their content to identify differences between the copies. This love of books spread to the highest levels of society, becoming a fashion that continued for centuries. Princes and nobles wanted to be seen as cultured, displaying their collections in libraries to impress visitors. In the early phase of this collecting craze, these books often lacked illustrations – it was the content that mattered. But this soon gave way to collecting books for their aesthetic appeal, to have as many as possible, or even for nationalistic reasons. Rich collectors, and in particular the princes of Italy, prized manuscripts that were especially rare or beautiful – manuscripts that made their libraries unique, that other collectors lacked, and that would impress people. Assembling libraries became a competition, a way of proclaiming status and learning, even if the owner never read the books or cared about their contents. This all made the buying and selling of manuscripts big business, with booksellers such as the famous Vespasiano da Bisticci of Florence (1421–98) employing book hunters and their own copyists.[48]

Notable among the Italian princes, the Duke of Urbino, Federico da Montefeltro (1422–82) invested a great deal of money in securing rare books for his collection; somewhat earlier, in Florence, Cosimo de Medici (1389–1464) began his own grand manuscript collection, despite probably not being able to read Latin, which was continued by his grandson Lorenzo de Medici (1449–92). An inventory written in 1436, detailing the collection of the princes of Ferrara, describes the appearance of their manuscripts at length, but says hardly anything about their contents – a telling insight into what they prized the most. Manuscripts were also often rebound to match the others in a prince's collection. The bindings had to look particularly attractive.[49]

Beyond works in Latin, collectors sought Greek manuscripts for their libraries, despite not being able to read the language.[50] There were few Greek manuscripts in libraries of the early fifteenth century, but their numbers increased as the years progressed, beginning primarily with the collection built by the humanist Niccolò Niccoli (1364–1437) in Florence. Later, it was not unusual to find hundreds of Greek manuscripts in a library, with the city of Ferrara becoming a major centre for their study. Hebrew was also of interest to collectors. The philosopher Giovanni Pico della Mirandola owned over a hundred Hebrew works, and the Duke of Urbino had nearly as many. Manuscripts in Arabic and Aramaic were much rarer, though Pico kept some in his library.

Italian princes also collected manuscripts written in the various dialects spoken across the country. Works of classical Latin and Greek were translated into these dialects, as well as contemporary texts composed in Latin. The dukes of Ferrara owned many such works, as well as manuscripts in French dialects, Catalan, and Spanish.[51] Some books in the collection of the dukes of Urbino were written in Coptic.[52] Occasionally, the language in which a manuscript was written was not clear to those compiling the inventories – two manuscripts in the collection of the Visconti family at Pavia in 1426, for example, were catalogued as written in Greek or Hebrew.[53]

Most collections in Italian princely libraries covered similar subjects: sacred literature, mathematics, geometry, and cosmography, and works classified as 'humane literature', consisting of philosophy, poetry, rhetoric, grammar, and history. Medicine could form its own category, fitted in after religious writings and before law and cosmography. Other collections included sections on natural philosophy, astrology, and geomancy. Federico, Duke of Urbino, is said to have owned works by every astrological author, and interest in this subject was widespread among his collecting contemporaries. Medical treatises were also popular among book collectors and humanists, particularly manuscripts written after the Black Death dedicated to preventing illnesses and improving hygiene, and works listing medical recipes and useful herbs. Medical works translated from Greek and

Arabic became fashionable in Italy too, with the academic Giorgio Valla owning a collection. The dukes of Este held many medical books in their library, likely out of a desire to keep themselves safe from the plague, which returned with alarming regularity. Finally, princely libraries contained books on magic, divination, and alchemy too.[54]

Although no one would have mistaken the Voynich Manuscript as a long-lost classical text, it would certainly have ticked the boxes for unusual content and rarity. This might have been enough to impress a prince eager to bolster his collection with works that his competitors did not own and could not find. It is a pity, then, that its original bindings do not survive, for these would have given us an insight into how attractive it once appeared. After all, it would not have mattered to most princes or wealthy collectors that no one could read its content.

UNBREAKABLE?

This book is not about solving the Voynich mystery, but rather about telling its story and exploring the stories of similarly mysterious manuscripts. However, it would be wrong to have journeyed so far and not to offer some thoughts. Here is my take – let's call it a contribution, rather than a solution – to add to the whirlpool of theories.

First, let's summarize what we have learned. The Voynich Manuscript was most probably produced in northern Italy during the early fifteenth century. Its script strongly resembles a cipher and is influenced by the types of characters used for enciphered communications in Italy, including Latin shorthand and alchemical symbols. It also features invented, creative characters, unknown from any other script. At this time in Europe, only the nobles of Italy were experimenting with increasingly complex ciphers, which again suggests this location as the manuscript's place of creation. If its content were copied from anywhere further afield, the script used (such as Arabic or Hebrew) would have been more than enough of a cipher to the vast majority of European readers, rendering special encipherment pointless.

The scribes, or whoever commissioned the manuscript, appear to have mined various sources to produce its content. They based the herbal section on the contemporary Italian tradition of alchemical herbals, while the bathing section was probably inspired by writings about therapeutic bathing, a popular subject in Italy from the mid-fourteenth century to the mid-fifteenth century. The astrological, astronomical, and cosmological content is built around features like rotae, common in medieval works on these subjects, where they usually communicated information about the movement of heavenly bodies to readers. Little sense can be taken from them in the Voynich Manuscript, however, beyond the presence of stars and the Sun. For the illustrations of the zodiac signs, the scribes may have drawn from manuscripts produced in Germanic-speaking territories. Other symbols and motifs were seemingly taken from diverse sources. In all cases, the artist took inspiration from these manuscripts and adapted them, creating something recognizable enough, but unusual and unique. This adds to the Voynich Manuscript's mystery, but not so much that it makes its content appear alien or inscrutable. A fifteenth-century reader would have understood much from glancing through its illustrations.

Taken as a whole, the manuscript appears to be a medical compendium, perhaps dedicated to women's health. The herbal, bathing, and recipes sections can all be tied together by herbal bathing for medical reasons, as mentioned in the popular *Trotula*. The cosmological, astronomical, and astrological content also match a medical function, for these would have provided the reader with the best times to create concoctions and herbal baths, or to better understand the progression of certain illnesses. None of this content would have been useful to its owner if they could not read the text, however; but, given that taboo, sexual, or potentially harmful topics in medical texts were routinely enciphered, this would not have appeared unusual, beyond its sheer extent.

Nonetheless, complex encipherment did not yet exist in Europe – at least, not to a level that could withstand over a century of attacks from professional codebreakers and modern computing power. As we have seen, the way that people used encipherment in the fifteenth century (and beyond) makes Voynichese unlikely to be a cipher. Authors did not employ such methods to write lengthy texts: it made reading and writing overly difficult, and there was little point in making all the content secret. In fact, it would realistically have brought unwanted attention to the text.

Furthermore, although artificial scripts did exist, it was rare for someone to write extensively using one (an exception might arise when a community without a script adopted one for religious reasons, usually following conversion to Christianity). Learning an artificial script to write an existing language is a massive effort, and it seems unlikely that a community would do this to produce a medical work on herbal therapeutic bathing and leave no other trace of their existence. Why endure such pain, when writing the language's words in a commonly understood script would have been much faster and simpler? Similarly, given its apparent themes, it is unlikely that the Voynich Manuscript would be an early artificial script and language, perhaps copied anew during the first half of the fifteenth century. On the whole, medieval scribes used ciphers and unusual scripts for fun – they were a playful way to add variety and beauty to their manuscripts – and Voynichese has little in common with the magical scripts, symbols, and 'exotic' alphabets popular in medieval and early modern Europe. In addition, attempts to invent a universal language and script are rare before the seventeenth century.

Could the Voynich Manuscript be a work of steganography? Ignoring the fact that Trithemius invented this method of concealed writing decades after the Voynich Manuscript was produced, the notion that it could hide content, spread out across its words with the rest simply being filler, has been raised over the years. It could be one reason why some statistical analyses of the text indicate nothing but gibberish.[55] Indeed, a study by Jürgen Hermes has shown that a method of encryption similar to those described by Trithemius in *Polygraphia*'s third book – replacing letters with invented words – can have statistical properties similar to those found in the Voynich text. But, as Hermes notes, using tables to produce a manuscript the length of the Voynich Manuscript would be a tremendous effort.[56] How steganography was meant to be used also needs to be considered. Trithemius invented his concealed writing for people to hide short messages in letters, not across the pages of a whole manuscript. Going to the expense of producing the Voynich Manuscript – the hours spent illustrating and writing, the cost of the parchment and other materials – to conceal a message for the restricted readership who would see the book makes little sense. It would be more believable if the manuscript had been copied and dispersed extensively, spreading a hidden message over great distances to initiates in its encryption method, but this is not the case.

The manuscript's illustrations might purposely give away clues about its content, while hinting that there is more to be learned from its text. But, if it is a hoax, its illustrations could be the 'way in' to the mystery, designed to intrigue a buyer. They are unusual, yet understandable. Rough yet mesmerizing. Just like today, they draw you in and make you want to know more. If the illustrations alone could intrigue, the content did not need to say anything – simply having the appearance of a cipher, with certain recognizable symbols, would be enough to appeal to a person's curiosity, building an expectation that they could break the cipher and release its secrets. This is important because, as a medical treatise, the manuscript would be useless without access to its content.

Whoever commissioned or produced the manuscript had enough money to buy good-quality (but not the highest quality) parchment, complete with impressive foldout sections, and perhaps had it all bound in wood and leather. It would not have looked cheap. Indeed, the use of parchment implies exclusivity and antiquity – a manuscript out of reach of regular people, who could not afford to buy or create it. If a group of scribes had used their own resources, this would have kept production costs low and sped up the production time, maximizing profit. Given that they knew the popular topics of their day, and drew on them for inspiration, they might have had access to a noble or university library, or to the manuscripts kept in book stores for copying by in-house scribes.

Could the Voynich Manuscript simply be an enciphered notebook of someone's thoughts and reading, copied from diverse sources? Given that five scribes shared the job of writing out its content, it would have to be a copy of a notebook that already existed. It was not unusual for notebooks to pass down through family lines, with different people adding to them over the years, and sometimes old notebooks were copied out onto parchment to make a good-quality edition for the family's library. Nonetheless, the Voynich Manuscript does not cover such a wide variety of topics as found in such notebooks. Instead, it appears to present material of interest to students, scholars, physicians, and book collectors, and has an organized structure, rather than being a collection of notes.[57] Also, if it were an enciphered notebook, in the early fifteenth century it would more likely have been written on paper, a much cheaper medium, and would be easy to decrypt. Likewise, if it was simply an attempt by someone to write some content for personal use in an artificial language and script, parchment would again have been an unnecessary extravagance, just as it would have been if someone simply found an unusual unreadable manuscript and made their own copy. The materials used argue against these interpretations.

Finally, in early fifteenth-century Italy, there would have been a large market for the Voynich Manuscript, one not present in earlier centuries. This was a time when rich collectors were searching for rare or unusual manuscripts that would separate them from their rivals, when book buying was an expanding activity, even among students, physicians, and academics. From this perspective, the world's most mysterious manuscript, appearing at the exact time and place when the rich were actively searching for the world's most mysterious manuscripts, appears too much of a coincidence.

So where does this leave us? Perhaps the Voynich Manuscript is a unique example of an otherwise unknown encryption method, designed by an equally unknown genius. Perhaps someone, or a group of people, experimented with developing an artificial language and script, then vanished from history. Perhaps its content comes from somewhere beyond Europe, but was recopied and interpreted through a European lens. Each is a possible explanation for the manuscript's unusual content – after all, we do not have all the pieces of the puzzle and, frankly, we never will.

This makes reaching conclusions a shaky undertaking. But, based on the current weight of the evidence, and the testimony of the manuscripts we have explored in this book, if I had to choose whether the Voynich Manuscript is an enciphered text, an artificial language and script, or a late medieval hoax, I would be forced to pick the hoax. As we have seen, hoaxers and frauds were just as common in the past as today. With this in mind, it is significant (and suspicious) that the manuscript's content reflects contemporary interests, particularly the herbal and bathing sections, which were fashionable in early fifteenth-century Italy. To a hoaxer, the inclusion of an apparent cipher text – again, a growing interest among the elite – would also have had the added benefit of generating more interest in the manuscript than if its content were simply a copy of existing, known material.

If we assume for the moment that the Voynich Manuscript is indeed a hoax, the scribes probably used the self-citation method to write the content. This appears to be the most sensible, simple, and elegant solution, and matches some of the statistical studies conducted in recent years. Why there appear to be two different 'languages' in the script is harder to explain. I suggest that the scribes closely drew from existing manuscripts for their inspiration; so, when writing in Voynichese, they might have been subliminally influenced by the words and sentences before them – their appearance, syntax, and grammar – which might have sometimes been Latin, sometimes vernacular Italian, and at other times German. Similarly, if one scribe was of a different cultural and linguistic background, this could potentially have influenced how, unconsciously, he might have expected the script to appear, compared to someone of Italian heritage.

Could the Voynich Manuscript therefore be unbreakable, a fraud created by a group of enterprising scribes wanting to earn some florins by cashing in on the interests of their day? If so, it might have been made to play on a noble's interest in unique and mysterious manuscripts, a rich man who judged his purchases based on a manuscript's rarity rather than its content. A wealthy buyer, or perhaps even a physician, would have seen an unknown compendium of medical treatises, perhaps dedicated to women's health, featuring unusual herbal illustrations and suggesting innovative cures; astrological, astronomical, and cosmological charts that could predict the best times to concoct medical recipes; and nude bathing women, appealing to the contemporary interest in writings on therapeutic bathing and sexological texts. The enciphered writing itself would appear familiar enough, implying hidden treasures behind the characters, but, in reality, it could never be cracked.

Another option is that a physician commissioned the Voynich Manuscript to generate interest in his knowledge while searching for a wealthy patron in Italy's competitive medical marketplace. This would be similar to how engineers produced manuscripts to show off their work. Although this was not a normal practice for doctors, some, like Fontana and Heckius, had an interest in engineering, showing how ideas like this might have travelled. If so, an itinerant physician might have applied the notion of engineering manuscripts as advertisements of skill to the medical world, using fake enciphered writing to hint at deeper knowledge, and illustrations inspired by manuscripts like the Italian alchemical herbals and German *Volkskalender* to highlight the extent of his learning without giving away any of the details. In this case, truly enciphered text was unnecessary – if you wanted access to this knowledge, you had to hire the physician. In either case, the Voynich Manuscript would be an example of secrecy as performance, designed to intrigue but holding no deeper meaning. It would be an elegant hoax.

All that said, we are far from having all the pieces of the puzzle, and new discoveries can quickly change the state of our knowledge. Experts will continue to investigate the Voynich Manuscript's folio pages for years to come. New research papers will be published. Theories will come and go. As a lover of the Voynich mystery, I would like nothing more than for the Voynich Manuscript to be a deviously complex cipher, hiding exotic secrets from far beyond Europe, or a mysterious language and script, unknown and potentially transformative of our knowledge of the late Middle Ages, all connected to a famous individual like John Dee or Roger Bacon. But to me, at least for the moment, the evidence sadly does not lead in that direction.

I sincerely hope I'm wrong.[58]

NOTES

INTRODUCTION

1. Raymond Clemens, 'The World's Most Mysterious Manuscript' in Raymond Clemens (ed.), *The Voynich Manuscript* (Yale University Press, New Haven and London, 2016), pp. 56–7.
2. Edwin Battistella, 'Codes and Ciphers', *OUPblog*, 5 January 2020, https://blog.oup.com/2020/01/codes-and-ciphers/.
3. Kirsten Møllegaard, Evangeline Lemieux, and Braden Savage, 'Posthumanism and the Search for Meaning in Luigi Serafini's *Codex Seraphinianus*', *International Journal of Literary Humanities,* 22 (2024), pp. 173–93; Jeffrey Christopher Stanley, 'To Read Images Not Words: Computer-Aided Analysis of the Handwriting in the *Codex Seraphinianus*', MSc dissertation, North Carolina State University (2010), pp. 6–9.
4. See, for example, Philip Neal, 'Voynich Sources', http://philipneal.net/voynichsources/, who also discusses Johannes Trithemius, John Dee, Giovanni Fontana, and Hildegard of Bingen.

1. THE *LINGUA IGNOTA* AND *LITTERAE IGNOTAE*

1. These events are found in Hildegard's *Scivias* and *Vita*. See Sabina Flanagan, *Hildegard of Bingen: A Visionary Life*, 2nd edn (Routledge, London and New York, 1998), pp. 18–19, 29; Mark Atherton, *Hildegard of Bingen: Selected Writings* (Penguin, London, 2001), pp. 190–2.
2. Michael Embach, 'The Life of Hildegard of Bingen (1098–1179)' in Jennifer Bain (ed.), *The Cambridge Companion to Hildegard of Bingen* (Cambridge University Press, Cambridge, 2021), pp. 11–19; Vincent J. Corrigan, 'Hildegard of Bingen' in Lister M. Matheson (ed.), *Icons of the Middle Ages: Rulers, Writers, Rebels, and Saints*, 2 vols (Greenwood, Santa Barbara, 2011), vol. 2, p. 363; Flanagan, *Hildegard of Bingen*, p. 19; Fiona Maddocks, *Hildegard of Bingen* (Review, London, 2002), pp. 27–30.
3. Embach, 'Life of Hildegard', p. 20; Flanagan, *Hildegard of Bingen*, pp. 2–3.
4. Hildegard, *Scivias*, preface. For the text, see the Library of Latin Texts; Atherton, *Hildegard of Bingen*, pp. 191–2.
5. Flanagan, *Hildegard of Bingen*, pp. 3, 148.
6. Flanagan, *Hildegard of Bingen*, pp. 3–4.

7. Flanagan, *Hildegard of Bingen*, pp. xi, 31–2, 39.
8. Embach, 'Life of Hildegard', pp. 23–5; Flanagan, *Hildegard of Bingen*, p. 4.
9. Maddocks, *Hildegard of Bingen*, p. 91.
10. Embach, 'Life of Hildegard', pp. 25–7; Maddocks, *Hildegard of Bingen*, pp. 93–5, 128.
11. Flanagan, *Hildegard of Bingen*, p. 5; Sarah L. Higley, *Hildegard of Bingen's Unknown Language: An Edition, Translation, and Discussion* (Palgrave Macmillan, New York, 2007), p. 22.
12. Honey Meconi, *Hildegard of Bingen* (University of Illinois Press, Urbana, 2018), p. 44; Higley, *Hildegard of Bingen's Unknown Language*, p. 21.
13. Laurence Moulinier, 'Un lexique "trilingue" du XIIe siècle: la "lingua ignota" de Hildegarde de Bingen' in Jacqueline Hamesse and Danielle Jacquart (eds), *Lexiques bilingues dans les domaines philosophique et scientifique (Moyen Âge–Renaissance)* (Brepols, Turnhout, 2001), pp. 89–111.
14. Higley, *Hildegard of Bingen's Unknown Language*, p. 23.
15. Higley, *Hildegard of Bingen's Unknown Language*, pp. 24–7; Michael Embach, *Die Schriften Hildegards von Bingen. Studien zu ihrer Überlieferung im Mittelalter und in der Frühen Neuzeit* (Akademie Verlag, Berlin, 2010), p. 261; Moulinier, 'Un lexique "trilingue"', pp. 89–111.
16. Jonathan P. Green, 'A New Gloss on Hildegard of Bingen's Lingua Ignota', *Viator*, 36 (2005), p. 226.
17. Higley, *Hildegard of Bingen's Unknown Language*, pp. 21–2, 60. Meconi, *Hildegard of Bingen*, p. 44.
18. This is found in the *Riesencodex* version: see Embach, *Die Schriften Hildegards*, p. 284.
19. Higley, *Hildegard of Bingen's Unknown Language*, pp. 60–2.
20. Joseph L. Baird and Radd K. Ehrman, *The Letters of Hildegard of Bingen*, vol. 3 (Oxford University Press, New York, 2004), pp. 40–1 (letter 241r).
21. Württembergische Landesbibliothek Stuttgart, Codex theol. et phil. 4° 253, folio 75v, line 5: see https://digital.wlb-stuttgart.de/sammlungen/sammlungsliste/werksansicht?id=6&tx_dlf%5Border%5D=title&tx_dlf%5Bid%5D=14413&tx_dlf%5Bpage%5D=162. See also Embach, *Die Schriften Hildegards*, p. 259.
22. Green, 'A New Gloss', pp. 225–6; Moulinier, 'Un lexique "trilingue"', pp. 89–111.
23. Green, 'A New Gloss', p. 226; Embach, *Die Schriften Hildegards*, p. 260; Moulinier, 'Un lexique "trilingue"', pp. 89–111.
24. Embach, *Die Schriften Hildegards*, pp. 261, 285.
25. The *Riesencodex* (Hochschul-und Landesbibliothek RheinMain, Wiesbaden, HS 2), the Berlin Manuscript, and the later copy of the now lost Vienna Codex.
26. Österreichische Nationalbibliothek, Vienna, Cod. 1016, folios 116r–121r; see Embach, *Die Schriften Hildegards*, pp. 282–3. For a description of the manuscripts that contain the unknown alphabet, see Higley, *Hildegard of Bingen's Unknown Language*, p. 146.
27. Higley, *Hildegard of Bingen's Unknown Language*, pp. 9, 22.
28. Embach, *Die Schriften Hildegards*, p. 253.
29. Flanagan, *Hildegard of Bingen*, p. 5 and p. 162, n. 2; Moulinier, 'Un lexique "trilingue"', pp. 89–111.
30. Green, 'A New Gloss', pp. 225, 229–32.

31. Green, 'A New Gloss', pp. 217–21, 225, 228; Embach, *Die Schriften Hildegards*, pp. 266–71; Higley, *Hildegard of Bingen's Unknown Language*, p. 5.
32. Moulinier, 'Un lexique "trilingue"', pp. 89–111; Patrizia Lendinara, 'The Poem "Nauta rudis . . ." in Anglo-Saxon Manuscripts: More than a Colophon' in Concetta Giliberto and Loredana Teresi (eds), *Limits to Learning: The Transfer of Encyclopaedic Knowledge in the Early Middle Ages* (Peeters, Leuven 2013), pp. 229–31.
33. Stephen Bax, 'A Proposed Partial Decoding of the Voynich Script', Stephenbax.net, 2014, p. 53, https://stephenbax.net/wp-content/uploads/2014/01/Voynich-a-provisional-partial-decoding-BAX.pdf; Phil Booth, 'Cyril and Methodius, Sts (826/7–69 and c.815–85)' in Andrew Louth (ed.), *The Oxford Dictionary of the Christian Church*, 4th edn (Oxford University Press, Oxford, 2022); Gordon Campbell, 'Slovakia, Christianity in' in Louth, *Oxford Dictionary of the Christian Church*.
34. Lendinara, 'The Poem "Nauta rudis . . ."', pp. 231–3; Raymond Ian Page, *An Introduction to English Runes*, 2nd edn (Boydell Press, Woodbridge, 1999), pp. 86–7.
35. Stephen J. Harris, 'Anglo-Saxon Ciphers' in Katherine Ellison and Susan Kim (eds), *A Material History of Medieval and Early Modern Ciphers: Cryptography and the History of Literacy* (Routledge, New York and London, 2017), pp. 65–79.
36. David A. King, *The Ciphers of the Monks: A Forgotten Number-Notation of the Middle Ages* (Franz Steiner, Stuttgart, 2001), p. 29 and chapter 1 for an explanation of the system with diagrams.
37. British Library, London, Add MS 9046, https://iiif.bl.uk/uv/#?manifest=https://bl.digirati.io/iiif/ark:/81055/vdc_100059142966.0x000001. See also Kate Thomas, 'How Many Alphabets?', Medieval Manuscripts Blog, *British Library*, 2019, https://blogs.bl.uk/digitisedmanuscripts/2019/05/how-many-alphabets.html.
38. Paul Henry Saenger, *Space Between Words: The Origins of Silent Reading* (Stanford University Press, Stanford, 1997), p. 118.
39. See, for example, Codex Igo (British Library, London, Sloane MS 1360) and a prayer book now in Montreal's McGill University, McClennan Library, MS G 177. Both are listed on Klaus Schmeh's Encrypted Book List, https://scienceblogs.de/klausis-krypto-kolumne/klaus-schmehs-list-of-encrypted-books/.
40. Katherine Ellison, *A Cultural History of Early Modern English Cryptography Manuals* (Routledge, Abingdon, 2017), pp. 48, 69–70, 159; John Dooley, *History of Cryptography and Cryptanalysis: Codes, Ciphers, and Their Algorithms* (Springer, Cham, 2018), pp. 15–18.
41. Ibrahim A. Al-Kadit, 'Origins of Cryptology: The Arab Contributions', *Cryptologia*, 16, no. 2 (1992), pp. 98–9, 104–13.
42. David Kahn, *The Codebreakers: The Story of Secret Writing*, rev. edn (Scribner, New York, 1996), chapter 2.
43. Al-Kadit, 'Origins of Cryptology', pp. 113–20.
44. Meconi, *Hildegard of Bingen*, pp. 41–3, 45–51; Atherton, *Hildegard of Bingen*, pp. 106, 108–10; Kenneth F. Kitchell and Irven M. Resnick, 'Hildegard as Medieval "Zoologist": The Animals of the Physica' in Maud Burnett McInerney (ed.), *Hildegard of Bingen: A Book of Essays* (Garland Publishing, New York and

London, 1998), pp. 27, 47; Lynn Thorndike, *A History of Magic and Experimental Science*, 8 vols (Columbia University Press, New York and London, 1923–58), vol. 2, pp. 134–5; Maddocks, *Hildegard of Bingen*, p. 198.

45. Maddocks, *Hildegard of Bingen*, p. 214.
46. Atherton, *Hildegard of Bingen*, pp. xxxiv–xxxvi.
47. Flanagan, *Hildegard of Bingen*, p. 108.
48. Embach, 'Life of Hildegard', pp. 28–30; Maddocks, *Hildegard of Bingen*, pp. 222–6.
49. Embach, 'Life of Hildegard', pp. 30–1, 34–5; Maddocks, *Hildegard of Bingen*, pp. 248, 253.
50. Higley, *Hildegard of Bingen's Unknown Language*, p. 146; Embach, *Die Schriften Hildegards*, p. 61. This manuscript was Wiener Handschrift Rec. 33.
51. Higley, *Hildegard of Bingen's Unknown Language*, p. 148. This manuscript is now Berlin State Library Lat. Quart. 674.
52. Embach, *Die Schriften Hildegards*, pp. 49–50, 52.
53. They can be found on folios 461v–464v. See Embach, *Die Schriften Hildegards*, p. 63.
54. Embach, *Die Schriften Hildegards*, p. 53. For the page, see folio 308r, after the seventh line: Hochschul- und Landesbibliothek RheinMain HS 2, https://hlbrm.digitale-sammlungen.hebis.de/handschriften-hlbrm/content/pageview/450244.
55. Embach, *Die Schriften Hildegards*, pp. 43–4, 55, 57.
56. Embach, *Die Schriften Hildegards*, pp. 58, 60, 254–5. Trithemius's copy of the manuscript is now in the British Library, London, Add MS 15102.
57. Embach, *Die Schriften Hildegards*, p. 60; Embach, 'Life of Hildegard', p. 34.
58. Embach, 'Life of Hildegard', pp. 30–1, 34–5; Maddocks, *Hildegard of Bingen*, pp. 248, 253.
59. Like the earlier addition, this too was written on the recto of the first folio: see Embach, *Die Schriften Hildegards*, p. 60.
60. Embach, *Die Schriften Hildegards*, p. 60.
61. Jennifer Bain, 'History of a Book: Hildegard of Bingen's "Riesencodex" and World War II', *Plainsong and Medieval Music*, 27, no. 2 (2018), pp. 143–4.
62. Bain, 'History of a Book', pp. 146–7, 150, 156.
63. Bain, 'History of a Book', p. 157.
64. Bain, 'History of a Book', pp. 158–61.
65. Bain, 'History of a Book', pp. 161–6.
66. A digital edition can be found here at https://hlbrm.digitale-sammlungen.hebis.de/handschriften-hlbrm/content/titleinfo/449618.

2. THE VOYNICH MANUSCRIPT

1. Paula Zyats et al., 'Physical Findings' in Raymond Clemens (ed.), *The Voynich Manuscript* (Yale University Press, New Haven and London, 2016), pp. 24, 26–7. Lisa Fagin Davis, 'How Many Glyphs and How Many Scribes: Digital Paleography and the Voynich Manuscript', *Manuscript Studies*, 5, no. 1 (2020), pp. 164–80. For northern Italy as the manuscript's most probable place of production, see Chapter 10 in this volume.
2. For a detailed overview of the manuscript, see MS 408 in Beinecke Rare Book and Manuscript Library, Yale University, https://pre1600ms.beinecke.library.

yale.edu/docs/pre1600.ms408.HTM. See also René Zandbergen, 'The Origin of the Voynich MS', 2022, https://www.voynich.nu/origin.html.

3. See, for example, Robert S. Brumbaugh, *The Most Mysterious Manuscript: The Voynich 'Roger Bacon' Cipher Manuscript* (Southern Illinois University Press, Carbondale, IL, 1978); Robert S. Brumbaugh, 'The Voynich Cipher Manuscript: A Current Report', *Yale University Library Gazette*, 61, nos 3–4 (1987), p. 93.
4. Folio 34v has roots that appear like two four-legged animals; folio 90v has animal-like roots with claws; folio 46v has roots that resemble wings. For a discussion of such features, see Mary E. D'Imperio, *The Voynich Manuscript: An Elegant Enigma* (National Security Agency/Central Security Service, Fort George E. Mead, MD, 1978), p. 15.
5. D'Imperio, *Voynich Manuscript*, p. 21.
6. D'Imperio, *Voynich Manuscript*, p. 17.
7. Robert S. Brumbaugh, 'The Solution of the Voynich "Roger Bacon" Cipher', *Yale University Library Gazette*, 49, no. 4 (1975), p. 349. Capricorn and Aquarius are missing, but were perhaps once present on the lost folio 74. Raymond Clemens, 'Preface' in Clemens, *The Voynich Manuscript*, p. xvi.
8. See D'Imperio, *Voynich Manuscript*, p. 20.
9. D'Imperio, *Voynich Manuscript*, pp. 15–16. For examples, see D'Imperio's section 8.8.
10. D'Imperio, *Voynich Manuscript*, pp. 94–5.
11. D'Imperio, *Voynich Manuscript*, pp. 23–5; René Zandbergen, 'Text Analysis: The Writing System', 2024, https://www.voynich.nu/writing.html; René Zandbergen, 'Text Analysis: Transliteration of the Text', 2023, https://www.voynich.nu/transcr.html; Davis, 'How Many Glyphs and How Many Scribes', pp. 168–9.
12. McCrone Associates, Inc., 'Materials Analysis of the Voynich Manuscript', 2009, https://beinecke.library.yale.edu/sites/default/files/files/voynich_analysis.pdf; Clemens, 'Preface', p. xiv; Davis, 'How Many Glyphs and How Many Scribes'.
13. Zyats et al., 'Physical Findings', pp. 25–6.
14. In a letter written by Johannes Marcus Marci to Athanasius Kircher on 19 August 1665 in Prague, the sale is recorded as 600 ducats. However, Stefan Guzy argues that this is too much for a single manuscript and that, because both ducats and florins are gold coins, the general sense of gold coins was meant in the Marci letter. Stefan Guzy, 'Book Transactions of Emperor Rudolf II, 1576–1612: New Findings on the Earliest Ownership of the Voynich Manuscript' in Colin Layfield and John Abela (eds), *International Conference on the Voynich Manuscript 2022*, CEUR Workshop Proceedings, 2022, https://ceur-ws.org/Vol-3313/paper16.pdf. See also Garry Shaw, 'Unknown History of 600-Year-Old, Coded Voynich Manuscript Revealed by Researcher', *Art Newspaper*, 13 January 2023, https://www.theartnewspaper.com/2023/01/13/unknown-history-of-600-year-old-coded-voynich-manuscript-revealed-by-researcher.
15. The amount paid and its ownership under Rudolf II are mentioned in Marci's letter to Kircher (see previous note), found with the manuscript. See Wilfrid M. Voynich, 'A Preliminary Sketch of the History of the Roger Bacon Cipher

Manuscript', *Transactions of the College of Physicians of Philadelphia*, 3rd series, 43 (1921), p. 417.

16. Guzy, 'Book Transactions of Emperor Rudolf II'; René Zandbergen, 'The Voynich MS – Biographies', 2024, http://www.voynich.nu/curricula.html.
17. Guzy, 'Book Transactions of Emperor Rudolf II'.
18. For this reconstruction of events, I have followed René Zandbergen, 'Special Topics: Related to the Origin of the MS', 2017, https://www.voynich.nu/extra/sp_origin.html and 'The Origin of the Voynich MS', https://www.voynich.nu/origin.html. For 'Rot', see folio 4r, with a potential, much fainter, example on folio 7r. For potential examples of 'G', see folios 1v and 9v. Because some of these are beneath the colour wash, they could date from the time of the manuscript's creation, or, more likely, shortly afterwards, added by an owner who wanted to introduce colour to the manuscript's illustrations.
19. Peter Marshall, *The Mercurial Emperor: The Magic Circle of Rudolf II in Renaissance Prague* (Pimlico, London, 2007), pp. 65, 87.
20. Suzanna Ivanič, *Cosmos and Materiality in Early Modern Prague* (Oxford University Press, Oxford, 2021), p. 20.
21. Jacob Wisse, 'Prague during the Rule of Rudolf II (1583–1612)' in *Heilbrunn Timeline of Art History*, Metropolitan Museum of Art, New York, November 2013, http://www.metmuseum.org/toah/hd/rupr/hd_rupr.htm.
22. Marshall, *The Mercurial Emperor*, p. 84. For the collection overall, see his chapter 6, 'The Kunstkammer'.
23. Though records of the content survive, not all books are mentioned. See René Zandbergen, 'The History of the Voynich MS', 2023, http://www.voynich.nu/history.html.
24. McCrone Associates, Inc., 'Materials Analysis', p. 1; Zyats et al., 'Physical Findings', p. 31; Zandbergen, 'History of the Voynich MS'; René Zandbergen, 'Earliest Owners' in Clemens, *The Voynich Manuscript*, p. 5.
25. František Martin Pelcl, *Abbildungen Böhmischer und Mährischer Gelehrten und Künstler, nebst kurzen Nachrichten von ihren Leben und Werken*, 3rd part (Prague, 1777), pp. 92–9.
26. Mentioned in the letter from Marci to Kircher (see n. 14 above): see Voynich, 'A Preliminary Sketch', p. 417.
27. Zandbergen, 'Earliest Owners', pp. 5–6; René Zandbergen, 'Voynich MS: 17th Century Letters Related to the MS', https://www.voynich.nu/letters.html.
28. Zandbergen, 'Earliest Owners', pp. 6–7; Zandbergen, 'Voynich MS: 17th Century Letters'; Zandbergen, 'Voynich MS – Biographies'.
29. Nathalie Lallemand-Buyssens, 'Les acquisitions d'Athanasius Kircher au musée du Collège Romain à la lumière de documents inédits', *Storia dell'arte*, 133 (2012), pp. 107–13; Roberto Buonanno, *The Stars of Galileo Galilei and the Universal Knowledge of Athanasius Kircher* (Springer, Cham, 2014), pp. 111–12; Jeremy Warren, book review of Anastasi Callinicos, Daniel Höhr, Jane Stevenson, and Peter Davidson, *The Celebrated Museum of the Roman College of the Society of Jesus. A Facsimile of the 1678 Amsterdam Edition of Giorgio de Sepi's Description of Athanasius Kircher's Museum, Musæum celeberrimum collegii romani societatis Jesu*, *Journal of the History of Collections*, 29, no. 3 (2017), pp. 516–17.
30. For a detailed overview of the later writings in the manuscript, see René Zandbergen, 'Extraneous Writing' in 'Text Analysis: the Writing System',

https://www.voynich.nu/writing.html#extr; Zandbergen, 'Origin of the Voynich MS'.

31. Lisa Fagin Davis, 'Multispectral Imaging and the Voynich Manuscript', *Manuscript Road Trip*, 8 September 2024, https://manuscriptroadtrip.wordpress.com/2024/09/08/multispectral-imaging-and-the-voynich-manuscript/.
32. Further possibly Greek writing is at the bottom left of folio 66r.
33. D'Imperio, *Voynich Manuscript*, p. 16.
34. The first example of this symbol is found on folio 68v, at the centre of the far left page. The second occurrence is at the centre of folio 86v, which is part of the foldout folios 85–86. The third example is on the main foldout page of folios 85–86, at the very top right of the foldout. See D'Imperio, *Voynich Manuscript*, pp. 19, 21, 120. The potential Arabic script is found on folios 85–86v; see D'Imperio, *Voynich Manuscript*, pp. 25–6.
35. Reconstruction based on the work of Zandbergen, 'Earliest Owners', pp. 7–8; René Zandbergen, 'The Vicissitudes of the Society of Jesus in Rome', 2024, https://www.voynich.nu/extra/socjesu.html; René Zandbergen, 'The "Discovery" of the Voynich MS by Wilfrid Voynich', 2023, https://www.voynich.nu/extra/mondragone.html.
36. Arnold Hunt, 'Voynich the Buyer' in Clemens, *The Voynich Manuscript*, pp. 12–15.
37. Zandbergen, 'Earliest Owners', p. 8; René Zandbergen, 'Wilfrid Voynich's Acquisition of the Voynich MS, Not in Villa Mondragone', 2023, https://www.academia.edu/106833983/Wilfrid_Voynichs_acquisition_of_the_Voynich_MS_not_in_Villa_Mondragone, 1–19; Zandbergen, 'The "Discovery" of the Voynich MS by Wilfrid Voynich'.
38. Voynich, 'A Preliminary Sketch', p. 415.
39. Voynich, 'A Preliminary Sketch', pp. 415–16.
40. Voynich, 'A Preliminary Sketch', pp. 416–17, 424–30.
41. Hunt, 'Voynich the Buyer', pp. 16–20; Clemens, 'The World's Most Mysterious Manuscript', pp. 53–4.
42. William Sherman, 'Cryptographic Attempts' in Clemens, *The Voynich Manuscript*, pp. 39–40; Clemens, 'The World's Most Mysterious Manuscript', pp. 55–6; William Romaine Newbold, *The Cipher of Roger Bacon* (University of Pennsylvania Press, Philadelphia, 1928).
43. Sherman, 'Cryptographic Attempts', pp. 41–2. Curt A. Zimansky, 'Editor's Note: William F. Friedman and the Voynich Manuscript', *Philological Quarterly*, 49, no. 4 (1970), pp. 433–43.
44. Sherman, 'Cryptographic Attempts', pp. 40–2; D'Imperio, *Voynich Manuscript*.
45. D'Imperio, *Voynich Manuscript*, p. 45; René Zandbergen, 'Papers on the Voynich Manuscript', 2004–15, https://www.voynich.nu/extra/curr_main.html.
46. D'Imperio, *Voynich Manuscript*, p. 14.
47. For Ethel Voynich's identifications, see René Zandbergen, 'Pre-1960's [*sic*] Tentative Herb Identifications', 2016, https://www.voynich.nu/extra/herb_oldid.html.
48. D'Imperio, *Voynich Manuscript*, pp. 8, 14. The supposed sunflower is on folio 93r, while the perceived pepper plant is on folio 100r.
49. See, for example, Brumbaugh, *The Most Mysterious Manuscript*.

50. Robert S. Brumbaugh, 'Botany and the Voynich "Roger Bacon" Manuscript Once More', *Speculum*, 49, no. 3 (1974), pp. 546–8; Brumbaugh, 'Solution of the Voynich "Roger Bacon" Cipher', pp. 351–3.
51. Robert S. Brumbaugh, 'The Voynich "Roger Bacon" Cipher Manuscript: Deciphered Maps of Stars', *Journal of the Warburg and Courtauld Institutes*, 39 (1976), pp. 139–50.
52. Brumbaugh, 'Solution of the Voynich "Roger Bacon" Cipher', pp. 347–55.
53. Brumbaugh, 'Voynich Cipher Manuscript: A Current Report', pp. 92–5.
54. It is still stored in their library, under call number K 114. To view the manuscript online, visit http://real-ms.mtak.hu/80/.
55. Benedek Láng, *The Rohonc Code: Tracing a Historical Riddle* (Pennsylvania State University Press, University Park, PA, 2021), pp. 3–4, 15, 22, 35–7.
56. Láng, *Rohonc Code*, pp. 21, 38, 42–3, 47, 49, 51.
57. Láng, *Rohonc Code*, pp. 24–34; Levente Zoltán Király and Gábor Tokai, 'Cracking the Code of the Rohonc Codex', *Cryptologia*, 42, no. 4 (2018), pp. 285–6.
58. Király and Tokai, 'Cracking the Code', pp. 285–315; Levente Zoltán Király, 'A Rohonci Kódex teológiai karaktere: közismert és idioszinkratikus mozzanatok azonosításával egy rejtélyes szerző kiléte felé' in Réka Kiss and Gábor Lányi (eds), *Hagyomány – Identitás – Történelem 2022* (Károli Gáspár Református Egyetem, Hittudományi Kar, Egyháztörténeti Kutatóintézet, Budapest, 2023), pp. 363–76
59. Some recent studies include, for example: Henriue F. de Arruda et al., 'Paragraph-Based Representation of Texts: A Complex Networks Approach', *Information Processing and Management*, 56 (2019), pp. 479–94; Vladimír Matlach, Barbora Anna Janeĉková, and Daniel Dostál. 'The Voynich Manuscript: Symbol Roles Revisited', *PLoS ONE*, 17, no. 1 (2022), https://doi.org/10.1371/journal.pone.0260948.
60. Luke Lindemann, 'Crux of the MATTR: Voynichese Morphological Complexity' in Layfield and Abela, *International Conference on the Voynich Manuscript*, https://ceur-ws.org/Vol-3313/paper9.pdf.
61. Ivan Zelinka et al., 'Softcomputing in Identification of the Origin of Voynich Manuscript by Comparison with Ancient Dialects', *Applied Soft Computing*, 138 (2023), https://doi.org/10.1016/j.asoc.2023.110217.
62. Sravana Reddy and Kevin Knight, 'What We Know about the Voynich Manuscript' in Kalliopi Zervanou and Piroska Lendvai (eds), *Proceedings of the 5th ACL–HLT Workshop on Language Technology for Cultural Heritage, Social Sciences, and Humanities* (The Association for Computational Linguistics, Portland, OR, 2011), pp. 78–86.
63. Claire L. Bowern and Luke Lindemann, 'The Linguistics of the Voynich Manuscript', *Annual Review of Linguistics*, 7 (2021), p. 289.
64. Andrew Caruana, Colin Layfield, and John Abela, 'An Analysis of the Relationship between Words within the Voynich Manuscript' in Layfield and Abela, *Internaional Conference on the Voynich Manuscript*, https://ceur-ws.org/Vol-3313/paper8.pdf.
65. Rainer Davis, 'How Many Glyphs and How Many Scribes'.
66. Hannig, 'Voynisch-Hebräisch: der Weg zur Entzifferung von Rainer Hannig', 2020, https://www.rainer-hannig.com/voynich/.

67. Gerard Cheshire, 'The Language and Writing System of MS408 (Voynich) Explained', *Romance Studies*, 37, no. 1 (2019), pp. 30–67; Gerard Cheshire, 'Voicing the Voynich: The Pronuncial Writing System and Graeco-Iberian Language of MS408 (Ischia/Voynich)', https://www.academia.edu/49263562/Voicing_the_Voynich_The_Pronuncial_Writing_System_and_Graeco_Iberian_Language_of_MS408_Ischia_Voynich.
68. Nicholas Gibbs, 'Voynich Manuscript: The Solution', *Times Literary Supplement*, 5971, 8 September 2017, https://www.the-tls.co.uk/articles/voynich-manuscript-solution/.
69. Jules Janick and Arthur O. Tucker, *Unraveling the Voynich Codex* (Springer, Cham, 2018), p. 248.
70. Arthur O. Tucker and Jules Janick, *Flora of the Voynich Codex: An Exploration of Aztec Plants* (Springer, Cham, 2019), p. 210.
71. Stephen Bax, 'A Proposed Partial Decoding of the Voynich Script', Stephenbax.net, 2014, https://stephenbax.net/wp-content/uploads/2014/01/Voynich-a-provisional-partial-decoding-BAX.pdf.
72. See, for example, Gordon Rugg, 'Applying the Bax Proposed Solution', *Hyde and Rugg: Neat Ideas from Unusual Places*, 23 February 2014, https://hydeandrugg.wordpress.com/2014/02/23/applying-the-bax-proposed-solution/.
73. See, for example, Torsten Timm and Andreas Schinner, 'The Voynich Manuscript: Discussion of Text Creation Hypotheses', *Cryptologia*, 48, no. 4 (2023), pp. 305–22, which looks at a variety of recently published articles and ultimately concludes that the argument for the Voynich text being gibberish remains the strongest explanation. See also Alexander Boxer, 'Fingerprinting Gibberish: A Quantitative Comparison of the Voynich and Sloane MS 3188' in Layfield and Abela, *International Conference on the Voynich Manuscript*, https://ceur-ws.org/Vol-3313/paper1.pdf.
74. See, for example, István Daruka, 'On the Voynich Manuscript', *Cryptologia*, 45, no. 1 (2021), pp. 44–80.
75. Andreas Schinner, 'The Voynich Manuscript: Evidence of the Hoax Hypotheses', *Cryptologia*, 31, no. 2 (2007), pp. 95–107.
76. Torsten Timm, 'Co-Occurrence Patterns in the Voynich Manuscript', *eprint arXiv* (2016), pp. 1–9, https://doi.org/10.48550/arXiv.1601.07435.
77. Torsten Timm and Andreas Schinner, 'A Possible Generating Algorithm of the Voynich Manuscript', *Cryptologia*, 44, no. 1 (2020), pp. 1–19; Timm and Schinner, 'Voynich Manuscript: Discussion of Text Creation Hypotheses', p. 15.
78. Gordon Rugg and Gavin Taylor, 'Hoaxing Statistical Features of the Voynich Manuscript', *Cryptologia*, 41, no. 3 (2017), pp. 247–68.
79. Daniel E. Gaskell and Claire L. Bowern, 'Gibberish After All? Voynichese Is Statistically Similar to Human Produced Samples of Meaningless Text' in Layfield and Abela, *International Conference on the Voynich Manuscript*, https://ceur-ws.org/Vol-3313/paper4.pdf.
80. Based on Zandbergen's summary of a 2016 article by Alain Touwaide. See René Zandbergen, 'Alain Touwaide on the Voynich – A Review by René Zandbergen', Stephenbax.net, 2016, https://stephenbax.net/?p=1814.
81. Zandbergen, 'Origin of the Voynich MS'; Zyats et al., 'Physical Findings', p. 27.

82. Koen Gheuens and Cary Rapaport, 'Above and Beyond Voynich Canopies: Tents as a Recurring Motif in Beinecke MS 408' in Layfield and Abela, *International Conference on the Voynich Manuscript*, https://ceur-ws.org/Vol-3313/paper2.pdf.
83. Keagan Brewer, '"I beg your grace that you suppress this chapter or else allow it to be written in secret letters": The Emotions of Encipherment in Late-Medieval Gynaecology' in Layfield and Abela, *International Conference on the Voynich Manuscript*, https://ceur-ws.org/Vol-3313/paper3.pdf.
84. Keagan Brewer and Michelle L. Lewis, 'The Voynich Manuscript, Dr Johannes Hartlieb and the Encipherment of Women's Secrets', *Social History of Medicine*, 37, no. 3 (2024), pp. 559–82.
85. Zyats et al., 'Physical Findings', pp. 23–37.
86. It is referred to as a cipher manuscript: see https://collections.library.yale.edu/catalog/2002046.

3. *BELLICORUM INSTRUMENTORUM LIBER*

1. Reconstruction based on the eyewitness accounts of Sister Bartolomea Riccoboni and Giovanni Fontana. See Sister Bartolomea Riccoboni and Daniel Bornstein, *Life and Death in a Venetian Convent: The Chronicle and Necrology of Corpus Domini, 1395–1436*, ed. and trans. Daniel Bornstein (University of Chicago Press, Chicago, 2000), pp. 43–4, where the date is given as 1409, though I follow the date as given by Karen McCluskey, 'When the Fury of the Proud Sea Re-Awoke' in Jenni Kuuliala, Rose-Marie Peake, and Päivi Räisänen-Schröder (eds), *Lived Religion and Everyday Life in Early Modern Hagiographic Material* (Springer, Cham, 2019), pp. 155–6. For the location of the convent, see Riccoboni and Bornstein, *Life and Death in a Venetian Convent*, p. 4, as well as maps 1 and 2. For Fontana's account, see: Pompilius Azalus, *Liber de omnibus rebus naturalibus quae continentur in mundo* (Venice, 1544), folio 71r and –v; Eugenio Battisti and Giuseppa Saccaro Battisti, *Le macchine cifrate di Giovanni Fontana. Con la riproduzione del Cod. icon. 242 della Bayerische Staatsbibliothek di Monaco di Baviera e la decrittazione di esso e del Cod. lat. nouv. acq. 635 della Bibliothèque nationale di Parigi* (Arcadia Edizioni, Milan, 1984), p. 9.
2. Battisti and Battisti, *Le macchine cifrate di Giovanni Fontana*, pp. 7–9.
3. Based on an estimate of the population by the 1330s. See Deborah Howard, *The Architectural History of Venice*, rev. edn (Yale University Press, New Haven and London, 2002), p. 26.
4. Battisti and Battisti, *Le macchine cifrate di Giovanni Fontana*, p. 39.
5. Ioanna Iordanou, *Venice's Secret Service: Organizing Intelligence in the Renaissance* (Oxford University Press, Oxford, 2019), pp. 28–9.
6. Iordanou, *Venice's Secret Service*, pp. 34–5.
7. Howard, *Architectural History of Venice*, pp. 45–50, 56, 89; Deborah Howard, in Eric R. Dursteler (ed.), *A Companion to Venetian History, 1400–1797* (Brill, Leiden and Boston, 2013), pp. 745–6.
8. Maria Beatrice Autizi, *L'università di Padova* (Editoriale Programma, Treviso, 2022), p. 9.
9. Autizi, *L'università di Padova*, p. 18.

10. From an account in Fontana's *Tractus de pisce, cane, et volucre*: see Battisti and Battisti, *Le macchine cifrate di Giovanni Fontana*, p. 40.
11. From the *Bellicorum instrumentorum liber*, folio 25v. See also Battisti and Battisti, *Le macchine cifrate di Giovanni Fontana*, pp. 39, 71.
12. Battisti and Battisti, *Le macchine cifrate di Giovanni Fontana*, p. 18.
13. Paula Findlen, 'The Renaissance of Science' in Gordon Campbell (ed.), *The Oxford History of the Renaissance* (Oxford University Press, Oxford, 2023), pp. 382–4, 386, 395.
14. Marshall Clagett, 'The Life and Works of Giovanni Fontana', *Annali dell'Istituto e Museo di Storia della Scienza di Firenze*, 1 (1976), p. 7.
15. Autizi, *L'università di Padova*, pp. 21, 51.
16. R.J. Mitchell, 'English Students at Padua, 1460–75', *Transactions of the Royal Historical Society*, 19 (1936), p. 109.
17. Hastings Rashdall, *The Universities of Europe in the Middle Ages, Vol. 1: Salerno, Bologna, Paris* (Clarendon Press, Oxford, 1895), p. 197, n. 1.
18. Alexander Birkenmajer, 'Zur Lebensgeschichte und wissenschaftlichen Tätigkeit von Giovanni Fontana (1395?–1455?)', *Isis*, 17, no. 1 (1932), pp. 35–6; Johannes Fontana, *Liber instrumentorum iconographicus / Ein illustriertes Maschinenbuch*, ed. and trans. Horst Kranz (Franz Steiner Verlag, Stuttgart, 2014), p. 9.
19. Österreichische Nationalbibliothek, Vienna, Cod. 5153. See Horst Kranz, 'Akademische Technik im 15. Jarhhundert: Inhalt und Terminologie einer wiederentdeckten Jugenschrift Johannes Fontanas', *Technikgeschichte*, 74, no. 2 (2007), pp. 119–47.
20. Deborah Howard, 'The Old, the Antique, and the Venerable in Venetian Renaissance Architecture' in Georg Christ and Franz-Julius Morche (eds), *Cultures of Empire: Rethinking Venetian Rule, 1400–1700. Essays in Honour of Benjamin Arbel* (Brill, Leiden and Boston, 2020), p. 64 with n. 5.
21. Fontana, *Liber instrumentorum iconographicus / Ein illustriertes Maschinenbuch*, p. 11; Battisti and Battisti, *Le macchine cifrate di Giovanni Fontana*, pp. 15, 40.
22. These three manuscripts are now bound together as MS 2705 in the University of Bologna's library: see Clagett, 'Life and Works of Giovanni Fontana', pp. 10–14. The Bologna manuscripts and the Vienna manuscript have been jointly published as Johannes Fontana, *Opera iuvenalia de rotis horologiis et mensuris / Jugendwerke über Räder, Uhren und Messungen*, ed. and trans. Horst Kranz (Franz Steiner Verlag, Stuttgart, 2011).
23. Kranz, 'Akademische Technik im 15. Jarhhundert', pp. 120–2, 146.
24. Battisti and Battisti, *Le macchine cifrate di Giovanni Fontana*, p. 39.
25. Joanne Marie Ferraro, *Venice: History of the Floating City* (Cambridge University Press, Cambridge, 2012), p. 61.
26. Iordanou, *Venice's Secret Service*, p. 29.
27. Paolo Galluzzi, *The Italian Renaissance of Machines* (Harvard University Press, Cambridge, MA, 2020), pp. vii–x; Fontana, *Liber instrumentorum iconographicus / Ein illustriertes Maschinenbuch*, pp. 17–18.
28. Battisti and Battisti, *Le macchine cifrate di Giovanni Fontana*, pp. 55, 56, 58–9, 63, 87–8.
29. Battisti and Battisti, *Le macchine cifrate di Giovanni Fontana*, pp. 67, 85, 69, 60–1.

30. Battisti and Battisti, *Le macchine cifrate di Giovanni Fontana*, pp. 76–7.
31. Battisti and Battisti, *Le macchine cifrate di Giovanni Fontana*, pp. 79, 66.
32. Battisti and Battisti, *Le macchine cifrate di Giovanni Fontana*, p. 78.
33. Battisti and Battisti, *Le macchine cifrate di Giovanni Fontana*, p. 88.
34. Battisti and Battisti, *Le macchine cifrate di Giovanni Fontana*, pp. 94–5.
35. Battisti and Battisti, *Le macchine cifrate di Giovanni Fontana*, pp. 96–7.
36. Battisti and Battisti, *Le macchine cifrate di Giovanni Fontana*, pp. 99–100.
37. Anthony Grafton, 'The Devil as Automaton: Giovanni Fontana and the Meanings of a Fifteenth-Century Machine' in Jessica Riskin (ed.), *Genesis Redux: Essays in the History and Philosophy of Artificial Life* (University of Chicago Press, Chicago and London, 2007), pp. 52–4; Lynn Thorndike, *A History of Magic and Experimental Science*, 8 vols (Columbia University Press, New York and London, 1923–58), vol. 4, pp. 169–70.
38. For an explanation of the system, see Battisti and Battisti, *Le macchine cifrate di Giovanni Fontana*, pp. 35–8, with a list of the symbols on p. 38.
39. Grafton, 'The Devil as Automaton', pp. 46, 48.
40. Battisti and Battisti, *Le macchine cifrate di Giovanni Fontana*, p. 53.
41. Battisti and Battisti, *Le macchine cifrate di Giovanni Fontana*, p. 36.
42. Battisti and Battisti, *Le macchine cifrate di Giovanni Fontana*, pp. 24, 36.
43. See Saverio Campanini, 'The Quest for the Holiest Alphabet in the Renaissance' in Nadia Vidro, Irene E. Zwiep, and Judith Olszowy-Schlanger (eds), *A Universal Art: Hebrew Grammar across Disciplines and Faiths* (Brill, Leiden, 2014), pp. 196–7.
44. Thorndike, *History of Magic and Experimental Science*, vol. 4, p. 175.
45. Fontana, *Liber instrumentorum iconographicus / Ein illustriertes Maschinenbuch*, p. 28. Johannes Fontana, *Methoden des Erinnerns und Vergessens. Johannes Fontanas Secretum de thesauro experimentorum ymaginationis hominum*, ed. and trans. Horst Kranz (Franz Steiner Verlag, Stuttgart, 2016), p. 20.
46. Mary E. D'Imperio, *The Voynich Manuscript: An Elegant Enigma* (National Security Agency/Central Security Service, Fort George E. Mead, MD, 1978), pp. 67 and 117, fig. 39. Aloys Meister, *Die Anfänge der modernen diplomatischen Geheimschrift* (Ferdinand Schöningh, Paderborn, 1902), pp. 16, 18.
47. David Kahn, *The Codebreakers: The Story of Secret Writing*, rev. edn (Scribner, New York, 1996), chapter 3; Nick Pelling, 'Fifteenth Century Cryptography Revisited', 2017, https://www.academia.edu/33813775/Fifteenth_Century_Cryptography_Revisited. For examples of early Italian ciphers, see Meister, *Die Anfänge der modernen diplomatischen Geheimschrift*, with the Simeone de Crema cipher on p. 41.
48. Thorndike, *History of Magic and Experimental Science*, vol. 4, p. 154. See Azalus, *Liber de omnibus rebus naturalibus*, folio 130v.
49. Iordanou, *Venice's Secret Service*, pp. 172–3 and n. 77.
50. See Bodleian Library, Oxford, MS Digby 47, https://medieval.bodleian.ox.ac.uk/catalog/manuscript_4384; and Bibliothèque nationale de France, Paris, Codex Paris, BnF ms Latin 9335, https://archivesetmanuscrits.bnf.fr/ark:/12148/cc77377g. See also Birkenmajer, 'Zur Lebensgeschichte und wissenschaftlichen Tätigkeit von Giovanni Fontana', pp. 46–7; Dietrich Lohrmann, 'Johannes Fontanas Traktat über Brennspiegel und der Codex Paris BnF ms. latin 9335', *Sudhoffs Archiv*, 100, no. 2 (2016), pp. 166–87.

51. Battisti and Battisti, *Le macchine cifrate di Giovanni Fontana*, pp. 32, 39.
52. Battisti and Battisti, *Le macchine cifrate di Giovanni Fontana*, pp. 141–5; Fontana, *Methoden des Erinnerns und Vergessens*, p. 14.
53. Fontana, *Methoden des Erinnerns und Vergessens*, pp. 17–18; Clagett, 'Life and Works of Giovanni Fontana', p. 17.
54. Fontana, *Methoden des Erinnerns und Vergessens*, p. 11.
55. Battisti and Battisti, *Le macchine cifrate di Giovanni Fontana*, p. 51.
56. Galluzzi, *Italian Renaissance of Machines*, pp. ix–x.
57. Battisti and Battisti, *Le macchine cifrate di Giovanni Fontana*, p. 39; Thorndike, *History of Magic and Experimental Science*, vol. 4, p. 157.
58. Thorndike, *History of Magic and Experimental Science*, vol. 4, pp. 163, 167–8; Battisti and Battisti, *Le macchine cifrate di Giovanni Fontana*, p. 51.
59. Horst Kranz, 'Johannes Fontana als Verfasser der *Speculi almukefi compositio* und sein Exkurs über den Stahl (ca. 1430)', *Sudhoffs Archiv*, 100, no. 2 (2016), pp. 150–65.
60. Bodleian Library, Oxford, MS Canon. Misc. 47, https://digital.bodleian.ox.ac.uk/objects/0da9eb2c-bc07-4365-9349-da35f340a71e/. The crossed-out page is folio 219v. See Clagett, 'Life and Works of Giovanni Fontana', pp. 19–20; Fontana, *Liber instrumentorum iconographicus / Ein illustriertes Maschinenbuch*, p. 16.
61. Battisti and Battisti, *Le macchine cifrate di Giovanni Fontana*, p. 39.
62. Thorndike, *History of Magic and Experimental Science*, vol. 4, pp. 158–9, 169–70.
63. Battisti and Battisti, *Le macchine cifrate di Giovanni Fontana*, pp. 43–5, 52.
64. Battisti and Battisti, *Le macchine cifrate di Giovanni Fontana*, p. 18.
65. Fontana, *Liber instrumentorum iconographicus / Ein illustriertes Maschinenbuch*, p. 19.
66. Battisti and Battisti, *Le macchine cifrate di Giovanni Fontana*, pp. 24, 40–1, 53; Fontana, *Liber instrumentorum iconographicus / Ein illustriertes Maschinenbuch*, p. 10. The transcription by Schulte is kept in the Bayerische Staatsbibliothek, Munich, BSB Cod.icon. 242a, https://opacplus.bsb-muenchen.de/title/BV 022759821.
67. Fontana, *Methoden des Erinnerns und Vergessens*, pp. 17–18; Clagett, 'Life and Works of Giovanni Fontana', p. 17.
68. Battisti and Battisti, *Le macchine cifrate di Giovanni Fontana*, pp. 41, 141–2; Birkenmajer, 'Zur Lebensgeschichte und wissenschaftlichen Tätigkeit von Giovanni Fontana', p. 41; Fontana, *Methoden des Erinnerns und Vergessens*, pp. 15–16, 21. This manuscript is now Cod. Lat. Nouv. Acq. 635 in the Bibliothèque nationale de France, Paris, https://archivesetmanuscrits.bnf.fr/ark:/12148/cc713449.
69. Lynn Thorndike, 'An Unidentified Work by Giovanni da' Fontana: *Liber de omnibus rebus naturalibus*', *Isis,* 15, no. 1 (1931), pp. 31–46; Thorndike, *History of Magic and Experimental Science*, vol. 4, pp. 150–82.
70. Copies of this work are today held by various libraries, including the Bibliothèque nationale de France and the British Library.
71. Kranz, 'Johannes Fontana als Verfasser der Speculi almukefi compositio'.
72. Bayerische Staatsbibliothek, Munich, https://opacplus.bsb-muenchen.de/title/BV022535440. See also https://www.digitale-sammlungen.de/en/view/bsb00013084?page=,1.

4. *STEGANOGRAPHIA*

1. Noel L. Brann, *The Abbot Trithemius (1462–1516): The Renaissance of Monastic Humanism* (Leiden, Brill, 1981), pp. 3–6; Anthony Grafton, *Worlds Made by Words: Scholarship and Community in the Modern West* (Harvard University Press, Cambridge, MA, and London, 2009), p. 57.
2. Brann, *The Abbot Trithemius*, pp. 6–7.
3. Noel L. Brann, *Trithemius and Magical Theology: A Chapter in the Controversy over Occult Studies in Early Modern Europe* (State University of New York Press, Albany, 1999), p. 6.
4. Brann, *The Abbot Trithemius*, pp. 3–6. Brann, *Trithemius and Magical Theology*, p. 5.
5. The pamphlet was called *De laude scriptorum manualium*. See Brann, *The Abbot Trithemius*, p. 144; Anthony Grafton, *Magus: The Art of Magic from Faustus to Agrippa* (The Belknap Press of Harvard University Press, Cambridge, MA, 2023), p. 131; Grafton, *Worlds Made by Words*, pp. 57, 62.
6. Brann, *The Abbot Trithemius*, pp. 9–14, 23, and 72.
7. Brann, *The Abbot Trithemius*, p. 243. See also Datenbank Gesamtkatalog der Wiegendrucke, 'Ursinus, Jason Alpheus', 2011, https://gesamtkatalogderwiegendrucke.de/docs/URSIJAS.htm.
8. Lynn Thorndike, *A History of Magic and Experimental Science*, 8 vols (Columbia University Press, New York and London, 1923–58), vol. 4, p. 525; Jim Reeds, 'Solved: The Ciphers in Book III of Trithemius's *Steganographia*', *Cryptologia*, 22, no. 4 (1998), pp. 293–4.
9. Trithemius wrote the *Clavis steganographiae* between 1498 to 1499, and the *Clavis generalis triplex* in 1499. See Thomas Ernst, 'The Numerical-Astrological Ciphers in the Third Book of Trithemius's *Steganographia*', *Cryptologia*, 22, no. 4 (1998), pp. 318–20.
10. Johannes Trithemius, *Steganographia* (Berner, Frankfurt, 1606), preface. For an English translation, see Alexander Boxer, '*Steganographia* and Other Occult Writings', https://web.archive.org/web/20210410093317/http://trithemius.com/steganographia-english/.
11. Trithemius, *Steganographia*, pp. 1–4.
12. Trithemius, *Steganographia*, pp. 9–10.
13. Trithemius, *Steganographia*, p. 10.
14. For the codes in Book III and how they were solved, see Reeds, 'Solved'; and Ernst, 'The Numerical-Astrological Ciphers'.
15. Brann, *Trithemius and Magical Theology*, pp. 101–2. For an overview of the letter, see Thorndike, *History of Magic and Experimental Science*, vol. 4, pp. 524–5. A full version can be found in Jean Jacques Boissard, *De divinatione et magicis praestigiis* (Typis Hieronymi Galleri, Oppenheim, 1615), p. 49.
16. Brann, *Trithemius and Magical Theology*, p. 7; Brann, *The Abbot Trithemius*, pp. 18–19.
17. Ernst, 'The Numerical-Astrological Ciphers', p. 321; Thomas Ernst, 'Schwarzweisse Magie: der Schlüssel zum dritten Buch der *Steganographia* des Trithemius', *Daphnis*, 25 (1996), p. 107.
18. Sarah L. Higley, *Hildegard of Bingen's Unknown Language: An Edition, Translation, and Discussion* (Palgrave Macmillan, New York, 2007), p. 62;

Vittoria Perrone Compagni, 'Heinrich Cornelius Agrippa von Nettesheim' in Edward N. Zalta (ed.), *The Stanford Encyclopedia of Philosophy* (Metaphysics Research Lab, Stanford University, Stanford, 2021), https://plato.stanford.edu/archives/spr2021/entries/agrippa-nettesheim/. The manuscript edition sent to Trithemius is now in the Universitätsbibliothek Würzburg, MS M.ch.q.50.

19. Paola Zambelli, *White Magic, Black Magic in the European Renaissance* (Brill, Leiden and Boston, 2007), pp. 3, 116, 245, 248, 251; Brann, *The Abbot Trithemius*, pp. 30–1; Brann, *Trithemius and Magical Theology*, pp. 152–6.
20. Brann, *Trithemius and Magical Theology*, pp. 7, 9–10, 88–9; Brann, *The Abbot Trithemius*, pp. 29–31; Grafton, *Magus*, pp. 137–8.
21. Grafton, *Magus*, pp. 126–8.
22. Zambelli, *White Magic, Black Magic*, pp. 2–3, 21–2, 27.
23. Zambelli, *White Magic, Black Magic*, pp. 7–8.
24. Grafton, *Magus*, pp. 150–4, 162; Brann, *Trithemius and Magical Theology*, pp. 61–2, 83.
25. Richard Kieckhefer, *Forbidden Rites: A Necromancer's Manual of the Fifteenth Century* (Pennsylvania State University Press, University Park, PA, 1997), pp. 1–21, 154–69.
26. Kieckhefer, *Forbidden Rites*, pp. 22–41. This manuscript is in the Bayerische Staatsbibliothek, Munich, Clm 849.
27. Brann, *Trithemius and Magical Theology*, pp. 33–42, 57.
28. Zambelli, *White Magic, Black Magic*, pp. 27, 60–9; Grafton, *Magus*, p. 132.
29. Brann, *Trithemius and Magical Theology*, pp. 76–9.
30. Brann, *Trithemius and Magical Theology*, pp. 51, 56–7.
31. Brann, *The Abbot Trithemius*, pp. 34–5, 37, 73–4.
32. Larry Silver, *Marketing Maximilian, The Visual History of a Holy Roman Emperor* (Princeton University Press, Princeton, 2008), p. 134; Brann, *The Abbot Trithemius*, pp. 42, 94; Brann, *Trithemius and Magical Theology*, p. 4.
33. Brann, *Trithemius and Magical Theology*, p. 64.
34. Brann, *The Abbot Trithemius*, p. 91.
35. Brann, *Trithemius and Magical Theology*, p. 9.
36. Brann, *The Abbot Trithemius*, pp. 91–2. Maximilian Gamer, *Die Polygraphia des Johannes Trithemius nach der handschriftlichen Fassung. Edition, Übersetzung und Kommentar*, 2 vols (Brill, Boston and Leiden, 2022), vol. 1, p. 39.
37. For a helpful summary of *Polygraphia*'s encipherment techniques, see Jürgen Hermes, '*Polygraphia* III: The Cipher That Pretends to be an Artificial Language' in Colin Layfield and John Abela (eds), *International Conference on the Voynich Manuscript 2022*, CEUR Workshop Proceedings, 2022, https://ceur-ws.org/Vol-3313/paper7.pdf.
38. For a recent publication of the tables, see Gamer, *Die Polygraphia des Johannes Trithemius*, vol. 2, pp. 46–237.
39. Grafton, *Magus*, p. 141.
40. For a German translation of Book 6, see Gamer, *Die Polygraphia des Johannes Trithemius*, vol. 1, pp. 108–27.
41. This edition is now in Vienna, in the Österreichische Nationalbibliothek, as Cod. 3308. See Gamer, *Die Polygraphia des Johannes Trithemius*, vol. 2, pp. 1–4.

42. This is now in Celle, Germany, at the Bibliothek des Oberlandesgerichts Celle, as Grupensche Stiftung C 23. See Gamer, *Die Polygraphia des Johannes Trithemius*, vol. 2, pp. 4–5.
43. Brann, *The Abbot Trithemius*, pp. 95–7.
44. Grafton, *Magus*, p. 167.
45. Zambelli, *White Magic, Black Magic*, pp. 74–5.
46. Ernst, 'Schwarzweisse Magie', p. 87.
47. Brann, *Trithemius and Magical Theology*, p. 33.
48. Grafton, *Magus*, p. 130.
49. Brann, *The Abbot Trithemius*, pp. 99–101.
50. Gamer, *Die Polygraphia des Johannes Trithemius*, vol. 2, pp. 14–23.
51. Ernst, 'Schwarzweisse Magie', p. 101.
52. Ernst, 'The Numerical-Astrological Ciphers', p. 321; Blaise de Vigenère, *Traicté des chiffres, ou secretes manieres d'escrire* (Abel L'Angelier, Paris, 1586), folios 12v, 13r, 182r; Thomas Ernst, 'Anatomie einer Fälschung', *Daphnis*, 30 (2001), pp. 538–9.
53. Ernst, 'The Numerical-Astrological Ciphers', p. 321 and n. 11; Johannes Reitsma, *Franciscus Junius. Een levensbeeld uit den eersten tijd der kerkhervorm-ingpage* (J.B. Huber, Netherlands, 1864), p. 103, n. 5. See also Ernst, 'Schwarzweisse Magie', pp. 72–3, with n. 418.
54. That is to say, Agrippa is known to have owned an original copy from at least 1520.
55. Ernst, 'Anatomie einer Fälschung', pp. 537, 541.
56. Peter Marshall, *The Mercurial Emperor: The Magic Circle of Rudolf II in Renaissance Prague* (Pimlico, London, 2007), p. 112.
57. This is now in the National Library of Wales, Cardiff, under reference number Peniarth MS 423D. For the manuscript's history, see https://www.library.wales/discover-learn/digital-exhibitions/manuscripts/early-modern-period/steganographia#?c=&m=&s=&cv=&xywh=-1249%2C0%2C6277%2C4866.
58. Zambelli, *White Magic, Black Magic*, p. 249.
59. Zambelli, *White Magic, Black Magic*, pp. 203–4.
60. Ernst, 'Anatomie einer Fälschung', pp. 538–9.
61. Copies of this edition can now be found in Halle and Leiden. The Halle edition is Universitäts- und Landesbibliothek Sachsen-Anhalt, call number 21 A 10. The Leiden edition is Universitaire Bibliotheken Leiden, VCF 14, https://digitalcollections.universiteitleiden.nl/view/item/1914511#page/4/mode/1up. The record says that it is only the third book, but it looks like the whole *Steganographia*. It is found on folios 16v–137 and is dated to '1577–1600?'. See also Ernst, 'Anatomie einer Fälschung', 542, n. 74.
62. Trithemius, *Steganographia*, p. 5.
63. Trithemius, *Steganographia*, p. 6.
64. Ernst, 'Anatomie einer Fälschung', pp. 513–95. This edition is now Codex 91.1 in the Herzog August Bibliothek, Wolfenbüttel.
65. Ernst, 'Schwarzweisse Magie', pp. 107–8.
66. Ernst, 'The Numerical-Astrological Ciphers', pp. 337–40, with nn. 44 and 45.
67. The solution was published by Thomas Ernst in German in 1996 and then in English in 1998. Simultaneously and independently from Ernst, another scholar, Jim Reeds, had also been working on breaking the code, and published

the solution in 1998. See Ernst, 'The Numerical-Astrological Ciphers'; Reeds, 'Solved'.

68. Ernst, 'The Numerical-Astrological Ciphers', pp. 337–40, with nn. 44 and 45.
69. The National Library of Wales, https://www.library.wales/discover-learn/digital-exhibitions/manuscripts/early-modern-period/steganographia#?c=&m=&s=&cv=&xywh=-1249%2C0%2C6277%2C4866.

5. THE ANGEL DIARIES OF JOHN DEE

1. Christopher Lionel Whitby, 'John Dee's Actions with Spirits: 22 December 1581 to 23 May 1583', 2 vols, PhD thesis, University of Birmingham (1982), vol. 2, pp. 230–8, and vol. 1, p. 447; Donald C. Laycock, *The Complete Enochian Dictionary: A Dictionary of the Angelic Language as Revealed to Dr. John Dee and Edward Kelley*, 3rd edn (Weiser Books, Newburyport, MA, 2023), pp. 28–9. The angel Raphael is also called Medicini Dei.
2. Whitby, 'John Dee's Actions with Spirits', vol. 2, pp. 241–2.
3. Whitby, 'John Dee's Actions with Spirits', vol. 2, pp. 258–67; Laycock, *Complete Enochian Dictionary*, pp. 31–4.
4. Whitby, 'John Dee's Actions with Spirits', vol. 1, pp. 143–4.
5. This is now Sloane MS 3189 in the British Library, London.
6. Benjamin Woolley, *The Queen's Conjurer: The Science and Magic of Dr Dee* (HarperCollins, London, 2001), pp. 12–15, 18–23.
7. Woolley, *Queen's Conjurer*, pp. 25–46, 52–8.
8. Deborah E. Harkness, *John Dee's Conversations with Angels: Cabala, Alchemy, and the End of Nature* (Cambridge University Press, Cambridge, 1999), pp. 71–7; Deborah E. Harkness, 'Managing an Experimental Household: The Dees of Mortlake and the Practice of Natural Philosophy', *Isis*, 88, no. 2 (1997), pp. 247–8; Woolley, *Queen's Conjurer*, pp. 49–50, 83–5.
9. Woolley, *Queen's Conjurer*, pp. 73–6; Harkness, *John Dee's Conversations with Angels*, pp. 82–3, 87–9; Nicholas H. Clulee, *John Dee's Natural Philosophy: Between Science and Religion* (Routledge, Abingdon, 2013), pp. 92–5.
10. Harkness, *John Dee's Conversations with Angels*, pp. 77–90; Saverio Campanini, 'The Quest for the Holiest Alphabet in the Renaissance' in Nadia Vidro, Irene E. Zwiep, and Judith Olszowy-Schlanger (eds), *A Universal Art: Hebrew Grammar across Disciplines and Faiths* (Brill, Leiden, 2014), pp. 217, 220–1.
11. Woolley, *Queen's Conjurer*, pp. 73–6.
12. Harkness, *John Dee's Conversations with Angels*, pp. 91–7.
13. Whitby, 'John Dee's Actions with Spirits', vol. 1, pp. 20–4; Woolley, *Queen's Conjurer*, p. 77.
14. Whitby, 'John Dee's Actions with Spirits', vol. 1, pp. 26–7; Deborah E. Harkness, 'Managing an Experimental Household: The Dees of Mortlake and the Practice of Natural Philosophy', *Isis*, 88, no. 2 (1997), p. 251.
15. Harkness, *John Dee's Conversations with Angels*, pp. 16–19.
16. Woolley, *Queen's Conjurer*, pp. 155–61.
17. Whitby, 'John Dee's Actions with Spirits', vol. 1, p. 145, and vol. 2, pp. 235–8 (and p. 391 for another copy of the alphabet, this time by Kelly); Harkness, *John Dee's Conversations with Angels*, p. 166; Laycock, *Complete Enochian Dictionary*, pp. 41, 45.

18. Whitby, 'John Dee's Actions with Spirits', vol. 1, p. 143.
19. This is one of the manuscripts now bound in British Library, London, Sloane MS 3189. Harkness, *John Dee's Conversations with Angels*, p. 41; Whitby, 'John Dee's Actions with Spirits', vol. 1, pp. 126, 142–3.
20. Stephen Clucas, 'False Illuding Spirits & Cownterfeiting Deuills: John Dee's Angelic Conversations and Religious Anxiety' in Joad Raymond (ed.), *Conversations with Angels: Essays Towards a History of Spiritual Communication, 1100–1700* (Palgrave Macmillan, Basingstoke, 2011), p. 169, n. 14.
21. Clucas, 'False Illuding Spirits & Cownterfeiting Deuills', p. 152.
22. Harkness, *John Dee's Conversations with Angels*, p. 96.
23. British Library, London, Sloane MS 3188, folio 30r.
24. Harkness, *John Dee's Conversations with Angels*, pp. 33–4 with n. 97.
25. Harkness, *John Dee's Conversations with Angels*, p. 35.
26. Harkness, *John Dee's Conversations with Angels*, pp. 37–8.
27. British Library, London, Sloane MS 3188, folios 49r and 57r; Whitby, 'John Dee's Actions with Spirits', vol. 2, pp. 159, 204.
28. Whitby, 'John Dee's Actions with Spirits', vol. 2, p. 151. Carmara here uses the name Ho.
29. Casaubon, *A True & Faithful Relation of What Passed for Many Yeers between Dr. John Dee . . . and Some Spirits* (D. Maxwell for T. Garthwait, London, 1659), p. 31.
30. Whitby, 'John Dee's Actions with Spirits', vol. 2, p. 288.
31. Whitby, 'John Dee's Actions with Spirits', vol. 2, p. 331.
32. Whitby, 'John Dee's Actions with Spirits', vol. 2, p. 130. Casaubon, *A True & Faithful Relation*, pp. 14, 17.
33. Whitby, 'John Dee's Actions with Spirits', vol. 2, pp. 24–6.
34. Whitby, 'John Dee's Actions with Spirits', vol. 2, p. 326.
35. Whitby, 'John Dee's Actions with Spirits', vol. 2, pp. 389–90.
36. Whitby, 'John Dee's Actions with Spirits', vol. 2, pp. 171, 172.
37. Casaubon, *A True & Faithful Relation*, p. 13. Whitby, 'John Dee's Actions with Spirits', vol. 2, pp. 330–1.
38. Whitby, 'John Dee's Actions with Spirits', vol. 2, pp. 321–5, 336–8, 391; Woolley, *Queen's Conjurer*, pp. 168–70, 175–7, 179, 181; Francis Young, 'Edward Kelley's Danish Treasure Hoax and Elizabethan Antiquarianism', *Intellectual History Review*, 30, no. 2 (2020), pp. 167–86.
39. Claire Fanger, 'Introduction: Theurgy, Magic, and Mysticism' in Claire Fanger (ed.), *Invoking Angels: Theurgic Ideas and Practices, Thirteenth to Sixteenth Centuries* (Pennsylvania State University Press, University Park, PA, 2012), pp. 3–7.
40. Gideon Bohak, 'Jewish Magic in the Middle Ages' in David J. Collins SJ (ed.), *The Cambridge History of Magic and Witchcraft in the West: From Antiquity to the Present* (Cambridge University Press, Cambridge, 2015), pp. 278–9.
41. Woolley, *Queen's Conjurer*, pp. 63–6; Harkness, *John Dee's Conversations with Angels*, p. 47, n. 153; Laycock, *Complete Enochian Dictionary*, p. 9. For the bookshop, see Stephen Clucas, 'John Dee, Alchemy, and Print Culture', *Ambix*, 64, no. 2 (2017), p. 113; and Manuel Mertens, 'Willem Silvius: "Typographical Parent" of John Dee's *Monas Hieroglyphica*', *Ambix*, 64, no. 2 (2017), pp. 175–89.
42. Whitby, 'John Dee's Actions with Spirits', vol. 2, p. 38.

43. Harkness, *John Dee's Conversations with Angels*, pp. 112–14 with n. 47.
44. Woolley, *Queen's Conjurer*, pp. 185–7; Glyn Parry, *The Arch-Conjuror of England: John Dee* (Yale University Press, New Haven and London, 2011), pp. 162–5, 167, 171.
45. Parry, *Arch-Conjuror of England*, pp. 173–4; Casaubon, *A True & Faithful Relation*, p. 69.
46. Rafał T. Prinke and Kamila Follprecht, 'John Dee and Edward Kelley in Crakow: Identifying the House of Enochian Revelations', *Polish Journal of the Arts and Culture*, 13, no. 1 (2015), p. 125; Whitby, 'John Dee's Actions with Spirits', vol. 1, p. 30.
47. The house was demolished in 1908 and replaced by the Art Nouveau building that still stands at no. 2 Plac Szczepański. Prinke and Follprecht, 'John Dee and Edward Kelley in Crakow', p. 130.
48. Whitby, 'John Dee's Actions with Spirits', vol. 1, pp. 141–2.
49. Sarah L. Higley, *Hildegard of Bingen's Unknown Language: An Edition, Translation, and Discussion* (Palgrave Macmillan, New York, 2007), pp. 67–71.
50. These are among the manuscripts bound together as British Library, London, Sloane MS 3191. Harkness, *John Dee's Conversations with Angels*, pp. 41–3; Parry, *Arch-Conjuror of England*, pp. 174–8.
51. Parry, *Arch-Conjuror of England*, pp. 180–8.
52. Seemingly 'Faust House' in Prague today. Woolley, *Queen's Conjurer*, pp. 241 and 323, n. 10.
53. Woolley, *Queen's Conjurer*, pp. 241–3; Parry, *Arch-Conjuror of England*, pp. 190–1. Dee's account was written in a pamphlet: see C.H. Josten, 'An Unknown Chapter in the Life of John Dee', *Journal of the Warburg and Courtauld Institutes*, 28, no. 1 (1965), pp. 223–57.
54. This event is recorded in the angel diaries, rather than in the pamphlet that says the books were burned. See Casaubon, *A True & Faithful Relation*, pp. 418–19; Woolley, *Queen's Conjurer*, pp. 243–4; Parry, *Arch-Conjuror of England*, p. 191.
55. Harkness, *John Dee's Conversations with Angels*, p. 44.
56. Woolley, *Queen's Conjurer*, p. 241.
57. Parry, *Arch-Conjuror of England*, pp. 196–7.
58. Laycock, *Complete Enochian Dictionary*, pp. 16–17, 49–50; Woolley, *Queen's Conjurer*, pp. 258–67; Parry, *Arch-Conjuror of England*, pp. 197–200, 203; Casaubon, *A True & Faithful Relation*, Actio Tertia, pp. 1–31. Certain details here are omitted from Casaubon's publication, but are present in the angel diary manuscript itself, with added information from Dee's personal diary. For the cipher, see Casaubon, *A True & Faithful Relation*, Actio Tertia, pp. 14–15.
59. Whitby, 'John Dee's Actions with Spirits', vol. 1, pp. 51, 117–18, 146–9, and vol. 2, pp. 338–9; Harkness, *John Dee's Conversations with Angels*, pp. 167–8, 170; Laycock, *Complete Enochian Dictionary*, pp. 30, 35–44, 49–50. The fate of the early spirit actions that Dee hid in his chimney at Mortlake is unknown.
60. Parry, *Arch-Conjuror of England*, pp. 204, 216; Woolley, *Queen's Conjurer*, pp. 271–2.
61. Parry, *Arch-Conjuror of England*, pp. 203, 205–6, 212, 228; Woolley, *Queen's Conjurer*, p. 283; Laycock, *Complete Enochian Dictionary*, p. 17.
62. Parry, *Arch-Conjuror of England*, pp. 212, 243, 246–7, 255; Harkness, *John Dee's Conversations with Angels*, p. 24.

63. Parry, *Arch-Conjuror of England*, p. 267; Whitby, 'John Dee's Actions with Spirits', vol. 1, p. 42; Lancashire OnLine Parish Clerk Project, 'Burials at the Cathedral in the City of Manchester', https://www.lan-opc.org.uk/Manchester/Manchester/cathedral/burials_1605-1608.html.
64. Parry, *Arch-Conjuror of England*, pp. 268–71; Woolley, *Queen's Conjurer*, pp. 289–90; Casaubon, *A True & Faithful Relation*, Actio Tertia, pp. 32–45.
65. John Aubrey, *Letters Written by Eminent Persons in the Seventeenth and Eighteenth Centuries*, 2 vols (Longman, Hurst, Rees, Orme, and Brown, Paternoster-Row, and Munday and Slatter, Oxford, London, 1813), vol. 2, part 1, p. 311; Whitby, 'John Dee's Actions with Spirits', vol. 1, p. 17, n. 18; William Sherman, *John Dee: The Politics of Reading and Writing in the English Renaissance* (University of Massachusetts Press, Amherst, MA, 1995), p. 30; S.L. Lee, 'Cotton, Sir Robert Bruce (1571–1631)' in Leslie Stephen (ed.), *Dictionary of National Biography*, vol. 12 (MacMillan and Co., New York, Smith, Elder, and Co., London, 1887), p. 312.
66. Casaubon, *A True & Faithful Relation*, Preface, folio F6.
67. Casaubon, *A True & Faithful Relation*, Preface; Whitby, 'John Dee's Actions with Spirits', vol. 1, p. 2.
68. Whitby, 'John Dee's Actions with Spirits', vol. 1, pp. 101–12.
69. Julian Harrison, 'Fire, Fire! The Tragic Burning of the Cotton Library', Medieval Manuscripts Blog, *British Library*, 2016, https://blogs.bl.uk/digitisedmanuscripts/2016/10/fire-fire-the-tragic-burning-of-the-cotton-library.html; Simon Keynes, 'The Reconstruction of a Burnt Cottonian Manuscript: The Case of Cotton MS. Otho A. I', *British Library Journal*, 22 (1996), p. 113.
70. It was also once catalogued as British Library, London, Add MS 5007. See https://searcharchives.bl.uk/primo_library/libweb/action/display.do?tabs=detailsTab&ct=display&doc=IAMS040-001104021&displayMode=-full&vid=IAMS_VU2.
71. It is British Library, London, Sloane MS 3189. British Library, https://searcharchives.bl.uk/primo-explore/fulldisplay?vid=IAMS_VU2&docid=IAMS040-002115573&context=L.
72. For the story, see British Library, London, Sloane MS 3188, folios 2r–3r. For a transcription of Ashmole's rather difficult handwriting, see Joseph H. Peterson, *John Dee's Five Books of Mystery: Original Sourcebook of Enochian Magic* (Weiser Books, Boston and York Beach, ME, 2003), pp. 47–9.
73. British Library, https://www.bl.uk/manuscripts/FullDisplay.aspx?ref=Sloane_MS_3188.
74. The *48 Claves angelicae*, *Liber scientiae auxilii et victoriae terrestris*, *Tabula bonorum angelorum invocationes*, and *De heptarchia mystica* are bound together as British Library, London, Sloane MS 3191. British Library, https://www.bl.uk/manuscripts/FullDisplay.aspx?ref=Sloane_MS_3191.

6. THE TURPIANA TOWER PARCHMENT

1. Mercedes García-Arenal and Fernando Rodriguez Mediano, *The Orient in Spain: Converted Muslims, the Forged Gospels of Granada, and the Rise of Orientalism* (Brill, Leiden, 2013), pp. 13–14; Claudia Colini, 'La invención del Sacromonte: How and Why Scholars Debated about the Lead Books of

Granada for Two Hundred Years' in Cécile Michel and Michael Friedrich (eds), *Fakes and Forgeries of Written Artefacts from Ancient Mesopotamia to Modern China* (De Gruyter, Berlin and Boston, 2020), pp. 215 and 217; Pieter Sjoerd van Koningsveld and Gerard A. Wiegers, *The Lead Books of the Sacromonte and the Parchment of the Torre Turpiana: Granada, 1588–1606* (Brill, Leiden, 2024), pp. 20–1 with fig. 4.

2. García-Arenal and Mediano, *The Orient in Spain*, p. 14; Pieter Sjoerd van Koningsveld and Gerard A. Wiegers, 'The Parchment of the "Torre Turpiana": The Original Document and Its Early Interpreters', *Al-Qantara*, 24, no. 2 (2003), pp. 329–30; Pieter Sjoerd van Koningsveld and Gerard A. Wiegers, *The Sacromonte Parchment and Lead Books: Critical Edition of the Arabic Texts and Analysis of the Religious Ideas* (Avondrood, Rijswijk, 2019), p. 6.
3. García-Arenal and Mediano, *The Orient in Spain*, pp. 14, 16–17; Koningsveld and Wiegers, 'Parchment of the "Torre Turpiana"', p. 345.
4. Colini, 'La invención del Sacromonte', pp. 212–14.
5. García-Arenal and Mediano, *The Orient in Spain*, pp. 97–98, 103, 155–6.
6. Koningsveld and Wiegers, 'Parchment of the "Torre Turpiana"', p. 345.
7. García-Arenal and Mediano, *The Orient in Spain*, p. 187; Koningsveld and Wiegers, 'Parchment of the "Torre Turpiana"', p. 332; Pieter Sjoerd van Koningsveld, 'Le parchemin et les livres de plomb de Grenade: écriture, langue et origine d'une falsification' in María Julieta Vega García-Ferrer, María Luisa García Valverde, and Antonio López Carmona (eds), *Nuevas aportaciones al conocimiento y estudio del Sacro Monte IV centenario fundacional (1610–2010)* (Fundación Euroárabe, Granada, 2011), pp. 184–6.
8. Koningsveld and Wiegers, 'Parchment of the "Torre Turpiana"', pp. 333–45; García-Arenal and Mediano, *The Orient in Spain*, p. 16.
9. García-Arenal and Mediano, *The Orient in Spain*, pp. 15, 19–20, 22; Colini, 'La invención del Sacromonte', p. 229.
10. García-Arenal and Mediano, *The Orient in Spain*, pp. 22–3; Colini, 'La invención del Sacromonte', pp. 217–18; Katie A. Harris, *From Muslim to Christian Granada: Inventing a City's Past in Early Modern Spain* (Johns Hopkins University Press, Baltimore, 2007), pp. 4, 156.
11. Harris, *From Muslim to Christian Granada*, pp. 4–7; Koningsveld and Wiegers, *Lead Books of the Sacromonte*, p. 14.
12. Harris, *From Muslim to Christian Granada*, p. 113.
13. Koningsveld and Wiegers, *Sacromonte Parchment and Lead Books*, p. 8; Colini, 'La invención del Sacromonte', p. 218.
14. Harris, *From Muslim to Christian Granada*, pp. 7, 29–33; García-Arenal and Mediano, *The Orient in Spain*, p. 24.
15. The Libro Mudo is Lead Book 17. Koningsveld and Wiegers, *Sacromonte Parchment and Lead Books*, pp. 12–14, 27–8.
16. Harris, *From Muslim to Christian Granada*, pp. 7, 33–4, 37, 128.
17. Colini, 'La invención del Sacromonte', pp. 234–5.
18. Harris, *From Muslim to Christian Granada*, pp. 41–5; Koningsveld and Wiegers, *Lead Books of the Sacromonte*, p. 80.
19. Harris, *From Muslim to Christian Granada*, pp. 46, 134, 149–50; Colini, 'La invención del Sacromonte', p. 221; Koningsveld and Wiegers, *Lead Books of the Sacromonte*, p. 152.

20. Rian Hagebeuk and Katherine Mueller, '"The Subtelty of Witches": A Reformation Era Cipher Mystery' in Carola Dahlke and Beáta Megyesi (eds), *Proceedings of the 5th International Conference on Historical Cryptology HistoCrypt 2022* (Linköping University Electronic Press, Linköping, 2022), pp. 101–10.
21. See the entry for Mellon MS 29 in the Beinecke catalogue, https://pre1600ms.beinecke.library.yale.edu/docs/pre1600.mell029.htm and https://collections.library.yale.edu/catalog/17388793. See also Agnieszka Rec, 'Ciphers and Secrecy among the Alchemists: A Preliminary Report', *Societas Magica Newsletter*, 31 (2014), pp. 5–6.
22. Ingrid Rowland, 'The Theatre of Forgery: Curzio Inghirami (Volterra, 1614–1655) and Giorgio Grognet de Vassé (Malta, 1774–1862)' in Philip Lavender and Matilda Amundsen Bergström (eds), *Faking It! The Performance of Forgery in Late Medieval and Early Modern Culture* (Brill, Leiden and Boston, 2023), pp. 232–5; Anthony Grafton, *Forgers and Critics: Creativity and Duplicity in Western Scholarship*, new edn (Princeton University Press, Princeton, 2019), p. 28.
23. Rowland, 'Theatre of Forgery', pp. 235–46.
24. Gerard González Germain, 'An Antiquarian Forger at Ferdinand's Court: On the Authorship of the Fake Inscriptions of Early 16th-Century Spain', *Bibliothèque d'Humanisme et Renaissance*, 79, no. 1 (2017), pp. 97–121.
25. Sari Kivistö, *The Vices of Learning: Morality and Knowledge at Early Modern Universities* (Brill, Leiden, 2014), pp. 122–3.
26. William McCuaig, *Carlo Sigonio: The Changing World of the Late Renaissance* (Princeton University Press, Princeton, 1989), p. 311.
27. Samantha Kelly, 'The Curious Case of Ethiopic Chaldean: Fraud, Philology, and Cultural (Mis)Understanding in European Conceptions of Ethiopia', *Renaissance Quarterly*, 68 (2015), pp. 1242–9.
28. Jack Lynch, 'Forgery as Performance Art: The Strange Case of George Psalmanazar', *1650–1850: Ideas, Aesthetics, and Inquiries in the Early Modern Era*, 11 (2005), pp. 22–3; Michael Keevak, *The Pretended Asian: George Psalmanazar's Eighteenth-Century Formosan Hoax* (Wayne State University Press, Detroit, 2004), p. 63.
29. Chien Hung-yi, 'The Psalmanazar Affair and the Birth of Taiwan Studies in Europe: A Reassessment of the Historic Hoax', *International Journal of Taiwan Studies*, 3 (2020), p. 115; Keevak, *Pretended Asian*, pp. 63–5.
30. Keevak, *Pretended Asian*, pp. 65–8, 71, 76–7. For the original drawings and writings, see MS 954, items 25 and 27, in the collection of Lambeth Palace, London.
31. Lynch, 'Forgery as Performance Art', pp. 23–4; Chien, 'Psalmanazar Affair', pp. 117, 123–6, 129. For the reference to Halley's map, see the entry for 26 April 1704 in the Meetings of the Royal Society, 1702–1707, https://ttp.royalsociety.org//ttp/ttp.html?id=92af9cc0-c0ec-4a8b-a03a-03b298a57f56&type=book.
32. Koningsveld and Wiegers, 'Parchment of the "Torre Turpiana"', p. 330; Colini, 'La invención del Sacromonte', pp. 236, 238; Harris, *From Muslim to Christian Granada*, pp. 154–6.
33. Harris, *From Muslim to Christian Granada*, p. 153.
34. Koningsveld and Wiegers, *Sacromonte Parchment and Lead Books*, pp. 25, 44–7.
35. Harris, *From Muslim to Christian Granada*, pp. 154–6.

36. Colini, 'La invención del Sacromonte', p. 215.
37. Harris, *From Muslim to Christian Granada*, pp. 150–1, 157–8.

7. 'AN UNIVERSALL ALPHABET'

1. John Sargeaunt, 'Busby's Account Book' in George Fisher Russell Barker, *Memoir of Richard Busby, D.D. (1606–1695) with Some Account of Westminster School in the Seventeenth Century* (Lawrence and Bullen, London, 1895), pp. 104–5. The manuscript page is now reference code GB 2014 WS-05-HAR-01 in the collection of Westminster School, London, https://collections.westminster.org.uk/index.php/gb-2014-ws-05-har-01.
2. Ethel Seaton, 'Thomas Hariot's Secret Script', *Ambix*, 5, nos 3–4 (1956), p. 111.
3. Seaton, 'Thomas Hariot's Secret Script', pp. 111–14.
4. Vivian Salmon, 'Thomas Harriot (1560–1621) and the Origins of Algonkian Linguistics' in Konrad Koerner (ed.), *Language and Society in Early Modern England: Selected Essays 1982–1994* (John Benjamins Publishing Company, Amsterdam and Philadelphia, 1996), pp. 150–2.
5. David Beers Quinn, 'Thomas Harriot and the Problem of America' in Robert Fox (ed.), *Thomas Harriot: An Elizabethan Man of Science* (Routledge, Abingdon and New York, 2017), pp. 10–13; Salmon, 'Thomas Harriot', pp. 144–5; David Beers Quinn, *The Roanoke Voyages, 1584–1590: Documents to Illustrate the English Voyages to North America under the Patent Granted to Walter Raleigh in 1584*, vol. 1 (Routledge, Abingdon and New York, 2016), pp. 6–7. Andrew Lawler, *The Secret Token: Myth, Obsession, and the Search for the Lost Colony of Roanoke* (Doubleday, New York, 2018), p. 33.
6. Quinn, 'Thomas Harriot', pp. 14–15; Salmon, 'Thomas Harriot', pp. 149–50; Quinn, *Roanoke Voyages*, pp. 94–100; Lawler, *Secret Token*, pp. 36–7.
7. Alden T. Vaughan, 'Sir Walter Ralegh's Indian Interpreters, 1584–1618', *William and Mary Quarterly*, 59, no. 2 (2002), pp. 344–6.
8. Michael Leroy Oberg, *The Head in Edward Nugent's Hand: Roanoke's Forgotten Indians* (University of Pennsylvania Press, Philadelphia, 2008), pp. 50–1.
9. Vaughan, 'Sir Walter Ralegh's Indian Interpreters', pp. 346–8; Oberg, *The Head in Edward Nugent's Hand*, p. 52.
10. Vaughan, 'Sir Walter Ralegh's Indian Interpreters', pp. 348–50; Oberg, *The Head in Edward Nugent's Hand*, pp. 57–60; Lawler, *Secret Token*, p. 50; Quinn, *Roanoke Voyages*, pp. 158–9. The five ships mentioned here do not include the two pinnaces.
11. Quinn, *Roanoke Voyages*, pp. 321, 380; Quinn, 'Thomas Harriot', p. 15; Salmon, 'Thomas Harriot', p. 146.
12. Vaughan, 'Sir Walter Ralegh's Indian Interpreters', pp. 350–1; Oberg, *The Head in Edward Nugent's Hand*, pp. 60–2; Lawler, *Secret Token*, p. 54.
13. Vaughan, 'Sir Walter Ralegh's Indian Interpreters', pp. 350–1; Oberg, *The Head in Edward Nugent's Hand*, pp. 63–7; Quinn, *Roanoke Voyages*, p. 191; Lawler, *Secret Token*, pp. 55–8.
14. Quinn, 'Thomas Harriot', p. 16; Quinn, *Roanoke Voyages*, p. 25; Lawler, *Secret Token*, p. 60.
15. Quinn, 'Thomas Harriot', pp. 15–16, 21; Salmon, 'Thomas Harriot', p. 146.
16. Oberg, *The Head in Edward Nugent's Hand*, pp. 6–9; Lawler, *Secret Token*, p. 38.

17. Salmon, 'Thomas Harriot', pp. 151–4; Xing Weiao, 'Linguistics and Epistemology in Thomas Harriot's North Atlantic World' in Jim Pearce, Ward J. Risvold, and William Given (eds), *Renaissance Papers 2021* (Camden House, Rochester, NY, 2022), p. 110.
18. Hilary Gatti, 'The Natural Philosophy of Thomas Harriot' in Fox, *Thomas Harriot*, pp. 73–4; Mordecai Feingold, *The Mathematician's Apprenticeship: Science, Universities and Society in England, 1560–1640* (Cambridge University Press, Cambridge, 1984), pp. 136–7. For the Arthur Dee alchemical manuscript, see MS 436 in the Wellcome Collection, London, https://wellcome collection.org/works/jbc2k756.
19. Thomas Harriot, *A Briefe and True Report of the New Found Land of Virginia: Of the Commodities and of the Nature and Manners of the Naturall Inhabitants* (Frankfurt, 1590), pp. 8–10, 25–27; Quinn, *Roanoke Voyages*, pp. 328–9, 333, 370, 372–5; Salmon, 'Thomas Harriot', p. 157.
20. Harriot, *A Briefe and True Report*, pp. 27–9; Oberg, *The Head in Edward Nugent's Hand*, pp. 37, 73–5, 78–80; Quinn, *Roanoke Voyages*, pp. 376–80.
21. Peter T. Daniels and William Bright (eds), *The World's Writing Systems* (Oxford University Press, Oxford and New York, 1996), p. 577.
22. George L. Campbell and Christoper Moseley, *The Routledge Handbook of Scripts and Alphabets*, 2nd edn (Routledge, Abingdon and New York, 2012), pp. 50, 82, 84, 96, 169, 177. Daniels and Bright, *World's Writing Systems*, p. 578; Ardit Bido, *The Albanian Orthodox Church: A Political History, 1878–1945* (Routledge, London, 2020), p. 13.
23. For these and further examples, see Campbell and Moseley, *Routledge Handbook of Scripts and Alphabets*, pp. 70, 117–18, 171, 173, 175, 180; Daniels and Bright, *World's Writing Systems*, p. 579.
24. Johanna Drucker, *Inventing the Alphabet: The Origins of Letters from Antiquity to the Present* (University of Chicago Press, Chicago and London, 2022), pp. 57–8, 60–1, 65, 71, 83–6; Patrizia Lendinara, 'The Poem "Nauta rudis . . ." in Anglo-Saxon Manuscripts: More than a Colophon' in Concetta Giliberto and Loredana Teresi (eds), *Limits to Learning: The Transfer of Encyclopaedic Knowledge in the Early Middle Ages* (Peeters, Leuven, 2013), pp. 228–31.
25. Oberg, *The Head in Edward Nugent's Hand*, pp. 81–6; Quinn, *Roanoke Voyages*, pp. 265–6.
26. Oberg, *The Head in Edward Nugent's Hand*, pp. 87–95; Lawler, *Secret Token*, pp. 67–8; Vaughan, 'Sir Walter Ralegh's Indian Interpreters', pp. 350–1; Quinn, *Roanoke Voyages*, pp. 270–1.
27. Oberg, *The Head in Edward Nugent's Hand*, pp. 96–102, 108; Quinn, *Roanoke Voyages*, pp. 286–8, 381–2.
28. Ralph W.V. Elliott, 'Isaac Newton's "Of an Universall Language"', *Modern Language Review*, 52, no. 1 (1957), p. 3; Jonathan Cohen, 'On the Project of a Universal Character', *Mind*, 63, no. 249 (1954), pp. 49–51; Umberto Eco, *The Search for the Perfect Language*, trans. James Fentress (Blackwell, Oxford, 1995), pp. 53–72.
29. Cohen, 'On the Project of a Universal Character', pp. 56–8; Jaap Maat and David Cram (eds), *George Dalgarno on Universal Language: The Art of Signs (1661), The Deaf and Dumb Man's Tutor (1680), and the Unpublished Papers* (Oxford University Press, Oxford, 2001), pp. 48, 139, 151, 272.

30. Cohen, 'On the Project of a Universal Character', pp. 58–9; Benedek Láng, *The Rohonc Code: Tracing a Historical Riddle* (Pennsylvania State University Press, University Park, PA, 2021), pp. 105–7.
31. Elliott, 'Isaac Newton's "Of an Universall Language"', pp. 1–18.
32. Vivian Salmon, 'Cave Beck: A Seventeenth-Century Ipswich Schoolmaster and His "Universal Character"', *Proceedings of the Suffolk Institute of Archaeology*, 33 (1976), pp. 295–6.
33. George E. McCracken, 'Athanasius Kircher's Universal Polygraphy', *Isis*, 39, no. 4 (1948), pp. 215–21.
34. Quinn, 'Thomas Harriot', p. 21; Vaughan, 'Sir Walter Ralegh's Indian Interpreters', pp. 351–2; Quinn, *Roanoke Voyages*, pp. 260, 293 with n. 4, 334 with n. 1, 302, 359; Lawler, *Secret Token*, pp. 70–5.
35. Salmon, 'Thomas Harriot', pp. 145, 147. Batho, 'Thomas Harriot and the Northumberland Household' in Fox, *Thomas Harriot*, p. 33. Xing, 'Linguistics and Epistemology', p. 113. For the map, see Royal Museums Greenwich, London, item reference P/49(29), https://www.rmg.co.uk/collections/archive/rmgc-object-541707.
36. Vaughan, 'Sir Walter Ralegh's Indian Interpreters', p. 356; Lawler, *Secret Token*, pp. 100–1.
37. British Library, London, Add MS 6788, folio 417v. See Salmon, 'Thomas Harriot', pp. 147–8. For the manuscript page itself, see, https://echo.mpiwg-berlin.mpg.de/ECHOdocuView?url=/permanent/library/AYB35Z4D/&start=830&viewMode=image&pn=834.
38. Salmon, 'Thomas Harriot', p. 148.
39. Quinn, 'Thomas Harriot', p. 26.
40. Batho, 'Thomas Harriot', pp. 33–8.
41. Batho, 'Thomas Harriot', p. 45; Alan Gallay, *Walter Ralegh: Architect of Empire* (Basic Books, New York, 2019); Lawler, *Secret Token*, p. 125; Andrew Fleck, '"At the time of his death": Manuscript Instability and Walter Ralegh's Performance on the Scaffold', *Journal of British Studies*, 48 (2009), pp. 6, 8–9, 12, 17, 19. The page itself is British Library, London, Add MS 6789, folio 533r. It can be viewed at https://echo.mpiwg-berlin.mpg.de/ECHOdocuView?url=/mpiwg/online/permanent/library/0VGM2B80&viewMode=text_image&start=1061&pn=1063&ws=3.
42. Quinn, 'Thomas Harriot', pp. 19–20.
43. Batho, 'Thomas Harriot', p. 38.
44. Salmon, 'Thomas Harriot', pp. 145, 158; Gordon R. Batho, 'Thomas Harriot's Manuscripts' in Fox, *Thomas Harriot*, pp. 286, 288–9; Robyn Arianrhod, *Thomas Harriot: A Life in Science* (Oxford University Press, New York, 2019), pp. 261–2; ECHO: Cultural Heritage Online, 'II History of the Manuscripts', Max Planck Institute for the History of Science, 2015, https://echo.mpiwg-berlin.mpg.de/content/scientific_revolution/harriot/project_infos/harriot-manuscripts; Rosalind C.H. Tanner, 'The Study of Thomas Harriot's Manuscripts I. Harriot's Will', *History of Science*, 6, no. 1 (1967), pp. 1–16.
45. John Aubrey, *Brief Lives, Chiefly of Contemporaries*, ed. Andrew Clark, 2 vols (Clarendon Press, Oxford, 1898), vol. 1, p. 285.
46. Aubrey, *Brief Lives*, vol. 1, p. 285; Salmon, 'Thomas Harriot', pp. 145–6; Arianrhod, *Thomas Harriot*, p. 261.

8. *FRUCTUS ITINERIS AD SEPTENTRIONALES*

1. Elisja M.R. Van Kessel, 'Johannes van Heeck (1579–?), Co-Founder of the Accademia dei Lincei in Rome: A Bio-Bibliographical Sketch', *Mededelingen van het Nederlands Instituut te Rome*, 38 (1976), p. 125; Ada Alessandrini, *Cimeli Lincei a Montpellier* (Accademia Nazionale dei Lincei, Rome, 1978), p. 74. Heckius's account is found in Bibliothèque universitaire historique de médecine, University of Montpellier, France, H 506, folios 1v–2r.
2. Giuseppe Gabrieli, 'Qualche altra notizia sugli scritti e sulla vita di Giovanni Ecchio Linceo', *Rediconti della Reale accademia nazionale dei Lincei, classe di scienze morali, storiche e filologiche*, 10 (1934), p. 481; Antonio Clericuzio and Silvia de Renzi, 'Medicine, Alchemy and Natural Philosophy in the Early Accademia dei Lincei' in D.S. Chambers and F. Quiviger (eds), *Italian Academies of the Sixteenth Century* (Warburg Institute, London, 1995), p. 178.
3. Antonio Cadei (ed.), *Il trionfo sul tempo. Manoscritti illustrati dell'Accademia nazionale dei Lincei* (Franco Cosimo Panini, Modena, 2002), p. 79. The notebook is in the Biblioteca Vallicelliana, Rome, R.57.
4. Clericuzio and Renzi, 'Medicine, Alchemy and Natural Philosophy', p. 180.
5. David Freedberg, *The Eye of the Lynx: Galileo, His Friends, and the Beginnings of Modern Natural History* (University of Chicago Press, Chicago, 2002), p. 197.
6. Gabrieli, 'Qualche altra notizia', p. 483.
7. Freedberg, *Eye of the Lynx*, pp. 196–7.
8. Van Kessel, 'Johannes van Heeck', pp. 109–13.
9. Domenico Carutti, *Di Giovanni Eckio e della instituzione dell'Accademia dei Lincei con alcune note inedite intorno a Galileo* (Coi tipi del Salviucci, Rome, 1877), p. 48.
10. Carutti, *Di Giovanni Eckio*, pp. 48–9. Also see Van Kessel, 'Johannes van Heeck', pp. 115–16.
11. Carutti, *Di Giovanni Eckio*, pp. 49–50.
12. Van Kessel, 'Johannes van Heeck', pp. 116–18; Freedberg, *Eye of the Lynx*, pp. 68–9.
13. The Lincean cipher was broken in 1822 by Domenico Morosini, at the request of Francesco Cancellieri. He explains his solution in a letter dated 15 July 1822. Domenico Morosini, *Lettere del conte Domenico Morosini, nobile veneziano, al signor abate Francesco Cancellieri di Roma, e di questo a quello intorno ad alcune cifre spettanti all'Accademia de' Lincei, e per la seconda volta pubblicate* (Stabilimento Tipo-Litografico di Gaetano Longo, Ceneda, 1865), pp. 25–7, with a drawing of the symbols on p. 24; Paolo Galluzzi, *The Lynx and the Telescope: The Parallel Worlds of Cesi and Galileo* (Brill, Leiden and Boston, 2017), pp. 41–5; Van Kessel, 'Johannes van Heeck', p. 128.
14. Stillman Drake, 'The Accademia dei Lincei', *Science*, 151 (1966), pp. 1195–6; Irene Baldriga, 'Reading the Universal Book of Nature: The Accademia dei Lincei in Rome (1603–1630)' in Arjan van Dixhoorn and Susie Speakman Sutch (eds), *The Reach of the Republic of Letters: Literary and Learned Societies in Late Medieval and Early Modern Europe*, vol. 1 (Brill, Leiden, 2008), pp. 353–8; Baldassare Odescalchi, *Memorie istorico critiche dell'Accademia de' Lincei e del principe Federico Cesi, secondo duca d'Aquasparta, fondatore e principe della Medesima* (Salvioni, Rome, 1806), pp. 28–31.

15. Carutti, *Di Giovanni Eckio*, p. 53; Van Kessel, 'Johannes van Heeck', pp. 119–20.
16. Simone Testa, *Italian Academies and Their Networks, 1525–1700: From Local to Global* (Palgrave Macmillan, New York, 2015), pp. 4–5, 10, 18, 26.
17. Neil Tarrant, 'Giambattista Della Porta and the Roman Inquisition: Censorship and the Definition of Nature's Limits in Sixteenth-Century Italy', *British Journal for the History of Science*, 46, no. 4 (2013), pp. 613–16, 619–23.
18. Tarrant, 'Giambattista Della Porta', pp. 613, 619–23.
19. Kristie Macrakis, 'Confessing Secrets: Secret Communication and the Origins of Modern Science', *Intelligence and National Security*, 25, no. 2 (2010), pp. 183–7.
20. Galluzzi, *Lynx and the Telescope*, pp. 54, 194.
21. Theodor Harmsen, 'Fiction or a Much Stranger Truth: Sources and Reception of the Geheime Figuren der Rosenkreuzer – Secret Symbols of the Rosicrucians in the 18th, 19th and 20th Centuries' in Monika Neugebauer-Wölk, Renko Geffarth, and Markus Meumann (eds), *Aufklärung und Esoterik. Wege in die Moderne* (De Gruyter, Berlin and Boston, 2013), pp. 726–52.
22. Kassel University, 'Anleitung zum Beschwören von Geistern: Unibibliothek entziffert Zauberhandschrift', 8 June 2013, https://www.uni-kassel.de/uni/en/aktuelles/sitemap-detail-news/post/detail/News/anleitung-zum-beschwoeren-von-geistern-unibibliothek-entziffert-zauberhandschrift. The manuscript is shelfmark 8° Ms. astron. 7, https://orka.bibliothek.uni-kassel.de/viewer/image/1374150101659/. For a translation and comments, see Brigitte Pfeil and Sabina Lüdemann, '"Man wirt ganz konfus von al Zeichen": die Handschrift 8° Ms. astron. 7 der Universitätsbibliothek Kassel – Landesbibliothek und Murhardsche Bibliothek der Stadt Kassel (Kasseler Zauberhandschrift)', Kassel, 2016, https://kobra.uni-kassel.de/items/8642ac8e-9ac5-44d4-8ac3-3db41581b413.
23. This manuscript is now in the István Sárközy Local History Museum in Nagybajom, Somogy county, Hungary. See Hanna Vámos, 'Leleplezett Titok, Pálóczi Horváth Ádám titkos, szabadkőműves dokumentuma' in Rumen István Csörsz and Béla Hegedüs (eds), *Magyar Arión. Tanulmányok Pálóczi Horváth Ádám műveiről* (Rec.iti, Budapest, 2011), pp. 41–55.
24. Andreas Önnerfors, 'Unveiling the Copiale-Manuscript: Layers of Fraternalism, Ritual and Politics in Eighteenth Century Germany', paper presented at the World Conference on Fraternalism, Freemasonry and History, 29–30 May 2015, http://dx.doi.org/10.13140/RG.2.1.1397.1367; Kevin Knight, Beáta Megyesi, and Christiane Schaefer, 'The Secrets of the Copiale Cipher', *Journal for Research into Freemasonry and Fraternalism*, 2, no. 2 (2011), pp. 315–24. For a translation of the Copiale manuscript, see https://web.archive.org/web/20230321151221/https://cl.lingfil.uu.se/~bea/copiale/copiale-translation.pdf.
25. Carutti, *Di Giovanni Eckio*, pp. 54–5; Freedberg, *Eye of the Lynx*, p. 70.
26. Van Kessel, 'Johannes van Heeck', pp. 120–1; Gabrieli, 'Qualche altra notizia', p. 500.
27. Van Kessel, 'Johannes van Heeck', pp. 121–2; Freedberg, *Eye of the Lynx*, pp. 69, 201–2; Gabrieli, 'Qualche altra notizia', p. 501.
28. Freedberg, *Eye of the Lynx*, p. 70; Lyke de Vries and Leen Spruit, 'Paracelsus and Roman Censorship: Johannes Faber's 1616 Report in Context', *Intellectual History Review*, 28, no. 2 (2018), p. 233.

29. Freedberg, *Eye of the Lynx*, pp. 91–7.
30. Clericuzio and Renzi, 'Medicine, Alchemy and Natural Philosophy', p. 183.
31. Van Kessel, 'Johannes van Heeck', pp. 122–4.
32. Freedberg, *Eye of the Lynx*, p. 199; Alessandrini, *Cimeli Lincei a Montpellier*, p. 68, n. 18; Gabrieli, 'Qualche altra notizia', p. 487. The two notebooks mentioned were recorded in the Albani library collection at the Quirinal Palace in Rome (see p. 190), but are now lost.
33. This is call number H 506 in the Bibliothèque universitaire historique de médecine, University of Montpellier, http://www.calames.abes.fr/pub/#details?id=D01042185.
34. This is call number H 507 in Montpellier, http://www.calames.abes.fr/pub/#details?id=D01042186.
35. This is call number H 508 in Montpellier, http://www.calames.abes.fr/pub/#details?id=D01042187. For the basilisk, see Cadei, *Il trionfo sul tempo*, p. 77.
36. Cadei, *Il trionfo sul tempo*, p. 76.
37. This notebook is now in the Bibliothèque universitaire historique de médecine of the University of Montpellier, France, call number H 505, http://www.calames.abes.fr/Pub/#details?id=D01042184. Alessandrini, *Cimeli Lincei a Montpellier*, pp. 68–73, 288–9; Freedberg, *Eye of the Lynx*, p. 444, n. 10. Cadei, *Il trionfo sul tempo*, p. 77.
38. Biblioteca Apostolica Vaticana, Vatican City, Borg.lat.898, https://digi.vatlib.it/view/MSS_Borg.lat.898/0002. The connection between this manuscript and Heckius was made by Nick Pelling, who deciphered it and made a translation, 'Johannes Van Heeck's Cipher Manuscript . . .', 8 February 2016, https://ciphermysteries.com/2016/02/08/johannes-van-heecks-cipher-manuscript. The text was also deciphered and translated by the DECODE team: Nada Aldarrab, Kevin Knight, and Beáta Megyesi, 'The Borg.lat.898 Cipher', 2018, https://web.archive.org/web/20231129122043/https://cl.lingfil.uu.se/~bea/borg/.
39. For the deciphered text in Latin and English, see Urban Örneholm, 'Interpretation of Decoding and English Translation', 2018, https://web.archive.org/web/20240223235659/https://cl.lingfil.uu.se/~bea/borg/corrected-Latin-translation.txthttps://web.archive.org/web/20240223230225/https://cl.lingfil.uu.se/~bea/borg/Comments.pdf.
40. Urban Örneholm, 'On the Translation/Paraphrase/Guesswork', 2018, https://web.archive.org/web/20240223230225/https://cl.lingfil.uu.se/~bea/borg/Comments.pdf.
41. Örneholm, 'Interpretation of Decoding and English Translation'.
42. Gabrieli, 'Qualche altra notizia', p. 501.
43. This is the *Magna mechanica*, now in the Biblioteca Medicea Laurenziana, Florence, Fondo Ashburnham Catalogo no. 1210. See entry in Bertram Ashburnham and Guillaume Libri, *A Catalogue of the Manuscripts at Ashburnham Place. Part the First, Comprising a Collection Formed by Professor Libri* (C.F. Hodgson, London, 1853). See also https://www.bmlonline.it/en/la-biblioteca/cataloghi/fondo-ashburnham-catalogo/. Gabrieli, 'Qualche altra notizia', p. 491; Giuseppe Gabrieli, 'Gli scritti inediti di Giovanni Ecchio Linceo (1577–1620)', *Rediconti della Reale accademia nazionale dei Lincei, classe di scienze morali, storiche e filologiche*, 6 (1930), pp. 390–1.

44. Macrakis, 'Confessing Secrets', pp. 191–3; Mario Biagioli, 'From Ciphers to Confidentiality: Secrecy, Openness and Priority in Science', *British Journal for the History of Science*, 45, no. 2 (2012), pp. 213–33. For Robert Boyle in particular, see Michael Hunter, 'Robert Boyle and Secrecy' in Elaine Leong and Alisha Rankin (eds), *Secrets and Knowledge in Medicine and Science, 1500–1800* (Routledge, New York and London, 2016), p. 104.
45. Biagioli, 'From Ciphers to Confidentiality'; Hannah Marcus and Paula Findlen, 'Deciphering Galileo: Communication and Secrecy before and after the Trial', *Renaissance Quarterly*, 72 (2019), pp. 953–95.
46. Elaine Leong and Alisha Rankin, 'Introduction: Secrets and Knowledge' in Leong and Rankin, *Secrets and Knowledge in Medicine and Science*, pp. 8–9; John Block Friedman, 'The Cipher Alphabet of John de Foxton's *Liber Cosmographiae*', *Scriptorium*, 36, no. 2 (1982), pp. 219–21.
47. Keagan Brewer, '"I beg your grace that you suppress this chapter or else allow it to be written in secret letters": The Emotions of Encipherment in Late-Medieval Gynaecology' in Colin Layfield and John Abela (eds), *International Conference on the Voynich Manuscript 2022*, CEUR Workshop Proceedings, 2022, https://ceur-ws.org/Vol-3313/paper3.pdf, p. 4, table 2.
48. Friedman, 'Cipher Alphabet of John de Foxton's *Liber Cosmographiae*', pp. 232–3. In another work, Friedman notes that there are 293 ciphered words in the manuscript: John Block Friedman, *John de Foxton's Liber Cosmographiae (1408): An Edition and Codicological Study* (E.J. Brill, Leiden and New York, 1988), p. xlvii.
49. This is Cod. III 2.8° 34 in Augsburg University Library. See Hans J. Vermeer, 'Technisch-naturwissenschaftliche Rezepte aus einer Harburger Handschrift', *Sudhoffs Archiv für Geschichte der Medizin und der Naturwissenschaften*, 45, no. 2 (1961), pp. 110–26; Hans J. Vermeer, 'Eine altdeutsche Sammlung medizinischer Rezepte in Geheimschrift', *Sudhoffs Archiv für Geschichte der Medizin und der Naturwissenschaften*, 45, no. 3 (1961), pp. 235–46.
50. Leong and Rankin, 'Introduction', pp. 9–10. The notebook is Stowe MS 1077 in the British Library, London.
51. Van Kessel, 'Johannes van Heeck', pp. 124–8; Freedberg, *Eye of the Lynx*, p. 253.
52. Gabrieli, 'Gli scritti inediti di Giovanni Ecchio Linceo', p. 364 and n. 1; Van Kessel, 'Johannes van Heeck', pp. 128–30; Carutti, *Di Giovanni Eckio*, p. 66.
53. Oddly, the enciphered notebook (H 505) never received the Cesiano-Lincea library stamp like the other Heckius notebooks, and neither did the enciphered Vatican notebook. Alessandrini, *Cimeli Lincei a Montpellier*, p. 69.
54. Maria Teresa Biagetti, 'Dispersed Collections of Scientific Books: The Case of the Private Library of Federico Cesi (1585–1630)' in Flavia Bruni and Andrew Pettegree (eds), *Lost Books: Reconstructing the Print World of Pre-Industrial Europe* (Brill, Leiden and Boston, 2016), pp. 390–3; Alessandrini, *Cimeli Lincei a Montpellier*, pp. 17–22.
55. *Mechanica et naturalia Ioannis Ecchi Lincaei* became Albani no. 1023. This is the notebook that would later become H 505 in Montpellier. Heckius's *De naturalium mixturis* was given call number Cod. 881 by the Albani librarian Francesco Cancellieri (1751–1826). This is still found written on the manuscript's last page. This notebook is listed among the Albani collection's Lincean manuscripts in a document now in the Vatican Library (Vat.lat.9205); see

M. Howard Rienstra, 'Gaetano Marini and the Historiography of the Accademia dei Lincei', *Archivo della Società romana di storia patria*, 94 (1971), pp. 231–3 (listed under Cod. 881). It may also bear an Albani collection number but, if so, it lies beneath the Vatican's library sticker at the top left of its first page, where we find examples of this number in other manuscripts that had been in the Albani collection. See, for example, H 507 in Montpellier.

56. Alessandrini, *Cimeli Lincei a Montpellier*, pp. 25–30, 41–2; Biagetti, 'Dispersed Collections of Scientific Books', pp. 393–4. BnF Comité d'histoire, 'Provenance. Albani', http://comitehistoire.bnf.fr/type-fiche/provenance?page=32.
57. Morosini, *Lettere del conte Domenico Morosini*, pp. 25–7, with a drawing of the symbols on p. 24.
58. Alessandrini, *Cimeli Lincei a Montpellier*, pp. 39–41.
59. Cecil H. Clough, 'The Albani Library and Pope Clement XI', *Librarium: Zeitschrift der Schweizerischen Bibliophilen-Gesellschaft*, 12 (1969), p. 17.
60. Fondo Ashburnham Catalogo no. 1210. Gabrieli, 'Gli scritti inediti di Giovanni Ecchio Linceo', p. 391.
61. Part of the blue stamp of the library of the Sacred Congregation for the Propagation of the Faith is at the bottom of the page, with the rest on the following page (folio 2r). Therefore, the remains of the ripped-out page must have been folded over on top of folio 2r when the librarian made the stamp, showing that the page was torn out earlier in its history. Interestingly, no stamp from the Cesi library, normally found on the title page, is present.
62. Francesco D'Aiuto and Paolo Vian, *Guida ai fondi manoscritti, numismatici, a stampa della Biblioteca vaticana*, 2 vols (Biblioteca Apostolica Vaticana, Vatican City, 2011), pp. 356–8, 376. For readers who want to investigate further: from digital inspection of the notebook, there is a number on the front cover beside its modern one. The older number reads 144?, with the final number smudged, possibly a zero. The spine, however, gives us a bit more information, bearing the numbers 4184 and 4307, each in a different hand, and again different from the number on the front cover. See https://digi.vatlib.it/view/MSS_Borg.lat.898/0002.
63. Gabrieli, 'Gli scritti inediti di Giovanni Ecchio Linceo', pp. 365–97. The title of the notebook is included in an article by Howard Rienstra in 1971 as part of the Albani collection under Cod. 881, but he does not connect it with Borg. Lat.898 or seem to know that it is in the Vatican library collection. See Rienstra, 'Gaetano Marini and the Historiography of the Accademia Dei Lincei', pp. 231–2 (listed under Cod. 881).
64. Pelling, 'Johannes Van Heeck's Cipher Manuscript . . .'. For the DECODE project's decryption, see Aldarrab et al., 'The Borg.lat.898 Cipher'.

9. *DE THEOSOPHIA AEGYPTIORUM* AND *ATALANTA FUGIENS*

1. Hereward Tilton, *The Quest for the Phoenix: Spiritual Alchemy and Rosicrucianism in the Work of Count Michael Maier (1569–1622)* (Walter de Gruyter, Berlin and New York, 2003), p. 40.
2. Tilton, *Quest for the Phoenix*, pp. 38–40, 44–5, 52–3; Olivia Jean Happel, 'That Which Is Not Yet Known: An Analysis of Michael Maier's Alchemical Work

through *Arcana arcanissima*', PhD thesis, Pacifica Graduate Institute (2019), p. 34.

3. Happel, 'That Which Is Not Yet Known', p. 39.
4. Maria Beatrice Autizi, *L'università di Padova* (Editoriale Programma, Treviso, 2022), pp. 72–6.
5. Autizi, *L'università di Padova*, pp. 71–2.
6. Tilton, *Quest for the Phoenix*, pp. 55, 57–9.
7. Ulrich Neumann, 'Michel Maier (1569–1622) "philosophe et médecin"' in Jean-Claude Margolin and Sylvain Matton (eds), *Alchimie et philosophie à la Renaissance* (Vrin, Paris, 1993), pp. 307–26; Nils Lenke, Nicolas Roudet, and Hereward Tilton, 'Michael Maier: Nine Newly Discovered Letters', *Ambix*, 61, no. 1 (2014), p. 5, n. 20; Karin Figala and Ulrich Neumann, 'Michael Maier (1569–1622): New Bio-Bibliographical Material' in Z.R.W.M. von Martels (ed.), *Alchemy Revisited: Proceedings of the International Conference on the History of Alchemy at the University of Groningen 17–19 April 1989* (Brill, Leiden, 1990), p. 39; Tilton, *Quest for the Phoenix*, p. 64.
8. Happel, 'That Which Is Not Yet Known', pp. 36–7, 40.
9. Figala and Neumann, 'Michael Maier', p. 41.
10. There is only one known copy of this book, which is kept in the Royal Danish Library, Copenhagen, 12,-159, 4°.
11. Tilton, *Quest for the Phoenix*, pp. 70, 86.
12. Tilton, *Quest for the Phoenix*, pp. 80–6; Peter J. Forshaw, 'Michael Maier and Mythoalchemy' in Tara Nummedal and Donna Bilak (eds), *Furnace and Fugue: A Digital Edition of Michael Maier's 'Atalanta fugiens' (1618) with Scholarly Commentary* (University of Virginia Press, Charlottesville, 2020), https://doi.org/10.26300/bdp.ff.forshaw; Hereward Tilton, 'The Egyptian Theosophy of Count Michael Maier', *Theosophical History*, 9 (2003), pp. 9–29; Neumann, 'Michel Maier'. The manuscript is now in the University of Leipzig's library, under call number MS 0396.
13. Tilton, *Quest for the Phoenix*, pp. 100–7.
14. Lawrence Principe, *The Secrets of Alchemy* (University of Chicago Press, Chicago, 2012), pp. 107–10.
15. Principe, *Secrets of Alchemy*, pp. 127–9, 131–3.
16. Principe, *Secrets of Alchemy*, p. 115–18.
17. Tara Nummedal, 'Sound and Vision: The Alchemical Epistemology of Michael Maier's *Atalanta fugiens*' in Nummedal and Bilak, *Furnace and Fugue*, https://doi.org/10.26300/bdp.ff.nummedal.
18. Figala and Neumann, 'Michael Maier', p. 50; Nummedal, 'Sound and Vision'; Forshaw, 'Michael Maier and Mythoalchemy'.
19. *Atalanta fugiens*, Emblem 11, https://furnaceandfugue.org/atalanta-fugiens/emblem11.html; Nummedal, 'Sound and Vision'.
20. Michael Gaudio, 'The Emblem in the Landscape: Matthäus Merian's Etchings for *Atalanta fugiens*' in Nummedal and Bilak, *Furnace and Fugue*, https://doi.org/10.26300/bdp.ff.gaudio; Happel, 'That Which Is Not Yet Known', p. 217.
21. Tilton, *Quest for the Phoenix*, p. 221.
22. Forshaw, 'Michael Maier and Mythoalchemy'.
23. Donna Bilak, 'Chasing Atalanta: Maier, Steganography, and the Secrets of Nature' in Nummedal and Bilak, *Furnace and Fugue*, https://doi.org/10.26300/

bdp.ff.bilak. For the history of magic squares, see Benedek Láng, *Unlocked Books: Manuscripts of Learned Magic in the Medieval Libraries of Central Europe* (Pennsylvania State University Press, University Park, PA, 2008), p. 91.

24. Principe, *Secrets of Alchemy*, p. 111.
25. Principe, *Secrets of Alchemy*, pp. 146, 151, 153.
26. Lawrence Principe, 'Robert Boyle's Alchemical Secrecy: Codes, Ciphers and Concealments', *Ambix*, 39, no. 2 (1992), pp. 65–6.
27. Principe, *Secrets of Alchemy*, p. 18.
28. Principe, *Secrets of Alchemy*, p. 18.
29. Principe, *Secrets of Alchemy*, pp. 75–9.
30. Anke Timmermann, *Verse and Transmutation: A Corpus of Middle English Alchemical Poetry (Critical Editions and Studies)* (Brill, Leiden and Boston, 2013), pp. 113–43.
31. For an example of one of the Ripley Scrolls, with explanation, see British Library, 'Exploring the Ripley Scroll', *Google Arts & Culture*, https://artsandculture.google.com/story/exploring-the-ripley-scroll-the-british-library/OwXBNEuJqIJzLg?hl=en. See also R.I. McCallum, 'Ripley's Alchemical Scrolls', *Royal College of Physicians of Edinburgh*, https://www.rcpe.ac.uk/heritage/ripleys-alchemical-scrolls; Timmermann, *Verse and Transmutation*, pp. 56 and 117, n. 11; Deborah E. Harkness, 'The Scientific Reformation: John Dee and the Restitution of Nature', PhD thesis, University of California (1994), p. 158.
32. Principe, 'Robert Boyle's Alchemical Secrecy', p. 68.
33. See Petro Borelli, *Bibliotheca chimica* (Samuel Broun, Heidelberg, 1656), p. 254.
34. Figala and Neumann, 'Michael Maier', pp. 34–5. For Newton's copy of the book, see Trinity College Library, Cambridge, https://lib-cat.trin.cam.ac.uk/Record/cd4e7e43-386d-453e-b04e-ac520290e8ab. For the enciphered writing in the 1618 copy of Maier's *Themis aurea*, see the final seven lines on p. 160.
35. Only one copy of this book now exists: see Figala and Neumann, 'Michael Maier', p. 35. For the cipher itself, see Karin Figala and Ulrich Neumann, '"Author cui nomen Hermes Malavici": New Light on the Bio-Bibliography of Michael Maier' in Piyo Rattansi and Antonio Clericuzio (eds), *Alchemy and Chemistry in the 16th and 17th Centuries* (Kluwer Academic, Dordrecht and London, 1994), p. 140, n. 12; Sarah Lang, 'Situating Ciphers among Alchemical Techniques of Secrecy' in Carola Dahlke and Matthias Göggerle (eds), *Proceedings of the 6th International Conference on Historical Cryptology HistoCrypt 2023* (Linköping University Electronic Press, Linköping, 2023), https://ecp.ep.liu.se/index.php/histocrypt/issue/view/77/80, pp. 97–8.
36. Tilton, *Quest for the Phoenix*, p. 41.
37. Lang, 'Situating Ciphers among Alchemical Techniques of Secrecy', pp. 96, 98, 101–2.
38. This is Codex Palatinus Germanicus 597 in Heidelberg. For the manuscript, see Bibliotheca Palatina – Digital, https://digi.ub.uni-heidelberg.de/diglit/cpg597/0010/image,info,thumbs. See also Wilhelm Wattenbach, 'Alchymey Teuczsch', *Anzeiger für Kunde der deutschen Vorzeit*, 16 (1869), pp. 264–8; Gerhard Eis, 'Alchymey Teuczsch', *Medizinische Fachprosa des späten Mittelalters und der frühen Neuzeit* (Rodopi, Amsterdam, 1982), pp. 307–15.

39. Gerd Mentgen, 'Jewish Alchemists in Central Europe in the Later Middle Ages: Some New Sources', *Aleph*, 9, no. 2 (2009), pp. 345–6; Agnieszka Rec, 'Ciphers and Secrecy among the Alchemists: A Preliminary Report', *Societas Magica Newsletter*, 31 (2014), pp. 3–4.
40. This is now in the Biblioteca nacional de España, Madrid, under call number RES/20. For the manuscript details, with a link to a digital edition, see http://bdh.bne.es/bnesearch/CompleteSearch.do?fechaFdesde=1401&showYearItems=&field=todos&advanced=false&exact=on&textH=&completeText=&text=tesoro&fechaFhasta=1500&pageSize=1&pageSizeAbrv=30&pageNumber=4.
41. James V. Williams, 'Recherches sur deux traités attribués abusivement a Enrique de Villena: *Del Tesoro* et *Libro de Astrologia*', *École pratique des hautes études. 4e section, Sciences historiques et philologiques. Annuaire 1977–1978* (1978), p. 1279.
42. Juan Carlos Galende Díaz, 'La criptografía medieval: el *Libro del Tresoro*' in Juan Carlos Galende Díaz (ed.), *II jornadas científicas sobre documentación de la corona de Castilla (siglos XIII–XIV)* (Universidad Complutense de Madrid, Madrid, 2003), p. 58.
43. Williams, 'Recherches sur deux traités', pp. 1278–9.
44. Díaz, 'La criptografía medieval', pp. 49–51, 53; Williams, 'Recherches sur deux traités', p. 1277.
45. Meredith K. Ray, *Daughters of Alchemy: Women and Scientific Culture in Early Modern Italy* (Harvard University Press, Cambridge, MA, 2015), pp. 14, 22, 24–5, and 175, n. 41.
46. This notebook is now in the British Library, London, Sloane MS 1902.
47. Megan Piorko, Sarah Lang, and Richard Bean. 'Deciphering the *Hermeticae Philosophiae Medulla*: Textual Cultures of Alchemical Secrecy', *Ambix*, 70, no. 2 (2023), pp. 153, 157.
48. The cipher is found on folio 13v and 13r, with the cipher table on folio 14r and the key text on folio 12v. Sarah Lang and Megan Piorko, 'An Alchemical Cipher in a Shared Notebook of John and Arthur Dee (Sloane MS 1902) [Work in Progress]' in Carola Dahlke (ed.), *Proceedings of the 4th International Conference on Historical Cryptology HistoCrypt 2021* (Linköping University Electronic Press, Linköping, 2021), pp. 90–3; Richard Bean, Sarah Lang, and Megan Piorko. 'Solving an Alchemical Cipher in a Shared Notebook of John and Arthur Dee' in Carola Dahlke and Beáta Megyesi (eds), *Proceedings of the 5th International Conference on Historical Cryptology HistoCrypt 2022* (Linköping University Electronic Press, Linköping, 2022), pp. 12–21. For an English translation of the cipher, see Piorko et al., 'Deciphering the *Hermeticae Philosophiae Medulla*', pp. 160–1, with p. 163 for the evidence that the text was copied from another source, and p. 177 for Arthur believing that he had discovered the philosopher's stone.
49. Tilton, *Quest for the Phoenix*, pp. 113–14; Happel, 'That Which Is Not Yet Known', p. 64.
50. Andrew Pettegree, *The Book in the Renaissance* (Yale University Press, New Haven and London, 2010), p. 257.
51. Tilton, *Quest for the Phoenix*, pp. 135–6, 143.

52. British Museum, museum number 1871,0812.4199, https://www.britishmuseum.org/collection/object/P_1871-0812-4199.
53. Lenke et al., 'Michael Maier', p. 18; Tilton, *Quest for the Phoenix*, pp. 181–2, 189–90, 202–8.
54. Lenke et al., 'Michael Maier', pp. 9–12, 16, 18.
55. Tilton, *Quest for the Phoenix*, pp. 208–15; Lenke et al., 'Michael Maier', pp. 20–1.
56. As observed by Mary E. D'Imperio, *The Voynich Manuscript: An Elegant Enigma* (National Security Agency/Central Security Service, Fort George E. Mead, MD, 1978), p. 61.
57. Sheila R. Canby, 'Dragons' in John Cherry (ed.), *Mythical Beasts* (British Museum Press, London, 1995), pp. 40–1; Barbara Obrist, 'Visualization in Medieval Alchemy', *HYLE – International Journal for Philosophy of Chemistry*, 9, no. 2 (2003), p. 151.
58. Jennifer M. Rampling, 'Alchemical Traditions' in Raymond Clemens (ed.), *The Voynich Manuscript* (Yale University Press, New Haven and London, 2016), p. 47. For an example, see John Rylands Library, University of Manchester, German MS 1, folio 6r, https://www.digitalcollections.manchester.ac.uk/view/MS-GERMAN-00001/17.
59. See, for example, John Rylands Library, German MS 1, folio 13v, https://www.digitalcollections.manchester.ac.uk/view/MS-GERMAN-00001/32.
60. Obrist, 'Visualization in Medieval Alchemy', p. 149.
61. Rampling, 'Alchemical Traditions', pp. 48–50.
62. Thomas Honegger, 'Allegorical Hares and Real Dragons: Animals in Medieval Literature and Beyond', *Anglistik*, 27, no. 2 (2016), p. 52.
63. Sarah Lang, Sergei Zotov, and Megan Piorko, 'Sources of Alchemical Cryptography' in Michelle Waldispühl and Beáta Megyesi (eds), *Proceedings of the 7th International Conference on Historical Cryptology HistoCrypt 2024* (Linköping University Electronic Press, Linköping, 2024), p. 162.
64. See University of Glasgow Library, shelfmark Ar-f.16; Sam Gilchrist, 'Colour Our Collections with *Atalanta fugiens*', *University of Glasgow Library Blog*, 7 February 2017, https://universityofglasgowlibrary.wordpress.com/2017/02/07/colour-our-collections-with-atalanta-fugiens/.
65. For an English edition, see Beinecke Rare Book and Manuscript Library, Yale University, Mellon MS 88, https://collections.library.yale.edu/catalog/15959780.
66. Tara Nummedal and Donna Bilak, 'Interplay: New Scholarship on *Atalanta fugiens*' in Nummedal and Bilak, *Furnace and Fugue*, https://doi.org/10.26300/bdp.ff.nummedal-bilak.
67. Tilton, *Quest for the Phoenix*, p. 115.
68. Tilton, *Quest for the Phoenix*, p. 81; Erik Leibenguth, *Hermetische Poesie des Frühbarock. Die 'Cantilenae intellectuales' Michael Maiers. Edition mit Übersetzung, Kommentar und Bio-Bibliographie* (Max Niemeyer Verlag, Tübingen, 2015), p. 491. See Universitätsbibliothek Leipzig, MS 0396 (previously 1435°), where it is given the subtitle 'De circulo artium', https://katalog.ub.uni-leipzig.de/Record/159-31611799.
69. For a digital edition, see https://digital.ub.uni-leipzig.de/object/viewid/0000049083.

70. See, for example, University of Glasgow Library, Sp Coll BD16-g.6, https://eleanor.lib.gla.ac.uk/record=b1566002; Sächsische Landesbibliothek – Staats- und Universitätsbibliothek Dresden, Chem.354, https://digital.slub-dresden.de/werkansicht/dlf/1419/1; Trinity College Dublin, Fag.K.6.4, https://digitalcollections.tcd.ie/concern/works/xp68kk38d?locale=fr.

10. CRYPTIC WRITINGS AND THE VOYNICH MYSTERY

1. For ciphers and the performance of secrecy, see Sarah Lang, 'Situating Ciphers among Alchemical Techniques of Secrecy' in Carola Dahlke and Matthias Göggerle (eds), *Proceedings of the 6th International Conference on Historical Cryptology HistoCrypt 2023* (Linköping University Electronic Press, Linköping, 2023), https://ecp.ep.liu.se/index.php/histocrypt/issue/view/77/80, pp. 93–104.
2. For an overview of the arguments regarding its origins, see René Zandbergen, 'The Origin of the Voynich MS', 2022, https://www.voynich.nu/origin.html.
3. Dominic Olariu, 'The Misfortune of Philippus de Lignamine's Herbal or New Research Perspectives in Herbal Illustrations from an Iconological Point of View' in *Early Modern Print Culture in Central Europe: Proceedings of the Young Scholars Section of the Wrocław Seminars, September 2013* (Wydawnictwo Uniwersytetu Wrocławskiego, Wrocław, 2014), pp. 39–46; Sivan Gottlieb, '"Already Verified": A Hebrew Herbal between Text and Illustration' in Petros Bouras-Vallianatos and Dionysios Stathakopoulos (eds), *Drugs in the Medieval Mediterranean: Transmission and Circulation of Pharmacological Knowledge* (Cambridge University Press, Cambridge, 2023), pp. 205–6; Sarah R. Kyle, *Medicine and Humanism in Late Medieval Italy: The Carrara Herbal in Padua* (Routledge, Abingdon and New York, 2017), p. 46. The earliest-known *tractatus de herbis* is in the British Library, London, Egerton MS 747.
4. Olariu, 'Misfortune of Philippus de Lignamine's Herbal', pp. 39–46.
5. For examples of alchemical herbals, see Biblioteca universitaria, Pavia, Aldini, Ms.Ald.211, https://www.internetculturale.it/it/16/search/detail?id=oai%3Awww.internetculturale.sbn.it%2FTeca%3A20%3ANT0000%3AN%3ACNMD0000292373. For an edition with a cipher on folio 2r (the first illustrated page), see Università degli Studi di Firenze-Biblioteca di Scienze, Florence, call number UFIE006694, https://www.internetculturale.it/it/16/search/detail?id=oai%3Awww.sba.unifi.it%3A12%3AIC0003%3AUFIE006694.
6. Gottlieb, '"Already Verified"', pp. 207–11. See also Philip Neal, 'Alchemical Herbals', http://philipneal.net/voynichsources/alchemical/; René Zandbergen, 'Analysis of the Illustrations', 2022, https://www.voynich.nu/illustr.html.
7. See Franklin Library, University of Pennsylvania, Philadelphia, Oversize LJS 419, https://franklin.library.upenn.edu/catalog/FRANKLIN_9958047623503681. For examples of faces in plants, see folios 42r and 77r.
8. Kyle, *Medicine and Humanism in Late Medieval Italy*, pp. 23 and 80, n. 2; Jean A. Givens, 'Reading and Writing the Illustrated *tractatus de herbis*, 1280–1526' in Jean A. Givens, Karen Reeds, and Alain Touwaide (eds), *Visualizing Medieval Medicine and Natural History, 1200–1550* (Ashgate, Aldershot, 2006), pp. 115–46; Gottlieb, '"Already Verified"', pp. 207–11; Mary E. D'Imperio, *The*

Voynich Manuscript: An Elegant Enigma (National Security Agency/Central Security Service, Fort George E. Mead, MD, 1978), p. 15.

9. Sarah R. Kyle, 'A More Modern Order: Virtual Collaboration in the Roccabonella Herbal' in Fabrizio Baldassarri (ed.), *Plants in 16th and 17th Century: Botany between Medicine and Science* (De Gruyter, Berlin and Boston, 2023), pp. 41–2.
10. Bibliothèque nationale de France, Paris, MS Latin 6823, https://archivesetmanuscrits.bnf.fr/ark:/12148/cc13456t.
11. Kyle, *Medicine and Humanism in Late Medieval Italy*, pp. 1, 4, 28, 30, 43, 46–7, 49, 67–8.
12. Many copies of this work survive. See, for example, a manuscript in the Biblioteca Apostolica Vaticana, Vatican City, Ross.379, https://digi.vatlib.it/view/MSS_Ross.379/0063. There is also one in the Bibliothèque nationale de France, Paris, MS Latin 8161. Loren C. MacKinney, *Medical Illustrations in Medieval Manuscripts* (University of California Press, Berkeley, 1965), pp. 96–8. For the Voynich similarities, see Zandbergen, 'Analysis of the Illustrations'; Raymond Clemens, 'Preface' in Raymond Clemens (ed.), *The Voynich Manuscript* (Yale University Press, New Haven and London, 2016), p. xv.
13. Ross King, *The Bookseller of Florence: Vespasiano da Bisticci and the Manuscripts that Illuminated the Renaissance* (Vintage, London, 2022), p. 34; Thomas G. Benedek, 'The Role of Therapeutic Bathing in the Sixteenth Century and Its Contemporary Scientific Explanations' in Albrecht Classen (ed.), *Bodily and Spiritual Hygiene in Medieval and Early Modern Literature: Explorations of Textual Presentations of Filth and Water* (De Gruyter, Berlin and Boston, 2017), p. 532.
14. Didier Boisseuil, 'La cure thermale dans l'Italie de la fin du Moyen Âge et du début du XVIe siècle' in John Scheid, Marilyn Nicoud, Didier Boisseuil, and Joël Coste (eds), *Le thermalisme. Approches historiques et archéologiques d'un phénomène culturel et médical* (CNRS Éditions, Paris, 2015), pp. 105–22.
15. Boisseuil, 'La cure thermale'.
16. Frank Fürbeth, 'Ein Moralist als Wilderer: Felix Hemmerlis "Tractatus de balneis naturalibus" (um 1450) und seine Rezeption in Deutschland', *Sudhoffs Archiv*, 77, no. 1 (1993), pp. 99–101; Katharine Park, 'Natural Particulars: Medical Epistemology, Practice, and the Literature of Healing Springs' in Anthony Grafton and Nancy Siraisi (eds), *Natural Particulars: Nature and the Disciplines in Renaissance Europe* (MIT Press, Cambridge, MA, 1999), pp. 349–51, 355.
17. Boisseuil, 'La cure thermale'.
18. Albrecht Classen, The "Dirty Middle Ages": Bathing and Cleanliness in the Middle Ages. With an Emphasis on Medieval German Courtly Romances, Early Modern Novels, and Art History: Another Myth-Buster' in Classen, *Bodily and Spiritual Hygiene* (De Gruyter, Berlin and Boston, 2017), p. 498.
19. See Biblioteca Apostolica Vaticana, Vatican City, Pal.lat.1295, folio 283v, https://digi.vatlib.it/view/MSS_Pal.lat.1295. There are much less Voynich-esque images of people in baths on folio 297v, including a person who is blindfolded. See also Heidelberg University Library, https://digi.ub.uni-heidelberg.de/diglit/bav_pal_lat_1295.
20. Fürbeth, 'Ein Moralist als Wilderer', pp. 99–101.

21. MacKinney, *Medical Illustrations in Medieval Manuscripts*, p. 96.
22. Cathleen Hoeniger, 'The Illuminated Tacuinum Sanitatis Manuscripts from Northern Italy ca. 1380–1400: Sources, Patrons, and the Creation of a New Pictorial Genre' in Givens et al., *Visualizing Medieval Medicine and Natural History*, pp. 51–81.
23. Monica Helen Green, *The Trotula: An English Translation of the Medieval Compendium of Women's Medicine* (University of Pennsylvania Press, Philadelphia, 2002), pp. 2, 52, 81, 91, 94, 96, 107.
24. Monica Azzolini, *The Duke and the Stars: Astrology and Politics in Renaissance Milan* (Harvard University Press, Cambridge, MA, 2013), pp. 2, 4, 9, 11–12, 17–18, 63, and 248, n. 141; Anthony Grafton and Nancy Siraisi, 'Between the Election and My Hopes: Girolamo Cardano and Medical Astrology' in William R. Newman and Anthony Grafton (eds), *Secrets of Nature: Astrology and Alchemy in Early Modern Europe* (Harvard University Press, Cambridge, MA, 2001), pp. 105–6 and 130, nn. 135–7; Helena Avelar de Carvalho, *An Astrologer at Work in Late Medieval France: The Notebooks of S. Belle* (Brill, Leiden and Boston, 2021), p. 32.
25. Brian Copenhaver, 'Astrology and Magic', 'Astrology and Magic' in Charles B. Schmitt, Quentin Skinner, Eckhard Kessler, and Jill Kraye (eds), *The Cambridge History of Renaissance Philosophy* (Cambridge University Press, Cambridge, 1988), pp. 270–1.
26. David A. Lines, *The Dynamics of Learning in Early Modern Italy: Arts and Medicine at the University of Bologna* (Harvard University Press, Cambridge, MA, 2022), pp. 86–7; Azzolini, *Duke and the Stars*, pp. 26–8.
27. Francis T. Marchese, 'Representing Abstraction: Information Visualization in the Middle Ages', *Leonardo*, 49, no. 5 (2016), p. 454. For examples of rotae, see https://gallica.bnf.fr/ark:/12148/btv1b8492138z/f1.item.
28. For a comparative example, see Gonville and Caius College, Cambridge, MS 428/428, folio 28v. This is shown as fig. 1.3 in Thijs Porck, 'The Ages of Man and the Ages of Woman in Early Medieval England: From Bede to Byrhtferth of Ramsey and the *Tractatus de quaternario*' in Thijs Porck and Harriet Soper (eds), *Early Medieval English Life Courses: Cultural-Historical Perspectives* (Brill, Leiden and Boston, 2022), pp. 17–46.
29. See, for example, the diagrams in Biblioteca Apostolica Vaticana, Vatican City, Reg.lat.1283.pt.A, https://digi.vatlib.it/view/MSS_Reg.lat.1283.pt.A. Zandbergen, 'Analysis of the Illustrations'.
30. See Biblioteca Apostolica Vaticana, Vatican City, Vat.gr.1291, https://digi.vatlib.it/view/MSS_Vat.gr.1291. For a discussion, see René Zandbergen, 'Vaticanus gr. 1291', 2018, https://www.voynich.nu/extra/vatg1291.html; and Zandbergen, 'Analysis of the Illustrations'.
31. René Zandbergen, 'Voynich MS: Quire 12', 2024, https://www.voynich.nu/q12/. See also Marco Ponzi, 'Parallels for the Voynich Zodiac as an Image Cycle', Stephenbax.net, 2016, https://stephenbax.net/?p=1755.
32. On *Picatrix*, see Dan Attrell and David Porreca, *Picatrix: A Medieval Treatise on Astral Magic* (Pennsylvania State University Press, University Park, PA, 2021), p. 5. The Voynich image resembles the *Picatrix* symbol for the Sun, but also a symbol found in strings of symbols representing Mars, Jupiter, and

Mercury. The symbol is also found in a spell used to create a storm. See Attrell and Porreca, *Picatrix*, pp. 104, 231–2, 254–5.

33. D'Imperio, *Voynich Manuscript*, pp. 21 and 120 (for images of the symbols).
34. Francis B. Brévart, 'The German Volkskalender of the Fifteenth Century', *Speculum*, 63, no. 2 (1988), pp. 312–42; Francis B. Brévart, 'Chronology and Cosmology: A German "Volkskalender" of the Fifteenth Century', *Princeton University Library Chronicle*, 57, no. 2 (1996), pp. 226–9. See also Nick Pelling, 'Cod. Sang. 760 and the "Iatromathematisches Hausbuch" Voynich Hypothesis . . .', *Cipher Mysteries*, 26 July 2017, https://ciphermysteries.com/2017/07/26/cod-sang-760-iatromathematisches-hausbuch-voynich-hypothesis. A good example is Cod. Sang. 760 in the Stiftsbibliothek, St Gallen, https://www.e-codices.unifr.ch/en/csg/0760/bindingA/0/. For examples bound with herbal texts, see Heidelberg, Cod. Pal. germ. 222, https://doi.org/10.11588/diglit.455; and Heidelberg, Cod. Pal. germ. 575, https://doi.org/10.11588/diglit.2845.
35. Tessa Storey, 'Face Waters, Oils, Love Magic and Poison: Making and Selling Secrets in Early Modern Rome' in Elaine Leong and Alisha Rankin (eds), *Secrets and Knowledge in Medicine and Science, 1500–1800* (Routledge, New York and London, 2016), pp. 146–9. Wellcome Collection, London, MS 327, https://wellcomecollection.org/works/ewew4tsu.
36. For the similarity to *mercantesca*, see Nick Pelling, 'Mercantesca, Leonardo, and the Voynich Manuscript . . .', 22 April 2009, https://ciphermysteries.com/2009/04/22/mercantesca-leonardo-and-the-voynich-manuscript. For overviews of *mercantesca*, see Ambrogio M. Piazzoni, 'Latin Paleography from Antiquity to the Renaissance', Vatican Library, §17, https://spotlight.vatlib.it/latin-paleography/feature/17-cancelleresca-minuscule-and-merchant-script; and Maddalena Signorini, 'Scripts and the Vernacular in Medieval and Renaissance Italy', trans. and ed. Isabella Magni, with Paul Gehl and Lia Markey, *Italian Paleography*, n.d., https://italian.newberry.t-pen.org/handbook. For examples of *mercantesca* script, see University of Philadelphia, MS Codex 254, https://openn.library.upenn.edu/Data/0002/html/mscodex254.html; Biblioteca Apostolica Vaticana, Vatican City, Pal.lat.940, https://digi.vatlib.it/view/MSS_Pal.lat.940; Beinecke Rare Book and Manuscript Library, Yale University, Beinecke MS 329, https://collections.library.yale.edu/catalog/2005033.
37. D'Imperio, *Voynich Manuscript*, pp. 23, 65, and 95, fig. 17.
38. D'Imperio, *Voynich Manuscript*, p. 120, fig. 42. For her source of the symbols, see G.W. Gessmann, *Die Geheimsymbole der Alchymie, Arzneikunde und Astrologie des Mittelalters* (Karl Siegismund, Berlin, 1922), plates V (white arsenic), XXV (urine), LIV (salt), LXXVIII (Jupiter, tin), CII (to prepare).
39. Biblioteca Apostolica Vaticana, Vatican City, Urb.lat.998, https://digi.vatlib.it/view/MSS_Urb.lat.998, folio 1v (under the letters 'v' and 'x'). A slightly similar one also occurs on folio 15v under the letter 'q'. In that same manuscript, for examples of a ligature leading to a symbol that appears like a 'P', see folio 19r under the 'nulles' and also folio 18r, again under the 'nulles'. For the three 'o's linked by a ligature, see folio 21v under 'geminate'. For the three linked 'c's and two linked 'c's, see folio 29v. Intriguing symbols can also be seen on folio 13v. See also D'Imperio, *Voynich Manuscript*, p. 117, fig. 39, for a selection of early Italian cryptographic systems.

40. Here, literacy is defined as knowing how to sign your own name. Eltjo Buringh and Jan Luiten Van Zanden, 'Charting the "Rise of the West": Manuscripts and Printed Books in Europe – A Long-Term Perspective from the Sixth through Eighteenth Centuries', *Journal of Economic History*, 69, no. 2 (2009), p. 434; Robert C. Allen, 'Progress and Poverty in Early Modern Europe', *Economic History Review*, 56, no. 3 (2003), pp. 415, 438–9; Robert Allan Houston, *Literacy in Early Modern Europe: Culture and Education 1500–1800*, 2nd edn (Routledge, London and New York, 2013), p. 153.
41. David N. Bell, 'Collectors and Collections: Libraries and Their Social and Private Functions' in Robert Demaria Jr, Heesok Chang, and Samantha Zacher (eds), *A Companion to British Literature*, vol. 1: *Medieval Literature 700–1450* (John Wiley & Sons, Oxford, 2014), p. 358. Daniel Hobbins, *Authorship and Publicity Before Print: Jean Gerson and the Transformation of Late Medieval Learning* (University of Pennsylvania Press, Philadelphia, 2009), p. 7; Malcolm Vale, 'Manuscripts and Books' in Christopher Allmand (ed.), *The New Cambridge Medieval History*, vol. 7: *c.1415–c.1500* (Cambridge, Cambridge University Press, 2008), p. 279; Ann Blair, 'Information in Early Modern Europe' in Ann Blair, Paul Duguid, Anja-Silvia Goeing, and Anthony Grafton (eds), *Information: A Historical Companion* (Princeton University Press, Princeton and Oxford, 2021), p. 64.
42. Andrew Griebeler, *Botanical Icons: Critical Practices of Illustration in the Premodern Mediterranean* (University of Chicago Press, Chicago and London, 2024), p. 131.
43. University of Pennsylvania, Franklin Library, Oversize LJS 419, https://franklin.library.upenn.edu/catalog/FRANKLIN_9958047623503681.
44. Joanne Filippone Overty, 'The Cost of Doing Scribal Business: Prices of Manuscript Books in England, 1300–1483', *Book History*, 11 (2008), pp. 2–7.
45. Vale, 'Manuscripts and Books', p. 279; King, *Bookseller of Florence*, p. 232.
46. Park, 'Natural Particulars', pp. 351, 355.
47. King, *Bookseller of Florence*, pp. 23–5, 37–9.
48. K. Lesley Knieriem, *Book-Fools of the Renaissance* (University of Illinois, Graduate School of Library and Information Science, Champaign, IL, 1993), pp. 7–14, 19–20, 22–3.
49. Knieriem, *Book-Fools of the Renaissance*, pp. 22–4, 30, 36.
50. Knieriem, *Book-Fools of the Renaissance*, p. 36.
51. Pearl Kibre, 'The Intellectual Interests Reflected in Libraries of the Fourteenth and Fifteenth Centuries', *Journal of the History of Ideas*, 7, no. 3 (1946), pp. 261–2, 266–8.
52. Cecil H. Clough, 'The Library of the Dukes of Urbino', *Librarium: Zeitschrift der Schweizerischen Bibliophilen-Gesellschaft*, 9 (1966), p. 102.
53. Dorothy M. Robathan, 'The Catalogues of the Princely and Papal Libraries of the Italian Renaissance', *Transactions and Proceedings of the American Philological Association*, 64 (1933), p. 139. For the catalogue entries, see Girolamo d'Adda, *Indagini storiche, artistiche e bibliografiche sulla libreria Viscontea-Sforzesca del castello di Pavia. Compilate ed illustrate con documenti inediti per cura di un bibliofilo* (Libreria Editrice Gaetano Brigola, Milan, 1875), pp. 13 (entry 122), 49 (entry 547).
54. Kibre, 'Intellectual Interests Reflected in Libraries', pp. 275–6, 286, 289–96.

55. See, for example, Daniel E. Gaskell and Claire L. Bowern, 'Gibberish After All? Voynichese Is Statistically Similar to Human Produced Samples of Meaningless Text' in Colin Layfield and John Abela (eds), *International Conference on the Voynich Manuscript 2022*, CEUR Workshop Proceedings, 2022, https://ceur-ws.org/Vol-3313/paper4.pdf, p. 8.
56. Jürgen Hermes, '*Polygraphia* III: The Cipher That Pretends to be an Artificial Language' in Layfield and Abela, *International Conference on the Voynich Manuscript*, https://ceur-ws.org/Vol-3313/paper7.pdf, p. 7.
57. See, for example, the 'Zibaldone da Canal': Beinecke Rare Book and Manuscript Library, Yale University, Beinecke MS 327, https://pre1600ms.beinecke.library.yale.edu/docs/pre1600.ms327.htm, and, https://collections.library.yale.edu/catalog/10269817. John H. Pryor, 'Merchant Culture in Fourteenth-Century Venice: The Zibaldone da Canal (Review)', *Parergon*, 12, no. 1 (1994), pp. 134–6.
58. The professor of medieval philosophy and Voynich researcher Robert Brumbaugh expressed a comparable sentiment when he reached a similar conclusion. Robert S. Brumbaugh, 'The Voynich Cipher Manuscript: A Current Report', *Yale University Library Gazette*, 61, nos 3–4 (1987), p. 95.

BIBLIOGRAPHY

MANUSCRIPTS

Bayerische Staatsbibliothek, Munich
BSB Cod.icon. 242
BSB Cod.icon. 242a
Clm 849
Beinecke Rare Book and Manuscript Library, Yale University
Beinecke MS 327
Beinecke MS 329
Beinecke MS 408
Mellon MS 29
Mellon MS 88
Biblioteca Apostolica Vaticana, Vatican City
Borg.lat.898
Pal.lat.940
Pal.lat.1295
Reg.lat.1283.pt.A
Ross.379
Urb.lat.998
Vat.gr.1291
Vat.lat.9205
Biblioteca nacional de España, Madrid
RES/20
Biblioteca Medicea Laurenziana, Florence
Fondo Ashburnham Catalogo no. 1210
Biblioteca Vallicelliana, Rome
R.57
Bibliothek des Oberlandesgerichts Celle, Germany
Grupensche Stiftung C 23
Bibliothèque nationale de France, Paris
Cod. Lat. Nouv. Acq. 635
MS Latin 6823
MS Latin 8161
MS Latin 9335
Bibliothèque universitaire historique de médecine, University of Montpellier
H 505–8

Biblioteca universitaria di Bologna
MS 2705
Biblioteca universitaria, Pavia
Aldini, Ms.Ald.211
Bodleian Library, Oxford
MS Canon. Misc. 47
MS Digby 47
British Library, London
Add MS 6788
Add MS 9046
Add MS 15102
Cotton MS Appendix XLVI (formerly Add MS 5007)
Egerton MS 747
Sloane MS 1360
Sloane MS 1902
Sloane MS 3188
Sloane MS 3189
Sloane MS 3191
Stowe MS 1077
Franklin Library, University of Pennsylvania, Philadelphia
Oversize LJS 419
Gonville and Caius College, Cambridge
MS 428/428
Herzog August Bibliothek, Wolfenbüttel
Codex 91.1
Hochschul- und Landesbibliothek RheinMain, Wiesbaden
HS 2
Hungarian Academy of Sciences, Budapest
K 114
John Rylands Library, Manchester
German MS 1
Lambeth Palace, London
MS 954
McClennan Library, McGill University, Montreal
MS G 177
National Library of Wales, Cardiff
Peniarth MS 423D
Österreichische Nationalbibliothek, Vienna
Cod. 1016
Cod. 3308
Cod. 5153
Royal Danish Library, Copenhagen
12,-159, 4°
Royal Museums Greenwich, London
P/49(29)
Sächsische Landesbibliothek – Staats- und Universitätsbibliothek Dresden
Chem.354

Staatsbibliothek, Berlin
Lat. Quart. 674
Stiftsbibliothek, St Gallen, Switzerland
Cod. Sang. 760
Trinity College, Cambridge
NQ.10.148[4]
Trinity College Dublin
Fag.K.6.4
Università degli Studi di Firenze-Biblioteca di Scienze, Florence
UFIE006694
Universitaire Bibliotheken Leiden
VCF 14
Universitäts- und Landesbibliothek Sachsen-Anhalt, Halle
21 A 10
Universitätsbibliothek Augsburg
Cod. III 2.8° 34
Universitätsbibliothek Heidelberg
Cod. Pal. germ. 222
Cod. Pal. germ. 575
Cod. Pal. germ. 597
Universitätsbibliothek Kassel
8° Ms. astron. 7
Universitätsbibliothek Leipzig
MS 0396
Universitätsbibliothek Würzburg
M.ch.q.50
University of Glasgow Library
Ar-f.16
Sp Coll BD16-g.6
University of Philadelphia
MS Codex 254
Wellcome Collection, London
MS 327
MS 436
Westminster School, London
GB 2014 WS-05-HAR-01
Württembergische Landesbibliothek, Stuttgart
Codex theol. et phil. 4° 253

PUBLISHED SOURCES

Aldarrab, Nada, Kevin Knight, and Beáta Megyesi. 'The Borg.lat.898 Cipher', 2018, https://web.archive.org/web/20231129122043/https://cl.lingfil.uu.se/~bea/borg/.

Alessandrini, Ada. *Cimeli Lincei a Montpellier*, Accademia Nazionale dei Lincei, Rome, 1978.

Al-Kadit, Ibrahim A. 'Origins of Cryptology: The Arab Contributions', *Cryptologia*, 16, no. 2 (1992), pp. 97–126.

BIBLIOGRAPHY

Allen, Robert C. 'Progress and Poverty in Early Modern Europe', *Economic History Review*, 56, no. 3 (2003), pp. 403–43.

Arianrhod, Robyn. *Thomas Harriot: A Life in Science*, Oxford University Press, New York, 2019.

Arruda, Henrique F. de, Vanessa Q. Marinhoa, Luciano da F. Costa, and Deigo R. Amancio. 'Paragraph-Based Representation of Texts: A Complex Networks Approach', *Information Processing and Management*, 56 (2019), pp. 479–94.

Ashburnham, Bertram and Guillaume Libri. *A Catalogue of the Manuscripts at Ashburnham Place. Part the First, Comprising a Collection Formed by Professor Libri*, C.F. Hodgson, London, 1853.

Atherton, Mark. *Hildegard of Bingen: Selected Writings*, Penguin, London, 2001.

Attrell, Dan, and David Porreca. *Picatrix: A Medieval Treatise on Astral Magic*, Pennsylvania State University Press, University Park, PA, 2021.

Aubrey, John. *Brief Lives, Chiefly of Contemporaries*, ed. Andrew Clark, 2 vols, Clarendon Press, Oxford, 1898.

Aubrey, John. *Letters Written by Eminent Persons in the Seventeenth and Eighteenth Centuries*, 2 vols, Longman, Hurst, Rees, Orme, and Brown, Paternoster-Row, and Munday and Slatter, Oxford and London, 1813.

Autizi, Maria Beatrice. *L'università di Padova*, Editoriale Programma, Treviso, 2022.

Azalus, Pompilius. *Liber de omnibus rebus naturalibus quae continentur in mundo*, Venice, 1544.

Azzolini, Monica. *The Duke and the Stars: Astrology and Politics in Renaissance Milan*, Harvard University Press, Cambridge, MA, 2013.

Bain, Jennifer. 'History of a Book: Hildegard of Bingen's "Riesencodex" and World War II', *Plainsong and Medieval Music*, 27, no. 2 (2018), pp. 143–70.

Baldriga, Irene. 'Reading the Universal Book of Nature: The Accademia dei Lincei in Rome (1603–1630)' in Arjan van Dixhoorn and Susie Speakman Sutch (eds), *The Reach of the Republic of Letters: Literary and Learned Societies in Late Medieval and Early Modern Europe*, vol. 1, Brill, Leiden, 2008, pp. 353–88.

Baird, Joseph L. and Radd K. Ehrman. *The Letters of Hildegard of Bingen*, vol. 3, Oxford University Press, New York, 2004.

Batho, Gordon R. 'Thomas Harriot and the Northumberland Household' in Robert Fox (ed.), *Thomas Harriot: An Elizabethan Man of Science*, Routledge, Abingdon and New York, 2017, pp. 28–47.

Batho, Gordon R. 'Thomas Harriot's Manuscripts' in Robert Fox (ed.), *Thomas Harriot: An Elizabethan Man of Science*, Routledge, Abingdon and New York, 2017, pp. 286–97.

Battistella, Edwin. 'Codes and Ciphers', *OUPblog*, 5 January 2020, https://blog.oup.com/2020/01/codes-and-ciphers/.

Battisti, Eugenio and Giuseppa Saccaro Battisti. *Le macchine cifrate di Giovanni Fontana. Con la riproduzione del Cod. icon. 242 della Bayerische Staatsbibliothek di Monaco di Baviera e la decrittazione di esso e del Cod. lat. nouv. acq. 635 della Bibliothèque nationale di Parigi*, Arcadia Edizioni, Milan, 1984.

Bax, Stephen. 'A Proposed Partial Decoding of the Voynich Script', Stephenbax.net, 2014, https://stephenbax.net/wp-content/uploads/2014/01/Voynich-a-provisional-partial-decoding-BAX.pdf.

Bean, Richard, Sarah Lang, and Megan Piorko. 'Solving an Alchemical Cipher in a Shared Notebook of John and Arthur Dee' in Carola Dahlke and Beáta Megyesi (eds), *Proceedings of the 5th International Conference on Historical Cryptology HistoCrypt 2022*, Linköping University Electronic Press, Linköping, 2022, pp. 12–21.

Bell, David N. 'Collectors and Collections: Libraries and Their Social and Private Functions' in Robert Demaria Jr, Heesok Chang, and Samantha Zacher (eds), *A Companion to British Literature*, vol. 1: *Medieval Literature 700–1450*, John Wiley & Sons, Oxford, 2014, pp. 355–68.

Benedek, Thomas G. 'The Role of Therapeutic Bathing in the Sixteenth Century and Its Contemporary Scientific Explanations' in Albrecht Classen (ed.), *Bodily and Spiritual Hygiene in Medieval and Early Modern Literature: Explorations of Textual Presentations of Filth and Water*, De Gruyter, Berlin and Boston, 2017, pp. 528–67.

Biagetti, Maria Teresa. 'Dispersed Collections of Scientific Books: The Case of the Private Library of Federico Cesi (1585–1630)' in Flavia Bruni and Andrew Pettegree (eds), *Lost Books: Reconstructing the Print World of Pre-Industrial Europe*, Brill, Leiden and Boston, 2016, pp. 386–99.

Biagioli, Mario. 'From Ciphers to Confidentiality: Secrecy, Openness and Priority in Science', *British Journal for the History of Science*, 45, no. 2 (2012), pp. 213–33.

Bido, Ardit. *The Albanian Orthodox Church: A Political History, 1878–1945*, Routledge, London, 2020.

Bilak, Donna. 'Chasing Atalanta: Maier, Steganography, and the Secrets of Nature' in Tara Nummedal and Donna Bilak (eds), *Furnace and Fugue: A Digital Edition of Michael Maier's 'Atalanta fugiens' (1618) with Scholarly Commentary*, University of Virginia Press, Charlottesville, 2020, https://doi.org/10.26300/bdp.ff.bilak.

Birkenmajer, Alexander. 'Zur Lebensgeschichte und wissenschaftlichen Tätigkeit von Giovanni Fontana (1395?–1455?)', *Isis*, 17, no. 1 (1932), pp. 34–53.

Blair, Ann. 'Information in Early Modern Europe' in Ann Blair, Paul Duguid, Anja-Silvia Goeing, and Anthony Grafton (eds), *Information: A Historical Companion*, Princeton University Press, Princeton and Oxford, 2021, pp. 61–85.

BnF Comité d'histoire, 'Provenance. Albani', http://comitehistoire.bnf.fr/type-fiche/provenance?page=32.

Bohak, Gideon. 'Jewish Magic in the Middle Ages' in David J. Collins SJ (ed.), *The Cambridge History of Magic and Witchcraft in the West: From Antiquity to the Present*, Cambridge University Press, Cambridge, 2015, pp. 268–99.

Boissard, Jean Jacques. *De divinatione et magicis praestigiis*, Typis Hieronymi Galleri, Oppenheim, 1615.

Boisseuil, Didier. 'La cure thermale dans l'Italie de la fin du Moyen Âge et du début du XVIe siècle' in John Scheid, Marilyn Nicoud, Didier Boisseuil, and Joël Coste (eds), *Le thermalisme. Approches historiques et archéologiques d'un phénomène culturel et médical*, CNRS Éditions, Paris, 2015, pp. 105–22.

Booth, Phil. 'Cyril and Methodius, Sts (826/7–69 and c.815–85)' in Andrew Louth (ed.), *The Oxford Dictionary of the Christian Church*, 4th edn, Oxford University Press, Oxford, 2022.

Borelli, Petro. *Bibliotheca chimica*, Samuel Broun, Heidelberg, 1656.

Bowern, Claire L. and Luke Lindemann. 'The Linguistics of the Voynich Manuscript', *Annual Review of Linguistics*, 7 (2021), pp. 285–308.

Boxer, Alexander. 'Fingerprinting Gibberish: A Quantitative Comparison of the Voynich and Sloane MS 3188' in Colin Layfield and John Abela (eds), *International Conference on the Voynich Manuscript 2022*, CEUR Workshop Proceedings, 2022, https://ceur-ws.org/Vol-3313/paper1.pdf.

Boxer, Alexander. '*Steganographia* and Other Occult Writings', https://web.archive.org/web/20210410093317/http://trithemius.com/steganographia-english/.

Brann, Noel L. *The Abbot Trithemius (1462–1516): The Renaissance of Monastic Humanism*, Leiden, Brill, 1981.

Brann, Noel L. *Trithemius and Magical Theology: A Chapter in the Controversy over Occult Studies in Early Modern Europe*, State University of New York Press, Albany, 1999.

Brévart, Francis B. 'Chronology and Cosmology: A German "Volkskalender" of the Fifteenth Century', *Princeton University Library Chronicle*, 57, no. 2 (1996), pp. 225–65.

Brévart, Francis B. 'The German Volkskalender of the Fifteenth Century', *Speculum*, 63, no. 2 (1988), pp. 312–42.

Brewer, Keagan. '"I beg your grace that you suppress this chapter or else allow it to be written in secret letters": The Emotions of Encipherment in Late-Medieval Gynaecology' in Colin Layfield and John Abela (eds), *International Conference on the Voynich Manuscript 2022*, CEUR Workshop Proceedings, 2022, https://ceur-ws.org/Vol-3313/paper3.pdf.

Brewer, Keagan and Michelle L. Lewis. 'The Voynich Manuscript, Dr Johannes Hartlieb and the Encipherment of Women's Secrets', *Social History of Medicine*, 37, no. 3 (2024), pp. 559–82.

British Library. 'Exploring the Ripley Scroll', *Google Arts & Culture*, https://artsandculture.google.com/story/exploring-the-ripley-scroll-the-british-library/OwXBNEuJqIJzLg?hl=en.

Brumbaugh, Robert S. 'Botany and the Voynich "Roger Bacon" Manuscript Once More', *Speculum*, 49, no. 3 (1974), pp. 546–8.

Brumbaugh, Robert S. *The Most Mysterious Manuscript: The Voynich 'Roger Bacon' Cipher Manuscript*, Southern Illinois University Press, Carbondale, IL, 1978.

Brumbaugh, Robert S. 'The Solution of the Voynich "Roger Bacon" Cipher', *Yale University Library Gazette*, 49, no. 4 (1975), pp. 347–55.

Brumbaugh, Robert S. 'The Voynich Cipher Manuscript: A Current Report', *Yale University Library Gazette*, 61, nos 3–4 (1987), pp. 92–5.

Brumbaugh, Robert S. 'The Voynich "Roger Bacon" Cipher Manuscript: Deciphered Maps of Stars', *Journal of the Warburg and Courtauld Institutes*, 39 (1976), pp. 139–50.

Buonanno, Roberto, *The Stars of Galileo Galilei and the Universal Knowledge of Athanasius Kircher*, Springer, Cham, 2014.

Buringh, Eltjo and Jan Luiten Van Zanden. 'Charting the "Rise of the West": Manuscripts and Printed Books in Europe – A Long-Term Perspective from the Sixth through Eighteenth Centuries', *Journal of Economic History*, 69, no. 2 (2009), pp. 409–45.

Cadei, Antonio (ed.). *Il trionfo sul tempo. Manoscritti illustrati dell'Accademia nazionale dei Lincei*, Franco Cosimo Panini, Modena, 2002.

Campanini, Saverio. 'The Quest for the Holiest Alphabet in the Renaissance' in Nadia Vidro, Irene E. Zwiep, and Judith Olszowy-Schlanger (eds), *A*

Universal Art: Hebrew Grammar across Disciplines and Faiths, Brill, Leiden, 2014, pp. 196–245.

Campbell, George L. and Christopher Moseley. *The Routledge Handbook of Scripts and Alphabets*, 2nd edn, Routledge, Abingdon and New York, 2012.

Campbell, Gordon. 'Slovakia, Christianity in' in *The Oxford Dictionary of the Christian Church*, 4th edn, Andrew Louth (ed.), Oxford University Press, Oxford, 2022.

Canby, Sheila R. 'Dragons' in John Cherry (ed.), *Mythical Beasts*, British Museum Press, London, 1995, pp. 14–43.

Caruana, Andrew, Colin Layfield, and John Abela. 'An Analysis of the Relationship Between Words within the Voynich Manuscript' in Colin Layfield and John Abela (eds), *International Conference on the Voynich Manuscript 2022*, CEUR Workshop Proceedings, 2022, https://ceur-ws.org/Vol-3313/paper8.pdf.

Carutti, Domenico. *Di Giovanni Eckio e della instituzione dell'Accademia dei Lincei con alcune note inedite intorno a Galileo*, Coi tipi del Salviucci, Rome, 1877.

Carvalho, Helena Avelar de. *An Astrologer at Work in Late Medieval France: The Notebooks of S. Belle*, Brill, Leiden and Boston, 2021.

Casaubon, Meric. *A True & Faithful Relation of What Passed for Many Yeers between Dr. John Dee . . . and Some Spirits*, D. Maxwell for T. Garthwait, London, 1659.

Cheshire, Gerard. 'The Language and Writing System of MS408 (Voynich) Explained', *Romance Studies*, 37, no. 1 (2019), pp. 30–67.

Cheshire, Gerard. 'Voicing the Voynich: The Pronuncial Writing System and Graeco-Iberian Language of MS408 (Ischia/Voynich)', https://www.academia.edu/49263562/Voicing_the_Voynich_The_Pronuncial_Writing_System_and_Graeco_Iberian_Language_of_MS408_Ischia_Voynich.

Chien Hung-yi. 'The Psalmanazar Affair and the Birth of Taiwan Studies in Europe: A Reassessment of the Historic Hoax', *International Journal of Taiwan Studies*, 3 (2020), pp. 112–36.

Clagett, Marshall. 'The Life and Works of Giovanni Fontana', *Annali dell'Istituto e Museo di Storia della Scienza di Firenze*, 1 (1976), pp. 5–28.

Classen, Albrecht. 'The "Dirty Middle Ages": Bathing and Cleanliness in the Middle Ages. With an Emphasis on Medieval German Courtly Romances, Early Modern Novels, and Art History: Another Myth-Buster' in Albrecht Classen (ed.), *Bodily and Spiritual Hygiene in Medieval and Early Modern Literature: Explorations of Textual Presentations of Filth and Water*, De Gruyter, Berlin and Boston, 2017, pp. 458–500.

Clemens, Raymond. 'Preface' in Raymond Clemens (ed.), *The Voynich Manuscript*, Yale University Press, New Haven and London, 2016, pp. xi–xvii.

Clemens, Raymond. 'The World's Most Mysterious Manuscript' in Raymond Clemens (ed.), *The Voynich Manuscript*, Yale University Press, New Haven and London, 2016, pp. 53–9.

Clericuzio, Antonio and Silvia de Renzi. 'Medicine, Alchemy and Natural Philosophy in the Early Accademia dei Lincei' in D.S. Chambers and F. Quiviger (eds), *Italian Academies of the Sixteenth Century*, Warburg Institute, London, 1995, pp. 175–94.

Clough, Cecil H. 'The Albani Library and Pope Clement XI', *Librarium: Zeitschrift der Schweizerischen Bibliophilen-Gesellschaft*, 12 (1969), pp. 13–21.

Clough, Cecil H. 'The Library of the Dukes of Urbino', *Librarium: Zeitschrift der Schweizerischen Bibliophilen-Gesellschaft*, 9 (1966), pp. 101–4.

Clucas, Stephen. 'False Illuding Spirits & Cownterfeiting Deuills: John Dee's Angelic Conversations and Religious Anxiety' in Joad Raymond (ed.), *Conversations with Angels: Essays Towards a History of Spiritual Communication, 1100–1700*, Palgrave Macmillan, Basingstoke, 2011, pp. 150–74.

Clucas, Stephen. 'John Dee, Alchemy, and Print Culture', *Ambix*, 64, no. 2 (2017), pp. 107–14.

Clulee, Nicholas H. *John Dee's Natural Philosophy: Between Science and Religion*, Routledge, Abingdon, 2013.

Cohen, Jonathan. 'On the Project of a Universal Character', *Mind*, 63, no. 249 (1954), pp. 49–63.

Colini, Claudia. 'La invención del Sacromonte: How and Why Scholars Debated about the Lead Books of Granada for Two Hundred Years' in Cécile Michel and Michael Friedrich (eds), *Fakes and Forgeries of Written Artefacts from Ancient Mesopotamia to Modern China*, De Gruyter, Berlin and Boston, 2020, pp. 209–61.

Compagni, Vittoria Perrone. 'Heinrich Cornelius Agrippa von Nettesheim' in Edward N. Zalta (ed.), *The Stanford Encyclopedia of Philosophy*, Metaphysics Research Lab, Stanford University, Stanford, 2021, https://plato.stanford.edu/archives/spr2021/entries/agrippa-nettesheim/.

Copenhaver, Brian. 'Astrology and Magic' in Charles B. Schmitt, Quentin Skinner, Eckhard Kessler, and Jill Kraye (eds), *The Cambridge History of Renaissance Philosophy*, Cambridge University Press, Cambridge, 1988, pp. 264–300.

Corrigan, Vincent J., 'Hildegard of Bingen' in Lister M. Matheson (ed.), *Icons of the Middle Ages: Rulers, Writers, Rebels, and Saints*, 2 vols, Greenwood, Santa Barbara, 2011, vol. 2, pp. 355–94.

d'Adda, Girolamo. *Indagini storiche, artistiche e bibliografiche sulla libreria Visconteo-Sforzesca del castello di Pavia. Compilate ed illustrate con documenti inediti per cura di un bibliofilo*, Libreria Editrice Gaetano Brigola, Milan, 1875.

D'Aiuto, Francesco and Vian, Paolo. *Guida ai fondi manoscritti, numismatici, a stampa della Biblioteca vaticana*, 2 vols, Biblioteca Apostolica Vaticana, Vatican City, 2011.

Daniels, Peter T. and William Bright (eds), *The World's Writing Systems*, Oxford University Press, Oxford and New York, 1996.

Daruka, István. 'On the Voynich Manuscript', *Cryptologia*, 45, no. 1 (2021), pp. 44–80.

Datenbank Gesamtkatalog der Wiegendrucke, 'Ursinus, Jason Alpheus', 2011, https://gesamtkatalogderwiegendrucke.de/docs/URSIJAS.htm.

Davis, Lisa Fagin. 'How Many Glyphs and How Many Scribes: Digital Paleography and the Voynich Manuscript', *Manuscript Studies*, 5, no. 1 (2020), pp. 164–80.

Davis, Lisa Fagin. 'Multispectral Imaging and the Voynich Manuscript', *Manuscript Road Trip*, 8 September 2024, https://manuscriptroadtrip.wordpress.com/2024/09/08/multispectral-imaging-and-the-voynich-manuscript/.

D'Imperio, Mary E. *The Voynich Manuscript: An Elegant Enigma*. National Security Agency/Central Security Service, Fort George E. Mead, MD, 1978.

Dooley, John. *History of Cryptography and Cryptanalysis: Codes, Ciphers, and Their Algorithms*, Springer, Cham, 2018.

Drake, Stillman. 'The Accademia dei Lincei', *Science*, 151 (1966), pp. 1194–200.

Drucker, Johanna. *Inventing the Alphabet: The Origins of Letters from Antiquity to the Present*, University of Chicago Press, Chicago and London, 2022.

ECHO: Cultural Heritage Online. 'II History of the Manuscripts', Max Planck Institute for the History of Science, 2015, https://echo.mpiwg-berlin.mpg.de/content/scientific_revolution/harriot/project_infos/harriot-manuscripts.

Eco, Umberto. *The Search for the Perfect Language*, trans. James Fentress, Blackwell, Oxford, 1995.

Eis, Gerhard. 'Alchymey Teuczsch', *Medizinische Fachprosa des späten Mittelalters und der frühen Neuzeit*, Rodopi, Amsterdam, 1982, pp. 307–15.

Elliott, Ralph W.V. 'Isaac Newton's "Of an Universall Language"', *Modern Language Review*, 52, no. 1 (1957), pp. 1–18.

Ellison, Katherine. *A Cultural History of Early Modern English Cryptography Manuals*, Routledge, Abingdon, 2017.

Embach, Michael. 'The Life of Hildegard of Bingen (1098–1179)' in Jennifer Bain (ed.), *The Cambridge Companion to Hildegard of Bingen*, Cambridge University Press, Cambridge, 2021, pp. 11–36.

Embach, Michael. *Die Schriften Hildegards von Bingen. Studien zu ihrer Überlieferung im Mittelalter und in der Frühen Neuzeit*, Akademie Verlag, Berlin, 2010.

Ernst, Thomas. 'Anatomie einer Fälschung', *Daphnis*, 30 (2001), pp. 513–95.

Ernst, Thomas. 'The Numerical-Astrological Ciphers in the Third Book of Trithemius's *Steganographia*', *Cryptologia*, 22, no. 4 (1998), pp. 318–41.

Ernst, Thomas. 'Schwarzweisse Magie: der Schlüssel zum dritten Buch der *Steganographia* des Trithemius', *Daphnis*, 25 (1996), pp. 1–205.

Fanger, Claire. 'Introduction: Theurgy, Magic, and Mysticism' in Claire Fanger (ed.), *Invoking Angels: Theurgic Ideas and Practices, Thirteenth to Sixteenth Centuries*, Pennsylvania State University Press, University Park, PA, 2012, pp. 1–33.

Feingold, Mordechai. *The Mathematician's Apprenticeship: Science, Universities and Society in England, 1560–1640*, Cambridge University Press, Cambridge, 1984.

Ferraro, Joanne Marie. *Venice: History of the Floating City*, Cambridge University Press, Cambridge, 2012.

Figala, Karin and Ulrich Neumann. '"Author cui nomen Hermes Malavici": New Light on the Bio-Bibliography of Michael Maier' in Piyo Rattansi and Antonio Clericuzio (eds), *Alchemy and Chemistry in the 16th and 17th Centuries*, Kluwer Academic, Dordrecht and London, 1994, pp. 121–47.

Figala, Karin and Ulrich Neumann. 'Michael Maier (1569–1622): New Bio-Bibliographical Material' in Z.R.W.M. von Martels (ed.), *Alchemy Revisited: Proceedings of the International Conference on the History of Alchemy at the University of Groningen 17–19 April 1989*, Brill, Leiden, 1990, pp. 34–50.

Findlen, Paula. 'The Renaissance of Science' in Gordon Campbell (ed.), *The Oxford History of the Renaissance*, Oxford University Press, Oxford, 2023, pp. 379–429.

Flanagan, Sabina. *Hildegard of Bingen: A Visionary Life*, 2nd edn, Routledge, London and New York, 1998.

Fleck, Andrew. '"At the time of his death": Manuscript Instability and Walter Ralegh's Performance on the Scaffold', *Journal of British Studies*, 48 (2009), pp. 4–28.

Fontana, Johannes. *Liber instrumentorum iconographicus / Ein illustriertes Maschinenbuch*, ed. and trans. Horst Kranz, Franz Steiner Verlag, Stuttgart, 2014.

Fontana, Johannes. *Methoden des Erinnerns und Vergessens. Johannes Fontanas Secretum de thesauro experimentorum ymaginationis hominum*, ed. and trans. Horst Kranz, Franz Steiner Verlag, Stuttgart, 2016.

Fontana, Johannes, *Opera iuvenalia de rotis horologiis et mensuris / Jugendwerke über Räder, Uhren und Messungen*, ed. and trans. Horst Kranz, Frank Steiner Verlag, Stuttgart, 2011.

Forshaw, Peter J. 'Michael Maier and Mythoalchemy' in Tara Nummedal and Donna Bilak (eds), *Furnace and Fugue: A Digital Edition of Michael Maier's 'Atalanta fugiens' (1618) with Scholarly Commentary*, University of Virginia Press, Charlottesville, 2020, https://doi.org/10.26300/bdp.ff.forshaw.

Fox, Robert (ed.). *Thomas Harriot: An Elizabethan Man of Science*, Routledge, Abingdon and New York, 2017.

Freedberg, David. *The Eye of the Lynx: Galileo, His Friends, and the Beginnings of Modern Natural History*, University of Chicago Press, Chicago, 2002.

Friedman, John Block. 'The Cipher Alphabet of John de Foxton's *Liber Cosmographiae*', *Scriptorium*, 36, no. 2 (1982), pp. 219–35.

Friedman, John Block. *John de Foxton's Liber Cosmographiae (1408): An Edition and Codicological Study*, E.J. Brill, Leiden and New York, 1988.

Fürbeth, Frank. 'Ein Moralist als Wilderer: Felix Hemmerlis "Tractatus de balneis naturalibus" (um 1450) und seine Rezeption in Deutschland', *Sudhoffs Archiv*, 77, no. 1 (1993), pp. 97–113.

Gabrieli, Giuseppe. 'Gli scritti inediti di Giovanni Ecchio Linceo (1577–1620)', *Rediconti della Reale accademia nazionale dei Lincei, classe di scienze morali, storiche e filologiche*, 6 (1930), pp. 363–97.

Gabrieli, Giuseppe. 'Qualche altra notizia sugli scritti e sulla vita di Giovanni Ecchio Linceo', *Rediconti della Reale accademia nazionale dei Lincei, classe di scienze morali, storiche e filologiche*, 10 (1934), pp. 479–508.

Galende Díaz, Juan Carlos. 'La criptografía medieval: el *Libro del tesoro*' in Juan Carlos Galende Díaz (ed.), *II jornadas científicas sobre documentación de la corona de Castilla (siglos XIII–XIV)*, Universidad Complutense de Madrid, Madrid, 2003, pp. 41–77.

Gallay, Alan. *Walter Ralegh: Architect of Empire*, Basic Books, New York, 2019.

Galluzzi, Paolo. *The Italian Renaissance of Machines*, Harvard University Press, Cambridge, MA, 2020.

Galluzzi, Paolo. *The Lynx and the Telescope: The Parallel Worlds of Cesi and Galileo*, Brill, Leiden and Boston, 2017.

Gamer, Maximilian. *Die Polygraphia des Johannes Trithemius nach der handschriftlichen Fassung. Edition, Übersetzung und Kommentar*, 2 vols, Brill, Boston and Leiden, 2022.

García-Arenal, Mercedes and Fernando Rodriguez Mediano. *The Orient in Spain: Converted Muslims, the Forged Gospels of Granada, and the Rise of Orientalism*, Brill, Leiden, 2013.

Gaskell, Daniel E. and Claire L. Bowern. 'Gibberish After All? Voynichese Is Statistically Similar to Human Produced Samples of Meaningless Text' in Colin Layfield and John Abela (eds), *International Conference on the Voynich Manuscript*

2022, CEUR Workshop Proceedings, 2022, https://ceur-ws.org/Vol-3313/paper4.pdf.

Gatti, Hilary. 'The Natural Philosophy of Thomas Harriot' in Robert Fox (ed.), *Thomas Harriot: An Elizabethan Man of Science*, Routledge, Abingdon and New York, 2017, pp. 64–92.

Gaudio, Michael. 'The Emblem in the Landscape: Matthäus Merian's Etchings for *Atalanta fugiens*' in Tara Nummedal and Donna Bilak (eds), *Furnace and Fugue: A Digital Edition of Michael Maier's 'Atalanta fugiens' (1618) with Scholarly Commentary*, University of Virginia Press, Charlottesville, 2020, https://doi.org/10.26300/bdp.ff.gaudio.

Germain, Gerard González. 'An Antiquarian Forger at Ferdinand's Court: On the Authorship of the Fake Inscriptions of Early 16th-Century Spain', *Bibliothèque d'Humanisme et Renaissance*, 79, no. 1 (2017), pp. 97–121.

Gessmann, G.W. *Die Geheimsymbole der Alchymie, Arzneikunde und Astrologie des Mittelalters*, Karl Siegismund, Berlin, 1922.

Gheuens, Koen and Cary Rapaport. 'Above and Beyond Voynich Canopies: Tents as a Recurring Motif in Beinecke MS 408' in Colin Layfield and John Abela (eds), *International Conference on the Voynich Manuscript 2022*, CEUR Workshop Proceedings, 2022, https://ceur-ws.org/Vol-3313/paper2.pdf.

Gibbs, Nicholas. 'Voynich Manuscript: The Solution', *Times Literary Supplement*, 5971, 8 September 2017, https://www.the-tls.co.uk/articles/voynich-manuscript-solution/.

Gilchrist, Sam. 'Colour Our Collections with *Atalanta fugiens*', *University of Glasgow Library Blog*, 7 February 2017, https://universityofglasgowlibrary.wordpress.com/2017/02/07/colour-our-collections-with-atalanta-fugiens/.

Givens, Jean A. 'Reading and Writing the Illustrated *tractatus de herbis*, 1280–1526' in Jean A. Givens, Karen Reeds, and Alain Touwaide (eds), *Visualizing Medieval Medicine and Natural History, 1200–1550*, Ashgate, Aldershot, 2006, pp. 115–46.

Gottlieb, Sivan. '"Already Verified": A Hebrew Herbal between Text and Illustration' in Petros Bouras-Vallianatos and Dionysios Stathakopoulos (eds), *Drugs in the Medieval Mediterranean: Transmission and Circulation of Pharmacological Knowledge*, Cambridge University Press, Cambridge, 2023, pp. 204–42.

Grafton, Anthony. 'The Devil as Automaton: Giovanni Fontana and the Meanings of a Fifteenth-Century Machine' in Jessica Riskin (ed.), *Genesis Redux: Essays in the History and Philosophy of Artificial Life*, University of Chicago Press, Chicago and London, 2007, pp. 46–62.

Grafton, Anthony. *Forgers and Critics: Creativity and Duplicity in Western Scholarship*, new edn, Princeton University Press, Princeton, 2019.

Grafton, Anthony. *Magus: The Art of Magic from Faustus to Agrippa*, The Belknap Press of Harvard University Press, Cambridge, MA, 2023.

Grafton, Anthony. *Worlds Made by Words: Scholarship and Community in the Modern West*, Harvard University Press, Cambridge, MA, and London, 2009.

Grafton, Anthony and Nancy Siraisi. 'Between the Election and My Hopes: Girolamo Cardano and Medical Astrology' in William R. Newman and Anthony Grafton (eds), *Secrets of Nature: Astrology and Alchemy in Early Modern Europe*, Harvard University Press, Cambridge, MA, 2001, pp. 69–131.

Green, Jonathan P. 'A New Gloss on Hildegard of Bingen's Lingua Ignota', *Viator*, 36 (2005), 217–34.

Green, Monica Helen. *The Trotula: An English Translation of the Medieval Compendium of Women's Medicine*, University of Pennsylvania Press, Philadelphia, 2002.

Griebeler, Andrew. *Botanical Icons: Critical Practices of Illustration in the Premodern Mediterranean*, University of Chicago Press, Chicago and London, 2024.

Guzy, Stefan. 'Book Transactions of Emperor Rudolf II, 1576–1612: New Findings on the Earliest Ownership of the Voynich Manuscript' in Colin Layfield and John Abela (eds), *International Conference on the Voynich Manuscript 2022*, CEUR Workshop Proceedings, 2022, https://ceur-ws.org/Vol-3313/paper16.pdf.

Hagebeuk, Rian and Katherine Mueller. '"The Subtelty of Witches": A Reformation Era Cipher Mystery' in Carola Dahlke and Beáta Megyesi (eds), *Proceedings of the 5th International Conference on Historical Cryptology HistoCrypt 2022*, Linköping University Electronic Press, Linköping, 2022, pp. 101–10.

Hannig, Rainer. 'Voynisch-Hebräisch: der Weg zur Entzifferung von Rainer Hannig', 2020, https://www.rainer-hannig.com/voynich/.

Happel, Olivia Jean. 'That Which Is Not Yet Known: An Analysis of Michael Maier's Alchemical Work through *Arcana arcanissima*', PhD thesis, Pacifica Graduate Institute, 2019.

Harkness, Deborah E. *John Dee's Conversations with Angels: Cabala, Alchemy, and the End of Nature*, Cambridge University Press, Cambridge, 1999.

Harkness, Deborah E. 'Managing an Experimental Household: The Dees of Mortlake and the Practice of Natural Philosophy', *Isis*, 88, no. 2 (1997), pp. 247–62.

Harkness, Deborah E. 'The Scientific Reformation: John Dee and the Restitution of Nature', PhD thesis, University of California, 1994.

Harmsen, Theodor. 'Fiction or a Much Stranger Truth: Sources and Reception of the Geheime Figuren der Rosenkreuzer – Secret Symbols of the Rosicrucians in the 18th, 19th and 20th Centuries' in Monika Neugebauer-Wölk, Renko Geffarth, and Markus Meumann (eds), *Aufklärung und Esoterik. Wege in die Moderne*, De Gruyter, Berlin and Boston, 2013, pp. 726–52.

Harriot, Thomas. *A Briefe and True Report of the New Found Land of Virginia: Of the Commodities and of the Nature and Manners of the Naturall Inhabitants*, Frankfurt, 1590.

Harris, Katie A. *From Muslim to Christian Granada: Inventing a City's Past in Early Modern Spain*, Johns Hopkins University Press, Baltimore, 2007.

Harris, Stephen J. 'Anglo-Saxon Ciphers' in Katherine Ellison and Susan Kim (eds), *A Material History of Medieval and Early Modern Ciphers: Cryptography and the History of Literacy*, Routledge, New York and London, 2017, pp. 65–79.

Harrison, Julian. 'Fire, Fire! The Tragic Burning of the Cotton Library', Medieval Manuscripts Blog, *British Library*, 2016, https://blogs.bl.uk/digitisedmanuscripts/2016/10/fire-fire-the-tragic-burning-of-the-cotton-library.html.

Hermes, Jürgen. '*Polygraphia* III: The Cipher That Pretends to be an Artificial Language' in Colin Layfield and John Abela (eds), *International Conference on the Voynich Manuscript 2022*, CEUR Workshop Proceedings, 2022, https://ceur-ws.org/Vol-3313/paper7.pdf.

Higley, Sarah L. *Hildegard of Bingen's Unknown Language: An Edition, Translation, and Discussion*, Palgrave Macmillan, New York, 2007.

Hobbins, Daniel. *Authorship and Publicity Before Print: Jean Gerson and the Transformation of Late Medieval Learning*, University of Pennsylvania Press, Philadelphia, 2009.

Hoeniger, Cathleen, 'The Illuminated Tacuinum Sanitatis Manuscripts from Northern Italy ca. 1380–1400: Sources, Patrons, and the Creation of a New Pictorial Genre' in Jean A. Givens, Karen M. Reeds, and Alain Touwaide (eds), *Visualizing Medieval Medicine and Natural History, 1200–1550*, Ashgate, Aldershot, 2006, pp. 51–81.

Honegger, Thomas. 'Allegorical Hares and Real Dragons: Animals in Medieval Literature and Beyond', *Anglistik*, 27, no. 2 (2016), pp. 47–57.

Houston, Robert Allan. *Literacy in Early Modern Europe: Culture and Education 1500–1800*, 2nd edn, Routledge, London and New York, 2013.

Howard, Deborah. *The Architectural History of Venice*, rev. edn, Yale University Press, New Haven and London, 2002.

Howard, Deborah. 'The Old, the Antique, and the Venerable in Venetian Renaissance Architecture' in Georg Christ and Franz-Julius Morche (eds), *Cultures of Empire: Rethinking Venetian Rule, 1400–1700. Essays in Honour of Benjamin Arbel*, Brill, Leiden and Boston, 2020, pp. 63–89.

Howard, Deborah. 'Venetian Architecture' in Eric R. Dursteler (ed.), *A Companion to Venetian History, 1400–1797*, Brill, Leiden and Boston, 2013, pp. 743–78.

Howard Rienstra, M. 'Gaetano Marini and the Historiography of the Accademia dei Lincei', *Archivo della Società romana di storia patria*, 94 (1971), pp. 209–33.

Hunt, Arnold. 'Voynich the Buyer' in Raymond Clemens (ed.), *The Voynich Manuscript*, Yale University Press, New Haven and London, 2016, pp. 11–21.

Hunter, Michael. 'Robert Boyle and Secrecy' in Elaine Leong and Alisha Rankin (eds), *Secrets and Knowledge in Medicine and Science, 1500–1800*, Routledge, New York and London, 2016, pp. 87–104.

Iordanou, Ioanna. *Venice's Secret Service: Organizing Intelligence in the Renaissance*, Oxford University Press, Oxford, 2019.

Ivanič, Suzanna. *Cosmos and Materiality in Early Modern Prague*, Oxford University Press, Oxford, 2021.

Janick, Jules and Tucker, Arthur O. *Unraveling the Voynich Codex*, Springer, Cham, 2018.

Josten, C.H. 'An Unknown Chapter in the Life of John Dee', *Journal of the Warburg and Courtauld Institutes*, 28, no. 1 (1965), pp. 223–57.

Kahn, David. *The Codebreakers: The Story of Secret Writing*, rev. edn, Scribner, New York, 1996.

Kassel University, 'Anleitung zum Beschwören von Geistern: Unibibliothek entziffert Zauberhandschrift', 8 June 2013, https://www.uni-kassel.de/uni/en/aktuelles/sitemap-detail-news/post/detail/News/anleitung-zum-beschwoeren-von-geistern-unibibliothek-entziffert-zauberhandschrift.

Keevak, Michael. *The Pretended Asian: George Psalmanazar's Eighteenth-Century Formosan Hoax*, Wayne State University Press, Detroit, 2004.

Kelly, Samantha. 'The Curious Case of Ethiopic Chaldean: Fraud, Philology, and Cultural (Mis)Understanding in European Conceptions of Ethiopia', *Renaissance Quarterly*, 68 (2015), pp. 1227–64.

Keynes, Simon. 'The Reconstruction of a Burnt Cottonian Manuscript: The Case of Cotton MS. Otho A. I', *British Library Journal*, 22 (1996), pp. 113–60.

Kibre, Pearl. 'The Intellectual Interests Reflected in Libraries of the Fourteenth and Fifteenth Centuries', *Journal of the History of Ideas*, 7, no. 3 (1946), pp. 257–97.

Kieckhefer, Richard. *Forbidden Rites: A Necromancer's Manual of the Fifteenth Century*, Pennsylvania State University Press, University Park, PA, 1997.

King, David A. *The Ciphers of the Monks: A Forgotten Number-Notation of the Middle Ages*, Franz Steiner, Stuttgart, 2001.

King, Ross. *The Bookseller of Florence: Vespasiano da Bisticci and the Manuscripts that Illuminated the Renaissance*, Vintage, London, 2022.

Király, Levente Zoltán. 'A Rohonci Kódex teológiai karaktere: közismert és idioszinkratikus mozzanatok azonosításával egy rejtélyes szerző kiléte felé' in Réka Kiss and Gábor Lányi (eds), *Hagyomány – Identitás – Történelem 2022*, Károli Gáspár Református Egyetem, Hittudományi Kar, Egyháztörténeti Kutatóintézet, Budapest, 2023, pp. 363–76.

Király, Levente Zoltán and Gábor Tokai, 'Cracking the Code of the Rohonc Codex', *Cryptologia*, 42, no. 4 (2018), pp. 285–315.

Kitchell, Kenneth F. and Irven M. Resnick 'Hildegard as Medieval "Zoologist": The Animals of the Physica' in Maud Burnett McInerney (ed.), *Hildegard of Bingen: A Book of Essays*, Garland Publishing, New York and London, 1998, pp. 25–52.

Kivistö, Sari, *The Vices of Learning: Morality and Knowledge at Early Modern Universities*, Brill, Leiden, 2014.

Knieriem, K. Lesley. *Book-Fools of the Renaissance*, University of Illinois, Graduate School of Library and Information Science, Champaign, IL, 1993.

Knight, Kevin, Beáta Megyesi, and Christiane Schaefer. 'The Secrets of the Copiale Cipher', *Journal for Research into Freemasonry and Fraternalism*, 2, no. 2 (2011), pp. 314–24.

Koningsveld, Pieter Sjoerd van. 'Le parchemin et les livres de plomb de Grenade: écriture, langue et origine d'une falsification' in María Julieta Vega García-Ferrer, María Luisa García Valverde, and Antonio López Carmona (eds), *Nuevas aportaciones al conocimiento y estudio del Sacro Monte IV centenario fundacional (1610–2010)*, Fundación Euroárabe, Granada, 2011, pp. 173–96.

Koningsveld, Pieter Sjoerd van and Gerard A. Wiegers. *The Lead Books of the Sacromonte and the Parchment of the Torre Turpiana: Granada, 1588–1606*, Brill, Leiden, 2024.

Koningsveld, Pieter Sjoerd van and Gerard A. Wiegers. 'The Parchment of the "Torre Turpiana": The Original Document and Its Early Interpreters', *Al-Qantara*, 24, no. 2 (2003), pp. 327–58.

Koningsveld, Pieter Sjoerd van and Gerard A. Wiegers. *The Sacromonte Parchment and Lead Books: Critical Edition of the Arabic Texts and Analysis of the Religious Ideas*, Avondrood, Rijswijk, 2019.

Kranz, Horst. 'Akademische Technik im 15. Jarhhundert: Inhalt und Terminologie einer wiederentdeckten Jugenschrift Johannes Fontanas', *Technikgeschichte*, 74, no. 2 (2007), pp. 119–47.

Kranz, Horst. 'Johannes Fontana als Verfasser der *Speculi almukefi compositio* und sein Exkurs über den Stahl (ca. 1430)', *Sudhoffs Archiv*, 100, no. 2 (2016), pp. 150–65.

Kyle, Sarah R. *Medicine and Humanism in Late Medieval Italy: The Carrara Herbal in Padua*, Routledge, Abingdon and New York, 2017.

Kyle, Sarah R. 'A More Modern Order: Virtual Collaboration in the Roccabonella Herbal' in Fabrizio Baldassarri (ed.), *Plants in 16th and 17th Century: Botany between Medicine and Science*, De Gruyter, Berlin and Boston, 2023, pp. 19–52.

Lallemand-Buyssens, Nathalie, 'Les acquisitions d'Athanasius Kircher au musée du Collège Romain à la lumière de documents inédits', *Storia dell'arte*, 133 (2012), pp. 107–29.

Lancashire OnLine Parish Clerk Project, 'Burials at the Cathedral in the City of Manchester', https://www.lan-opc.org.uk/Manchester/Manchester/cathedral/burials_1605-1608.html.

Láng, Benedek, *The Rohonc Code: Tracing a Historical Riddle*, Pennsylvania State University Press, University Park, PA, 2021.

Láng, Benedek. *Unlocked Books: Manuscripts of Learned Magic in the Medieval Libraries of Central Europe*, Pennsylvania State University Press, University Park, PA, 2008.

Lang, Sarah. 'Situating Ciphers among Alchemical Techniques of Secrecy' in Carola Dahlke and Matthias Göggerle (eds), *Proceedings of the 6th International Conference on Historical Cryptology HistoCrypt 2023*, 2023, https://ecp.ep.liu.se/index.php/histocrypt/issue/view/77/80, pp. 93–104.

Lang, Sarah and Megan Piorko. 'An Alchemical Cipher in a Shared Notebook of John and Arthur Dee (Sloane MS 1902) [Work in Progress]' in Carola Dahlke (ed.), *Proceedings of the 4th International Conference on Historical Cryptology HistoCrypt 2021*, Linköping University Electronic Press, Linköping, 2021, pp. 90–3.

Lang, Sarah, Sergei Zotov, and Megan Piorko. 'Sources of Alchemical Cryptography' in Michelle Waldispühl and Beáta Megyesi (eds), *Proceedings of the 7th International Conference on Historical Cryptology HistoCrypt 2024*, Linköping University Electronic Press, Linköping, Sweden, 2024, pp. 161–73.

Lawler, Andrew. *The Secret Token: Myth, Obsession, and the Search for the Lost Colony of Roanoke*, Doubleday, New York, 2018.

Laycock, Donald C. *The Complete Enochian Dictionary: A Dictionary of the Angelic Language as Revealed to Dr. John Dee and Edward Kelley*, 3rd edn, Weiser Books, Newburyport, MA, 2023.

Lee, S.L. 'Cotton, Sir Robert Bruce (1571–1631)' in Leslie Stephen (ed.), *Dictionary of National Biography*, vol. 12, MacMillan and Co., New York, Smith, Elder, and Co., London, 1887, pp. 308–15.

Leibenguth, Erik. *Hermetische Poesie des Frühbarock. Die 'Cantilenae intellectuales' Michael Maiers. Edition mit Übersetzung, Kommentar und Bio-Bibliographie*, Max Niemeyer Verlag, Tübingen, 2015.

Lendinara, Patrizia. 'The Poem "Nauta rudis . . ." in Anglo-Saxon Manuscripts: More than a Colophon' in Concetta Giliberto and Loredana Teresi (eds), *Limits to Learning: The Transfer of Encyclopaedic Knowledge in the Early Middle Ages*, Peeters, Leuven, 2013, pp. 219–41.

Lenke, Nils, Nicolas Roudet, and Hereward Tilton. 'Michael Maier: Nine Newly Discovered Letters', *Ambix*, 61, no. 1 (2014), pp. 1–47.

Leong, Elaine and Alisha Rankin. 'Introduction: Secrets and Knowledge' in Elaine Leong and Alisha Rankin (eds), *Secrets and Knowledge in Medicine and Science, 1500–1800*, Routledge, New York and London, 2016, pp. 1–20.

Lindemann, Luke. 'Crux of the MATTR: Voynichese Morphological Complexity' in Colin Layfield and John Abela (eds), *International Conference on the Voynich Manuscript 2022*, CEUR Workshop Proceedings, 2022, https://ceur-ws.org/Vol-3313/paper9.pdf.

Lines, David A. *The Dynamics of Learning in Early Modern Italy: Arts and Medicine at the University of Bologna*, Harvard University Press, Cambridge, MA, 2022.

Lohrmann, Dietrich. 'Johannes Fontanas Traktat über Brennspiegel und der Codex Paris BnF ms. latin 9335', *Sudhoffs Archiv*, 100, no. 2 (2016), pp. 166–87.

Lynch, Jack. 'Forgery as Performance Art: The Strange Case of George Psalmanazar', *1650–1850: Ideas, Aesthetics, and Inquiries in the Early Modern Era*, 11 (2005), pp. 21–35.

Maat, Jaap and David Cram (eds). *George Dalgarno on Universal Language: The Art of Signs (1661), The Deaf and Dumb Man's Tutor (1680), and the Unpublished Papers*, Oxford University Press, Oxford, 2001.

McCallum, R.I. 'Ripley's Alchemical Scrolls', *Royal College of Physicians of Edinburgh*, https://www.rcpe.ac.uk/heritage/ripleys-alchemical-scrolls.

McCluskey, Karen. 'When the Fury of the Proud Sea Re-Awoke' in Jenni Kuuliala, Rose-Marie Peake, and Päivi Räisänen-Schröder (eds), *Lived Religion and Everyday Life in Early Modern Hagiographic Material*, Springer, Cham, 2019, pp. 153–87.

McCracken, George E. 'Athanasius Kircher's Universal Polygraphy', *Isis*, 39, no. 4 (1948), pp. 215–28.

McCrone Associates, Inc., 'Materials Analysis of the Voynich Manuscript', 2009, https://beinecke.library.yale.edu/sites/default/files/files/voynich_analysis.pdf.

McCuaig, William. *Carlo Sigonio: The Changing World of the Late Renaissance*, Princeton University Press, Princeton, 1989.

MacKinney, Loren C. *Medical Illustrations in Medieval Manuscripts*, University of California Press, Berkeley, 1965.

Macrakis, Kristie. 'Confessing Secrets: Secret Communication and the Origins of Modern Science', *Intelligence and National Security*, 25, no. 2 (2010), pp. 183–97.

Maddocks, Fiona. *Hildegard of Bingen: The Woman of Her Age*, Review, London, 2002.

Maier, Michael. *Themis aurea*, Lucas Jennis, Frankfurt, 1618.

Marchese, Francis T. 'Representing Abstraction: Information Visualization in the Middle Ages', *Leonardo*, 49, no. 5 (2016), pp. 454–5.

Marcus, Hannah and Paula Findlen. 'Deciphering Galileo: Communication and Secrecy before and after the Trial', *Renaissance Quarterly*, 72 (2019), pp. 953–95.

Marshall, Peter. *The Mercurial Emperor: The Magic Circle of Rudolf II in Renaissance Prague*, Pimlico, London, 2007.

Matlach, Vladimír, Barbora Anna Janečková, and Daniel Dostál. 'The Voynich Manuscript: Symbol Roles Revisited', *PLoS ONE*, 17, no. 1 (2022), https://doi.org/10.1371/journal.pone.0260948.

Meconi, Honey. *Hildegard of Bingen*, University of Illinois Press, Urbana, 2018.

Meister, Aloys. *Die Anfänge der modernen diplomatischen Geheimschrift*, Ferdinand Schöningh, Paderborn, 1902.

Mentgen, Gerd. 'Jewish Alchemists in Central Europe in the Later Middle Ages: Some New Sources', *Aleph*, 9, no. 2 (2009), pp. 345–52.

Mertens, Manuel. 'Willem Silvius: "Typographical Parent" of John Dee's *Monas Hieroglyphica*', *Ambix*, 64, no. 2 (2017), pp. 175–89.

Mitchell, R.J. 'English Students at Padua, 1460–75', *Transactions of the Royal Historical Society*, 19 (1936), pp. 101–17.

Møllegaard, Kirsten, Evangeline Lemieux, and Braden Savage. 'Posthumanism and the Search for Meaning in Luigi Serafini's *Codex Seraphinianus*', *International Journal of Literary Humanities*, 22 (2024), pp. 173–93.

Morosini, Domenico. *Lettere del conte Domenico Morosini, nobile veneziano, al signor abate Francesco Cancellieri di Roma, e di questo a quello intorno ad alcune cifre spettanti all'Accademia de' Lincei, e per la seconda volta pubblicate*, Stabilimento Tipo-Litografico di Gaetano Longo, Ceneda, 1865.

Moulinier, Laurence. 'Un lexique "trilingue" du XIIe siècle: la "Lingua ignota" de Hildegarde de Bingen' in Jacqueline Hamesse and Danielle Jacquart (eds), *Lexiques bilingues dans les domaines philosophique et scientifique (Moyen Âge-Renaissance)*, Brepols Publishers, Turnhout, 2001, pp. 89–111.

Neal, Philip. 'Alchemical Herbals', http://philipneal.net/voynichsources/alchemical/.

Neal, Philip. 'Voynich Sources', http://philipneal.net/voynichsources/.

Neumann, Ulrich. 'Michel Maier (1569–1622) "philosophe et médecin"' in Jean-Claude Margolin and Sylvain Matton (eds), *Alchimie et philosophie à la Renaissance*, Vrin, Paris, 1993, pp. 307–26.

Newbold, William Romaine. *The Cipher of Roger Bacon*, University of Pennsylvania Press, Philadelphia, 1928.

Nummedal, Tara. 'Sound and Vision: The Alchemical Epistemology of Michael Maier's *Atalanta fugiens*' in Tara Nummedal and Donna Bilak (eds), *Furnace and Fugue: A Digital Edition of Michael Maier's 'Atalanta fugiens' (1618) with Scholarly Commentary*, University of Virginia Press, Charlottesville, 2020, https://doi.org/10.26300/bdp.ff.nummedal.

Nummedal, Tara and Donna Bilak. 'Interplay: New Scholarship on *Atalanta fugiens*' in Tara Nummedal and Donna Bilak (eds), *Furnace and Fugue: A Digital Edition of Michael Maier's 'Atalanta fugiens' (1618) with Scholarly Commentary*, University of Virginia Press, Charlottesville, 2020, https://doi.org/10.26300/bdp.ff.nummedal-bilak.

Oberg, Michael Leroy. *The Head in Edward Nugent's Hand: Roanoke's Forgotten Indians*, University of Pennsylvania Press, Philadelphia, 2008.

Obrist, Barbara. 'Visualization in Medieval Alchemy', *HYLE – International Journal for Philosophy of Chemistry*, 9, no. 2 (2003), pp. 131–70.

Odescalchi, Baldassare. *Memorie istorico critiche dell'Accademia de' Lincei e del principe Federico Cesi, secondo duca d'Aquasparta, fondatore e principe della Medesima*, Salvioni, Rome, 1806.

Olariu, Dominic. 'The Misfortune of Philippus de Lignamine's Herbal or New Research Perspectives in Herbal Illustrations from an Iconological Point of View' in *Early Modern Print Culture in Central Europe: Proceedings of the Young Scholars Section of the Wrocław Seminars, September 2013*, Wydawnictwo Uniwersytetu Wrocławskiego, Wrocław, 2014, pp. 39–62.

Önnerfors, Andreas. 'Unveiling the Copiale-Manuscript: Layers of Fraternalism, Ritual and Politics in Eighteenth Century Germany', paper presented at the

World Conference on Fraternalism, Freemasonry and History, 29–30 May 2015, http://dx.doi.org/10.13140/RG.2.1.1397.1367.

Örneholm, Urban. 'Interpretation of Decoding and English Translation', n.d., https://web.archive.org/web/20240223235659/https://cl.lingfil.uu.se/~bea/borg/corrected-Latin-translation.txt.

Örneholm, Urban. 'On the Translation/Paraphrase/Guesswork', 2018, https://web.archive.org/web/20240223230225/https://cl.lingfil.uu.se/~bea/borg/Comments.pdf.

Overty, Joanne Filippone. 'The Cost of Doing Scribal Business: Prices of Manuscript Books in England, 1300–1483', *Book History*, 11 (2008), pp. 1–32.

Page, Raymond Ian. *An Introduction to English Runes*, 2nd edn, Boydell Press, Woodbridge, 1999.

Park, Katharine. 'Natural Particulars: Medical Epistemology, Practice, and the Literature of Healing Springs' in Anthony Grafton and Nancy Siraisi (eds), *Natural Particulars: Nature and the Disciplines in Renaissance Europe*, MIT Press, Cambridge, MA, 1999, pp. 347–67.

Parry, Glyn. *The Arch-Conjuror of England: John Dee*, Yale University Press, New Haven and London, 2011.

Pelcl, František Martin. *Abbildungen Böhmischer und Mährischer Gelehrten und Künstler, nebst kurzen Nachrichten von ihren Leben und Werken*, 3rd part, Prague, 1777.

Pelling, Nick. 'Cod. Sang. 760 and the "Iatromathematisches Hausbuch" Voynich Hypothesis . . .', *Cipher Mysteries*, 26 July 2017, https://ciphermysteries.com/2017/07/26/cod-sang-760-iatromathematisches-hausbuch-voynich-hypothesis.

Pelling, Nick. 'Fifteenth Century Cryptography Revisited', 2017, https://www.academia.edu/33813775/Fifteenth_Century_Cryptography_Revisited.

Pelling, Nick. 'Johannes Van Heeck's Cipher Manuscript . . .', *Cipher Mysteries*, 8 February 2016, https://ciphermysteries.com/2016/02/08/johannes-van-heecks-cipher-manuscript.

Pelling, Nick. 'Mercantesca, Leonardo, and the Voynich Manuscript . . .', *Cipher Mysteries*, 22 April 2009, https://ciphermysteries.com/2009/04/22/mercantesca-leonardo-and-the-voynich-manuscript.

Peterson, Joseph H. *John Dee's Five Books of Mystery: Original Sourcebook of Enochian Magic*, Weiser Books, Boston and York Beach, ME, 2003.

Pettegree, Andrew. *The Book in the Renaissance*, Yale University Press, New Haven and London, 2010.

Pfeil, Brigitte and Sabina Lüdemann. '"Man wirt ganz konfus von al Zeichen": die Handschrift 8° Ms. astron. 7 der Universitätsbibliothek Kassel – Landesbibliothek und Murhardsche Bibliothek der Stadt Kassel (Kasseler Zauberhandschrift)', Kassel, 2016, https://kobra.uni-kassel.de/items/8642ac8e-9ac5-44d4-8ac3-3db41581b413.

Piazzoni, Ambrogio M. 'Latin Paleography from Antiquity to the Renaissance', Vatican Library, §17, https://spotlight.vatlib.it/latin-paleography/feature/17-cancelleresca-minuscule-and-merchant-script.

Piorko, Megan, Sarah Lang, and Richard Bean. 'Deciphering the *Hermeticae Philosophiae Medulla*: Textual Cultures of Alchemical Secrecy', *Ambix*, 70, no. 2 (2023), pp. 150–83.

Ponzi, Marco. 'Parallels for the Voynich Zodiac as an Image Cycle', Stephenbax.net, 2016, https://stephenbax.net/?p=1755.

Porck, Thijs. 'The Ages of Man and the Ages of Woman in Early Medieval England: From Bede to Byrhtferth of Ramsey and the *Tractatus de quaternario*' in Thijs Porck and Harriet Soper (eds), *Early Medieval English Life Courses: Cultural-Historical Perspectives*, Brill, Leiden and Boston, 2022, pp. 17–46.

Principe, Lawrence. 'Robert Boyle's Alchemical Secrecy: Codes, Ciphers and Concealments', *Ambix*, 39, no. 2 (1992), pp. 63–74.

Principe, Lawrence. *The Secrets of Alchemy*, University of Chicago Press, Chicago, 2012.

Prinke, Rafał T., and Kamila Follprecht. 'John Dee and Edward Kelley in Crakow: Identifying the House of Enochian Revelations', *Polish Journal of the Arts and Culture*, 13, no. 1 (2015), pp. 119–36.

Pryor, John H. 'Merchant Culture in Fourteenth-Century Venice: The Zibaldone da Canal (Review)', *Parergon*, 12, no. 1 (1994), pp. 134–6.

Quinn, David Beers. *The Roanoke Voyages, 1584–1590: Documents to Illustrate the English Voyages to North America under the Patent Granted to Walter Raleigh in 1584*, vol. 1, Routledge, Abingdon and New York, 2016.

Quinn, David Beers. 'Thomas Harriot and the Problem of America' in Robert Fox (ed.), *Thomas Harriot: An Elizabethan Man of Science*, Routledge, Abingdon and New York, 2017, pp. 9–27.

Rampling, Jennifer M. 'Alchemical Traditions' in Raymond Clemens (ed.), *The Voynich Manuscript*, Yale University Press, New Haven and London, 2016, pp. 45–51.

Rashdall, Hastings. *The Universities of Europe in the Middle Ages, Vol. 1: Salerno, Bologna, Paris*, Clarendon Press, Oxford, 1895.

Ray, Meredith K. *Daughters of Alchemy: Women and Scientific Culture in Early Modern Italy*, Harvard University Press, Cambridge, MA, 2015.

Rec, Agnieszka. 'Ciphers and Secrecy among the Alchemists: A Preliminary Report', *Societas Magica Newsletter*, 31 (2014), pp. 1–6.

Reddy, Sravana and Kevin Knight. 'What We Know about the Voynich Manuscript' in Kalliopi Zervanou and Piroska Lendvai (eds), *Proceedings of the 5th ACL–HLT Workshop on Language Technology for Cultural Heritage, Social Sciences, and Humanities*, The Association for Computational Linguistics, Portland, OR, 2011, pp. 78–86.

Reeds, Jim. 'Solved: The Ciphers in Book III of Trithemius's *Steganographia*', *Cryptologia*, 22, no. 4 (1998), pp. 291–317.

Reitsma, Johannes. *Franciscus Junius. Een levensbeeld uit den eersten tijd der kerkhervormingpage*, J.B. Huber, Netherlands, 1864.

Riccoboni, Sister Bartolomea. *Life and Death in a Venetian Convent: The Chronicle and Necrology of Corpus Domini, 1395–1436*, ed. and trans. Daniel Bornstein, University of Chicago Press, Chicago, 2000.

Robathan, Dorothy M. 'The Catalogues of the Princely and Papal Libraries of the Italian Renaissance', *Transactions and Proceedings of the American Philological Association*, 64 (1933), pp. 138–49.

Rowland, Ingrid. 'The Theatre of Forgery: Curzio Inghirami (Volterra, 1614–1655) and Giorgio Grognet de Vassé (Malta, 1774–1862)' in Philip Lavender and Matilda Amundsen Bergström (eds), *Faking It! The Performance of Forgery in*

Late Medieval and Early Modern Culture, Brill, Leiden and Boston, 2023, pp. 231–61.

Rugg, Gordon. 'Applying the Bax Proposed Solution', *Hyde and Rugg: Neat Ideas from Unusual Places*, 23 February 2014, https://hydeandrugg.wordpress.com/2014/02/23/applying-the-bax-proposed-solution/.

Rugg, Gordon and Gavin Taylor. 'Hoaxing Statistical Features of the Voynich Manuscript', *Cryptologia*, 41, no. 3 (2017), pp. 247–68.

Saenger, Paul Henry. *Space Between Words: The Origins of Silent Reading*, Stanford University Press, Stanford, 1997.

Salmon, Vivian. 'Cave Beck: A Seventeenth-Century Ipswich Schoolmaster and His "Universal Character"', *Proceedings of the Suffolk Institute of Archaeology*, 33 (1976), pp. 285–98.

Salmon, Vivian. 'Thomas Harriot (1560–1621) and the Origins of Algonkian Linguistics' in Konrad Koerner (ed.), *Language and Society in Early Modern England: Selected Essays 1982–1994*, John Benjamins Publishing Company, Amsterdam and Philadelphia, 1996, pp. 143–72.

Sargeaunt, John. 'Busby's Account Book' in George Fisher Russell Barker, *Memoir of Richard Busby, D.D. (1606–1695) with Some Account of Westminster School in the Seventeenth Century*, Lawrence and Bullen, London, 1895, pp. 104–27.

Schinner, Andreas. 'The Voynich Manuscript: Evidence of the Hoax Hypotheses', *Cryptologia*, 31, no. 2 (2007), pp. 95–107.

Schmeh, Klaus. 'Klaus Schmeh's Encrypted Book List (EBL)', https://scienceblogs.de/klausis-krypto-kolumne/klaus-schmehs-list-of-encrypted-books/.

Seaton, Ethel. 'Thomas Hariot's Secret Script', *Ambix*, 5, nos 3–4 (1956), pp. 111–14.

Shaw, Garry. 'Unknown History of 600-Year-Old, Coded Voynich Manuscript Revealed by Researcher', *Art Newspaper*, 13 January 2023, https://www.theartnewspaper.com/2023/01/13/unknown-history-of-600-year-old-coded-voynich-manuscript-revealed-by-researcher.

Sherman, William. 'Cryptographic Attempts' in Raymond Clemens (ed.), *The Voynich Manuscript*, Yale University Press, New Haven and London, 2016, pp. 39–43.

Sherman, William H. *John Dee: The Politics of Reading and Writing in the English Renaissance*, University of Massachusetts Press, Amherst, MA, 1995.

Signorini, Maddalena. 'Scripts and the Vernacular in Medieval and Renaissance Italy', trans. and ed. Isabella Magni, with Paul Gehl and Lia Markey, *Italian Paleography*, n.d., https://italian.newberry.t-pen.org/handbook.

Silver, Larry. *Marketing Maximilian, The Visual History of a Holy Roman Emperor*, Princeton University Press, Princeton, 2008.

Stanley, Jeffrey Christopher. 'To Read Images Not Words: Computer-Aided Analysis of the Handwriting in the *Codex Seraphinianus*', MSc dissertation, North Carolina State University, 2010.

Storey, Tessa. 'Face Waters, Oils, Love Magic and Poison: Making and Selling Secrets in Early Modern Rome' in Elaine Leong and Alisha Rankin (eds), *Secrets and Knowledge in Medicine and Science, 1500–1800*, Routledge, New York and London, 2016, pp. 143–63.

Tanner, Rosalind C.H. 'The Study of Thomas Harriot's Manuscripts I. Harriot's Will', *History of Science*, 6, no. 1 (1967), pp. 1–16.

Tarrant, Neil. 'Giambattista Della Porta and the Roman Inquisition: Censorship and the Definition of Nature's Limits in Sixteenth-Century Italy', *British Journal for the History of Science*, 46, no. 4 (2013), pp. 601–25.

Testa, Simone. *Italian Academies and Their Networks, 1525–1700: From Local to Global*, Palgrave Macmillan US, New York, 2015.

Thomas, Kate. 'How Many Alphabets?', Medieval Manuscripts Blog, *British Library*, 2019, https://blogs.bl.uk/digitisedmanuscripts/2019/05/how-many-alphabets.html.

Thorndike, Lynn. *A History of Magic and Experimental Science*, 8 vols, Columbia University Press, New York and London, 1923–58.

Thorndike, Lynn. 'An Unidentified Work by Giovanni da' Fontana: *Liber de omnibus rebus naturalibus*', *Isis,* 15, no. 1 (1931), pp. 31–46.

Tilton, Hereward. 'The Egyptian Theosophy of Count Michael Maier', *Theosophical History*, 9 (2003), pp. 9–29.

Tilton, Hereward. *The Quest for the Phoenix: Spiritual Alchemy and Rosicrucianism in the Work of Count Michael Maier (1569–1622)*, Walter de Gruyter, Berlin and New York, 2003.

Timm, Torsten. 'Co-Occurrence Patterns in the Voynich Manuscript', *eprint arXiv* (2016), pp. 1–9, https://doi.org/10.48550/arXiv.1601.07435.

Timm, Torsten and Andreas Schinner. 'A Possible Generating Algorithm of the Voynich Manuscript', *Cryptologia*, 44, no. 1 (2020), pp. 1–19.

Timm, Torsten and Andreas Schinner. 'The Voynich Manuscript: Discussion of Text Creation Hypotheses', *Cryptologia*, 48, no. 4 (2023), pp. 305–22.

Timmermann, Anke. *Verse and Transmutation: A Corpus of Middle English Alchemical Poetry (Critical Editions and Studies)*, Brill, Leiden and Boston, 2013.

Trithemius, Johannes. *Steganographia*, Berner, Frankfurt, 1606.

Tucker, Arthur O. and Jules Janick. *Flora of the Voynich Codex: An Exploration of Aztec Plants*, Springer, Cham, 2019.

Vale, Malcolm. 'Manuscripts and Books' in Christopher Allmand (ed.), *The New Cambridge Medieval History*, vol. 7: *c.1415–c.1500*, Cambridge, Cambridge University Press, 2008, pp. 278–86.

Vámos, Hanna. 'Leleplezett Titok, Pálóczi Horváth Ádám titkos, szabadkőműves dokumentuma' in Rumen István Csörsz and Béla Hegedüs (eds), *Magyar Arión. Tanulmányok Pálóczi Horváth Ádám műveiről*, Rec.iti, Budapest, 2011, pp. 41–55.

Van Kessel, Elisja M.R. 'Johannes van Heeck (1579–?), Co-Founder of the Accademia dei Lincei in Rome: A Bio-Bibliographical Sketch', *Mededelingen van het Nederlands Instituut te Rome*, 38 (1976), pp. 109–34.

Vaughan, Alden T. 'Sir Walter Ralegh's Indian Interpreters, 1584–1618', *William and Mary Quarterly*, 59, no. 2 (2002), pp. 341–76.

Vermeer, Hans J. 'Eine altdeutsche Sammlung medizinischer Rezepte in Geheimschrift', *Sudhoffs Archiv für Geschichte der Medizin und der Naturwissenschaften*, 45, no. 3 (1961), pp. 235–46.

Vermeer, Hans J. 'Technisch-naturwissenschaftliche Rezepte aus einer Harburger Handschrift', *Sudhoffs Archiv für Geschichte der Medizin und der Naturwissenschaften*, 45, no. 2 (1961), pp. 110–26.

Vigenère, Blaise de. *Traicté des chiffres, ou secretes manieres d'escrire*, Abel L'Angelier, Paris, 1586.

Voynich, Wilfrid M. 'A Preliminary Sketch of the History of the Roger Bacon Cipher Manuscript', *Transactions of the College of Physicians of Philadelphia*, 3rd series, 43 (1921), pp. 415–30.

Vries, Lyke de and Leen Spruit. 'Paracelsus and Roman Censorship: Johannes Faber's 1616 Report in Context', *Intellectual History Review*, 28, no. 2 (2018), pp. 225–54.

Warren, Jeremy. Book review of Anastasi Callinicos, Daniel Höhr, Jane Stevenson, and Peter Davidson, *The Celebrated Museum of the Roman College of the Society of Jesus. A Facsimile of the 1678 Amsterdam Edition of Giorgio de Sepi's Description of Athanasius Kircher's Museum, Musæum celeberrimum collegii romani societatis Jesu*, *Journal of the History of Collections*, 29, no. 3 (2017), pp. 516–17.

Wattenbach, Wilhelm. 'Alchymey Teuczsch', *Anzeiger für Kunde der deutschen Vorzeit*, 16 (1869), pp. 264–8.

Whitby, Christopher Lionel. 'John Dee's Actions with Spirits: 22 December 1581 to 23 May 1583', 2 vols, PhD thesis, University of Birmingham, 1982.

Williams, James V. 'Recherches sur deux traités attribués abusivement a Enrique de Villena: *Del Tesoro* et *Libro de Astrologia*', *École pratique des hautes études. 4e section, Sciences historiques et philologiques. Annuaire 1977–1978* (1978), pp. 1275–81.

Wisse, Jacob, 'Prague during the Rule of Rudolf II (1583–1612)' in *Heilbrunn Timeline of Art History*, Metropolitan Museum of Art, New York, November 2013, http://www.metmuseum.org/toah/hd/rupr/hd_rupr.htm.

Woolley, Benjamin. *The Queen's Conjurer: The Science and Magic of Dr Dee*, HarperCollins, London, 2001.

Xing Weiao. 'Linguistics and Epistemology in Thomas Harriot's North Atlantic World' in Jim Pearce, Ward J. Risvold, and William Given (eds), *Renaissance Papers 2021*, Camden House, Rochester, NY, 2022, pp. 107–21.

Young, Francis. 'Edward Kelley's Danish Treasure Hoax and Elizabethan Antiquarianism', *Intellectual History Review*, 30, no. 2 (2020), pp. 167–86.

Zambelli, Paola. *White Magic, Black Magic in the European Renaissance*, Brill, Leiden and Boston, 2007.

Zandbergen, René. 'Alain Touwaide on the Voynich – A Review by René Zandbergen', Stephenbax.net, 2016, https://stephenbax.net/?p=1814.

Zandbergen, René. 'Analysis of the Illustrations', 2022, https://www.voynich.nu/illustr.html.

Zandbergen, René. 'The "Discovery" of the Voynich MS by Wilfrid Voynich', 2023, https://www.voynich.nu/extra/mondragone.html.

Zandbergen, René. 'Earliest Owners' in Raymond Clemens (ed.), *The Voynich Manuscript*, Yale University Press, New Haven and London, 2016, pp. 3–9.

Zandbergen, René. 'Extraneous Writing' in 'Text Analysis: The Writing System', 2024, https://www.voynich.nu/writing.html#extr.

Zandbergen, René. 'The History of the Voynich MS', 2023, http://www.voynich.nu/history.html.

Zandbergen, René. 'The Origin of the Voynich MS', 2022, https://voynich.nu/origin.html.

Zandbergen, René. 'Papers on the Voynich Manuscript', 2004–15, https://www.voynich.nu/extra/curr_main.html.

Zandbergen, René. 'Pre-1960's [*sic*] Tentative Herb Identifications', 2016, https://www.voynich.nu/extra/herb_oldid.html.

Zandbergen, René. 'Special Topics: Related to the Origin of the MS', 2017, https://www.voynich.nu/extra/sp_origin.html.

Zandbergen, René. 'Text Analysis: The Writing System', 2024, https://www.voynich.nu/writing.html.

Zandbergen, René. 'Text Analysis: Transliteration of the Text', 2023, https://www.voynich.nu/transcr.html.

Zandbergen, René. 'Vaticanus gr. 1291', 2018, https://www.voynich.nu/extra/vatg1291.html.

Zandbergen, René. 'The Vicissitudes of the Society of Jesus in Rome', 2024, https://www.voynich.nu/extra/socjesu.html.

Zandbergen, René. 'Voynich MS: 17th Century Letters Related to the MS', 2019, https://www.voynich.nu/letters.html.

Zandbergen, René. 'The Voynich MS – Biographies', 2024, http://www.voynich.nu/curricula.html.

Zandbergen, René. 'Voynich MS: Quire 12', 2024, https://www.voynich.nu/q12/.

Zandbergen, René. 'Wilfrid Voynich's Acquisition of the Voynich MS, Not in Villa Mondragone', 2023, https://www.academia.edu/106833983/Wilfrid_Voynichs_acquisition_of_the_Voynich_MS_not_in_Villa_Mondragone, pp. 1–19.

Zelinka, Ivan, Melvin Lara, Leah C. Windsor, and René Lozi. 'Softcomputing in Identification of the Origin of Voynich Manuscript by Comparison with Ancient Dialects', *Applied Soft Computing* 138 (2023), https://doi.org/10.1016/j.asoc.2023.110217.

Zimansky, Curt A. 'Editor's Note: William F. Friedman and the Voynich Manuscript', *Philological Quarterly*, 49, no. 4 (1970), pp. 433–43.

Zyats, Paula, Erin Mysak, Jens Stenger, Marie-France Lemay, Anikó Bezur, and David D. Driscoll. 'Physical Findings' in Raymond Clemens (ed.), *The Voynich Manuscript*, Yale University Press, New Haven and London, 2016, pp. 23–37.

ILLUSTRATIONS

PLATES

1. Hildegard of Bingen experiences a vision, from *Scivias*. Niday Picture Library / Alamy.
2. Tironian Notes in a ninth-century psalter. British Library, Add MS 9046, folio 71r. From the British Library archive / Bridgeman Images.
3. The cover of Hildegard of Bingen's *Riesencodex*. Hochschul- und Landesbibliothek, Cover, Hs. 2. Hochschul- und Landesbibliothek RheinMain / CC BY 4.0.
4. A plant with roots entangled with snakes or worms, from the Voynich Manuscript. Beinecke Rare Book and Manuscript Library, Yale University, General Collection, MS 408, folio 49r.
5. Plants and pots, from the Voynich Manuscript. Beinecke Rare Book and Manuscript Library, Yale University, General Collection, MS 408, folio 99v.
6. A castle with swallowtail merlons, from the Voynich Manuscript. Beinecke Rare Book and Manuscript Library, Yale University, General Collection, MS 408, top right panel of folio 86r6.
7. A gigantic tower-shaped battering ram on wheels, from Giovanni Fontana's *Bellicorum instrumentorum liber*. Bayerische Staatsbibliothek, Cod.icon. 242, folios 1v/2r. München. Bayerische Staatsbibliothek / CC-BY-NC 4.0.
8. A fire-breathing witch, from Giovanni Fontana's *Bellicorum instrumentorum liber*. Bayerische Staatsbibliothek, Cod.icon. 242, folios 63v/64r. Bayerische Staatsbibliothek / CC-BY-NC 4.0.
9. A memory device, from Giovanni Fontana's *Secretum de thesauro experimentorum ymaginationis hominum*. Bibliothèque nationale de France, Cod. Lat. Nouv. Acq. 635, folio 32r.
10. A portrait of Johannes Trithemius. DE 899, Château de Chantilly. © GrandPalaisRmn (Domaine de Chantilly) / René-Gabriel Ojeda.
11. Wolfgang Ernst Heidel's enciphered solution in *Steganographia vindicata*. Reprinted edition from 1721. 26.Q.50, Austrian National Library.
12. A portrait of John Dee by an anonymous artist. © Ashmolean Museum.
13. The cover of John Dee's *Monas hieroglyphica*. Beinecke Rare Book and Manuscript Library, Yale University, Mellon Alchemical 38.
14. A page from the *Ars notoria*. Bibliothèque nationale de France, Latin 9336, folio 19v.

IN THE TEXT

INDEX

INDEX